Top 10
of
London

OVER 250 LONDON LISTS
THAT WILL SIMPLY
AMAZE YOU!

ALEXANDER ASH

Top 10
of
London

OVER 250 LISTS
ABOUT LONDON
THAT WILL SIMPLY
AMAZE YOU!

ALEXANDER ASH

DEDICATION

To Russell John Ash (1946–2010)

'Your razor wit and charming smile are an honour to recall,
as friend, husband and loving father, you died beloved by all'

And to his granddaughter

Leonie Flora Page (2011–)

An Hachette UK Company
www.hachette.co.uk

First published in Great Britain in 2012 by
Hamlyn, a division of Octopus Publishing Group Ltd
Endeavour House
189 Shaftesbury Avenue
London
WC2H 8JY
www.octopusbooks.co.uk

ISBN 13: 978-0-600-62064-8

A CIP catalogue record for this book is available from the British Library.

Printed and bound in China.

10 9 8 7 6 5 4 3 2 1

Executive Editor: Trevor Davies
Editor: Jo Wilson
Designer: Jeremy Tilston
Production Controller: Caroline Alberti

CONTENTS

Infrastructure & Property

Politics & Society

Historical London

Transport

Tourism

Trade & Industry

Sport

Miscellaneous

INTRODUCTION

INTRODUCTION

'By seeing London, I have seen as much of life
as the world can show.'
SAMUEL JOHNSON

Dr Samuel Johnson, who wrote the above, and whose quote is often paraphrased, is
a man who knows what he is talking about; he did after all write the *Dictionary of the*
English Language (1785). I have had the pleasure of both being born in London and
studying at its oldest university, University College London. It has therefore been my
privilege to continue my late father's legacy in helping compile this compendium on
perhaps the most famous city in the world.

'London is a modern Babylon.'
BENJAMIN DISRAELI

London is a city that has stood the test of time. Happily, it was also chosen, (after
fierce competition from other international centres of civilization, science and
culture), to be the very marker of time: the Prime Meridian.

   Although archaeologists are digging up ever older evidence of the first settlers
on the River Thames, the Romans are often credited with establishing the first major
permanent settlement, Londinium, around the year AD 43. The surrounding tribes,
united by Boudica, subsequently burnt it to the ground. At that time, Latin was
the official language and London was not the capital of the collection of tribes and
cultures that made up the population of our islands.

   The Romans reorganized themselves and over the next couple of centuries built
a wall to surround their precious settlement. Remains of the wall can today be seen
at the Museum of London, and its influence is evident in the names of roads and
areas, for example Aldgate and the road imaginatively named London Wall. This area
is today known as the City of London (and colloquially as 'the City' or 'the Square
Mile'), run by the City of London Corporation.

   In the Dark Ages that followed the collapse of the Roman Empire, London's
inhabitants spent less of their time writing and building in stone, and more of it

fighting and keeping the Saxon pirates and invaders at bay. By the time of the Norman Conquest of England in 1066 London had became the capital of England. After William the Conqueror had defeated Harold, just outside present day Hastings, it was towards London that he and his army then marched, where William was crowned William I at Westminster Abbey.

At that time, Westminster was entirely separate from The City of London itself, which was overcrowded, noisy and without adequate sanitation. But it was still sufficiently important for William to build the Tower of London to keep an eye on it. Though many tried, London and England were never again invaded.

There followed a long period of relative peace and prosperity, when flourishing trade at the port of London allowed the transportation of goods from around the world. Of course this newfound international outlook was indirectly responsible for the rats on which the fleas lived that spread the Black Death for which London remains notorious. As trade developed and the city grew, London's streets became congested and overcrowded. Three hundred years later, in 1666, the Great Fire of London laid waste to 87 parishes and an estimated 13,000 houses. Although it was a humanitarian disaster, it proved to be the catalyst for a great architectural rebirth, with the restructured City taking the shape we know today. The new City had wider streets, better hygiene and, needless to say, better fire safety. Christopher Wren was at the forefront of rejuvenating the City's churches including the building of a magnificent new St Paul's Cathedral. New London flourished and in 1703 The Duke of Buckingham built Buckingham House, later purchased by George III for his Royal Palace. Buckingham Palace was built soon after, though it was not the monarch's official residence for another hundred years.

As skilled workers and intellectuals flowed into and stayed in London during the eighteenth century, its rulers decided to explore and conquer overseas. As the capital of the world's largest empire, London became the world's biggest city for a time. Many systems, ideals and inventions were hatched, incubated and spread throughout the English-speaking world. The sandwich, cash machine and jigsaw puzzle, for example, can all trace their roots to London.

'The man who can dominate a London dinner-table can dominate the world.'
OSCAR WILDE

After the Industrial Revolution, wealthy Victorian Londoners found they had more leisure time, and disposable income, than ever before. With their new wealth, some of these Victorian Londoners practiced philanthropy on an industrial scale, arguably laying the roots for many of today's social systems. As the working day became more regulated, Big Ben was forged with its clock that the people of the world could set their watches to.

And so to living memory, and the dark days of World War II, where Londoners faced a new threat from above: the Luftwaffe. The Blitz was intended to intimidate, but London and its people stood united and strong. The vulnerable were evacuated, those who stayed took shelter when the sirens rang, often in the Underground stations expertly built just a few decades earlier. The baby boomer generation soon followed, taking root in the suburbs, and Greater London was formed, as inner London shrank and outer London grew. American banks engulfed many of the older English merchant banks, and international money pours into the city, still, though as I write not to the extent of recent years. Today, London remains as cosmopolitan a city as ever, and bears the honour of the first city to entertain the world three times by hosting the modern Olympic Games.

In the writing of this book I jumped at the chance to visit the plethora of museums dotted around London, and I encourage you to do the same and to wonder around its streets. I have strived to ensure that all the information contained within this book is accurate but it is intended for enjoyment – to make you raise an eyebrow, feel more at home in your city, more confident in quizzes, or perhaps simply pause for thought. If nothing else they should emphasize what a unique and amazing city London is.

ALEXANDER ASH
London, 2011

BOROUGHS & NEIGHBOURHOODS

BOROUGHS WITH THE HIGHEST FERTILITY RATE

	Borough	Fertility rate*	Children per female
1	Newham	103.0	2.87
2	Barking and Dagenham	90.5	2.66
3	Brent	89.7	2.57
4	Waltham Forest	87.3	2.54
5	Greenwich	82.7	2.35
6	Hounslow	77.9	2.14
7	Ealing	77.1	2.12
8	Enfield	76.1	2.27
9	Hackney	76.0	2.13
10	Haringey	74.2	2.08
	London average	69.5	1.95

*Live births in 2010 per 1,000 women aged 15–44

Source – Office for National Statistics
The most common age for childbirth across London is 31, although in Hackney and Newham it is significantly lower at 24 and 26 respectively. Newham has one of the highest fertility rates in the UK, yet even this is low compared to Victorian London, when the rate was roughly 180.

YOUNGEST BOROUGHS

	Borough	Percentage of residents under 20	Under 4
1	Newham	30.6	8.8
2	Barking and Dagenham	28.9	7.7
3	Hackney	27.6	8.5
4	Redbridge	26.4	6.6
5	Tower Hamlets	26.1	7.8
6	Enfield	26.0	7.0
7	Waltham Forest	25.9	7.4
8	Croydon	25.7	6.3
9	Bexley	25.6	5.9
10	Hillingdon	25.5	6.4
	London	24.2	6.6
	UK	24.5	5.6

Source – Office for National Statistics
London's population is forecast to reach nearly 9 million by 2030. Projections suggest that while the proportion of residents under both 20 and 4 years old will remain constant, London will be home to fewer 20–40 year olds and relatively more over of the over 60s.

MOST DENSELY POPULATED BOROUGHS

	Borough	Population per hectare (2.5 acres)
1	City of London	34
2	Tower Hamlets	95
3	Hammersmith and Fulham	97
4	Southwark	98
5	Lambeth	105
6	Camden	106
7	Westminster	112
8	Hackney	113
9	Islington	129
10	Kensington and Chelsea	137
	London	49

Source – Office for National Statistics
Kensington and Chelsea, the most densely populated borough when all space is considered, has more residents per hectare than Jakarta, New York and Tokyo. London as a whole is on a par with Madrid and Bangkok, and the population is slightly more spread out than Hong Kong, Mexico City and Rio de Janeiro.

LEAST DENSELY POPULATED BOROUGHS

	Borough	Population per hectare (2.5 acres)
1	Bromley	1
2	Havering	21
3	Hillingdon	23
4	Bexley	32
=	Richmond upon Thames	32
6	Croydon	40
=	Barnet	40
8	Sutton	44
9	Harrow	45
=	Kingston upon Thames	45
	London	*49*

Source – Office for National Statistics
Bromley, the largest London borough, is less densely populated than the towns Cambridge and Exeter, while only slightly more so than Bolton.

TOP 10
LONGEST LIVING NEIGHBOURHOODS

	Neighbourhood	Average age at death
1	Golders Green	78.5
2	Chislehurst	77.8
=	Cockfosters	77.8
4	Coulsdon	77.6
5	Sutton	77.5
6	Beckenham East	77.4
7	Fortis Green	77.1
8	Woodford Green	77.0
=	Wimbledon North	77.0
10	Barnet West	76.9
=	Sidcup	76.9
	London Average	*73.6*
	England Average	*74.6*

Source – University of Sheffield
Improvements in healthcare have meant that for the past 150 years, life expectancy has risen by three months every year; the life expectancy in Kensington & Chelsea is now 83.3 years. Other studies show that the majority of babies born in Britain today will live past the age of 100.

SHORTEST LIVING NEIGHBOURHOODS

	Neighbourhood	Average age at death
1	Harlesden	68.6
2	Vauxhall North	69.4
3	Vauxhall South	69.5
4	Hackney North	69.6
5	Poplar	69.9
6	Deptford North	70.0
=	Peckham	70.0
8	Kensal Town	70.4
9	Shepherds Bush	70.5
=	Stepney	70.5
	London Average	*73.6*
	England Average	*74.6*

Source – University of Sheffield
Although London has a higher life expectancy than New York, it lags behind other world cities such as Paris, Sydney and Tokyo, particularly for female life expectancy.

BOROUGHS WITH THE BEST EXAM RESULTS

	Borough	Average pupil A-level points
1	Sutton	340
2	Havering	303
3	Barnet	296
4	Ealing	284
5	Kingston upon Thames	280
6	Bromley	279
7	Bexley	276
=	Redbridge	276
9	Hillingdon	272
10	Harrow	267
	London average	*260*

Source – Department for Education and Skills
Under the 'UCAS tariff', which is the measure used for entry to universities, an A* is worth 140 points, an A worth 120, a B 100, and so on in intervals of 20. The most popular A-level subjects in the country are English, Mathematics, Biology, Psychology and History.

BOROUGHS WITH THE WORST EXAM RESULTS

	Borough	A–C pass rate (%)
1	Islington	68
=	Westminster	68
3	Waltham Forest	67
=	Newham	67
5	Croydon	66
6	Greenwich	62
=	Barking and Dagenham	62
8	Southwark	62
9	Tower Hamlets	62
10	Lambeth	62
	London average	*74*

Source – Department for Education and Skills
GCE A-level examination results of 16–18 year olds by number of A–C grade passes.

BOROUGHS WITH THE MOST MARRIAGES

	Borough	Number of marriages	First marriages for both partners
1	Westminster	2,032	1,491
2	Kensington and Chelsea	1,529	1,033
3	Richmond upon Thames	1,184	808
4	Croydon	1,080	790
5	Wandsworth	1,065	815
6	Brent	1,021	806
7	Bromley	1,008	638
8	Barnet	994	730
9	Havering	975	549
10	Bexley	964	586
	London	*27,333*	*19,617*

Source – Office for National Statistics, 2009
The number of weddings in London has dropped by around a third in the past 25 years and is at nearly the lowest rate since records began in 1837. Saturday is by far the most popular day to get married, with 43% of weddings on that day. Sunday, the least popular, hosts just 4%.

BOROUGHS WITH THE MOST STREET TREES

		Estimated total street trees in 2011	Trees planted in boroughs, 2009–10	Estimated street trees in 2007
1	Bromley	36,000	962	38,000
2	Croydon	33,000	400	33,000
3	Barnet	29,119	508	36,000
4	Enfield	25,000	1,410	20,000
5	Ealing	24,511	431	26,500
6	Havering	23,000	412	23,500
7	Redbridge	21,195	795	20,872
8	Brent	20,000	100	18,000
9	Waltham Forest	20,000	158	22,000
10	Sutton	19,848	530	22,000
	London	*497,686*	*14,926*	*508,825*

BOROUGHS WITH THE MOST OVERWEIGHT SCHOOLCHILDREN

	Borough	Percentage of 10–11 year-olds overweight*	Of which obese+
1	Westminster	43.6	28.6
2	Kensington and Chelsea	41.9	24.7
3	Lambeth	41.6	24.7
4	Tower Hamlets	41.4	25.7
5	Lewisham	40.6	24.4
6	Hackney	40.4	25.5
7	Southwark	40.3	26.0
=	Newham	40.3	25.9
9	Hounslow	40.2	24.6
=	Hammersmith and Fulham	40.2	24.0
	London average	*36.8*	*21.8*

* Above the 85th centile of the BMI scale
+ Above the 95th centile of the BMI scale

Source – NHS

The obesity rate has nearly tripled in the last 25 years, with the cost of treatment forecast to double by 2050. One in ten school children across all years in London are obese, which is the worst rate in the country. Despite government action to provide healthy school meals, takeaway meals, which are often sold near the school gates, can contain three times the recommended allowance of saturated fat.

BOROUGHS WITH THE MOST CHILD TOOTH DECAY

	Borough	Average number of decayed teeth*
1	Westminster	2.58
2	Hillingdon	2.36
=	Newham	2.36
4	Kensington and Chelsea	2.20
5	Tower Hamlets	2.16
6	Ealing	2.15
=	Hammersmith and Fulham	2.15
8	Hounslow	2.05
9	Harrow	1.96
10	Brent	1.71
	London	*1.66*
	England	*1.47*

* In five-year-olds. Includes teeth missing, decayed or filled.

Source – British Association for the Study of Community Dentistry (data for Greenwich and Bexley missing), 2010
London has more dentists than the national average, but London's children are the least likely in the country to use them. The profession of dentistry was first recorded in 1860, prior to which barbers and blacksmiths would extract teeth.

BOROUGHS WITH THE MOST ALCOHOL-RELATED HOSPITAL ADMISSIONS

	Borough	Admission rate*	Admissions
1	Ealing	2,144.1	6,384
2	Islington	1,995.5	3,073
3	Newham	1,989.2	3,956
4	Hammersmith and Fulham	1,978.5	2,916
5	Hounslow	1,933.8	4,163
6	Barking and Dagenham	1,844.5	3,016
7	Hillingdon	1,804.1	4,842
8	Lewisham	1,719.0	3,999
9	Waltham Forest	1,675.6	3,447
10	Brent	1,663.0	4,203
	London	*1,489.9*	*111,040*
	England	*1,582.4*	*945,469*

* Per 100,000 people

Source – North West Public Health Observatory, 2009
Around two thirds of those admitted to hospital for drinking are men, with the worst rates amongst females occurring in Croydon, Bromley and Camden. Among under 18s, residents of Ealing, Croydon and Sutton are the most frequent patients.

BINGE DRINKING BOROUGHS

	Borough	Binge drinkers Percentage	Total
1	Lambeth	16.8	36,000
2	Hammersmith and Fulham	16.4	24,000
3	Westminster	15.7	32,000
4	Camden	15.3	28,000
=	Islington	15.3	23,000
6	Southwark	14.8	30,000
=	Tower Hamlets	14.8	24,000
8	Kensington and Chelsea	14.7	23,000
9	Haringey	13.9	26,000
=	Wandsworth	13.9	33,000
	London	*12.7*	*762,000*

Source – NHS, 2005

Binge drinking is defined by the NHS as eight units (four pints of beer) for men and six units (two large glasses of wine) for women. Every London borough is below the average rate for binge drinking in England, however, which currently stands at 18% of the population.

BOROUGHS SPENDING
THE MOST ON SEXUAL HEALTH

	Borough	Spend per head* (£)
1	Camden	57.67
2	Kensington and Chelsea	42.40
3	Tower Hamlets	40.47
4	Hackney	34.13
5	Westminster	32.50
6	Lambeth	32.31
7	Southwark	28.87
8	Hammersmith and Fulham	26.46
9	Wandsworth	26.35
10	Lewisham	20.17

* Including contraceptives prescribed by GPs

Source – NHS, 2009

London has the highest rate for chlamydia screening in England, but it is still the most common STI. Londoners have the highest rates nationally for syphilis and herpes.

BOROUGHS WITH THE HIGHEST RATE OF TEEN PREGNANCY

	Borough	Pregnancy rate*	Conceptions
1	Southwark	69.3	781
2	Lambeth	68.3	760
3	Lewisham	65.2	842
4	Greenwich	63.6	708
5	Haringey	58.3	604
6	Barking and Dagenham	56.0	592
7	Hackney	55.7	582
8	Wandsworth	52.8	430
9	Waltham Forest	52.7	611
10	Croydon	52.0	1,026
	London	*43.7*	*16,181*

* Per 1,000 women aged 15–17

Source – Office for National Statistics, 2009
Southwark has the highest rate in the entire country, with one in 13 teenage girls getting pregnant. These figures make the UK second only to the USA for its rate of teenage pregnancies in the developed world.

WORST BOROUGHS FOR CRIME

	Borough	Total offenses, 2010	Percentage change on previous year
1	Westminster	63,367	−0.8
2	Southwark	36,934	+0.4
3	Ealing	35,577	+7.1
4	Lambeth	35,405	+0.9
5	Newham	35,294	+5.7
6	Camden	33,755	−0.6
7	Croydon	32,553	−1.7
8	Brent	29,285	+1.5
9	Lewisham	29,009	−2.7
10	Tower Hamlets	28,101	+3.5
	*London**	*824,601*	*−1.0*

* Excluding City of London

Source – Metropolitan Police, 2010
These figures only show reported crimes. Surveys have indicated that 40% of those witnessing a crime do not report it to the police. Despite having over one million CCTV cameras in operation in the capital to help tackle criminal activity, only around one crime is solved by every 1,000 cameras. Nevertheless, captured footage has helped in an estimated 70% of murder investigations.

WORST BOROUGHS FOR MURDER

	Borough	Murders
1	Newham	14
2	Lambeth	8
=	Lewisham	8
4	Barnet	7
5	Brent	6
=	Croydon	6
=	Ealing	6
=	Islington	6
=	Southwark	6
=	Tower Hamlets	6
	London total	*120*

Source – Metropolitan Police, 2010
2010 saw the fewest murders in the capital since 1978, reflecting an overall downward trend over the last decade. A knife was the most common weapon, accounting for 49 cases, followed by gun murders, of which there were 29.

WORST BOROUGHS FOR RESIDENTIAL BURGLARY

	Borough	Burglary in a dwelling	Burglary in other buildings
1	Barnet	3,097	1,248
2	Croydon	2,833	1,432
3	Ealing	2,653	1,112
4	Redbridge	2,629	724
5	Brent	2,610	998
6	Enfield	2,452	971
7	Waltham Forest	2,431	1,025
8	Lambeth	2,410	876
9	Haringey	2,395	876
10	Newham	2,346	1,296
	London	*58,761*	*32,043*

Source – Metropolitan Police, 2010
Even though Camden as a borough does not feature on the list, Cantelowes ward in Camden is the worst-hit hot spot, suffering 24 burglaries for every 1,000 residents. Kensington & Chelsea and Kingston upon Thames suffered the least burglaries, with some areas 15 times less likely to be burgled than those worst hit.

WORST BOROUGHS FOR
DRUG TRAFFICKING

	Borough	Trafficking offenses	Total drug offenses
1	Southwark	382	4,866
2	Tower Hamlets	369	3,202
3	Westminster	288	5,883
4	Enfield	212	1,804
5	Camden	202	2,610
6	Haringey	198	1,767
7	Ealing	187	2,648
8	Hackney	156	2,738
9	Hounslow	154	1,846
10	Islington	150	1,899
	London	*4,356*	*64,590*

Source – Metropolitan Police, 2010
Drug use rates in London are roughly in line with the rest of the UK, the notable exception being cocaine which is double the national rate. Drug possession offenses have risen sharply in recent years, with the increase mostly attributed to cannabis related charges.

WORST BOROUGHS FOR POLICE CAR CRASHES

	Borough	Claims	Injuries*
1	Westminster	109	21
2	Lambeth	98	25
3	Barnet	86	15
4	Croydon	81	24
5	Southwark	75	23
6	Newham	73	26
7	Wandsworth	65	20
8	Ealing	64	22
9	Tower Hamlets	63	19
10	Hackney	62	20
	London total	*1,627*	*446*

* Civilian and police officer

Source – Metropolitan Police
Around £10 million has been paid out in compensation to motorists and pedestrians by the Metropolitan Police over the past five years. An average of four accidents per day occur, which have tragically resulted in 21 deaths.

BOROUGHS WITH THE MOST PARKING PENALTIES

	Borough	Total parking penalties (£)	Per head (£)
1	Westminster	35,410,000	62.46
2	Camden*	26,468,950	90.97
3	Kensington and Chelsea	12,881,864	85.29
4	Islington	10,709,295	55.15
5	Lambeth	8,792,329	47.17
6	Newham	8,662,934	52.08
7	Wandsworth	8,053,274	62.97
8	Haringey	7,449,000	57.41
9	Hammersmith and Fulham	6,959,902	47.38
10	Southwark	6,234,001	28.66
	London	*182,929,815*	*34.03*

* 2008 data, all other 2009

Source – Tax Payers' Alliance, 2009
Only around 1% of parking tickets in London are contested, although when they are, drivers in Westminster are most likely to win their appeals (with a 93% success rate). During the last five years clamping has significantly decreased, from a high of 140,000 to around 40,000, but towing incidents have increased across the capital.

SLOWEST BOROUGHS

	Borough	Average road speed* kph	mph
1	City of London	13.1	8.1
2	Camden	15.1	9.4
3	Islington	16.7	10.4
4	Westminster	16.8	10.4
5	Hackney	17.3	10.7
=	Southwark	17.3	10.7
7	Lewisham	17.4	10.8
8	Lambeth	17.8	11.1
9	Hammersmith and Fulham	18.0	11.2
10	Tower Hamlets	18.1	11.2

* During weekday afternoon peak traffic times

Source – Transport for London, 2009
Vehicles in London collectively travel around 32 billion kilometres (20 billion miles) a year, creating 120,000 potholes on 14,000 kilometres (9,000 miles) of road. The world's first traffic light was built near the Houses of Parliament in 1868. Today, there are over 5,000 signalized road junctions and pedestrian crossings.

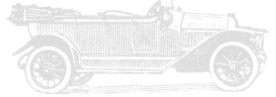

BOROUGHS FOR TRAFFIC JAMS

	Borough	Total	Annual vehicle delay Per km of road*
1	Barnet	618,000,000	5,140,000
2	Ealing	550,000,000	6,330,000
3	Enfield	452,600,000	4,520,000
4	Wandsworth	426,100,000	6,260,000
5	Westminster	408,700,000	4,200,000
6	Croydon	392,300,000	3,940,000
7	Hounslow	383,600,000	4,260,000
8	Brent	376,400,000	5,220,000
9	Bromley	349,200,000	2,720,000
10	Greenwich	342,800,000	3,800,000

* Measured in minutes, between the hours of 7am and 7pm

Source – Transport for London
Second only to Paris as Europe's most gridlocked city, London contains 5 of the top 10 UK congestion hotspots. Around a third of London's traffic uses just 5% of its roads, and estimates of the costs of being stuck in traffic (for example lost wages) range from £2 billion to £4 billion.

TOP10

EARNING BOROUGHS

	Borough	Average earnings (£)
1	Kensington and Chelsea	151,000
2	City of London	102,000
3	Westminster	82,600
4	Camden	69,800
5	Richmond upon Thames	59,600
6	Wandsworth	49,500
7	Hammersmith and Fulham	48,600
8	Islington	43,300
=	Merton	43,300
10	Barnet	38,700
	London	*37,400*

Source – Office for National Statistics

Kensington and Chelsea's prominence is heavily influenced by its preponderance of multi-millionaire residents. The median income in the borough is much lower, at £27,500.

LONGEST WORKING BOROUGHS

	Borough	Average hours worked per week
1	Hounslow	36.2
2	City of London	36.1
3	Tower Hamlets	35.4
4	Camden	35.3
=	Kensington and Chelsea	35.3
=	Westminster	35.3
7	Hillingdon	35.0
=	Newham	35.0
9	Wandsworth	34.9
10	Southwark	34.8
	London	*34.4*

Source – Office for National Statistics, 2010
Around 40% of males and 20% of females in London work over 45 hours a week. Workaholics are most likely to live in the City of London, Westminster and Kensington and Chelsea.

BOROUGHS WITH THE MOST OFFICE SPACE

	Borough	Office space m²	Office space sq ft
1	Westminster	7,897,000	85,003,000
2	City of London	5,162,000	55,563,000
3	Tower Hamlets	3,967,000	42,700,000
4	Hillingdon	3,347,000	36,027,000
5	Camden	3,287,000	35,381,000
6	Ealing	3,089,000	33,250,000
7	Southwark	2,713,000	29,202,000
8	Hounslow	2,550,000	27,448,000
9	Croydon	2,400,000	25,833,000
10	Brent	2,335,000	25,134,000

Source – Office for National Statistics
Prime office space in London is now the most expensive in the world, overtaking Tokyo, with rent costing £90 per square foot. Around £10 billion is invested each year in buying London's office buildings. A third of this is from overseas purchasers, with Germans the biggest buyers.

BOROUGHS FOR FAILED BUSINESSES

	Borough	Business deaths*	Total
1	Westminster	6,475	47,010
2	Camden	3,140	25,175
3	Barnet	3,075	19,920
4	Wandsworth	2,280	15,270
5	Ealing	1,930	14,150
6	Southwark	1,920	13,240
7	Brent	1,825	12,475
8	Tower Hamlets	1,820	11,880
9	Islington	1,785	14,010
10	Hammersmith and Fulham	1,775	11,850
	London	*55,100*	*402,315*
	UK	*279,180*	*2,341,900*

* Excludes merger and restructuring activity

Source – Office for National Statistics, 2009
In total 13.7% of London businesses failed in 2009, at a rate of over 150 a day, as the recession made itself felt. It was the first year on record when business failures outweighed 'business births', which were down over 10%. Business administration and support services were the hardest hit industries.

TOP10
BOROUGHS WITH THE MOST BLUE PLAQUES

	Borough	Blue plaques
1	Westminster	295
2	Kensington and Chelsea	157
3	Camden	153
4	City of London	152
5	Lambeth	24
6	Wandsworth	23
7	Hammersmith and Fulham	21
=	Richmond upon Thames	21
9	Tower Hamlets	20
10	Greenwich	15
=	Islington	15
	London	*1,003*

Source – English Heritage

The scheme, the first in the world, uses commemorative 'blue plaque' markers to link a location with a famous person or event. The original plaque honoured the poet Lord Byron in Cavendish Square, although the building has since been demolished, and the oldest surviving plaque commemorates Napoleon in King Street. The figures include plaques erected by English Heritage (1986–2011), the Royal Society of Arts (1866–1901), London County Council (1901–65) and Greater London Council (1965–86).

BOROUGHS WITH THE MOST SHOPS AND RESTAURANTS

	Borough	Shops and restaurants	Floorspace (thousand m^2)
1	Westminster	8,660	1,940
2	Camden	4,280	572
3	Barnet	3,420	512
4	Croydon	3,340	620
5	Wandsworth	3,070	478
6	Kensington and Chelsea	2,980	404
7	Islington	2,950	338
8	Bromley	2,870	472
9	Brent	2,820	380
=	Ealing	2,820	441
	London	*85,080*	*13,475*

Source – Greater London Authority
London is the highest grossing city for retail sales in the world, with £64 billion being spent in 2010. Its eateries boast a range of influences, with over 50 cuisines represented in London's 12,000 restaurants. They serve up around 400 million meals a year.

HEALTHY-EATING BOROUGHS

	Borough	Proportion of adults eating healthily (%)
1	Kensington and Chelsea	48.1
2	Camden	43.2
3	Barnet	42.8
4	Westminster	42.5
5	Hammersmith and Fulham	41.8
6	Hackney	39.8
7	Harrow	39.6
8	Haringey	39.5
9	Brent	39.2
10	Wandsworth	39.1
	London	*36.4*
	England	*28.9*

Source – The Health Survey of England
As defined by the Department of Health, healthy eating is constituted by consuming five or more portions of fruit and vegetables per day.

PROPERTY & INFRASTRUCTURE

TOP10
MOST EXPENSIVE MONOPOLY LOCATIONS

	Property area	Average price (£)
1	Mayfair	2,102,583
2	Oxford Street	1,309,375
3	Marlborough Street	1,257,700
4	Park Lane	919,138
5	Bow Street	768,200
6	Piccadilly	738,531
7	Pall Mall	651,313
8	Regent Street	510,222
9	Strand	472,929
10	Fleet Street	366,244

Monopoly has been one of the world's best-selling games since it was released in the 1930s, featuring a number of iconic London streets. Of the real-life locations, Old Kent Road is still the cheapest location on the board, with the average property costing £158,000. Marlborough Street is the highest climber, where the average house is nearly 7,000 times its value on the original board.

MOST EXPENSIVE HOTEL SUITES

		Price per suite per night (£)
1	Royal Suite at The Lanesborough Hotel	8,000
2	Infinity Suite at The Langham London	6,189
3	Royal Suite at The Savoy	5,500
4	Royal Suite at The Mandarin Oriental	5,287
5	The Brook Penthouse at Claridge's	4,584
6	Price of Wales Suite at The Ritz	4,435
7	Pavilion Conservatory at The Berkeley	4,000
8	Lowndes Suite at Sheraton Park Tower	3,500
9	London Suite at The Intercontinental	3,400
10	Oliver Messel Suite at The Dorchester	2,950

A favourite with visiting royalty and heads of state, the Royal Suite at The Lanesborough boasts butler service and views of Buckingham Palace gardens. Suites aside, standard rooms in London's five-star hotels are relatively cheap at around £212 per night – nearly half the price of New York.

TOP10

MOST EXPENSIVE HOUSES

	Property	Price (£)
1	20 Grosvenor Square	250,000,000
2	Penthouse, One Hyde Park	136,000,000
3	17 Upper Phillmore Gardens	80,000,000
4	18–19 Kensington Palace Gardens	78,000,000
5=	Toprak Mansion	50,000,000
=	Witanhurst Estate	50,000,000
7	Beechwood House Estate	48,000,000
8	15 Kensington Palace Gardens	42,000,000
9	100 Park Lane	37,000,000
10	31 Belgrave Square	33,000,000

At 166,000 square feet, the 20 Grosvenor Square property was the former headquarters of the United States Naval Forces, Europe. London's most expensive apartment, the penthouse of One Hyde Park, cost over £6,000 per square foot (over 11 times the city average).

NATIONALITIES FOR BUYING PRIME PROPERTY

	Country	Average purchase (£)
1	China	6,477,000
2	Malaysia	6,164,000
3	Hong Kong	5,477,000
4	Russia	5,381,000
5	Egypt	5,092,000
6	UAE	4,835,000
7	India	4,031,000
8	USA	3,815,000
9	UK	3,156,000
10	Nigeria	3,145,000

Source – Knight Frank

Prime property is the most desirable, and often most expensive, property in a given area. In London it is at an all time peak, yet favourable exchange rates can provide foreign buyers with pre-crisis prices. The British account for just under half of prime property purchases, with Russians, Emiratis and Americans being the largest foreign buyers (with 5.9%, 4.4% and 3.7% of purchases respectively).

10

DEROGATORY PLACE NAMES

		Meaning
1	Addle Street	Rotten place
2	Chalk Farm	Cold cottages
3	Fetter Lane	False beggars
4	Houndsditch	Dead dogs
5	Laystall Street	Muck heap
6	Love Lane	Prostitutes
7	Pudding Lane	Entrails
8	Scadbury	Thieves' fort
9	Sherborne Lane	Toilet
10	Shernhall Street	Sewer

Many instances exist where a descriptive name later became ignominious and was changed to avoid negative associations; Aldersbrook was once Nakedhall, Belmont used to be Little Hell while King Edwards Street previously existed as Stinking Lane.

RUDE STREET NAMES

1   Bishops Butt Close, Orpington

2   Bollocks Terrace, Tooting

3   Clitheroe Road, Lambeth

4   Clitterhouse Road, Barnet

5   Cock Lane, City

6   Cumming Street, Islington

7   Gaywood Street, Elephant & Castle

8   Knobs Hill Road, Waltham Forest

9   Mincing Lane, City

10 Penistone Road, Streatham

Medieval London had many rude street names which have since been changed to something less unsavoury. Among them, XX Place, E1 and Shiteburn Lane (the site of cess pits in 1273).

TOP 10
BUSIEST PARTS OF OXFORD STREET

	Junction/crossing	Pedestrians*
1	Argyll Street	231,000
2	Oxford Circus	187,000
3	Davies Street	171,000
4	Dering Street	166,000
5	Hollies Street	132,000
6	Ramilles Street	131,000
7	Berwick Street	117,000
8	Dean Street	109,000
9	Tottenham Court Road	105,000
10	Binney Street	101,000

* Total counted on a trading Saturday

Source – Greater London Authority
Frequented by 2.6 million shoppers a week, and attracting 50 million international visitors a year, Oxford Street is the busiest shopping street in Europe. The combined turnover of its multiple chain, department and flagship stores is around £6 billion a year.

BUSIEST STREETS IN VICTORIAN LONDON

	Street	Vehicles*
1	London Bridge	13,099
2	Cheapside	11,053
3	Temple Bar Gate	7,741
4	Holborn Hill	6,906
5	Ludgate Hill	6,829
6	Newgate Street	6,375
7	Blackfriars Bridge	6,263
8	Leadenhall Street	5,930
9	Cornhill	4,916
10	Gracechurch Street	4,887

* Carriages drawn by one or more horses, passing between 9am and 9pm

Source – City Surveyor records, 1853
In 1853, London had an estimated 1,000 omnibuses, 3,000 cabs and 10,000 private carts in the city itself, with the same number again driving into the capital from elsewhere each day. By comparison, there are 21,000 cabs in London today.

TOP10
MOST COMMON STREET NAMES

1   Victoria Road

2   Church Road

3   Green Lane

4   Park Road

5   Kings Road

6   Alexandra Road

7   Stanley Road

8   Queens Road

9   Warwick Road

10 Manor Road

Many of London's streets were renamed during the Victorian period, hence the monarch's prominence on the list (Victoria Green, Place and Terrace are also commonplace). Despite being the most popular name in the UK, London only possesses half a dozen High Streets.

MOST EXPENSIVE STREETS

	Street, area*	Postcode	Average house price (£)+
1	Parkside, Merton	SW19	5,058,000
2	Wycombe Square	W8	4,415,000
3	Blenheim Crescent	W11	4,346,000
4	Mallord Street	SW3	4,091,000
5	Drayton Gardens	SW10	4,011,000
6	Hampstead Lane, Camden	N3	3,657,000
7	Cedar Park Gardens, Merton	SW19	3,596,000
8	Chester Square, Westminster	SW1	3,461,000
9	Duchess of Bedfords Walk	W8	3,423,000
10	Chelsea Park Gardens	SW3	3,197,000

* Royal Borough of Kensington and Chelsea unless indicated
+ Based on sales from 2003–2010

Source – The Land Registry
The average house price for Greater London is £409,000, but houses in Kensington and Chelsea change hands for, on average, £1,342,000. Barking and Dagenham is the cheapest borough in London, where the average property costs £180,000.

TOP 10

FIRST TUNNELS UNDER
THE THAMES

	Tunnel	Year built
1	Thames Tunnel, Wapping to Rotherhithe	1843
2	Tower Subway, Tower Hill to Vine Lane	1870
3	Northern Line Tunnels, City Branch*	1890
4	Blackwall Tunnels, Poplar to Greenwich	1897
5	Waterloo & City Line Tunnels	1898
6	Northern Line Tunnels, Bank Branch	1900
7	Bakerloo Line Tunnels	1906
8	Rotherhithe Tunnel, Limehouse to Rotherhithe	1908
9	Woolwich Foot Tunnel, North Woolwich to Woolwich	1912
10	Northern Line Tunnels, Charing Cross Branch	1926

* Became disused in 1900, was replaced by the Bank branch tunnel

The Thames Tunnel, described as the Eighth Wonder of the World when it opened, was the first tunnel built under a navigable river. Built by Marc Brunel (father of Isambard Kingdom Brunel), the tunnel saw one million people pass through within ten weeks of opening; half the population of London at the time.

OLDEST BRIDGES

		Year first built	Last rebuilt
1	London Bridge	50	1972
2	Putney Bridge	1729	1886
3	Westminster Bridge	1750	1862
4	Kew Bridge	1759	1903
5	Blackfriars Bridge	1769	1869
6	Battersea Bridge	1771	1886
7	Richmond Bridge	1777	n/a
8	Vauxhall Bridge	1816	1906
9	Waterloo Bridge	1817	1936
10	Southwark Bridge	1819	1921

Before Putney Bridge was built in 1729, London Bridge was the only crossing over the Thames, and it could often take up to an hour to cross due to extensive overcrowding. In medieval times, shops and houses built on the bridge left just 3.5 m (12 feet) in width for two lanes of traffic. Excavations have revealed burnt remains of the original London Bridge, which was built by Roman legionaries after swimming across the Thames.

TOP10
TALLEST BUILDINGS

	Building	Height (m)	(ft)
1	Shard London Bridge (completed 2012)	310	1,016
2	Bishopsgate Tower (to complete 2013)	288	945
3	One Canada Square	236	774
4	Heron Tower	230	755
5	The Leadenhall Building (to complete 2014)	225	737
6	25 Canada Square	201	659
7	8 Canada Square	200	655
8	Tower 42	183	600
9	One St. George Wharf (to complete 2014)	181	593
10	30 St. Mary Axe	180	590

Source – Council for Tall Buildings and Urban Habitat
The Shard's facade is made from 11,000 glass panels, covering an area larger than the base of the Great Pyramid of Giza.

LATEST STRUCTURES TO BE THE TALLEST IN LONDON

	Structure	Height (m)	(ft)	Period
1	Shard London Bridge	310	1,016	2010–
2	One Canada Square	235	771	1991–2010
3	Crystal Palace Transmitter	219	720	1950–1991
4	Battersea Power Station	113	370	1939–1950
5	St. Paul's Cathedral	111	365	1710–1939
6	St. Mary-le-Bow	72	236	1683–1710
7	The Monument	62	202	1677–1683
8	Southwark Cathedral	50	163	1666–1677
9	Old St. Paul's Cathedral	150	493	1310–1666
10	White Tower	27	90	1098–1310

Source – Council for Tall Buildings and Urban Habitat

Excluding antennas and chimneys, the first building in London to be taller than St Paul's Cathedral was the BT Tower, completed in 1964. Despite being one of the most visible buildings in London, the Official Secrets Act meant that it was unmarked on any maps of London until the mid-1990s.

TOP 10

BUILDINGS BY
SIR CHRISTOPHER WREN

1   Old Royal Naval College

2   St. Paul's Cathedral

3   Monument to the Great Fire of London

4   Fountain Court, Hampton Court

5   St. Mary-le-Bow

6   The Royal Hospital Chelsea

7   Royal Observatory

8   Custom House*

9   Theatre Royal, Drury Lane*

10   St. Clement Danes

* Redesigned in later years

Appointed by King Charles II to rebuild the city after the Great Fire of London, Christopher Wren designed 51 churches along with many other grand buildings. His gravestone in St. Paul's Cathedral is inscribed with the epitaph, 'If you seek his memorial, look about you'.

BUILDINGS BY RICHARD ROGERS

1   Lloyd's Building

2   Millennium Dome

3   Channel 4 Headquarters

4   Reuters Data Centre

5   Heathrow Terminal 5

6   One Hyde Park

7   Leadenhall Building

8   88 Woods Street

9   Broadwick House

10 Paddington Waterside

After the completion of the controversial Pompidou Centre in Paris in 1977, Richard Rogers (Lord Rogers of Riverside) was commissioned to redesign the Lloyd's Building, his first major work in London. Rejecting a traditional classical approach, his trademark of placing most of the building's mechanical systems on the exterior in order to leave uninterrupted interiors has won him numerous awards. From 2001 to 2008 he was chief advisor on architecture to then Mayor of London, Ken Livingstone.

10
BUILDINGS NOMINATED FOR THE STERLING PRIZE

	Building	Architect
1	30 St. Mary Axe*	2004, Foster and Partners
2	British Library	1998, Colin St. John Wilson
3	British Museum Great Court	2003, Foster and Partners
4	Canary Wharf Station	2000, Foster and Partners
5	Laban Dance Centre*	2003, Herzog & de Meuron
6	Lloyd's Register of Shipping	2002, Richard Rogers Partnership
7	Lord's Media Centre*	1999, Future Systems
8	Maggie's Centre*	2009, Rogers Stirk Harbour+
9	Peckham Library*	2000, Alsop & Stormer
10	Portcullis House	2001, Michael Hopkins & Partners

* Denotes winner of the prize
+ Formerly Richard Rogers partnership

Awarded annually by the Institute of British Architects, the Sterling Prize recognizes the buildings making the greatest contribution to British architecture.

BUILDINGS NOMINATED AS
THE UGLIEST IN THE UK

	Building	Location
1	Bezier Apartments	Old Street
2	Blue Fin Building	Bankside
3	Broadgate Tower	Bishopsgate
4	City Hall / More London	South Bank
5	Nido Student Housing	Pentonville Road
6	Serpentine Pavilion	Hyde Park
7	St. George Wharf	Lambeth
8	Strata*	Elephant & Castle
9	University College Hospital	Bloomsbury
10	Westfield Shopping Centre	Shepherd's Bush

* Winner of 2010 award

The Carbuncle Cup, awarded annually by *Building Design* magazine, celebrates the ugliest building completed in the UK in the prior 12 months.

PROJECTS THAT WERE NEVER BUILT

1   Royal Palace next to Downing Street
    Designed by Inigo Jones for Charles I in 1638.

2   A symmetrical and piazza-filled Square Mile
    Proposed by Sir Christopher Wren after the Great Fire, the plan centred on the Royal
    Exchange. Other plans included a grid style layout, with each of the 55 blocks being a
    separate parish with a church at its centre.

3   A Triumphal bridge between Lambeth and Westminster
    Heavily featuring Corinthian columns designed by Sir John Soane.

4   An arched span on Tower Bridge
    Horace Jones's original design would not allow larger ships to pass beneath it.

5   A 91-m (300-ft) pyramid in Trafalgar Square
    Proposed by Colonel Trench in 1815, it would have covered almost all of the square at a
    cost of £1 million.

6   A 300-m (1000-ft) Crystal Palace Tower at Hyde Park
To save space it was proposed to turn the hall on its side.

7   Cleopatra's Needle in Parliament Square
Favoured by John Dixon, the engineer who transported the obelisk from Egypt.

8   An elevated cable car railway
Proposed by John Pym before work had started on the London Underground, to be
named the Metropolitan Super-Way.

9   A Viaduct Railway along the middle of the Thames
To avoid paying compensation for demolition, the route was to run from London Bridge
to Westminster with stations on each bridge.

10   The Eiffel Tower at Wembley Park
The project ran out of funds, reaching only 46 m (150 ft) before being demolished in
1907.

BIGGEST PARKS AND GREEN SPACES

		Area (hectares)	(acres)
1	Richmond Park	955	2,360
2	Wimbledon Common	460	1,137
3	Bushy Park	445	1,100
4	Hampstead Heath	320	791
5	The Regent's Park	166	410
6	Hyde Park	142	351
7	Kensington Gardens	111	274
8	Clapham Common	89	220
9	Victoria Park	86	213
10	Battersea Park	83	205

Richmond Park, which is home to around 650 free-roaming deer, has a royal connection dating back to King Edward I in the 13th century, when it was known as the Manor of Sheen. Its name was changed to Richmond during the reign of Henry VII, and was residence to Charles I during the plague.

LARGEST PRISONS

	Prison, type	Capacity	Date built
1	Wandsworth, male	1,665	1851
2	Wormwood Scrubs, male	1,277	1891
3	Pentonville, male	1,250	1842
4	Highdown, male	1,103	1992
5	Belmarsh, high security	910	1991
6	Brixton, male	798	1819
7	Feltham, youth	762	1910
8	Holloway, female	501	1852
9	Isis, youth	480	2010
10	Downview, female	358	1989
	London	*9,311*	

Source – HM Prison Service
Wandsworth, the largest prison in the UK, played host to some of the country's most infamous murderers, spies and traitors (and Oscar Wilde).

FIRST PRIME MINISTERS AT
10 DOWNING STREET

	Prime Minister	Ruling years
1	Sir Robert Walpole	1735–42
2	George Grenville	1763–65
3	Lord North	1770–82
4	The Duke of Portland	1782
5	William Pitt The Younger	1783–1801 & 1804–06
6	Henry Addington	1801–04
7	Lord Grenville	1806–07
8	Spencer Perceval	1809–12
9	The Earl of Liverpool	1812–27
10	George Canning	1827

Robert Walpole, who held the title First Lord of the Treasury, was originally presented with two adjacent houses by King George II which he joined together and completely refurbished to form the building currently known as Number 10. What was his study is now the Cabinet Room.

OLDEST TAILORS ON SAVILE ROW

	Tailor, building number	Founded
1	Gieves & Hawks, No. 1	1771
2	Davies & Son, No. 38	1803
3	Henry Poole & Co, No. 15	1806
4	Norton & Sons, No. 16	1821
5	Holland & Sherry*, No. 9/10	1836
6	H. Huntsman & Sons, No. 11	1849
7	Dege & Skinner, No. 10	1865
8	Kilgor, No. 8	1870
9	Anderson & Sheppard+	1906
10	Chester Barrie, No. 19	1935

* Cloth suppliers
+ Moved to Old Burlington Street in 2005

Royalty, celebrities, world leaders and the business elite have all worn the bespoke suits made by tailors on Savile Row (which was also the site for the Beatles' last ever live performance). The oldest tailor in London, and possibly the world, is Ede & Ravenscroft on Chancery Lane. It was established in 1689, well before Savile Row was built in 1733.

ROMAN ROADS STILL IN USE

		Original destination
1	Brixton Road	Weald mines
2	Edgware Road	Shrewsbury
3	Fleet Street	Burial site
4	Kennington Road	Chichester
5	Kensington Road	Bath
6	Kingsland Road	Lincoln
7	Old Kent Road	Canterbury
8	Oxford Street	Oxford
9	Shoreditch High Street	York
10	Strand	Silchester

Source – Museum of London

Six key routes radiated out of Roman London, primarily to link up and aid communication with military forts. The longest, Ermine Street which connected London to York, stretched further than the M1 does today.

SLOWEST ROADS

TOP10

Road, borough	Hours congested per week
1 Bedford Road, Clapham	92
2 Trinity Road, Wandsworth	85
= Uxbridge Road, Ealing	85
4 Eversholt Street, Camden	84
= Burntwood Lane, Wandsworth	84
6 Rocks Lane, Richmond upon Thames	83
= High Street, Bromley	83
8 Court Road, Greenwich	82
= Regent's Park Road, Barnet	82
10 Pope's Lane, Ealing	81

Source – TomTom
London boroughs (who are responsible for nine of the ten roads) cite roadworks as the main cause of congestion; a record 370,000 sets of roadworks occurred last year, which is over four times the actual number of streets in London.

OLDEST HOSPITALS

		Date founded
1	**St. Bartholomew's Hospital** The oldest surviving hospital in England was founded by philanthropists who felt that London's poor should have access to free healthcare.	1123
2	**St. Thomas' Hospital** Originally built in Southwark, it is now located in Lambeth.	12th century
3	**Westminster Hospital** This became Chelsea & Westminster Hospital in 1994.	1719
4	**Guy's Hospital** Now part of Guys and St. Thomas' Hospital NHS Trust.	1721
5	**St. George's Hospital** The medical school was established in 1834, when the hospital was at Hyde Park Corner.	1733

TOP10

BOROUGHS WITH THE FEWEST PUBLIC TOILETS

	Borough	Number of toilets
1	Merton	2
2	Havering	8
3	Barking and Dagenham	10
=	Harrow	10
5	Newham	10
6	Kensington and Chelsea	12
7	Hackney	13
8	Sutton	14
9	Bexley	16
=	Hammersmith and Fulham	16

POLITICS &
SOCIETY

IN LINE TO THE BRITISH THRONE

1   HRH The Prince of Wales (Prince Charles Philip Arthur George)
b. 14 November 1948
then his elder son:

2   HRH Prince William of Wales (Prince William Arthur Philip Louis)
b. 21 June 1982
then his younger brother:

3   HRH Prince Henry of Wales (Prince Henry Charles Albert David)
b. 15 September 1984
then his uncle:

4   HRH The Duke of York (Prince Andrew Albert Christian Edward)
b. 19 February 1960
then his elder daughter:

5   HRH Princess Beatrice of York (Princess Beatrice Elizabeth Mary)
b. 8 August 1988
then her younger sister:

6   HRH Princess Eugenie of York (Princess Eugenie Victoria Helena)
b. 23 March 1990
then her uncle:

7   HRH Prince Edward (Prince Edward Antony Richard Louis)
b. 10 March 1964
then his son:

8   Viscount Severn (Prince James Alexander Philip Theo)
b. 17 December 2007
then his sister:

9   Lady Louise Alice Elizabeth Mary Mountbatten Windsor
b. 8 November 2003
then her aunt:

10   HRH The Princess Royal (Princess Anne Elizabeth Alice Louise)
b. 15 August 1950

Although Princess Anne is the second oldest child of the Queen, as she is female and males take precedence, the children of her brothers come before her in the order of succession.

LONGEST-REIGNING BRITISH MONARCHS

	Monarch	Reign	Age at accession	Age at death	Reign (years)
1	Victoria	1837–1901	18	81	63
2	Elizabeth II	1952–	25	n/a	59*
3	George III	1760–1820	22	81	59**
4	Henry III	1216–72	9	64	56
5	Edward III	1327–77	14	64	50
6	Elizabeth I	1558–1603	25	69	44
7	Henry VI	1422–61 (deposed; d.1471)	8 months	49	38
8	Henry VIII	1509–47	17	55	37
9	Charles II	1649–85	19	54	36
10	Henry I	1100–35	31–32+	66–67+	35

* The Queen has reigned for 59 years, 9 months and 25 days as of 31 November 2011
** George III reigned for 59 years, 3 months and 4 days
+ Henry I's birthdate is unknown, so his age at accession and death are uncertain

This list excludes the reigns of monarchs before 1066, so omits such rulers as Ethelred II (Ethelred the Unready) who reigned for 37 years from 978.

GREATEST LONDONERS

	Name	Dates
1	Winston Churchill	1874–1965
2	Isambard Kingdom Brunel	1806–1859
3	Diana Spencer	1961–1997
4	Charles Darwin	1809–1882
5	Isaac Newton	1642–1727
6	Queen Elizabeth I	1926–
7	Oliver Cromwell	1599–1658
8	Captain James Cook	1728–1779
9	The Duke of Wellington	1769–1852
10	Margaret Thatcher	1925–

Source – BBC's 100 Greatest Britons poll
More than one million votes were cast in the BBC poll, with Churchill claiming just under half. Other Londoners nominated included Charles Dickens and Guy Fawkes. Channel 4 later sponsored a poll to find the 100 worst Britons, which also featured Margaret Thatcher in the top 10.

ALL-PARTY PARLIAMENTARY GROUPS

	Group	Donations (£)
1	Nuclear Disarmament and Non-Proliferation	181,000
2	Health	148,050
3	Extraordinary Rendition	111,000
4	America	110,000
5	Population, Development and Reproductive Health	80,412
6	Corporate Governance	73,750
7	Choir	60,000
8	Beer	52,747
9	Information Technology	46,300
10	Scientific	46,300

Source – *Guardian*

With no formal place in the legislator, all-party parliamentary groups allow non-governmental organisations to become involved in discussion with Members of the House of Commons and House of Lords. The groups cover a diverse set of subjects, including bingo, brass bands, jazz appreciation and greyhounds.

LONDON MPS' EXPENSE CLAIMS

	MP, constituency	Total expenses claimed (£)*
1	Glenda Jackson, Hampstead & Highgate	166,309
2	Paul Burstow, Sutton & Cheam, Lib Dem	165,691
3	Robert Neill, Bromely & Chislehurst, Con	153,439
4	Barry Gardiner, Brent North	150,400
5	Andrew Dismore, Hendon	150,322
6	Andrew Slaughter, Ealing Acton and Shepherd's Bush	148,056
7	Malcolm Wicks, Croydon North	146,055
8	Stephen Pound, Ealing North	145,766
9	Siobhain McDonagh, Mitcham & Morden	145,487
10	Martin Linton, Battersea	145,282
	Average	*140,456*

* 2009/2010

The expenses scandal of 2010, in which MPs expenses claims were leaked to newspapers and made public for the first time, caused a furore. The maximum that could be claimed during the period was £168,327, of which over £100,000 is allowed for staffing costs, which is paid directly by the Commons finance department. Liberal Democrats MPs had the largest average claim total, at £153,281.

TOP10
COUNTRIES OF BIRTH FOR LONDONERS

	Country	Population	Proportion of group's UK's population (%)
1	United Kingdom	5,080,000	9
2	India	220,000	34
3	Ireland	114,000	29
4	Bangladesh	112,000	56
5	Poland	105,000	20
6	Nigeria	95,000	61
7	Pakistan	81,000	18
=	Jamaica	81,000	57
9	Kenya	75,000	53
10	Sri Lanka	70,000	66
	Total	*7,680,000*	*13*

Source – Greater London Authority
London can rightfully lay claim to the being the most cosmopolitan city on Earth, with 300 languages spoken and at least 50 non-indigenous communities larger than 10,000. Over half of the live births in London are to a mother born outside the UK.

NATIONALITIES WORKING IN LONDON

	Country	Employment rate (%)
1	Australia	90
2	Romania	88
3	South Africa	86
4	France	84
5	Italy	83
6	USA	77
=	Nigeria	77
8	UK	76
=	Portugal	76
=	Ghana	76
	Average	*73*

Source – Annual Population Survey, 2009
The countries with the lowest rates are Bangladesh (44%), Turkey (42%) and Somalia (25%). The levels of employment correlate significantly to the number in higher education and qualifications possessed (held by 63% of Australians compared to 12% of Somalis).

OCCUPATIONS IN VICTORIAN LONDON

	Occupation	
1	Domestic servant	168,701
2	Dress Maker	29,780
3	Shoemakers	28,574
4	Tailor	21,517
5	Commercial clerk	20,417
6	Carpenter	18,321
7	Laundry keeper	16,220
8	Messengers	13,103
9	Painter or plumber	11,507
10	Baker	9,100

Source – London Census, 1861

The opening of the railways brought a rush of servants from around the country to London, where 'the wages were high and the dress and pleasures plentiful and cheap'. Despite around a fifth of servants being under 15 (and some, reportedly, as young as eight), the hours were gruelling, the rules strict and the work arduous.

TOP 10 LONDON JOBS

	Sector	Jobs	Percentage in inner London
1	Health and social work	390,400	58
2	Retail	378,200	49
3	Financial intermediation	331,800	86
4	Transport and communication	307,000	42
5	Education	309,600	46
6	Hotels and restaurants	303,000	62
7	Public administration and defence	223,500	58
8	Manufacturing	178,200	46
9	Human resources	170,000	62
10	Wholesale	151,500	40
	Total	*4,168,500*	*57*

Source – Annual Business Inquiry, 2008
Professional and technical occupations represent well over a third of London's jobs, while managerial and senior official positions account for nearly one fifth.

HISTORICAL BOYS' NAMES

	c.1120		c.1610
1	Willelm	1	John
2	Robert	2	William
3	Ricard	=	Thomas
4	Radulf	4	Richard
5	Roger	5	Samuel
6	Herbert	6	Henry
7	Hugo	7	Edward
8	Johannes	8	James
9	Anschetill	9	Joseph
=	Drogo	10	Robert

Source – sample of Doomsday book as well as parish records
Willelm, the Old English version of William, was hugely boosted in popularity following the Norman conquest in 1066. The invasion also brought with it the French name Jean, which was anglicised over the centuries to John.

TOP10

HISTORICAL GIRLS' NAMES

	13th century	17th century
1	Alice	Elizabeth
2	Matilda	Mary
3	Joanna	Ann
4	Agnes	Sarah
5	Emma	Joanna
6	Isabella	Jane
7	Margery	Alice
8	Christiana	Susan
9	Rohesia	Catherine
10	Juliana	Margaret

Source – Doomsday book and parish records
Many 13th century names are still in existence, though some have failed to stand the test of time, with the top 20 including Basilia, Gunnora, Hawsia and Wymarc.

TOP10
BOYS' NAMES

	Name	Number*
1	Oliver	826
2	Daniel	815
3	Joshua	741
4	Mohammed	666
5	Thomas	643
6	Harry	592
7	Jack	591
8	Samuel	582
9	James	579
10	Alexander	573
	Total	*66,020*

* Born in 2009

Source – Office for National Statistics
James, Thomas and Jack were the top 3 names a decade ago, but Oliver did not even feature in the top 10.

GIRLS' NAMES

	Name	Number*
1	Olivia	587
2	Sophie	479
3	Emily	477
4	Chloe	474
5	Jessica	469
6	Isabella	433
7	Amelia	413
8	Sophia	413
9	Ruby	401
10	Grace	384
	Total	*63,219*

* Born in 2009

Source – Office for National Statistics
Girls' names appear to fall in and out of fashion more than boys'; just four of the top ten featured 10 years ago, with Olivia, Jessica, Isabella, Amelia, Sophia, Ruby and Grace replacing Charlotte, Hannah, Rebecca, Megan, Lauren and Lucy.

SURNAMES

	Surname	Number
1	Brown	40,575
2	Smith	39,971
3	Patel	38,884
4	Jones	33,697
5	Williams	21,862
6	Johnson	20,034
7	Taylor	19,217
8	Thomas	18,249
9	Roberts	17,663
10	Khan	14,502

Source – London Electoral Role

London's cosmopolitan nature is reflected in its residents surnames: the top 25 contains names of English, Welsh, Scottish, Pakistani, Indian, Sikh, Bangladeshi, Irish and Greek origin.

BOROUGHS WHERE ENGLISH IS NOT THE FIRST LANGUAGE

	Borough	Percentage of residents
1	Newham	54.7
2	Tower Hamlets	38.1
3	Hounslow	35.9
4	Brent	35.8
5	Harrow	35.5
6	Redbridge	33.4
7	Ealing	29.9
8	Westminster	29.2
9	Waltham Forest	29.0
10	Kensington & Chelsea	28.1
	London	*21.8*
	UK	*6.7*

Source – Labour Force Survey
Bengali and Panjabi were the most common languages spoken at home other than English, with Greek the most common European first language.

LARGEST CEMETERIES IN
LONDON

Cemetery, Postcode, founded	Area (hectares)	(acres)
1 St Pancras and Islington, N2 (1854)	173.5	82
2 City of London, E12 (1856)	52.5	130*
3 Kensal Green, NW19 (1832)	31	77
4 Battersea New, SM4 (1891)	28	70
= Streatham Park, SW16 (1909)	28	70
6 Lee, SE6 (1873)	26	65
7 Camberwell New, SE23 (1927)	24.5	61
8 Great Northern, N11 (1861)	24	60
9 Merton and Sutton, Morden (1947)	23	57+
10 Tottenham, N17 (1856)	22.5	56

* Plus 46 in reserve
+ Of which 22 are in use

Due to public outcry over the appalling overcrowding of inner-city church graveyards (St. Martin-in-the-fields contained an estimated 70,000 bodies within an area just under an acre), Parliament authorised seven public cemeteries in 1841, which are now known as the 'Magnificent Seven'.

CAUSES OF DEATH

		Proportion of all deaths (%)
1	Neoplasms (e.g. cancer)	28
2	Heart disease	23
3	Diseases of the repository system	14
4	Other diseases of the circulatory system	7
5	Disease of the digestive system	5
6	Stroke	4
7	Disease of the nervous system	3
8	Mental and behavioural disorders	3
9	Disease of the genitourinary system	3
10	Infections and parasitic diseases	2

Source – Office for National Statistics, 2007
Each year around 2,000 deaths are related to alcohol, 4,000 to obesity and 10,000 to smoking.

LARGEST POLITICAL DEMONSTRATIONS

	Protest, cause	Estimated demonstrators	Date
1	Stop the War, Iraq	750,000	15 Feb 2003
2	Liberty & Livelihood, Hunting	410,000	23 Sep 2002
3	March for the Alternative, Cuts	400,000	26 Mar 2011
4	CND march for peace, Nuclear weapons	400,000	22 Oct 1983
5	Peace march, Vietnam War	200,000	27 Oct 1968
6	All Britain anti-poll tax, Poll tax	200,000	31 Mar 1990
7	Tamil Eelam, Tamil rights	100,000	31 Jan 2009
8	Stop the War, Afghanistan	100,000	18 Nov 2001
9	Fund Our Future, Education cuts	50,000	10 Nov 2010
10	Jobs, Justice and Climate, G20	35,000	28 Mar 2009

Source – Metropolitan Police

Across the globe up to 10 million people in 60 countries took part in coordinated anti-war protests on 15 February 2003. The peaceful three mile march in London culminated in Hyde Park and resulted in just three arrests.

LONDON RIOT CHARGES

	Offence	Proportion of all charges (%)
1	Burglary	62.2%
2	Public order act offences	11.7%
3	Miscellaneous	7.2%
4	Handling Stolen Goods	5.4%
5	Possession of Offensive Weapon	4.5%
6	Drug Offences	2.7%
=	Robbery	2.7%
8	Assault on police	1.8%
9	Criminal damage	0.9%
10	Going equipped	0.9%

*After the first week, there were 1,802 arrests of which 1,032 were charged.

Source – Metropolitan Police
Following the police shooting of Mark Duggan, the London Riots from 6–10 August 2011 caused an estimated £100 million worth of damage.

DECADES OF MIGRATION TO LONDON

	Decade	Net migration
1	1900s	931,381
2	1880s	855,896
3	1860s	807,787
4=	1850s	807,782
=	1870s	807,782
6	1890s	660,638
7	1920s	545,416
8	1910s	395,651
9	1840s	369,596
10	1990s	284,756

Source – London Census records

In the 1820s London overtook Beijing to become the world's largest city, succeeded by New York 100 years later. London's population peaked at over 8.6 million just before the outbreak of the Second World War, declining by nearly 2 million over the following 40 years.

HISTORICAL LONDON

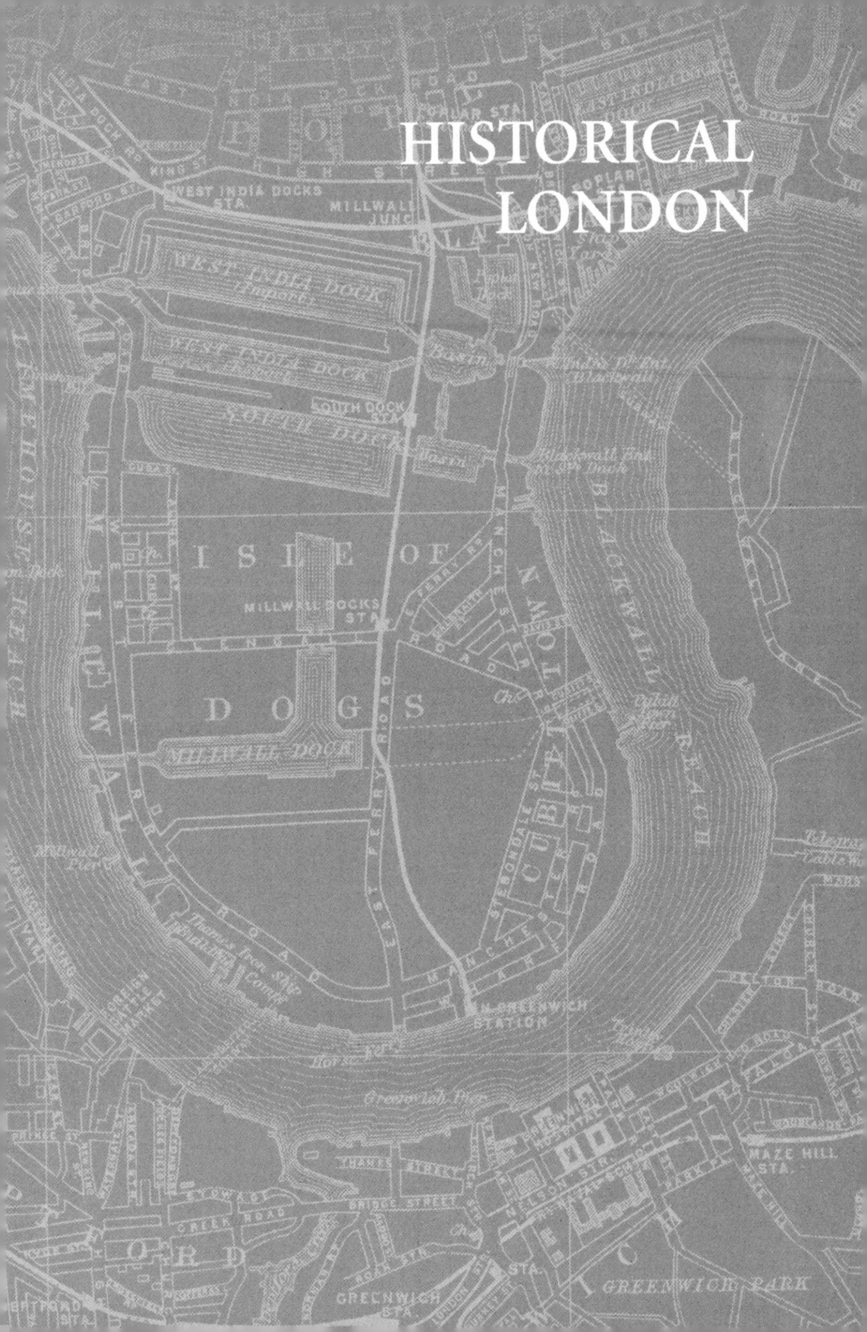

LONDON'S POPULATION AT THE BEGINNING OF THE LAST 10 CENTURIES

		Population
1	12th century	*c.*18,000
2	13th century	*c.*25,000
3	14th century	*c.*50,000
4	15th century	*c.*80,000
5	16th century	*c.*130,000
6	17th century	*c.*220,000
7	18th century	*c.*630,000
8	19th century	1,096,784
9	20th century	6,506,889
10	21st century	7,172,036

In a period when 400 million people were added to the British Empire, 19th century London's population increased six fold (averaging 1.8% per year). The city grew outward with the introduction of the metropolitan railway network, spreading past Islington, Paddington, Southwark and Lambeth.

WORST YEARS FOR
PLAGUE DEATHS

	Year	Deaths
1	1665	68,596
2	1603	30,578
3	1349	c.25,000
4	1563	c.15,000
5	1593	10,675
6	1636	10,400
7	1350	c.8,000
8	1472	c.5,000
9	1609	4,240
10	1647	3,597

Source – Bills of Mortality
Carried by the fleas on rats, the bubonic plague killed up to 7,000 Londoners a week during its peak in 1665, the year of the last major outbreak. It has since been named the Great Plague. In an effort to contain the disease, watchmen locked and kept guard over infected houses, while those who could fled the city.

IMPORTS IN THE 16TH CENTURY

	Product	Value (£)
1	Linen cloth	61,679
2	Wine	57,952
3	Canvas	39,072
4	Oil	38,020
5	Woad (dye)	33,431
6	Cotton cloth	23,349
7	Iron	19,559
8	Sugar	18,237
9	Worsted (yarn)	17,314
10	Hops	16,925
	Total	*643,319*

Source – London Port Book of Orders
In 1560 the majority of London's imports originated in the ports of Rouen, Bordeaux, La Rochelle and Antwerp. Following the defeat of the Spanish Armada in 1588, merchants petitioned for permission to sail to the Indian Ocean, establishing the East India Trading Company in 1600.

DEBTORS TO LONDON IN THE 16TH CENTURY

	County	Debts
1	Yorkshire	515
2	Devon	372
3	Kent	311
4	Essex	218
5	Staffordshire	173
6	Hertfordshire	160
7	Northamptonshire	131
8	Oxfordshire	124
9	Bedfordshire	119
10	Berkshire	77
	Total	*4,609*

Source – Debt cases in the Court of Common Pleas, 1570
Londoners supplied goods on extended credit to their countrymen, resorting to the Court of Common Pleas held in Westminster Hall when they were not paid their dues. The average size of debt in 1570 was £31, with residents of Newcastle, Norwich and Coventry owing the most.

BEHEADINGS AT TOWER HILL

	Name	Date	Crime
1	Simon Fraser, Lord Lovat (Jacobite)	9 Apr 1747	High treason
2	Charles Radcliffe, Earl of Derwentwater	8 Dec 1746	High treason
3=	Arthur Elphonstone, Baron Balmerino	18 Aug 1746	High treason
=	General William Boyd	18 Aug 1746	High treason
5=	William Gordon, Viscount Kenmure	24 Feb 1716	High treason
=	Sir James Radcliffe, Earl of Derwentwater	4 Feb 1716	High treason
7	Sir John Fenwick	28 Jan 1697	Privy to plot to assassinate William III
8	Sir William Perkins	13 May 1696	Plotting to assassinate William III
9	James Scott, Duke of Monmouth	15 May 1685	Rebellion
10	Algernon Sidney	7 Dec 1683	Popish plot

Between 1388 and 1780 a total of 118 prisoners were executed at Tower Hill: 93 by beheading, 12 hangings, 11 hung drawn and quartered and 2 burned at the stake.

LAST PEOPLE TO BE HANGED IN LONDON

	Name	Date	Place
1	Henryk Niemasz	8 Sep 1961	Wandsworth
2	Edwin Bush	6 Jul 1961	Pentonville
3	Victor John Terry	25 May 1961	Wandsworth
4=	Francis Forsyth	10 Nov 1960	Wandsworth
=	Norman Harris	10 Nov 1960	Pentonville
6	Guenther Podola	5 Nov 1959	Wandsworth
7	Ronald Marwood	8 May 1959	Pentonville
8	Joseph Chrimes	28 Apr 1959	Pentonville
9	Ruth Ellis	13 Jul 1955	Holloway
10	Sydney Clarke	14 Apr 1955	Wandsworth

All of the above were hanged for the crime of murder. Conducted promptly at 9am, often only those required to be, by law, were present. The last executions in London were a far cry from the public hangings carried out at Tyburn (near present day Marble Arch) up until the 18th century.

OLD BAILEY PUNISHMENTS

1 ## Hanging
In front of large crowds, convicts were hanged at Tyburn village, near present day Marble Arch. Known as 'dancing the Tyburn jig', executions occurred here from 1196 to 1783.

2 ## Branding
For less serious offences, convicts were branded on the thumb; a T for thief, F for felon or M for manslaughter. For a period (1699–1707), in order to increase the deterrent effect, convicts were branded on the cheek.

3 ## Burned at the stake
This punishment for women found guilty of treason was abolished in 1790. It was common practice for the executioner to strangle the condemned victim first.

4 ## Hung, drawn and quartered
A rare punishment for men convicted of high treason, this was considered the ultimate sanction of the law. Convicts were hanged, cut down while still alive, disembowelled, castrated, then beheaded and quartered.

5 ## Hanging in chains
To act as a deterrent, the bodies of those convicted of egregious acts were left hanging in chains near the scene of their crime. The practice was abolished in 1834.

6 ## Pillory
For crimes of sodomy, perjury and fraud, the convict's head and arms were locked in a wooden frame on a busy street, such as Cheapside or Charing Cross, for one hour. Crowds would then pelt the offender with rotten vegetables, dead cats and even excrement.

7 ## Whipping
Stripped down and tied to the back of a cart, offenders convicted of theft were flogged 'until his back be bloody' along a public street near the scene of the crime.

8 ## Military / naval duty
A practice used frequently during War of Grand Alliance (1688–97), War of American Independence (1775–83) and Napoleonic wars (1793–1815).

9 Imprisonment
Though not perceived to be a form of punishment in itself, convicts were sent into solitary confinement to reflect on their sins and reform themselves.

10 Hard labour
In an attempt to teach them to be industrious, convicts were set to dredge the Thames and naval dockyards, or beat hemp with a mallet to make rope.

Source – The Old Bailey

Many statutes specified death as the penalty for even minor offences such as stealing a handkerchief. However, some mechanisms existed to mitigate the sentence, such as claiming 'benefit of clergy'. This was the right for the church to deal its own, less severe, punishment upon its members. Convicts were required to read a passage from the Bible to prove their affiliation.

Women could 'plead the belly', claiming pregnancy and postponing their punishment until after childbirth. Out of sympathy for the newborn baby, the woman was often later pardoned.

SAMUEL PEPYS DIARY ENTRIES

1 **23 May 1660**
The King, with his two Dukes and Queen of Bohemia, Princess Royal and Prince of Orange, came on board, where I in their coming in kissed the King's, Queen's and Princess's hands, having done the other before. Infinite shooting off of the guns. All day nothing but Lords and persons of honour on board that we were exceedingly full. Dined in a great deal of state, the Royal company by themselves in the coach, which was a blessed sight to see.

2 **13 October 1660**
I went out to Charing Cross, to see Major-general Harrison hanged, drawn and quartered; which was done there, he looked as cheerful as any man could do in that condition. He was presently cut down, and his head and heart shown to the people, at which there were great shouts of joy.

3 **23 April 1661**
Then the Duke, and the King with a scepter (carried by my Lord Sandwich) and sword and mond before him, and the crown too. The King in his robes, bare headed, which was very fine. The crown being put upon his head, a great shout begun, and he came forth to the throne, and there passed more ceremonies.

4 **24 April 1661**
Waked in the morning with my head in a sad taking through the last night's drink, which I am very sorry for; so rose and went out with Mr Creed to drink our morning draft, which he did give me in chocolate to settle my stomach.

5 **30 April 1665**
The fleete, with about 106 ships upon the coast of Holland, in sight of the Dutch, within the Texel. Great fears of the sickenesse here in the city, it being said that two or three houses are already shut up. God preserve us all!

6 **3 September 1665**
It is a wonder what will be the fashion after the plague is done as to periwiggs, for nobody will dare buy any hair for fear of infection, that it had been cut off the heads of people dead of the plague.

7 **12 September 1665**
The people die so, that now it seems they are fain to carry the dead to be buried by daylight, the nights not sufficing to do it in.

8 2 September 1666

Jane comes and tells me that she hears 300 houses have been burned down overnight by the fire we saw, and that it is now burning down all of Fish Street, by London Bridge.

...in an hour's time seen the fire rage every way, and nobody, to my sight, endeavouring to quench it, but to remove their goods, and leave all to the fire.

9 5 September 1666

...down by Poundry's boat to Woolwich; but Lord! What a sad sight it was by moonlight to see, the whole city almost on fire.

...Thence homeward, having passed through Cheapside and Newgate Market, all burned, and seen Anthony Joyce's house in fire, And took up a piece of glass of Mercers' Chappell in the street, where much more was, so melted and buckled with the heat of the fire like parchment.

10 7 September 1666

Walked thence, and saw, all the town burned, and the miserable sight of St. Paul's church; with all the roofs fallen, and the body of the quire fallen into St. Fayth's; Paul's school also, Ludgate, and Fleet Street, my father's house , and the church, and a good part of the Temple the like.

TOP10

PRICES IN THE 18TH CENTURY

		Price
1	One day's allowance of coal, candles and firewood	1d
2	Enough Gin to get dead drunk on	2d
3	Cost of blood letting (for a poor person)	3d
4	A quart of Beer	4d
5	One pound of hair powder	5d
6	Price to sweep one chimney	6d
7	Dinner for a government clerk	7d
8	Toll for a coach and four horses	8d
9	Cost of an Almanac	9d
10	One pound of bacon or a dozen Seville oranges	10d

Source – *Dr Johnson's London* by Liza Picard

A penny, which was silver at this point, was the hourly wage for many unskilled tasks in the city. Yearly wages could be as low as £2 (480 pennies) a year for a domestic servant, around £20 for a coachman, while the First Lord of the Treasury enjoyed an annual salary of £4,000.

SOURCES FOR DR JOHNSON'S DICTIONARY

	Quoted source	Estimated references
1	William Shakespeare	11,676
2	John Dryden	8,150
3	John Milton	4,813
4	Joseph Addison	4,456
5	Alexander Pope	4,170
6	Francis Bacon	3,765
7	Jonathan Swift	3,360
8	The Bible	3,241
9	John Locke	2,788
10	Edmund Spenser	2,645
	Total	*114,000*

Source – Dictionary of the English Language
Almost nine years in the making, Dr Samuel Johnson's *Dictionary of the English Language* was published in 1755. Regarded as the most important British cultural monument of the 18th century, around 1,700 of his 42,773 definitions remain in the Oxford English Dictionary (which was first published 173 years later).

CAUSES OF DEATH IN 18TH CENTURY LONDON

	Cause	Deaths
1	Seizure (convulsion)	4,417
2	Tuberculosis (consumption)	3,411
3	Fever	2,472
4	Aged	1,397
5	Smallpox	1,273
6	Measles	696
7	Edema (dropsy)	682
8	Teeth	644
9	Abortive & stillborn	597
10	Asthma	294
	London total	*17,576*

Source – Bills of Mortality in the City, 1758
Convulsion, an especially common occurrence in young children, was attributed to both poor diet and bad air, as were many of the diseases on the list.

CAUSES OF DEATH IN VICTORIAN LONDON

	Cause	Deaths
1	Tuberculosis (phthisis)	7,146
2	Pneumonia	6,705
3	Bronchitis	5,342
4	Cancer	5,101
5	Diarrhoea	2,658
6	Urinary diseases	2,525
7	Premature birth	2,467
8	Digestive diseases	1,763
9	Measles	1,539
10	Influenza	1,350
	London total	*70,380*

Source – Registrar General's annual survey, 1901
A major contributor to tuberculosis, air quality and fogs in London had become so bad during Victorian times that shopkeepers had to routinely turn their lights on at noon. The 'pea soup' fogs were caused by a mixture of smoke and soot from burning coal.

AREAS WITH THE MOST PROSTITUTES IN VICTORIAN LONDON

		Prostitutes	Of which 'well dressed'
1	Stepney	1,015	310
2	Whitechapel	811	135
3	Southwark	661	193
4	Lambeth	657	354
5	Greenwich	570	296
6	Holborn	511	241
7	Westminster	469	194
8	Islington	441	226
9	St. Marylebone	428	276
10	Hampstead	331	70
	Total	*7,261*	*3,023*

Source – Magistrate Authorities, 1858
Unofficial estimates proclaimed the number of prostitutes in London to be as high as 50,000. The listed figures represent the number known to the police, though Stepney had no entry given for brothels, only 'those who walk the streets'. The areas of Covent Garden, St. James's and Westminster experienced the biggest decreases since previous counts, although London's total had risen from 6,598.

FIRST JACK THE RIPPER VICTIMS

		Date	Location
1	Emma Elizabeth Swan	3 Apr 1888	Osborn Street
2	Martha Tabram	7 Aug 1888	George Yard
3	Mary Ann Nichols	31 Aug 1888	Buck's Row
4	Annie Chapman	8 Sep 1888	Hanbury Street
5=	Elizabeth Stride	30 Sep 1888	Berner Street
=	Catherine Eddowes	30 Sep 1888	Mitre Square
7	Mary Jane Kelly	9 Nov 1888	Dorset Street
8	Rose Mylett	20 Dec 1888	Clarke's Yard
9	Alice McKenzie	17 Jul 1889	Castle Alley
10	Unknown female	10 Sep 1889	Pinchin Street

Source – Metropolitan Police

Over 2,000 people were interviewed and 300 investigated in connection with the Whitechapel murders, especially butchers, surgeons and physicians due to the nature of the mutilations. Only four men were nominated as the potential murderer by contemporary police officers, but as there was no hard evidence, no one was ever convicted.

TYPES OF MEAT IN VICTORIAN LONDON

	Country	Annual consumption
1	Sheep	1,480,000
2	Poultry	1,266,000
3	Rabbit	680,000
4	Pigeon	284,000
5	Bullock	277,000
6	Duck	235,000
7	Lark	213,000
8	Geese	188,000
9	Partridge	84,000
10	Turkey	60,000
	Total	*5,173,000*

Source – London World Exposition
Such was the appetite of the city's population that the overcrowded Smithfield's cattle market, then 600 years old, had to be moved outside the city. In addition, carnivorous Londoners ate over 200,000 tonnes of fish (sole and oysters were especially popular) washed down with 43 million gallons of ale and 2 million gallons of spirits.

TOP 10
VEGETABLES IN VICTORIAN LONDON

	Vegetable	Weight sold (tonnes)
1	Potatoes	400,000
2	Cabbages	110,000
3	Turnips	60,000
4	Onions	50,000
5	Cauliflower and broccoli	30,000
6	Green peas	20,000
7	Brussels sprouts	15,000
8	Carrots and parsnips	14,000
9	Beans	13,000
10	Marrows	2,000

Source – *The Leisure Hour*, 1889

At the time, the Covent Garden Market was by far the largest source of produce in the country, spanning some 30 acres (12 hectares). Today, at its new location in Battersea, it remains the largest fruit, vegetable and flower market in the UK.

TYPES OF THEFT AND ROBBERY IN VICTORIAN LONDON

		Value of goods stolen (£)
1	Theft by servants	8,866
2	Doors left open	4,500
3	Pickpockets	3,018
4	Theft by lodgers	2,936
5	Forced entry	2,848
6	Plunder with violence	2,845
7	Theft by prostitutes	2,024
=	Using false keys	2,024
9	Fraud	1,615
10	Theft from carriages	1,597
	Total	*41,988*

Source – Constabulary Commissioners report, 1853

Common thieves, or *sneaks-men*, were often labelled in accordance with how they stole: *cracksmen* broke into houses, *bludgers* robbed in the company of low women, *bug-hunter*s plundered drunken men, *sawney-hunters* stole cheese, *mudlarks* stole from barges and *toshers* purloined copper from ships.

PLACES OF WORSHIP IN VICTORIAN LONDON

	Religion	Seats	Buildings
1	Church of England	409,184	371
2	Independents	100,436	140
3	Methodists	60,696	154
4	Baptists	54,234	130
5	Roman Catholics	35,994	35
6	The New Church	18,833	94
7	Presbyterians	18,221	23
8	Jewish	3,692	11
9	Unitarians	3,300	9
10	Quakers	3,151	4
	Total	*708,831*	*973*

Source – Handbook to places of worship, 1851

Victorian values and morals were very much rooted in the Bible and Anglican Church. However, the Church of England often focused on appeasing the elite with little care for the lower classes, resulting in the emergence of the Methodist, Presbyterian and Quaker churches. The publication of Charles Darwin's *On the Origin of Species* in 1859 was highly controversial and began a crisis of faith in many areas of religious life.

LARGEST CITIES IN 1858

		Population
1	London	2,363,263
2	Beijing	1,648,000
3	Paris	1,314,000
4	Vienna	900,998
5	Guangzhou	875,000
6	Istanbul	785,000
7	St. Petersburg	590,559
8	New York	515,547
9	Madrid	472,447
10	Berlin	429,000

Source – Based on Census data where available

London was already the biggest city in Europe by 1700, growing mainly through migration from other parts of the British Isles. By 1858, the population of the British Empire was estimated to be 175 million. Lured by the capital's prosperity and opportunities, the foreign-born population boomed.

MOST POPULATED BOROUGHS IN VICTORIAN LONDON

	Borough	Population	Per acre (2.5 hectares)
1	Islington	334,991	108.4
2	Lambeth	301,895	74.0
3	Stepney	298,600	169.1
4	Camberwell	259,339	57.9
5	St. Pancras	235,317	87.4
6	Wandsworth	231,926	25.5
7	Hackney	219,111	66.6
8	Southwark	206,180	182.3
9	Westminster	183,011	73.1
10	Kensington	176,628	77.1
	London	*4,536,272*	*60.6*

Source – 1901 Census
In 1900 the County of London was divided into 28 metropolitan boroughs (the City of London remained a separate county, under the control of the Corporation of London). The areas were amalgamated into the current 12 Inner London boroughs in 1965, joining with the 20 Outer London boroughs to create Greater London.

MOST BOMBED AREAS ON THE FIRST DAY OF THE BLITZ

	Area	Raids
1	Royal Arsenal, Woolwich	13
2	Royal Dockyard, Woolwich	9
3	Rotherhithe Street, Southwark	7
4	Manchester Road, Cubitt Town	5
=	Tunnel Avenue, Greenwich	5
=	West Ferry Road, Millwall	5
7	Barrow Road, Streatham	3
=	Deptford Church Street, Deptford	3
=	Southey Road, Brixton	3
=	Blackwall Lane, Greenwich	3
=	Commercial Road, Stepney	3

Source – based on London Fire Brigade call-outs on 7 September 1940.
Just a few short weeks after the Battle of Britain, an estimated 350 bombers escorted by over 600 fighters raided London. The Luftwaffe attacks continued for 76 consecutive nights, dropping over 12,000 tonnes of high explosives and nearly 1,000,000 incendiary bombs.

BUILDINGS BOMBED DURING THE BLITZ

Building

1 Arsenal Stadium

2 Big Ben

3 The British Museum

4 Broadcasting House

5 Buckingham Palace

6 The Great Synagogue of London

7 The London Library

8 The National Portrait Gallery

9 The Old Bailey

10 Westminster Abbey

Many of Christopher Wren's churches were destroyed during the Blitz and required substantial reconstruction. However, despite being targeted, St Paul's Cathedral survived the war. It is estimated that over one million buildings in London were damaged, with the East End worst hit.

BOROUGHS WITH THE MOST HISTORIC BUILDINGS

	Borough	Listed Buildings	Of which Grade 1	Ancient monuments
1	Westminster	3,826	199	3
2	Camden	3,320	95	1
3	Kensington & Chelsea	1,136	15	2
4	Islington	941	11	4
5	Lambeth	893	6	0
6	Southwark	848	4	7
7	Tower Hamlets	835	17	7
8	Richmond upon Thames	753	38	4
9	City of London	600	83	50
10	Greenwich	511	27	7
	London	*19,129*	*605*	*152*

Source – Department for Culture, Media and Sport
To qualify for listed status, a building can be considered important for either its architectural or historic aspects, taking into account age, rarity, aesthetic merits and national interest. Grade 1 buildings are considered of exceptional interest, usually judged to be of national importance.

TOP10

HISTORICAL ATTRACTIONS

	Attraction	Annual visitors
1	Tower of London	2,414,541
2	St. Paul's Cathedral	1,892,467
3	Westminster Abbey	1,394,472
4	Old Royal Naval College	1,274,957
5	Houses of Parliament	703,255
6	Hampton Court Palace	550,225
7	Buckingham Palace	413,000
8	Churchill War Rooms	328,621
9	Kensington Palace	251,817
10	HMS Belfast	240,769

Source – Association of Leading Visitor Attractions, 2010
Completed by 1100 by William the Conqueror, the Tower of London has served as a palace, prison, armoury, treasury, menagerie and royal mint during its history.

HOTTEST SUMMERS IN LONDON*

	Month, year	Average maximum daily temperature °C	Average maximum daily temperature °F
1	July 2006	28.2	82.8
2	July 1983	27.6	81.7
3	August 1995	27.0	80.6
4	July 1976	26.6	79.9
5	August 2003	26.4	79.5
6	July 1995	26.3	79.3
7	July 1994	26.2	79.2
8	August 1990	26.0	78.8
9	August 1975	25.9	78.6
10=	August 1997	25.8	78.4
=	July 1987	25.8	78.4

* Since 1948

Source – Met Office
The hottest temperature ever recorded in London was 38.1°C (100.6°F) at Kew Gardens on 10 August 2003. In an average year, the capital will experience 28 days that are warmer than 25°C (77°F) and 4 days where the temperature is over 30°C (86°F).

COLDEST WINTERS IN LONDON*

	Month, year	Average minimum daily temperature	
		°C	°F
1	January 1963	-4.6	23.7
2	February 1956	-3.6	25.5
3	February 1986	-2.7	27.1
4	January 1979	-2.6	27.3
5	February 1963	-2.2	28.0
6	January 1985	-1.8	28.8
7	December 2010	-1.5	29.3
8	February 1991	-1.3	29.7
9=	December 1962	-1.1	30.0
=	January 1959	-1.1	30.0

* Since 1948

Source – Met Office
The most severe winter months from previous centuries are thought to have been during 1683 and 1739. During these and many other years the Thames completely froze over, prompting Londoners to hold frost fairs on the ice which featured streets of booths and horse racing.

BIGGEST HEISTS

Location, year	Estimated value (£)
1 **City of London, 1990** Carrying Bank of England Treasury bills, a 58-year-old messenger was mugged at knifepoint.	292,000,000
2 **Millennium Dome, 2000** Foiled mid-way through the act, robbers used a JCB digger to smash through a vault containing diamonds.	200,000,000
3 **Knightsbridge, 1987** With inside help, 120 safe deposit boxes were broken into at a warehouse opposite Harrods.	60,000,000
4 **Bond Street, 2009** After using a professional make-up artist to disguise themselves, two men held up the Graff Diamonds branch, making off with 43 items.	40,000,000

5   Heathrow Airport, 1983   26,000,000
    Robbers broke into a warehouse, taking three tonnes of gold.

6   Bond Street, 2003   23,000,000
    Members of the Pink Panther international jewel thief network
    stole 47 pieces of jewellery from Graff Diamonds.

7   Sloane Street, 2007   10,000,000
    Two men held up a Graff Diamonds branch, taking jewellery.

8   Mayfair, 1975   8,000,000
    A gang raided a Bank of America branch using inside help.

9   Hatton Gardens, 1993   7,000,000
    Graff Diamonds workshop was targeted.

10 Shoreditch, 1983   6,000,000
    A gang broke into the Security Express depot, taking cash.

CRIMES IN LONDON

		Offences Number	(%)
1	Other theft*	121,962	14.4
2	Theft from motor vehicle	85,554	10.1
3	Actual bodily harm	66,958	7.9
4	Possession of drugs	66,759	7.9
5	Burglary in a dwelling	59,837	7.1
6	Criminal damage to motor vehicle	48,972	5.8
7	Harassment	44,435	5.3
8	Common assault	40,787	4.8
9	Theft from shops	34,420	4.1
10	Burglary in other buildings	34,057	4.0
	London total	848,500	100.0

* Excludes theft from/of motor vehicles, cycles and shops

Source – Metropolitan Police, 2007–8
These figures, for London, where over 50,000 people passed away in 2007. The figure is dropping (well under 50,000 in 2009). Nearly one in every five crimes in England and Wales occurs in London, including just under half the robberies and one third of drug offenses.

NIGHTLIFE & CULTURE

FIRST PUBLICATIONS PRINTED IN LONDON

Author/book

1   *Propositio ad Carolum ducem Burgundiae* (Proposition to Charles, Duke of Burgundy)

2   Cato, *Disticha de Moribus* (Distichs on Morality)

3   Geoffrey Chaucer, *The Canterbury Tales*

4   *Ordinale seu Pica ad usem Sarum* ('Sarum Pie')

5   John Lydgate, *The Temple of Glass*

6   John Lydgate, *Stans puer mensam* (Table Manners for Children)

7   John Lydgate, *The Horse, the Sheep and the Goose*

8   John Lydgate, *The Churl and the Bird*

9   *Infantia Salvatoris*

10 William Caxton, advertisement for '*Sarum Pie*'

All the first known publications in England were printed by William Caxton (*c*.1422–*c*.1491) at Westminster. He had previously printed books in Bruges, where in about 1474 he printed the first book in English, *Recuyell of the Historyes of Troye*, followed by *The Game and Playe of the Chesse*. He then moved to England where *Propositio ad Carolum ducem Burgundiae* was printed some time before September 1476; the others were all printed at unknown dates in either 1476 or 1477. It is likely that Chaucer's *The Canterbury Tales* was the first book in English to be printed in England.

FIRST NOVELS
BY CHARLES DICKENS

	Novel	Serial	Book
1	*The Pickwick Papers*	Mar 1836 – Oct 1837	17 Nov 1837
2	*The Adventures of Oliver Twist*	Feb 1837 – Apr 1839	9 Nov 1838
3	*The Life and Adventures of Nicholas Nickleby*	Mar 1838 – Sep 1839	23 Oct 1839
4	*The Old Curiosity Shop*	Apr 1840 – Feb 1841	15 Dec 1841
=	*Barnaby Rudge*	Feb – Nov 1841	15 Dec 1841
6	*The Life and Adventures of Martin Chuzzlewit*	Jan 1843 – Jul 1844	16 Jul 1844
7	*Dombey and Son*	Oct 1846 – Apr 1848	12 Apr 1848
8	*David Copperfield*	May 1849 – Nov 1850	14 Nov 1850
9	*Bleak House*	Mar 1852 – Sep 1853	12 Sep 1853
10	*Hard Times*	Apr – Aug 1854	7 Aug 1854

Dickens' novels were serialized in monthly magazines before being published as books, with readers anxiously awaiting the appearance of each new episode. As well as these full-length novels, *A Christmas Carol* and four other short 'Christmas Books' were published annually from 1843 to 1848.

FILMS SET IN LONDON

	Film	Year	Worldwide takings ($)
1	*Sherlock Holmes*	2009	524,028,679
2	*The Kings Speech*	2010	421,039,684
3	*Notting Hill*	1999	363,728,226
4	*Austin Powers: The Spy Who Shagged Me*	1999	310,332,636
5	*101 Dalmatians*	1996	304,200,000
6	*Bridget Jones's Diary*	2001	281,527,158
7	*Shakespeare in Love*	1998	279,500,000
8	*Bridget Jones: The Edge of Reason*	2004	263,894,551
9	*Love Actually*	2003	247,967,903
10	*Four Weddings and a Funeral*	1994	242,895,809

Source – The Numbers

The top grossing movie filmed in London is Christopher Nolan's *The Dark Knight*. While it is set in the fictional Gotham City, it features Battersea power station, the Criterion Theatre and University College London.

BEST-SELLING ALBUMS
RECORDED IN LONDON

	Album, artist	Year	Studio
1	*The Dark Side of the Moon*, Pink Floyd	1973	Abbey Road Studios
2	*Led Zeppelin IV*, Led Zeppelin	1971	Basing Street Studios
3	*Abbey Road*, The Beatles	1969	Abbey Road Studios
4	*Sgt. Pepper's Lonely Hearts Club Band*, The Beatles	1967	Abbey Road Studios
5	*Brothers in Arms*, Dire Staits	1985	AIR Studios
6	*Faith*, George Michael	1987	Sarm Studios
7	*Spice*, Spice Girls	1996	Olympic Studios
8	*The White Album*, The Beatles	1968	Abbey Road Studios
9	*Houses of the Holy*, Led Zeppelin	1973	Olympic Studios
10	*Promise*, Sade	1985	Power Plant Studios

Source – Billboard
Pink Floyd's eighth album has sold an estimated 45 million copies worldwide, staying in the charts for over 14 years. Abbey Road Studios was a sixteen-roomed residence before being converted into a recording facility in 1931, when it hosted the London Symphony Orchestra conducted by Sir Edward Elgar.

MOST EXPENSIVE ARTWORKS SOLD AT A LONDON AUCTION HOUSE

	Painting	Artist	Sale	Price (£)
1	*L'homme Qui Marche I*	Alberto Giacometti (Swiss; 1901–66)	Sotheby's London, 3 Feb 2010	£65,001,250
2	*The Massacre of the Innocents*	Sir Peter Paul Rubens (Flemish; 1577–1640)	Sotheby's London, 10 Jul 2002	£49,506,648
3	*Le Bassin aux Nymphéas*	Claude Monet (French; 1840–1926)	Christie's London, 24 Jun 2008	£40,921,250
4	*Portrait d'Angel Fernández de Soto*	Pablo Picasso (Spanish; 1881–1973)	Christie's London, 23 Jun 2010	£34,761,250
5	*Modern Rome – Campo Vaccino*	Joseph Mallord William Turner (British; 1775–1851)	Sotheby's London, 7 Jul 2010	£29,721,250

6	*Head of a muse*	Raphael (Italian; 1483–1520)	Christie's London, 8 Dec 2009	£29,161,250
7	*Kirche In Cassone*	Gustav Klimt (Austrian, 1862–1918)	Sotheby's London, 3 Feb 2010	£26,921,250
8	*Triptych 1974–1977*	Francis Bacon (British; 1909–92)	Christie's London, 6 Feb 2008	£26,340,500
9	*La Lecture*	Pablo Picasso	Sotheby's London, 8 Feb 2011	£25,241,250
10	*Three Studies for Portrait of Lucian Freud*	Francis Bacon	Sotheby's London, 10 Feb 2011	£23,001,250

Sotheby's is the world's oldest auction house outside of Sweden, with its first sale of several hundred rare books in 1744. Its rival, Christie's, was established 22 years later in 1766, and was quick to take advantage of the fine art flowing through London following the French Revolution.

BEST-ATTENDED EXHIBITIONS AT THE BRITISH MUSEUM, LONDON

	Exhibition	Year	Total attendance
1	*Treasures of Tutankhamun**	1972–3	1,694,117
2	*Turner Watercolours*	1975	585,046
3	*The Vikings**	1980	465,000
4	*Thracian Treasures from Bulgaria*	1976	424,465
5	*From Manet to Toulouse-Lautrec: French Lithographs 1860–1900*	1978	355,354
6	*The Ancient Olympic Games*	1980	334,354
7	*Treasures for the Nation**	1988–9	297,837
8	*Excavating in Egypt*	1982–3	285,736
9	*Heraldry*	1978	262,183
10	*Drawings by Michelangelo*	1975	250,000
=	*Exploring the City: the Foster Studio*	2001	250,000

* Admission charged, all others free

The world's first national public museum, the British Museum was founded after the death of collector Sir Hans Sloane (1660-1753), who bequeathed over 71,000 objects to King George II. The collection today contains over 13 million objects, some of which are over 2 million years old.

BEST-ATTENDED EXHIBITIONS AT THE ROYAL ACADEMY OF ARTS

	Exhibition	Year	Total attendance
1	*The Genius of China*	1974	771,466
2	*Monet in the 20th Century*	1999	739,324
3	*Monet: The Series Paintings*	1990	658,289
4	*Pompeii AD79*	1977	633,347
5	*Post-Impressionism*	1980	558,573
6	*The Great Japan Exhibition*	1982	523,005
7	*The Genius of Venice*	1983	452,885
8	*Aztecs*	2002–3	436,276
9	*J.M.W. Turner*	1975	424,629
10	*The Real Van Gogh*	2010	411,475

The Academy was founded by George III in 1768 to promote the arts of design. Past Academicians include John Constable and J.M.W. Turner, with Norman Foster, David Hockney and Antony Gormley amongst current members.

BEST-ATTENDED EXHIBITIONS AT THE TATE MODERN

	Exhibition	Year	Total attendance
1	*Matisse/Picasso*	2002	467,166
2	*Edward Hopper*	2004–5	429,909
3	*Frida Kahlo*	2005	369,249
4	*Rothko*	2008–9	327,244
5	*Kandinsky: The Path to Abstraction*	2006	282,439
6	*Andy Warhol*	2002	218,801
7	*Between Cinema and a Hard Place*	2000	200,937
8	*Pop Life: Art in a Material World*	2009–10	192,745
9	*Henri Rousseau: Jungles in Paris*	2005–6	190,795
10	*Surrealism: Desire Unbound*	2001–2	168,825

Housed in a former oil-fired power station, the Tate Modern is now the world's most popular modern art gallery, with 60,000 pieces that are displayed on rotation.

BEST-ATTENDED EXHIBITIONS AT THE NATIONAL GALLERY*

	Exhibition	Year	Total attendance
1	*Manet to Picasso*	2006–7	1,110,044
2	*Seeing Salvation: The Image of Christ*	2000	355,175
3	*Velázquez*	2006–7	302,520
4	*Vermeer and the Delft School*	2001	276,164
5	*Titian*	2003	267,939
6	*Raphael: From Urbino to Rome*	2004–5	230,649
7	*Picasso Prints: Challenging the Past*	2009	227,831
8	*Kienholz: The Hoerengracht*	2009–10	223,183
9	*El Greco*	2004	219,000
10	*Picasso: Challenging the Past*	2009	204,862

* In the 21st century

The world's fourth (and London's second) most popular art gallery houses paintings dating from the mid-13th century to 1900.

BALLETS MOST FREQUENTLY PERFORMED BY THE ROYAL BALLET AT THE ROYAL OPERA HOUSE*

	Ballet	Choreographer	First performance by RB at ROH	Total performances
1	*Swan Lake*	Marius Petipa, Lev Ivanov	19 Dec 1946	959
2	*The Sleeping Beauty*	Marius Petipa	20 Feb 1946	840
3	*Giselle*	Jules Perrot, Jean, Coralli, Marius Petipa	12 Jun 1946	551
4	*Romeo and Juliet*	Kenneth MacMillan	9 Feb 1965	435
5	*Cinderella*	Frederick Ashton	23 Dec 1948	409
6	*Les Sylphides*	Michel Fokine	16 May 1946	373
7	*Les Patineurs*	Frederick Ashton	20 Mar 1946	346
8	*La Fille Mal Gardée*	Frederick Ashton	28 Jan 1960	336
9	*The Nutcracker*	Lev Ivanov	29 Feb 1968	326
10	*Symphonic Variations*	Frederick Ashton	24 Apr 1946	249

* 1946 to 7 June 2011

The Royal Ballet was founded in 1931 as the Vic-Wells Ballet, later known as the Sadler's Wells Ballet. It became the resident ballet company of the Royal Opera House, located in Covent Garden, in 1946.

OPERAS MOST FREQUENTLY PERFORMED AT THE ROYAL OPERA HOUSE

	Opera	Composer	First performance	Total performances*
1	La Bohème	Giacomo Puccini	2 Oct 1897	580
2	Carmen	Georges Bizet	27 May 1882	534
3	Aïda	Giuseppi Verdi	22 Jun 1876	495
4	Rigoletto	Giuseppi Verdi	14 May 1853	490
5	Faust	Charles Gounod	2 Jul 1863	448
6	Tosca	Giacomo Puccini	12 Jul 1900	447
7	La Traviata	Giuseppi Verdi	25 May 1858	437
8	Don Giovanni	Wolfgang Amadeus Mozart	17 Apr 1834	434
9	Madama Butterfly	Giacomo Puccini	10 Jul 1905	387
10	Le Nozze di Figaro	Wolfgang Amadeus Mozart	6 Mar 1819	370

* To 7 June 2011

Most of the works listed were first performed at the Royal Opera House, Covent Garden, within a few years of their world premieres (in the case of *Tosca*, in the same year). Although some of them were considered controversial at the time, all are now regarded as important works within the operatic canon.

TOP10
MUSIC VENUES PUTTING ON THE MOST SHOWS

Venue

1   Southbank Centre

2   Wigmore Hall

3   St Martin-In-The-Fields

4   Jazz Cafe

5   O2 Academy Islington

6   Fairfield Halls

7   Underworld

8   Barbican Centre

9   Royal Albert Hall

10 St James's Church

Source – PRS for Music

Welcoming visitors 364 days of the year, the Southbank Centre occupies a 21-acre site and is one of the largest arts centres in the world. It put on 634 shows in 2009, hundreds of which were free. Across the capital, nearly half of musical performances were rock and pop, with one fifth jazz and latin, and one eighth classical.

LARGEST MUSIC VENUES IN LONDON

	Venue	Capacity
1	The O2 Arena	20,000
2	Earl's Court One	17,500
3	Wembley Arena	13,000
4	Earl's Court 2	6,000
5	Royal Albert Hall	5,250
6	Hammersmith Apollo	5,000
7	Brixton Academy	4,900
8	Royal Festival Hall	2,500
9	Coliseum Theatre	2,400
10	London Palladium	2,300

This list excludes parks and stadiums. Wembley, the second largest stadium in Europe, has held over 80,000 fans while estimates of the crowd size for the Rolling Stones concert at Hyde Park in 1969 range from 250,000 to 500,000.

OLDEST LONDON THEATRES

	Theatre	Date opened
1	Theatre Royal, Drury Lane	7 May 1663
2	Sadler's Wells, Rosebery Avenue	3 June 1683
3	The Haymarket (Theatre Royal), Haymarket	29 Dec 1720
4	Royal Opera House, Covent Garden	7 Dec 1732
5	The Adelphi (originally Sans Pareil), Strand	27 Nov 1806
6	The Old Vic (originally Royal Coburg), Waterloo Road	11 May 1818
7	The Vaudeville, Strand	16 Apr 1870
8	The Criterion, Piccadilly Circus	21 Mar 1874
9	The Savoy, Strand	10 Oct 1881
10	The Comedy, Panton Street	15 Oct 1881

These theatres are the 10 oldest still operating in London on their original sites – although most of them have been rebuilt, some several times. The Lyceum, built in 1771 as 'a place of entertainment', was not originally licensed as a theatre and in its early years was used for such events as circuses and exhibitions, with only occasional theatrical performances. The Savoy was gutted by fire in 1990, but was completely rebuilt and reopened in 1993.

ANDREW LLOYD WEBBER MUSICALS IN LONDON

	Show/run	Performances
1	*The Phantom of the Opera* (1986–)	10,000*
2	*Cats* (1981–2002)	8,949
3	*Starlight Express* (1984–2002)	7,406
4	*Jesus Christ Superstar* (1972–80)	3,358
5	*Evita* (1978–86)	2,900
6	*Sunset Boulevard* (1993–97)	1,529
7	*Aspects of Love* (1989–92)	1,325
8	*Whistle Down the Wind* (1998–2001)	1,044
9	*Song and Dance* (1982–84)	781
10	*Joseph and the Amazing Technicolor Dreamcoat* (2003–5)	·768

* Still running, total as of 31 May 2011

Now in its 25th year, *The Phantom of the Opera* is second only to *Les Miserables* as the longest running West End musical.

RESTAURANTS IN LONDON

	Restaurant	UK rank
1	The Ledbury	1
2	Bistrot Bruno Loubet	3
3	Hibiscus	4
4	Bar Boulud	7
5	The Square	8
6	Galvin La Chapelle	10
7	Pied a Terre	12
8	Hix	14
9	L'Anima	15
10	Terroirs	17

Source – *Restaurant Magazine*, **National Restaurant Awards 2010**
The Ledbury's Brett Graham won Chef of the Year, with the Notting Hill restaurant also winning the Front of House award. 53 of the UK's top 100 were in London, with Terroirs awarded Best Wine List.

RESTAURANTS WITH THE MOST MICHELIN STARS

	Restaurant	Michelin stars
1	Alain Ducasse at the Dorchester	3
=	Gordon Ramsay at Claridge's	3
3	Helene Darroze at the Connaught	2
=	Hibiscus	2
=	L'Ateleir de Joel Robochon	2
=	Le Gavroche	2
=	Marcus Wareing at the Berkeley	2
=	Pied a Terre	2
=	The Ledbury	2
=	The Square	2

London's restaurants boast 65 Michelin stars collectively, offering the greatest variety of cuisines (namely British, Chinese, French, Indian, Italian and Japanese) of any city. Tokyo is the world's most starred city, at 240, which is more than London, Paris and New York combined.

TOP10
ARTS COUNCIL BENEFICIARIES

	Organisation	Funding (£)
1	Royal Opera House	26,342,464
2	Southbank Centre	20,643,408
3	Royal National Theatre	18,285,780
4	English National Opera	17,078,058
5	English National Ballet	6,387,857
6	Crafts Council	2,601,718
7	Sadler Well's Theatre	2,286,395
8	London Symphony Orchestra	2,193,283
9	Royal Court Theatre	2,139,360
10	Rambert Dance Company	2,070,646

Source – Arts Council 2011/12
The Arts Council is a national body concerned with 'developing, promoting and investing in the arts'. Its funding covers, on average, one third of an organisation's income. Tickets and merchandise typically account for half of revenue with the remainder coming from private and local authority donations.

LARGEST HIGHER EDUCATION INSTITUTIONS FOR THE ARTS

	Institution	Students	Founded
1	Goldsmiths, University of London	7,651	1891
2	London College of Communication*	5,432	1894
3	London College of Fashion*	5,113	1906
4	Central Saint Martins College of Art and Design*	5,113	1854
5	Chelsea College of Art and Design*	1,751	1895
6	Camberwell College of Arts*	1,746	1898
7	Royal College of Art	1,205	1896
8	Wimbledon College of Art*	1,124	1890
9	Central School of Speech and Drama	855	1906
10	Guildhall School of Music and Drama	762	1880
	London	*50,130*	

* Part of University of the Arts London

Source – Higher Education Statistics Agency
The University of the Arts London brought together five previously independent colleges in 1986 (with Wimbledon College of Art joining in 2006), forming Europe's largest provider of education in art, communication, design, fashion and performing arts.

TOP10

ANIMALS AT LONDON ZOO

	Animal*	Number
1	Seba's Short-tailed Bat (*Carollia perspicillata*)	140
2	Sacred Ibis (*Threskiornis aethiopicus*)	72
3	Jackass Penguin (*Spheniscus demersus*)	40
4	Blue Spiny Lizard (*Sceloporus serrifer cyanogenys*)	39
5	Lake Oku Clawed Frog (*Xenopus longipes*)	33
6	Greater Flamingo (*Phoenicopterus roseus*)	27
=	Jamaican Boa (*Epicrates subflavus*)	27
8	Red-necked Wallaby (*Macropus rufogriseus rufogriseus*)	25
=	Domestic Rat (*Rattus norvegicus*)	25
10	Abdim's Stork (*Ciconia abdimii*)	23
	Total	*1601*

* Excludes fish and invertebrates

The world's oldest scientific zoo, which opened in 1828, is home to 752 different species. As it was believed that they could not survive London's cold weather, the tropical animals were kept indoors until 1902. This included the first hippopotamus to be seen in Europe since the days of the Roman Empire.

ITEMS ON LONDON ZOO'S FOOD SHOPPING LIST

	Food	Tonnes per year
1	Hay	47
2	Bananas	29
=	Apples	29
4	Straw	28
5	Clovers	26
6	Fish	19
7	Food pellets	18
8	Carrots	13
9	Meat	9
10	Oranges	5

Feeding the zoo's 16,000 mouths is certainly a mammoth task. The animals' diet must be similar to what they would eat in the wild, and require as much effort to 'catch' in order to keep the animals healthy, and their natural hunting instincts honed.

LONDON LIFESTYLE LEAGUE LEADERS

	Indicator	London	New York	Paris	Shanghai
1	Museums	184	101	157	106
2	Public Libraries	395	255	303	248
3	UNESCO World Heritage Sites	4	1	2	0
4	Major Theatres	55	39	43	19
5	Theatre Performances	17,285	12,045	15,598	3,117
6	Music Venues	400	151	122	148
7	Music Performances	32,292	22,204	3,612	11,736
8	Bars	3,117	1,800	2,618	2,996
9	International Students	85,718	64,253	50,158	26,190
10	Festivals	200	81	40	22

Source – London Development Agency
London and New York are constantly exchanging the number one and two spot of the numerous global city rankings. London does however consistently emerge a clear winner within the category of culture, regardless of the metrics or methods used.

TRANSPORT

OLDEST LONDON
UNDERGROUND LINES

	Line	First operated	Original terminuses
1	Metropolitan	1863	Paddington and Farringdon
2	District	1868	South Kensington and Westminster
3	Circle	1884	Circular route
4	Northern	1890	Stockwell and King William Street*
5	Waterloo and City	1898	Waterloo and Bank
6	Central	1900	Shepherd's Bush and Bank
7	Bakerloo	1906	Baker Street and Lambeth North
8	Piccadilly	1906	Finsbury Park and Hammersmith
9	Victoria	1968	Walthamstow Central and Highbury
10	Jubilee	1979	Stanmore and Charing Cross

* Now disused

Source – Transport for London

When a Royal Commission declared central London a no-go area to railway companies in 1846, solicitor Charles Pearson proposed the notion of 'trains in drains'. Construction began in 1860, with a trench dug the length of Euston Road which was lined with bricks and then covered. The line was laid with three rails, to accommodate both broad and standard gauge steam trains (electric trains were not used until 1890). The line officially opened on 9 January 1863, stopping at Edgware Road, Baker Street, Portland Road (now Great Portland Street), Gower Street (now Euston Square) and King's Cross, covering the 6 km (3.5 mile) route in 18 minutes.

UNDERGROUND LINES BY OPERATING DISTANCE

	Line	Distance travelled (km)	(miles)
1	Central	11,834,063	7,353,346
2	Northern	11,765,670	7,310,848
3	Piccadilly	11,659,384	7,244,805
4	District	9,081,236	5,642,818
5	Metropolitan	6,694,500	4,159,769
6	Jubilee	6,166,231	3,831,518
7	Bakerloo	3,490,575	2,168,943
8	Circle	3,411,074	2,119,543
=	Hammersmith & City	3,411,074	2,119,543
10	Waterloo & City	279,399	173,610

Source – Transport for London, 2010
The Central line, which opened in 1900, carries over half a million people each weekday on 72 trains. Travelling its length between West Ruislip and Epping is the longest journey possible without change on the London Underground, at 54.9 km (34.1 miles) taking just under an hour and a half.

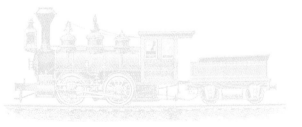

ITEMS LOST ON LONDON TRANSPORT

	Item	Number lost
1	Books	129,158
2	Bags	116,749
3	Clothing	103,966
4	Valuables	73,998
5	Phones	65,912
6	Keys	39,011
7	Glasses	31,174
8	Umbrellas	30,378
9	Gloves	29,147
10	Jewellery	20,444

Source – Transport for London, 2005–10

The sheer volume of items that are misplaced on London buses, tubes and trains means that the lost property office at Baker Street requires 39 full time staff. Amongst the more unusual items that have been lost are a case full of dentures, breast implants, a wedding dress, six full sized mannequins, a 14-foot boat, an outboard motor and a Grandfather clock.

WORDS OCCURRING ON THE TUBE MAP*

	Word	Occurrences
1	Park	31
2	Road	21
3	West	15
4=	Hill/Hills	12
=	South	12
6=	Green	11
=	Street	11
8	East	9
9	Lane/Lanes	8
10	Central	7

* Includes the Underground, Overground and DLR

Source – Transport for London
Although there are 287 tube stations in total, only two feature all five vowels (Mansion House and South Ealing) and only one stop does not contain any letters from the word 'mackerel' (St. John's Wood).

ORIGINS OF TUBE STATION NAMES

1   Angel
    Named after a 17th-century coaching inn.

2   Blackfriars
    From the colour of the habits worn by the monks of a 13th-century Dominican
    monastery.

3   Burnt Oak
    The site where Romans used to light fires as a navigational guide.

4   Covent Garden
    The area was originally a walled garden used by the monks of Westminster Abbey.

5   Highgate
    A toll collection point for travellers using the Bishop of London's road.

6   King's Cross St. Pancras
    The site of the Roman battle with Boudicca, the station took its name from a statue of
    King George IV.

7   Knightsbridge
    Believed to have once been the site of jousting tournaments.

Many of the tube lines take their names from the stations they serve. These include the
Bakerloo Line – an amalgamation of Baker Street and Waterloo, Hammersmith & City – this
line runs from Hammersmith at its west end end through the City.The Piccadilly Line is
named after Piccadilly Circus. The Victoria Line is named after Victoria station; Waterloo &
City runs from a station that used to be known as City, and is now part of Bank, to Waterloo
station.

8 Mansion House
   The residence of the Lord Mayor of London since 1753.

9 Piccadilly Circus
   Named after the house of a merchant who made his fortune selling a type of ruff known as a pickadilly.

10 Swiss Cottage
   Named after the Swiss Tavern, once the largest pub in London.

10

BUSIEST UNDERGROUND STATIONS*

	Station	Passengers per year**
1	Oxford Circus	73,971,000
2	Bank and Monument	40,655,000
3	Canary Wharf	39,616,000
4	Piccadilly Circus	38,567,000
5	Bond Street	36,851,000
6	Leicester Square	35,556,000
8	Tottenham Court Road	34,869,000
9	Holborn	30,098,000
10	Green Park	28,259,000
	Total	*2,426,740,000*

* This excludes stations attached to mainline train stations
** Includes entries and exits

Source – Transport for London
With 526 trains crossing the capital at an average of 33 km/h (20.5 mph), the world's oldest underground railway is used by an estimated 28 million individuals each year.

STATIONS OVERCHARGING OYSTER CARDS

	Station	Total*
1	Waterloo National Rail	£2,452,000
2	London Bridge National Rail	£2,300,000
3	Liverpool Street National Rail	£1,615,000
4	Bank Underground	£1,339,000
5	King's Cross Underground	£1,073,000
6	Victoria Underground	£982,000
7	Stratford	£877,000
8	Oxford Circus Underground	£862,000
9	Wimbledon	£825,000
10	Liverpool Street Underground	£670,000
	London Total	£61,800,000

* Based on incomplete and autocomplete maximum fares in 2010

The maximum £7.40 fare is deducted from an Oyster card when the user fails to swipe at the start or end of their trip. The problem arises during rush hours, when the stations frequently become overcrowded and the barriers are left open, or when the gates are broken. Underground passengers were overcharged around £30 million, National Rail users £25 million and £3 million on the Docklands Light Railway in 2010.

TOP 10

BUSIEST STATIONS IN EDWARDIAN LONDON

	Stations	Daily departures
1	Piccadilly Circus	1,772
2	Bank	1,220
3	Moorgate	965
4	Charing Cross	794
5	Mansion House	711
6	Liverpool Street	427
7	Victoria	404
8	Broad Street*	325
=	Waterloo	325
10	London Bridge	303
	London Total	*8,622*

* Closed in 1986

Source – London Census, 1909
Opened in 1906, Piccadilly Circus tube station served the Baker Street & Waterloo Railway and the Great Northern, Piccadilly & Brompton Railway (now the Bakerloo and Piccadilly lines). A busy thoroughfare, it was around this time that the first illuminated advertising hoardings were erected here, with Bovril and Schweppes among the first brands to take advantage of this powerful new advertising space.

BUSIEST RAIL STATIONS

	Station	Passengers per year
1	Waterloo	86,397,666
2	Victoria	70,224,543
3	Liverpool Street	51,596,155
4	London Bridge	48,723,068
5	Charing Cross	36,459,945
6	Euston	30,068,092
7	Paddington	29,104,198
8	King's Cross	24,817,616
9	Cannon Street	20,229,239
10	East Croydon	19,881,243
	London Total	*947,569,166*

Source – Office of Rail Regulation, 2009/10
Waterloo is the second busiest station outside of Asia (after Gare du Nord in Paris), handling more passengers than Heathrow airport. The oldest terminal station is London Bridge, built in 1836, just six years after Liverpool Station, the oldest station in the world.

CRIMES ON THE LONDON UNDERGROUND*

	Crime	Offenses	Rate+
1	Theft of passenger property	6,134	5.3
2	Violence against the person	2,158	1.9
3	Serious public order	1,892	1.6
4	Drugs	1,616	1.4
5	Criminal damage	1,615	1.4
6	Cycle offenses	359	0.3
7	Sexual offences	338	0.3
8	Serious fraud	230	0.2
9	Robbery	136	0.1
10	Trespass	118	0.1
	Total	*15,109*	*13.1*

* And Docklands Light Railway
+ Per million journeys

Source – Transport for London, 2009
Over 700 British Transport Police officers and 12,000 CCTV cameras monitor London Underground. Trains on the London Underground are now one person operated, with just the driver. In the past, a train guard would also be present, responsible for looking after passengers and assisting the driver in emergencies. 12,000 CCTV cameras now help prevent crime on the London Underground, including serious fraud of tampering with cash and ticket machines.

BOROUGHS WITH THE MOST STOLEN BICYCLES

	Borough	Offences per year*
1	Westminster	1,898
2	Islington	1,632
3	Camden	1,566
4	Hackney	1,509
5	Tower Hamlets	1,422
6	Southwark	1,305
7	Hammersmith and Fulham	1,303
8	Wandsworth	1,293
9	Lambeth	1,138
10	Kensington and Chelsea	922
	London Total	*21,954*

Source – Metropolitan Police, 2010
Around half a million bicycle journeys are made across London every day. The West End and Euston Station are the biggest hot-spots for bike theft, based on recorded crimes, although only half of stolen bikes are thought to be reported.

BUS ROUTES WITH THE MOST DRIVER INCIDENT REPORTS

	Number	Route
1	38	Clapton Pond to Victoria
2	25	Oxford Circus to Hainault Street
3	29	Lordship Lane to Trafalgar Square
4	73	Victoria to Seven Sisters
5	51	Woolwich High Street to Orpington
6	149	Edmonton Green to London Bridge
7	18	Sudbury and Harrow to Euston
8	5	Romford Market to Canning Town
9	8	Bow Church to Holles Street
10	176	Penge to Tottenham Court Road

Source – Transport for London
A Driver Incident Report is a radio call from a London Bus driver to the control centre. The most common anti-social behaviour incidents to be reported are disturbances, forgery and criminal damage.

MOST UNRELIABLE BUS ROUTES*

	Number	Route	Probability of waiting over 10 minutes (%)
1	194	Bell Green to West Croydon	33.1
2	66	Romford to Leytonstone	32.8
3	C10	Canada Water to Victoria	32.5
=	217	Waltham Cross to Turnpike Lane	32.5
5	154	West Croydon to Morden	32.2
6	179	Chingford to Hainault Street	31.7
7	81	Slough to Hounslow	31.3
8	425	Stratford to Kenninghall Road	31.0
9	P4	Lewisham to Brixton	30.5
10	152	Yorkshire Road to Walton Avenue	30.4
	All buses average		*15.3*

* Among those scheduled to run every six minutes or less

Source – Transport for London
Londoners are the nations most frequent bus users, averaging approximately 200 trips per year. This is more than double that of the average Parisian and treble that of a New Yorker.

OTHER COLOURS OF BLACK CABS

	Colour
1	Atlantic Blue
2	British Racing Green
3	City Blue
4	Diamond White
5	Nightfire Red
6	Oxford Blue
7	Platinum Silver
8	Sherwood Green
9	Storm Grey
10	Sunburst Yellow

Originating in the 17th century as the hackney coach, London's 21,000 taxis make nearly a quarter of a million journeys a day. The association with the colour black originated in the 1950s, when the Austin Motor Company charged more for colours other than the standard black. Few drivers were prepared to pay extra, and so it became the norm over the next three decades.

COMPONENTS OF A TAXI FARE

	Component	Pence per mile	Proportion of cost (%)
1	Drivers' wage	128	60.2
2	Fuel	22	10.1
3	Vehicle cost	18	8.5
4	The Knowledge	12	5.5
5	Parts	9	4.1
6	Insurance	8	4.0
7	Social cost	6	2.8
8	Servicing	5	2.4
9	Miscellaneous	2	1.1
10	Tyres	1	0.5
	Total	*212*	*100*

Source – Transport for London
Taxi fares are set by parliament, as they have been since the invention of the taximeter in 1891 (derived from French *taxe*, price, and Greek *metron*, measure). When the standard fare was imposed, it initially proved unpopular with drivers who did not want a machine telling them how much to charge. There are even reports of the inventor, German Wilhelm Bruhn, being thrown in the Thames by angry drivers.

GOODS TRANSPORTED BY HGVS IN LONDON

	Commodity	Tonnes
1	Processed food	18,710,000
2	Other crude minerals	16,077,000
3	Cements	9,432,000
4	Other building materials	7,472,000
5	Sand, gravel and clay	7,073,000
6	Machinery	6,118,000
7	Beverages	6,108,000
8	Agricultural products	4,581,000
9	Petroleum products	3,470,000
10	Chemicals	2,023,000
	Total	*139,239,000*

Source – Department for Transport, 2009
Food, drink and tobacco products travel an average of 115 km (71 miles) to London, with the average heavy goods vehicle laden with 8.6 tonnes. Trucks within, to and from London collectively travel over 1.6 billion km (62 million miles) a year.

TYPES OF CARGO STOLEN FROM TRUCKS

	Type of Cargo	Incidents
1	Building and industrial	111
2	Fuel	64
3	Alcohol	45
4	Household goods	32
5	Electronics	31
6	Food and beverages	25
7	Clothes and shoes	24
8	Metals	20
9	Mobile phones	2
10	Art and antiques	1
	Total	*389*

Source – TruckPol
In addition to theft from trucks, 143 large goods vehicles were themselves stolen, with the total cost of goods and vehicles estimated to exceed £12 million.

IMPORTS TO THE PORT OF LONDON

	Cargo	Tonnes
1	Oil products	10,668,636
2	Other dry bulk	7,600,598
3	Crude oil	4,976,326
4	Agricultural products	1,747,834
5	Coal	1,240,621
6	Forestry products	984,507
7	Other liquid bulk	520,217
8	Motor vehicles	472,225
9	Liquefied gas	370,483
10	Iron & steel products	189,000
	London total	*38,568,050*

Source – Department for Transport
In its heyday in the 1960s, the Port of London handled over 60 million tonnes of cargo and had a total quayside length of 58 km (36 miles). Today it is the largest port in the UK for non-fuel cargo and employs over 29,000 people.

BIGGEST COMMUTES
WITHIN LONDON*

	Journey	Commuters
1	Wandsworth to Westminster	26,010
2	Lambeth to Westminster	25,650
3	Camden to Westminster	23,940
4	Southwark to Westminster	19,350
5	Brent to Westminster	18,060
6	Kensington & Chelsea to Westminster	17,640
7	Hammersmith & Fulham to Westminster	16,530
8	Barnet to Westminster	16,290
9	Wandsworth to City of London	15,300
10	Islington to Westminster	14,880

* Excludes commutes within one borough

Source – Census data
Westminster's population more than doubles in the daytime as commuters arrive at its 45,000 workplaces; the most of any borough in the UK.

PEDESTRIAN ACCIDENTS IN EDWARDIAN LONDON

	Vehicle	Casualties	Fatal
1	Pedal cycles	4,519	17
2	Uncovered vehicles	3,914	121
3	Motor powered tramcar	2,092	26
4	Covered vehicles	1,925	53
5	Motor powered omnibus	1,362	62
6	Horse-drawn cab	941	8
7	Motor powered cab	859	8
8	Private carriages	497	13
9	Motorcycle	312	2
10	Horse-drawn omnibus	273	10
	London total	*17,000*	*326*

Source – London Census, 1908
With many competing omnibus companies in operation, there are several reports of fatalities occurring whilst the drivers were racing against each other. London also had the largest tram network in Europe at the beginning of the century.

PEDESTRIAN ACCIDENTS

	Vehicle	Casualties	Fatal
1	Car	3,543	49
2	Bus	437	17
3	Light commercial vehicle	298	10
4	Motorcycle (>500cc)	193	5
5	Motorcycle (50–125cc)	180	3
6	Taxi	161	1
7	Motorcycle (125–500cc)	78	4
8	Pedal cycle	71	3
9	Motorcycle (<50cc)	65	0
10	Heavy goods vehicle	63	11
	Total	*5,252*	*109*

Source – Transport for London, 2008

Roads in London have become significantly safer over the years; 20 years previously, over 12,000 pedestrians were injured. T-junctions and crossroads are the most dangerous spots while Westminster is the most collision-prone borough, with 419 casualties and 1,390 crashes.

TOP10
BOROUGHS WITH THE MOST TRAFFIC

Borough	Traffic flow (million vehicle km)	(million vehiclemiles)
1 Hillingdon	2,277	1415
2 Barnet	1,747	1086
3= Hounslow	1,615	1004
= Enfield	1,615	1004
5 Havering	1,559	969
6 Bromley	1,356	843
7 Croydon	1,323	822
8 Ealing	1,321	821
9 Greenwich	1,158	720
10 Redbridge	1,064	661
London Total	*32,154*	*19,980*
UK Total	*508,871*	*316,198*

Source – Department for Transport
Car ownership rates are nearly twice as high in outer London compared to the inner city, with South London residents the most likely to make a trip by car.

BOROUGHS WITH THE LEAST TRAFFIC

	Borough	Traffic flow (million vehicle km)	(million vehicle miles)
1	City of London	188	117
2	Islington	467	290
3	Camden	528	328
4=	Kensington and Chelsea	561	349
=	Hackney	561	349
6	Hammersmith and Fulham	587	365
7	Barking and Dagenham	596	370
8	Haringey	618	384
9	Harrow	645	400
10	Merton	672	418
	London Total	*32,154*	*19,980*
	UK Total	*508,871*	*316,198*

Source – Department for Transport
The congestion charge is a fee automatically imposed on certain types of vehicle travelling through busy areas of central London at peak times. It saves an estimated 15 million litres (4 million gallons) of fuel a year, as there are 70,000 fewer cars a day using the roads in Central London. Inner London represents just over 8 billion of the 32 billion vehicle kilometres completed in Greater London.

EMBASSIES OWING PARKING FINES

	Embassy	Number of fines	Outstanding amount (£)*
1	Kazakhstan	1,715	189,640
2	Sudan	1,005	108,240
3	Afghanistan	676	75,860
4	China	668	72,780
5	Saudi Arabia	597	58,460
6	Turkey	468	50,640
7	Egypt	410	49,980
8	Cyprus	449	47,700
9	Pakistan	239	35,360
10	UAE	327	34,760

* As of January 2011

Around 100 embassies have outstanding parking debts, with roughly 60% of diplomatic vehicles ignoring tickets. The worst offender is the driver of a BMW 318i from the Kazakhstan office, who single-handedly has racked up 471 tickets totalling £53,820 in fines.

EMBASSIES OWING CONGESTION CHARGE FINES

	Embassy	Number of fines	Outstanding amount (£) *
1	USA	45,326	5,017,500
2	Japan	31,273	3,476,220
3	Nigeria	23,492	2,565,030
4	India	15,522	1,758,940
5	Sudan	14,391	1,545,540
6	Poland	12,427	1,400,160
7	Kenya	10,088	1,086,990
8	Tanzania	8,361	894,700
9	South Africa	6,674	724,720
10	South Korea	5,979	685,740
	Total	*220,811*	*24,302,150*

* As of February 2011

Source – Transport for London
Embassies and diplomats claim that the congestion charge is a tax, and they therefore have immunity, whilst Transport for London argue that it is a charge for a service, from which they are not exempt.

HEATHROW DESTINATIONS

	Destination	Passengers
1	New York	2,478,722
2	Dubai	1,745,005
3	Dublin	1,620,044
4	Hong Kong	1,528,886
5	Amsterdam	1,509,787
6	Paris	1,338,307
7	Los Angeles	1,235,549
8	Chicago	1,218,516
9	Frankfurt	1,201,534
10	Madrid	1,127,369
	Total	*65,881,660*

Source – Civil Aviation Authority
Starting life as a military training aerodrome in the First World War, today Heathrow handles
1,231 aircraft and 180,000 passengers on an average day.

DOMESTIC FLIGHTS TO LONDON

	London airport	Destination	Passengers
1	Heathrow	Edinburgh	1,306,065
2	Heathrow	Glasgow	1,079,970
3	Heathrow	Manchester	908,723
4	Gatwick	Edinburgh	647,908
5	Heathrow	Aberdeen	641,294
6	Gatwick	Jersey	555,971
7	Heathrow	Belfast	522,676
8	Gatwick	Glasgow	514,660
9	Heathrow	Newcastle	475,432
10	Stansted	Edinburgh	373,714

Just over 20 million people took domestic flights around the UK in 2010, with Gatwick connecting to the most destinations at 19. Certain routes have experienced rises and falls in popularity over the past 20 years. In the early 90s, Gatwick to Edinburgh carried under 20,000 passengers, while over a million people travelled to Belfast from Heathrow.

TOP 10 AIRPORT DIVERSIONS

	Intended arrival airport	Actual arrival airport	Occurrences in 2009
1	Stansted	Birmingham	59
2	Luton	Birmingham	24
3	Gatwick	Birmingham	17
4	Luton	East Midlands	14
=	Stansted	East Midlands	14
6	Gatwick	Manchester	12
7	Gatwick	East Midlands	11
8	Heathrow	Manchester	7
=	Heathrow	Prestwick	7
10	Gatwick	Bournemouth	6

Source – Civil Aviation Authority
London's airports experienced a total of 510 diversions in 2009, primarily during February and December when the country was subject to heavy snowfall which affected a number of public services and transport throughout the country.

TOURISM

LONDON-LOVING NATIONS

	Country	Proportion of UK visits involving London (%)
1	Venezuela	87.4
2	Brazil	85.7
3	Argentina	84.2
4	Kuwait	82.0
5	Israel	80.0
6	Mexico	77.0
7	Taiwan	76.7
8	Japan	76.0
9	South Korea	75.1
10	Nigeria	75.0
	Average	*51.9*

Source – Visit Britain
Around two thirds of visitors to London have no desire to visit anywhere else in the UK, citing either 'not enough time' or 'enough here in London' as the main reasons.

TOURIST ARRIVALS

	Country	Arrivals per year
1	USA	2,370,000
2	France	1,313,000
3	Germany	1,217,000
4	Spain	936,000
5	Italy	822,000
6	Ireland	745,000
7	Netherlands	622,000
8	Australia	607,000
9	Canada	487,000
10	Poland	427,000
	Total	

Source – Office for National Statistics
Although many of London's visitors hail from G7 nations, the fastest growing contingents are from emerging economies. In 2010 Russian, Brazilian, Indian and Chinese visitor numbers were up 37%, 36%, 31% and 17% respectively compared to the previous year.

BIGGEST TOURIST SPENDERS

	Country	Spend (£)	Spend per visitor (£)
1	USA	1,598,000,000	674
2	Germany	399,000,000	328
3	France	394,000,000	300
=	Spain	394,000,000	421
5	Italy	356,000,000	433
6	Australia	335,000,000	552
7	Canada	263,000,000	540
8	Ireland	251,000,000	337
9	Russia	199,000,000	1,199
10	Switzerland	181,000,000	493
	Total	*8,238,000,000*	*537*

Source – Office for National Statistics
In terms of spending per visitor, Saudi Arabians top the league with an average of £1,627 each, but the lower visitor numbers mean that the country doesn't make the Top 10. At the opposite end of the scale, Belgians are the lowest at under £300 per person. Visitors to London from elsewhere in the UK spend an average of £217.

SHOPAHOLIC NATIONS

	Country	Average West End spend per visitor (£)
1	Saudi Arabia	1,974
2	Kuwait	1,780
3	Nigeria	1,648
4	China	1,310
5	Japan	1,295
6	UAE	1,267
7	Thailand	1,183
8	Russia	988
9	Hong Kong	906
10	Singapore	896
	UK	*120*

Source – New West End Company
The retail capital of the world, sales in London are greater than Los Angeles, Milan, Rome, Madrid and Berlin combined. Quantity and quality of shops are a key reason, with more global brands on offer than in any other city, featuring more complete collections and the earlier release of lines and products.

BOROUGHS FOR TOURIST SPENDING

	Borough	Total	Visitor spend (£) from overseas
1	Westminster	6,824,904,000	2,926,597,000
2	Kensington and Chelsea	2,091,536,000	985,857,000
3	Camden	1,533,147,000	588,855,000
4	Hammersmith and Fulham	710,060,000	183,210,000
5	Southwark	707,237,000	162,271,000
6	Hillingdon	696,510,000	325,636,000
7	City of London	682,012,000	239,753,000
8	Barnet	649,803,000	16,936,000
9	Lambeth	645,406,000	148,174,000
10	Tower Hamlets	643,846,000	176,210,000
	London Total	*22,579,983,000*	*8,192,407,000*

Source – London Development Agency
Despite the concentration of attractions in central London, the outer boroughs receive about a third of overall visitor spending. London accounts for over half of all spending by overseas visitors in the UK.

NATIONS KEEN TO SEE
BUCKINGHAM PALACE

	Country	Proportion of tourists (%)
1	Russia	85.7
2	Mexico	81.4
=	India	81.4
4	Hungary	80.0
5	China	78.6
=	Malaysia	78.6
7	Czech Republic	74.3
8	Singapore	72.9
=	South Korea	72.9
=	Poland	72.9

Source – London Visitor Survey

Originally built for a politician on the site of King James I's mulberry garden, Buckingham Palace was first used by a monarch in 1837 when Queen Victoria moved in. It features 775 rooms, including its own chapel, post office and doctor's surgery. It is not the property of the Queen as an individual, but like Windsor Castle, is property of the Queen as a sovereign.

TOP10

ATTRACTIONS IN LONDON

	Attraction	Visitors per year
1	British Museum	5,842,138
2	Tate Modern	5,061,172
3	National Gallery	4,954,914
4	Natural History Museum	4,647,613
5	The London Eye	2,850,000
6	Science Museum	2,751,902
7	Victoria & Albert Museum	2,629,065
8	Madame Tussauds	2,500,000
9	National Maritime Museum	2,419,802
10	Tower of London	2,414,515

Source – Association of Leading Visitor Attractions, 2010

Tourist attractions in London are some of the most popular in the world. Each of the Top 10 attract more visitors than the Taj Mahal, while the top four exceed the number visiting the Statue of Liberty, the Vatican and the Sydney Opera House (which have 4.3, 4.2 and 4 million visitors respectively).

TOURIST ACTIVITIES

	Activity	Proportion of tourists (%)
1	Eating in restaurants	83
2	Shopping for clothes	70
=	Sightseeing	70
4	Shopping for souvenirs	60
5	Visiting a museum	55
6	Going to a pub	49
7	Visiting parks & gardens	48
8	Visiting religious monuments & buildings	41
9	Visiting an art gallery	32
10	Visiting a historic house	31

Source – London visitor survey
Other popular activities included going to the theatre, going on a tour and socialising with the locals (although only 30% of respondents in London said they did this, compared to 39% in other parts of the country).

'ONLY IN LONDON' ACTIVITIES

1   Admire the world's largest cut and polished white diamond, The First Star of Africa, at the Tower of London.

2   Discover where the Gunpowder Plot was contrived at Eastbury Manor House.

3   Indulge in strawberries and cream at Wimbledon Centre Court.

4   Observe the world's oldest fossil insect at the Natural History Museum.

5   Recreate the Beatles album cover on Abbey Road.

6   See the original wooden prototype of the red telephone box at the entrance to the Royal Academy of Arts.

7   Shop around at the world's largest antiques market on Portobello Road.

8   Stock up on delicacies at the Queen's grocer, Fortnum & Masons.

9   Tour Harrow Public School, which boasts eight former Prime Ministers among its alumni.

10 Visit 'the golden mile of tailoring', Savile Row.

ICONIC LONDON PHOTOGRAPHS

		Proportion of visitors that chose as most iconic (%)
1	Double-decker red bus	24
2	Queen Elizabeth II	11
3	Red telephone booths	10
4	The Union Jack	8
5	The London Eye	5
6	Football match	3
=	Draught beer	3
8	Beefeaters	2
9	Tea	1
=	Fish and chips	1

Source – London Visitor survey
Introduced in 1956, the Routemaster was in continuous service until 2005. Nearly 3,000 of the original model were built, outlasting several replacement types. A new version is currently under development which uses a diesel-electric hybrid drive system, making it 40% more fuel efficient.

LONDON EXCURSIONS IN VICTORIAN LONDON

1   Botanic Gardens at Kew

2   Dulwich Gallery

3   Greenwich Hospital

4   Hampstead and Highbury

5   Hampton Court

6   Holland House

7   Lord's Cricket Ground

8   The Thames at Twickenham

9   Windsor Castle

10 Woolwich Arsenal

Source – *Handbook of London* by Peter Cunningham, 1850

These are all described as celebrated places near to, but outside of, London which a stranger should see. In the 1850s London only covered an area that extended to Hyde Park to the west, Regents Park to the north, Mile End to the east and Kennington Oval to the south.

ROUTES RECOMMENDED TO SIGHTSEERS TO VICTORIAN LONDON

Route, notable sites	Omnibus fare
1 London Bridge to Charing Cross Billingsgate Fish Market, Custom House	7d
2 London Bridge to New Oxford Street Newgate Market, College of Physicians	9d
3 London Bridge to Shoreditch Church East India House, Royal Exchange	2d
4 London Bridge to Kennington Gate Guy's Hospital, Horsemonger Lane Gaol	4d
5 Charing Cross to Regent's Park Haymarket Theatre, Regent Street shops	4d
6 Charing Cross to Vauxhall Bridge The Horse Guards, The Treasury	4d

7	Charing Cross to Buckingham Palace Pall Mall, Green Park	3d
8	Charing Cross to Hyde Park Corner The Royal Academy, Burlington Arcade	3d
9	New Oxford Street to Edgware Road Oxford Street shops, Hyde Park	5d
10	The 'Angel' Islington to Marylebone Road King's Cross, Regents Park	4d

Source – *A Handbook for Strangers,* 1865
Visitors to London were recommended that a minimum of eight days (with the nights spent at the theatre and art galleries) were necessary to obtain a thorough knowledge of the capital.

TOP 10

VISITORS TO LONDON THEATRES

	Country	Proportion of tourists who visit the theatre (%)
1	Denmark	31
2	Brazil	29
3	Norway	28
4	New Zealand	26
5	South Korea	25
6	Greece	24
7	Malaysia	23
=	Austria	23
=	Canada	23
=	Australia	23

Source – International Passenger Survey

Around 2.2 million visits are made each year to London's theatres by international tourists. Few cite it as their main reason for visiting the capital, with nearly half the tickets booked on the day of or day before the performance. Musicals are the most popular (representing 64% of sales), especially amongst Europeans, while Asian and Latin American visitors prefer more serious theatre.

NIGHTLIFE-LOVING NATIONS

	Pubs	Nightclubs
1	New Zealand	Brazil
2	Australia	Greece
3	Sweden	Norway
4	Canada	Czech Republic
5	South Africa	UAE
6	Finland	Argentina
7	Norway	Australia
8	USA	New Zealand
9	Denmark	Spain
10	Ireland	Sweden

Source – Office for National Statistics
A recent New Zealander tradition to celebrate Waitangi Day (6 February) in London is to undertake the Circle Line pub crawl, performing the haka at Westminster.

'CULTURE VULTURE' NATIONS

	Most attendees to museums and galleries	Most concert-loving nations*
1	Argentina	Brazil
2	Mexico	South Africa
3	South Korea	New Zealand
4	Brazil	Denmark
5	New Zealand	USA
6	Russia	Australia
7	Australia	Greece
8	Japan	Singapore
9	USA	Mexico
10	China	Canada

* Includes ballet, opera and theatre

Source – Office for National Statistics
With 184 museums, 92 art galleries and over 32,000 concert performances a year, visitors to London are spoilt for choice (New York, the closest rival, can only boast 20,000 performances).

BUSINESS TOURIST NATIONS

	Country	Visitors	Spend (£)
1	USA	441,228	491,748,000
2	Germany	247,341	108,832,000
3	France	221,749	88,257,000
4	Spain	139,532	71,225,000
5	Italy	137,130	70,017,000
6	Netherlands	126,556	71,827,000
7	Ireland	121,760	54,097,000
8	Poland	79,368	30,077,000
9	Belgium	78,020	38,643,000
10	Sweden	77,934	48,569,000
	Total	*2,751,168*	*2,216,790,000*

Source – Office for National Statistics

Business tourism, including conferences and corporate events, is a lucrative market with the average visitor spending double the amount spent by leisure tourists. Indian businessmen stay the longest, with the average trip lasting 15 nights. The average Belgian stays for only two.

PROTECTED VIEWS

	View	Location	Landmarks seen
1	Alexandra Palace	The Viewing Terrace	St Paul's Cathedral, The London Eye
2	Blackheath Point	The Point	Tower Bridge, The Old Bailey
3	Greenwich Park	The General Wolfe Statue	Greenwich Observatory, Tower Bridge
4	Kenwood	The Gazebo	Guy's Hospital, 30 St Mary Axe
5	King Henry VIII's	The Viewing Point Mound	St Paul's Cathedral, Broadgate Tower
6	The Mall	Admiralty Arch	Buckingham Palace, Queen Victoria Memorial
7	Parliament Hill	The Summit	St Pancras Station, Palace of Westminster
8	Parliament Hill	East of the Summit	St Paul's Cathedral, Palace of Westminster

| 9 | Primrose Hill | The Summit | BT Tower, University College Hospital |
| 10 | Westminster Pier | The Viewing Point | St Paul's Cathedral, Royal Festival Hall |

Source – London View Management Framework
These protected vistas, principally of London's UNESCO World Heritage sites, have been enforced since 1991. The protected view corridors are mostly 300 metres wide (with the exception of Westminster Pier) and mean new developments within them have to be approved by English Heritage, Historic Royal Palaces and the Commission for Architecture and the Built Environment.

VISITORS ATTENDING ENGLISH LANGUAGE COURSES

	Country	Visitors
1	France	75,000
2	Italy	59,000
3	Germany	50,000
4	Spain	48,000
5	Austria	24,000
6	Poland	23,000
7	Switzerland	20,000
8=	Japan	18,000
=	Nordic	18,000
10	Russia	10,000

Source – International Passenger Survey
It is estimated that around a billion people worldwide are learning English, but it's not just for tourism. London accounted for just under a third of the UK's English for Speakers of Other Languages (ESOL) budget in 2008, with an estimated 600,000 residents lacking fluency.

HOTEL CHAINS IN LONDON

	Group	Establishments	Rooms
1	Thistle	21	5,969
2	Hilton	14	4,662
3	Premier Inn	27	3,658
4	Holiday Inn	12	3,164
5	Travelodge	17	2,495
6	Novotel	8	2,072
7	Marriott	8	1,920
8	Radisson Edwardian	10	1,786
9	Jurys Inn	7	1,603
10	Accor Group	9	1,571
	*Total**	*184*	*35,749*

* Includes all chains with over 1,000 rooms

Source – Visit London
Around 40% of London's hotel bedrooms are provided by major hotel groups and brands. With a world-leading occupancy rate of over 80%, and an average room rate of over £100, it is no wonder that an extra 20,000 rooms are planned or under construction in the capital over the next few years.

TOP10

OLDEST HOTELS

	Hotel	Year opened
1	Brown's Hotel, Albemarle Street	1837
2	Claridge's, Brook Street	1854
3	The Great Northern Hotel, Cheney Road	1855
4	Grosvenor Hotel, Buckingham Palace Road	1860
5	The Langham, Portland Place	1865
6	Charing Cross Hotel, Strand	1865
7	Andaz Liverpool Street, Liverpool Street	1884
8	Savoy Hotel, Strand	1889
9	Cadogan Hotel, Sloane Street	1895
10	The Connaught, Carlos Place	1897

Hotels in London were virtually non-existent before the railways; visitors would either rent houses or stay in coaching inns. Brown's was known for its sophistication and luxury, while others were more innovative. The Grosvenor was the first hotel to feature lifts (or 'ascending rooms' as they were then called), while the Savoy was the first to be lit by electricity and offer private en suite bathrooms to all guests.

TYPES OF VISITOR ACCOMMODATION

	Type	Rooms	Establishments
1	4 Star hotels	32,939	146
2	Guesthouses & B&Bs	22,896	1,058
3	Universities and colleges	16,396	46
4	3 Star hotels	14,071	86
5	5 Star hotels	9,274	54
6	Branded services hotels	8,469	73
7	Youth groups	5,315	83
8	Self-catering holiday homes	3,257	145
9	Hotels with no rating	3,028	18
10	Serviced apartments	2,944	64
	London Total	*121,993*	*1,852*

Source – Visit London

London's hotels are relatively small by international standards with the largest, the Royal National Hotel on Bedford Way containing 1,630 rooms. In comparison, the largest hotel in the world, the Izmailovo Hotel in Moscow, boasts 7,500 across four towers, and hotels in Las Vegas regularly contain over 2,000 rooms. Las Vegas is home to two thirds of the world largest largest 30 hotels.

TYPES OF OVERSEAS VISITOR ACCOMMODATION

	Type	Proportion of visitors (%)
1	Staying with friends	24
2	Hotel, 3 star	19
3	Staying with relatives	14
4	Hotel, 2 star or less	12
5	Hostel or University	9
6	Hotel, 4 or 5 star	8
7	Bed & breakfast or guesthouse	5
=	Rented apartment	5
9	Other	3
10	Paying guest at private house	1

Source – London Visitor Survey
Staying with friends and relatives is the most common accommodation type for UK visitors to London too, with 32% and 23% of respondents respectively.

HOLIDAY DESTINATIONS
FOR LONDONERS

	Country	Visits	Spend (£)
1	France	2,343,000	824,000,000
2	Spain	1,603,000	707,000,000
3	USA	915,000	923,000,000
4	Italy	771,000	342,000,000
5	Germany	558,000	167,000,000
6	Ireland	514,000	226,000,000
7	Netherlands	417,000	122,000,000
8	Poland	395,000	172,000,000
9	Belgium	390,000	105,000,000
10	Portugal	358,000	167,000,000
	Total	*13,462,000*	*7,438,000,000*

Source – Office for National Statistics
European destinations account for over 70% of Londoners' holidays, at a total cost of £4,078,000. The most expensive destinations are Australia and Thailand, with the average trip costing £1,412 and £1,363 per person respectively.

DAYS OUT FOR LONDONERS

	Place	Visited in the last 12 months (%)
1	Seaside	48
2	Town or City	42
3	Museum or Art Gallery	37
4	Retail outlet	36
5	A Beauty spot	33
6	Gardens	31
7	Stately Home	27
=	Zoo or Aquarium	27
9	Leisure Complex	24
=	Theme Park	24

Source – Days Out, Mintel
Compared to the rest of the UK, Londoners are more likely to visit museums and art galleries, gardens and theme parks.

DOMESTIC VISITORS TO LONDON

	Region	Visitors	Spend (£)
1	South East England	1,600,000	202,000,000
2	South West England	1,540,000	313,000,000
3	North West England	1,180,000	371,000,000
4	East of England	1,130,000	195,000,000
5	East Midlands	880,000	197,000,000
6	Yorkshire & Humberside	830,000	197,000,000
7	West Midlands	730,000	148,000,000
8	Scotland	510,000	191,000,000
9	Wales	450,000	191,000,000
10	North East England	410,000	98,000,000
	Total	*9,460,000*	*2,230,000,000*

Source – Office for National Statistics
Despite being the second most likely nation to take a foreign holiday (after the Swiss), British tourists are significant spenders in London, too. Northern Irish and Welsh visitors spend the most per head, at £550 and £424 respectively.

LONDON'S QUALITIES WITH THE HIGHEST SATISFACTION RATINGS

	Activity	Mean satisfaction score (out of 5)
1	Museums & galleries	3.96
2	History & heritage	3.94
3	Parks & gardens	3.87
4	Theatre & the arts	3.76
5	Shopping & markets	3.64
6	Visitor information	3.40
7	Eating & drinking out	3.34
8	Public transport	3.25
9	Customer service	3.22
10	Accommodation	3.18

Source – London Visitor Survey

The qualities with the lowest satisfaction scores include general cleanliness and the cost of taxis. When visitors were asked, unprompted, what they would like seen improved, the most popular answers were to make transport less expensive, reduce rubbish and smog, and to lift the smoking ban. Thousands of face-to-face interviews are conducted each year as part of the London visitor survey, designed to better understand and improve visitors' experience.

TRADE & INDUSTRY

TOP 10

OLDEST BUSINESSES IN LONDON

	Company	Founded
1	Whitechapel Bell Foundry	1570
2	London Gazette, journal	1665
=	Firmin, button makers	1665
3	Spink, numismatists	1666
4	Hoares, private banking	1672
5	Lock & Co, hat makers	1676
6	Toye, Kenning & Spencer, jewellery and clothing	1685
7	Lloyds of London, insurance	1688
8	Ede and Ravenscroft, tailors	1689
9	Coutts, private banking	1692
10	Berry, Bros & Rudd, wine merchant	1698

Established during the reign of Queen Elizabeth I and the only business in London to celebrate a quatercentenary (400-year anniversary), the Whitechapel Bell Foundry cast the original Liberty Bell and, most famously, Big Ben.

LARGEST COMPANIES WITH HEADQUARTERS IN LONDON

	Company	Global rank	Sales (2010) ($)
1	BP	4	246,138,000,000
2	HSBC Holdings	39	103,736,000,000
3	Lloyds Banking Group	42	102,967,000,000
4	Aviva	53	92,140,000,000
5	Prudential	72	75,010,000,000
6	Legal & General Group	90	68,290,000,000
7	Barclays	96	66,533,000,000
8	Rio Tinto Group	173	41,825,000,000
9	Old Mutual	220	34,072,000,000
10	BT Group	222	33,860,000,000

Source – Fortune 500

If it were a country, BP (formally British Petroleum) would have the 36th largest GDP, ahead of Finland, Malaysia and Ireland. In 2010 BP contributed $20 billion to a compensation fund for those affected by the Deepwater Horizon oil spill in the USA.

FINANCIAL MARKETS IN WHICH LONDON IS A MAJOR PLAYER

	Market	London's share of global market (%)
1	Non-ferrous metals trading	90
2	International bond trading	70
3	Ship broking	50
4	Off-exchange derivatives	46
5	Foreign exchange trading	37
6	Marine insurance	21
7	Hedge fund assets	20
8	Cross boarder bank lending	18
9	Foreign equities	17
10	Private equity	13

Even London's financial markets have a cosmopolitan flavour, with 250 foreign banks operating in the capital (of which only a third are European). Its exchanges list the highest proportion of foreign companies in the world.

WEALTHIEST LONDONERS

	Name	Wealth (£ millions)
1	Lakshmi Mittal and family, steel	17,514
2	Alisher Usmanov, steel	12,400
3	Roman Abramovich, oil	10,300
4	Ernesto and Kirsty Bertarelli, pharmaceuticals	7,000
5	Leonard Blavatnik, investments	6,237
6	John Fredriksen and family, shipping	6,200
7	David and Simon Reuben, investments	6,176
8	Gopi and Sri Hinduja, investments	6,000
=	Galen and George Weston, retailing	6,000
10	Charlene and Michel de Carvalho, brewing	5,400

Source – The *Sunday Times* Rich List
The Top 10's collective wealth grew by over £16 billion in the last year, with 20 new sterling billionaires created nationwide. Also featuring in the Top 20 are Sir Philip Green (£4.2 billion), Sir Richard Branson (£3.1 billion) and Bernie Ecclestone (£2.5 billion).

FTSE 100 ONE DAY DROPS

	Date	Fall (%)	Fall points
1	20 Oct 1987	12.22	250.70
2	19 Oct 1987	10.84	249.60
3	10 Oct 2008	8.83	381.70
4	6 Oct 2008	7.85	391.10
5	26 Oct 1987	6.16	111.10
6	11 Sep 2001	5.71	287.70
7	22 Oct 1987	5.69	110.60
8	21 Jan 2008	5.48	323.50
9	15 Jul 2002	5.43	229.60
10	1 Mar 2009	5.33	204.30

Black Monday, on 19 October 1987, began with a crash in Hong Kong and Tokyo, followed by a wave of panic selling once the markets opened in London. Due to a huge storm the previous Friday which crippled the transport system, only a few traders were at their desks. The FTSE 100 took just under two years to recover its position.

WEALTHIEST FUND MANAGERS
IN LONDON

	Name, fund	Wealth (£)
1	Robert Miller, Sail Advisors	1,000,000,000
=	Nat Rothschild, Attara	1,000,000,000
3	Alan Howard, Brevan Howard	975,000,000
4	Michael Hintze, CQS	550,000,000
5	Michael Platt, Man Group	525,000,000
6	Crispin Odey, Odey Asset Management	453,000,000
7	David Harding, Winton Capital	410,000,000
8	Sir John and Peter Beckwith, Thames River Capital	350,000,000
9	Pierre Lagrange, Man Group	331,000,000
10	Stephen Butt, Silchester Partners	325,000,000

Source – Sunday Times Rich List, 2011

Finance was the second most common source of wealth, behind property and land, amongst London's wealthiest residents. Nat Rothschild saw his personal fortune more than treble over the past year due to his starting of a new hedge fund and floating a holding company.

METALS STOCKED BY THE LONDON METAL EXCHANGE

	Metal	Stock (tonnes)
1	Aluminium	4,450,209
2	Zinc	708,804
3	Copper	383,848
4	Lead	243,318
5	Nickel	135,020
6	Aluminium alloy	71,414
7	Steel	55,669
8	Tin	17,248
9	Cobalt	290
10	Molybdenum	285
	Total	*6,205,482*

Source – London Metal Exchange

Primarily dealing in the hedging of risk through options and futures, the London Metal Exchange still features open-outcry trading (where traders sit in what is known as 'The Ring' with positions at fixed points around a circle and shout their orders). Over 600 warehouses around the globe house the exchange's stocks of metals, with over $10 trillion worth of contracts traded annually.

CURRENCY PAIRS TRADED IN LONDON

	Currency pair*	Average daily volume ($)	Proportion of total (%)
1	Euro–US Dollar	634,400,000,000	34.8
2	Sterling–US Dollar	218,700,000,000	12.0
3	Yen–US Dollar	203,200,000,000	11.2
4	Australian Dollar–US Dollar	115,000,000,000	6.3
5	Swiss Franc–US Dollar	74,800,000,000	4.1
6	Sterling–Euro	66,900,000,000	3.7
7	Canadian Dollar–US Dollar	60,600,000,000	3.3
8	Euro–Swiss Franc	39,700,000,000	2.2
9	Euro–Yen	35,600,000,000	2.0
10	Swedish Krona–US Dollar	28,000,000,000	1.5
	Total	*1,821,000,000,000*	*100.0*

Source – Bank of England
*Foreign exchange, or forex, is the simultaneous buying of one currency while selling another. As it sits on the Prime Meridian, London's markets are open 24 hours a day and trade twice as many dollars than in the US forex markets, as well as double the volume of Euros than in all the Euro-area countries combined.

TOP10

CITIES FOR HUMAN CAPITAL
AND CULTURAL EXPERIENCE

	Human capital	Cultural experience
1	London	London
2	New York	Paris
3	Los Angeles	New York
4	Chicago	Tokyo
5	Hong Kong	Moscow
6	Tokyo	Los Angeles
7	Sydney	San Francisco
8	Boston	Berlin
9	Toronto	Buenos Aires
10	San Francisco	Chicago

Source – A.T. Kearney Global Cities Index, 2010
The A.T. Kearney index assesses the global connectivity of the world's most populous cities. Human capital takes into account the city's foreign-born population, international students and residents' education, while cultural experience is defined by the sports events, arts venues, museums and restaurants. London is second to New York in the overall index, but is lagging in the rankings of political engagement and information exchange.

TOP10

CITIES LINKED TO LONDON

	City	Linkage score
1	New York	87
2	Paris	68
3	Hong Kong	64
4	Tokyo	61
5	Brussels	59
6	Singapore	58
7	Sydney	57
8	Milan	55
9	Frankfurt	54
=	Los Angeles	54

Source – The Global Capacity of a World City report
The scores are based upon accountancy, adverting, banking and law firms' office locations around the world. London has approximately 12,000 office networks, ahead of New York (11,000) and Tokyo (8,500).

BUSINESS ACTIVITIES
CONCENTRATED IN LONDON*

	Business	Specialisation index	Employees
1	Management consultancy	5.0	83,900
2	Engineering research and development	4.3	16,809
3	Software consultancy	4.2	88,719
4	Newspaper publishing	3.8	11,579
=	Monetary intermediation	3.8	141,047
6	Non-life insurance	3.6	15,849
7	Real estate agencies	3.4	27,170
8	Legal activities	3.3	83,500
9	Accounting and auditing	3.2	61,300
10	Activities of religious organisations	3.0	12,957

* Sectors with over 10,000 employees

Source – Annual Business Inquiry
The specialisation index compares the number of employees in an industry within London to the rest of the UK. Many smaller sectors exist which are very exclusive to the capital, including central banking, financial market regulation and foreign affairs (with 88%, 63% and 60% respectively of the UK jobs in the market).

UNIVERSITIES FOR LEAVERS WORKING IN LONDON

	University	(%)	Leavers coming to London* number
1	King's College London	63	2,600
2	University College London	62	2,500
3	London School of Economics	58	750
4	Imperial College London	57	1,650
5	University of Oxford	39	1,500
6	University of Cambridge	33	1,300
7	University of Warwick	25	1,000
8	University of Bristol	23	950
9	University of Nottingham	20	1,500
10	University of Leeds	17	1,300
	Russell Group	*21*	*15,750*

* Russell Group University graduates finding their first graduate job in London

Source – Higher Education Statistics Agency, 2010
86 of the top 100 graduate employers have offices in London (the largest of which, PricewaterhouseCoopers, takes on 1,200 graduates a year). Each position had, on average, a record 45 applications.

BUSINESS SERVICES

	Industry	Jobs	Share of UK jobs (%)
1	Labour recruitment	161,000	21
2	Real estate	109,100	23
3	Information technology	105,100	25
4	Industrial cleaning	96,900	22
5	Consultancy	83,900	30
6	Legal activities	83,500	31
7	Accounting and tax	61,300	29
8	Architecture and engineering	55,600	18
9	Investigation and security	38,600	23
10	Advertising	30,300	38
	Total	*1,016,000*	*23*

Source – Office for National Statistics
Forecast to double in size over the next two decades, business services are already London's largest employment sector.

MANUFACTURING INDUSTRIES IN LONDON

	Industry	Jobs	Share of UK
1	Food, drink & tobacco	28,000	7
2	Printing	25,200	16
3	Electrical & optical equipment	15,200	5
4	Metals	10,900	3
=	Textiles & clothing	10,900	9
6	Machinery & equipment	9,400	4
7	Chemicals	9,100	5
8	Transport equipment	8,800	3
9	Rubber & plastics	6,600	4
10	Wood & wood products	3,100	4
	Total	*204,500*	*7*

Source – Office for National Statistics

Losing approximately 24,000 manufacturing jobs per year over the last three decades, London now has the lowest rate of manufacturing employment in the country. However, due to the concentration of high value added manufacturing, employees are more productive, contributing over 10% of the UK's output.

LONDON TAXES

	Tax	Total (£)	Proportion of total tax revenue (%)
1	Income	27,900,000,000	25.6
2	National Insurance	15,300,000,000	14.1
3	VAT	11,800,000,000	10.8
4	Corporation	8,500,000,000	7.8
5	Business Rates	4,500,000,000	4.1
6	Fuel Duties	3,600,000,000	3.3
7	Council	2,800,000,000	2.6
8	Stamp Duty	1,700,000,000	1.6
9	Alcohol Duties	1,200,000,000	1.1
=	Tobacco Duties	1,200,000,000	1.1
	Total	*91,900,000,000*	*100.0*

Source – HM Treasury
Taxes were first introduced to London by the Romans, chiefly on imports and inheritance (although it is not clear if their infamous urine tax was implemented in Britain). Odd taxes have included a levy on playing cards, top hats and wigs. The unpopular window tax, introduced in 1696, resulted in many households simply bricking over unessential windows (of which there are plentiful examples around London today).

LONDON EXPORTS

	Export	Value (£)
1	Fund management and securities broking	11,200,000,000
2	Monetary finance	10,800,000,000
3	Personal travel	7,100,000,000
4	Air transport	5,700,000,000
5	Management consulting	2,100,000,000
6	Insurance	1,700,000,000
7	Computer and information services	1,600,000,000
8	Advertising and market research	1,200,000,000
9	Engineering and technical services	1,100,000,000
10	Legal services	1,000,000,000

Source – Greater London Authority
The Square Mile alone accounts for 1% of the world's GDP, with the city's fund managers controlling nearly £2 trillion worth of assets.

COUNTRIES INVESTING IN LONDON

	Country	Annual foreign direct investment (£)	Share of total foreign owned stock (%)
1	USA	16,120,000,000	50

London and partners has two offices in the USA, in San Francisco and New York. The others, aside from London, are in Beijing, Mumbai and Shanghai.

2	India	8,320,000,000	<1

There are up to 10,000 Indian-owned businesses in London. Roughly one million passengers a year fly directly between the airports of India and London.

3	France	3,640,000,000	12

French investment in Eurostar International Limited now give London access to over 100 destinations in Europe.

4	Canada	3,120,000,000	1

The London and Toronto Stock Exchanges nearly merged in 2011, which would have created an exchange containing the largest number of listed companies in the world.

=	China	3,120,000,000	3

Chinese investors benefit from the Olympic Games Legacy in London from the Beijing competition in 2008.

=	Japan	3,120,000,000	5

Relations with Japan stem from the Anglo-Japanese Treaty of Amity and Commerce in 1858.

7	Australia	2,600,000,000	3

Being situated on the meridian is considered a significant advantage
when australian companies decide where to invest abroad.

8	South Korea	2,080,000,000	<1

London has a bigger Korean population of any European city.

9	Spain	1,560,000,000	<1

The capital secured more foreign business projects than Spain in 2007.

10	Germany	1,040,000,000	4

London secured more Foreign direct investment than any city in Germany,
and only narrowly less than the whole country.

=	Italy	1,040,000,000	<1

Many Italian fashion companies appreciate London's creative centre and
design schools.

=	Sweden	1,040,000,000	<1

The Swedish Chamber of Commerce for the United Kingdom was founded
in 1906 in London.

	Total	52,000,000,000	100

Source – Think London
Access to markets, time zone advantages, qualified staff and a stable business environment are
the preeminent factors attracting investment in London, the world's top ranking business city.

TOP 10
LOW CARBON INDUSTRIES

	Industry	Value (£)	Companies	Employees
1	Geothermal	2,360,000,000	1,040	17,460
2	Alternative fuels	2,150,000,000	1,060	19,340
3	Wind	2,100,000,000	1,100	14,760
4	Building technologies	1,980,000,000	830	15,560
5	Photovoltaic	1,190,000,000	370	8,720
6	Waste management	1,180,000,000	430	9,950
7	Biomass	930,000,000	350	7,840
8	Recycling	850,000,000	170	5,160
9	Energy management	320,000,000	60	1,790
10	Renewable consulting	80,000,000	10	520
	Total	*13,390,000,000*	*5,520*	*102,620*

Source – Greater London Authority, 2009
Other environmental sectors in London include Carbon Finance, which is worth over £5 billion, and Waste Water Treatment, valued at £1.5 billion. Across the capital there are 17 universities and 80 departments focusing on low carbon related research.

BOROUGHS WITH THE MOST START-UPS

	Borough	Start-ups
1	Westminster	6,745
2	Camden	3,035
3	Barnet	2,610
4	Wandsworth	2,570
5	Ealing	2,155
6	Tower Hamlets	2,045
7	Southwark	2,025
8	City of London	2,005
9	Hammersmith & Fulham	1,960
10	Islington	1,940
	London	*57,955*

Source – Office for National Statistics
London's entrepreneurs benefit from the largest venture capital market outside of the US, a plethora of business services and world class research universities. A recent survey suggested that 15% of Londoners expect to start a business within the next three years.

BOROUGHS WITH THE WORST BUSINESS SURVIVAL RATES

	Borough	Proportion of businesses surviving over five years (%)
1	Hammersmith & Fulham	35.4
2	Wandsworth	36.5
3	Waltham Forest	37.2
4	Newham	38.5
5	Barking & Dagenham	39.0
6	Brent	39.1
7	Ealing	39.2
8	Merton	39.4
9	Redbridge	40.0
10	Lambeth	40.5
	London	*41.9*

Source – Office for National Statistics
91% of London's businesses survive their first year, dropping to 67% after the first three. Late payments and bad debts are amongst the most frequently cited problems for businesses.

FIRST ROYAL WARRANTS TO LONDON COMPANIES

	Company	Warrant
1	Charles Farris Ltd	Candles
2	DAKS Ltd	Outfitters
3	Ede & Ravenscroft Ltd	Robe Makers
4	Fortnum & Mason Plc	Grocers & Provisions
5	James Purdey & Sons Ltd	Gun & Cartridge Makers
6	Justerini & Brooks Ltd	Wine Merchants
7	Tanqueray Gordon & Co Ltd	Gin Distillers
8	Thomas Goode & Co Ltd	China & Glass
9	Toye, Kenning & Spencer Ltd	Gold & Silver Laces
10	Yardley of London	Toiletry Products

All of the above warrants were granted by the Queen in 1955 and 1956 as a mark of recognition of supplying the royal household for at least four years. Over 800 have since been appointed to individuals and companies globally, including Aston Martin, Bollinger and Xerox.

TOP10

LIVERY COMPANIES BY
ORDER OF PRECEDENCE

	Company	Date founded
1	The Worshipful Company of Mercers	1394
2	The Worshipful Company of Grocers	1345
3	The Worshipful Company of Drapers	1361
4	The Worshipful Company of Fishmongers	1537
5	The Worshipful Company of Goldsmiths	1327
6	The Worshipful Company of Merchant Taylors*	1327
7	The Worshipful Company of Skinners*	1327
8	The Worshipful Company of Haberdashers	1448
9	The Worshipful Company of Salters	1559
10	The Worshipful Company of Ironmongers	1463

* Alternate every year

Established to foster their respective trades and enforce standards, there are now 108 livery companies. After much dispute the order of precedence was settled in 1515, though the Merchant Taylors and Skinners exchange places every year, giving origin to the phrase 'at sixes and sevens'.

INSURANCE POLICIES ISSUED BY LLOYD'S OF LONDON

1   Food critic Egon Ronay's taste buds

2   Against a prize for the capture of the Loch Ness Monster

3   The tongue of Gennaro Pelliccia, a coffee taster

4   Keith Richards' fingers

5   Jewellery worn by the stars at the Oscars

6   Formula One drivers

7   Against death from excessive laughter at theatres

8   Star of *Ugly Betty* America Ferrara's smile

9   Bruce Springsteen's voice

10   The Titanic

The world's leading specialised insurance market (or brand, but not a company) is a society of members who underwrite and accept risk from clients and brokers across the globe. The hull and machinery alone of the Titanic was insured for over £1,000,000 in 1912, with total payouts exceeding three times this figure.

FORTNUM & MASON'S BESTSELLING LINES

1   Hampers

2   Royal Blend tea

3   Champagne truffles

4   Christmas pudding

5   Fortnum & Mason Blancs de Blancs Champagne

6   Royal Christmas cracker

7   *Debrett's Correct Form* (etiquette book)

8   Fortnum's Pickle

9   Piccadilly honey

10   Fortnum's Apron & Chef's Hat

Fortnum & Mason Ltd of Piccadilly dates from the 18th century when William Fortnum, a former footman in Queen Anne's household, joined forces with Hugh Mason to form a grocery store that soon became one of the most famous in the world.

FASHION PRODUCTS SOLD

		Spend (£)
1	Women's clothing	4,828,000,000
2	Men's clothing	3,261,000,000
3	Children's clothing	1,649,000,000
4	Footwear	1,444,000,000
5	Jewellery & watches	1,090,000,000
6	Lingerie	793,000,000
7	Accessories	564,000,000
8	Hair	417,000,000
9	Luggage & bags	329,000,000
10	Cosmetics	196,000,000
	Total	*14,570,000,000*

Source – British Fashion Council

London accounted for just over a quarter of the UK's fashion spending. Compared to the rest of the country, Londoners spend proportionally less on cosmetics and more on jewellery and watches. Residents spent a further £9.9 billion online, topping the global e-retail rankings.

RETAIL CENTRES IN LONDON

	Centre	Turnover (£)	Floor space (m^2)
1	West End	7,520,000,000	1,581,456
2	Knightsbridge	1,710,000,000	167,742
3	Bromley	980,000,000	176,495
4	Kingston	924,000,000	246,969
5	Croydon	923,000,000	266,981
6	Westfield	840,000,000	149,461
7	Brent Cross	704,000,000	86,388
8	Purley Way	544,000,000	133,400
9	Kensington	488,000,000	94,125
10	Romford	465,000,000	197,033

Source – London Town Centre Assessment Report

Sales in the West End are projected to reach upwards of £11 billion per annum in the next 20 years, with London requiring an additional 3 million m^2 of retail floor space.

SPORT

LAST MEN TO SCORE A
HAT-TRICK AT WEMBLEY*

	Player	Team	Score	Date
1	Scott Sinclair	Swansea City v. Reading	4–2	30 May 2011
2	Jermain Defoe	England v. Bulgaria	4–0	3 Sep 2010
3	Alan Shearer	England v. Luxembourg	6–0	4 Sep 1999
4	Paul Scholes	England v. Poland	3–0	27 Mar 1999
5	Clive Mendonca	Charlton Athletic v. Sunderland	4–4	25 May 1998
6	David Platt (4)	England v. San Marino	6–0	17 Feb 1993
7	Gary Lineker	England v. Turkey	8–0	14 Oct 1987
8	Gary Lineker	England v. Turkey	5–0	16 Oct 1985
9	Luther Blissett	England v. Luxembourg	9–0	15 Dec 1982
10	Malcolm Macdonald (5)	England v. Cyprus	5–0	16 Apr 1975

* In a senior competitive match

Giampaolo Pazzini scored the first goal at the new Wembley Stadium on 24 March 2007, after just 28 seconds, in an England Under-21 friendly against Italy. Pazzini went on to score the first hat-trick at the new Wembley Stadium in that match, which ended 3–3. The first man to score a hat-trick at the old Wembley was Alex Jackson, a member of the famous Scottish Wembley Wizards who beat England 5–1 on 31 March 1928.

Gary Lineker (above), Geoff Hurst (1966 and 1969) and Jimmy Greaves (1961 and 1963) are the only men ever to score two hat-tricks at Wembley.

Whilst the 'Matthews Final', as it became known, really belonged to two men, Stan Matthews and Stan Mortensen, the 1966 World Cup final belonged to eleven heroes but one man's name will be etched into World Cup history forever, that of Geoff Hurst, the only man to score a hat trick in a World Cup Final.

West Germany opened the scoring through a defensive error after 12 minutes but England levelled when Geoff Hurst met a Bobby Moore free kick after 20 minutes to score his first goal.

Moore's West Ham teammate Martin Peters put England back into the lead deep into the game after 78 minutes and with victory in sight they saw it snatched from them with a last minute equaliser from Weber.

With four minutes of the first half of extra time remaining, Alan Ball crossed the ball to Geoff Hurst who turned and hit the ball against the underside of the crossbar. The ball bounced down and back into play.

Roger Hunt who was closest to the incident raised his hand immediately to celebrate the 'goal'. He made no effort to help it over the line 'again' as he was adamant it had already crossed the line.

After much deliberation between the referee and linesman the referee, Gottfried Dienst of Switzerland signalled a goal.

Towards the closing stages of the second period of extra time West Germany went in search of another late equaliser but on leaving themselves exposed at the back Geoff Hurst picked up a ball from Bobby Moore and had no problems adding England's fourth goal in the last minute as he completed that first ever World Cup Final hat-trick.

SPORTS CONTESTED AT WEMBLEY STADIUM*

Sport	Major event at Wembley
American Football	NFL International Series
Athletics	The 1948 Olympics athletics events
Boxing	Henry Cooper v Cassius Clay 1963 and Frank Bruno v Oliver McCall 1995
Greyhound Racing	Trafalgar Cup 1929–98
Hockey	The 1948 Olympic tournament semi-finals and final
Rugby League	Challenge Cup Final, 1992 and 1995 World Cup Finals
Rugby Union	Wales home venue for the 1998 and 1999 Five Nations Championship
Show Jumping	The 1948 Olympic show jumping competition
Speedway	Speedway world championship and the Wembley Lions home stadium
Wrestling	The 1992 WWF Summer Slam

* Other than football.

At both the old Wembley (1923–2000) and New Wembley since 2007
In addition, Wembley has played host to many pop concerts including the Live Aid Concert on 13 July 1985.

BIGGEST LONDON
SPORTS STADIUMS *

	Stadium	Capacity
1	Wembley Stadium	90,000
2	Twickenham	82,000
3	Olympic Stadium	80,000
4	Emirates Stadium (Arsenal FC)	60,361
5	Stamford Bridge (Chelsea FC)	41,841
6	White Hart Lane (Tottenham Hotspur FC)	36,534
7	Boleyn Ground (West Ham United FC)	35,303
8	Lord's Cricket Ground	32,000
9	The Valley (Charlton Athletic FC)	27,111
10	Selhurst Park (Crystal Palace FC)	26,225

* By capacity as at 1 June 2011

The All-England Club at Wimbledon has a capacity of over 40,000 for the entire complex, with Centre Court holding over 15,000.

OLDEST LONDON FOOTBALL CLUBS*

	Club	Year formed
1	Fulham	1879
2	Leyton Orient	1881
3	Tottenham Hotspur	1882
4	Millwall	1885
5	Queens Park Rangers	1886
6	Arsenal	1886
7	Barnet	1888
8	Brentford	1889
9	West Ham United	1895
10	Chelsea	1905

* Premier League and Football League teams 2011–12

There are currently 14 London teams in the Premier League and Football League. The youngest is AFC Wimbledon who were formed in 2002 after Wimbledon FC moved to Milton Keynes. Chelsea (10 March, at a pub), Charlton Athletic (9 June, by teenagers) and Crystal Palace (10 September, by the builders of the Crystal Palace) were all formed in 1905.

MOST SUCCESSFUL LONDON CLUBS*

		1	2	3	4	FAC	FLC	TOTAL
1	Arsenal	13	0	0	0	10	2	25
2	Chelsea	4	2	0	0	6	4	16
=	Tottenham Hotspur	2	2	0	0	8	4	16
4	Brentford	0	1	2	3	0	0	6
5	Queens Park Rangers	0	2	2	0	0	1	5
=	West Ham United	0	2	0	0	3	0	5
=	Wanderers	0	0	0	0	5	0	5
8	Fulham	0	2	2	0	0	0	4
=	Millwall	0	1	2	1	0	0	4
=	Charlton Athletic	0	1	2	0	1	0	4

Key: 1 = Top level of English football, 2 = second tier, 3 = third tier, 4 = fourth tier, FAC = FA Cup, FLC = Football League Cup

* Based on senior domestic trophies won: League titles (all divisions), FA Cup and Football League Cup up to the end of the 2010–11 season.

The first London team to win a domestic trophy were the Wanderers who were the first winners of the FA Cup in 1872. The club was founded in 1859 as Forest FC and used Battersea Park and Kennington Oval for most of their home games.

TRANSFERS PAID BY LONDON FOOTBALL CLUBS

	Player	Transfer	Year	Price
1	Fernando Torres	Liverpool to Chelsea	2011	£50,000,000
2	Andriy Schevchenko	AC Milan to Chelsea	2006	£30,800,000
3	Michael Essien	Olympique Lyon to Chelsea	2005	£24,430,000
4	Didier Drogba	Marseille to Chelsea	2004	£24,000,000
5	David Luiz	Benfica to Chelsea	2011	£21,440,000
6	Shaun Wright-Phillips	Manchester City to Chelsea	2005	£21,000,000
7	Ricardo Carvalho	FC Porto to Chelsea	2004	£19,850,000
8	Yuri Zhirkov	CSKA Moscow to Chelsea	2009	£18,000,000
=	Ramires	Benfica to Chelsea	2010	£18,000,000
10	Damien Duff	Blackburn Rovers to Chelsea	2003	£17,000,000
=	David Bentley	Blackburn Rovers to Tottenham Hotspur	2008	£17,000,000

Source – figures widely quoted in the press

The record for London's other Premier League clubs are £15,000,000 paid by Arsenal to Zenit Saint Petersburg for Andriy Arshavin in 2009, £11,500,000 by Fulham to Lyon for Steve Marlet in 2001, and £3,500,000 paid by Queens Park Rangers to Instituto de Córdoba for Alejandro Faurlin in 2009.

BIGGEST RUGBY WINS BY ENGLAND AT TWICKENHAM*

	Opponent	Date	Score
1	Romania	17 Nov 2001	134–0
2	USA	21 Aug 1999	106–8
3	Tonga	15 Oct 1999	101–10
4	Italy	17 Feb 2001	80–23
5	Canada	13 Nov 2004	70–0
6	Italy	2 Oct 1999	67–7
7	Wales	4 Aug 2007	62–5
8	Canada	10 Dec 1994	60–19
=	Wales	21 Feb 1998	60–26
10	Italy	12 Feb 2011	59–13

* Correct as of 7 June 2011

England's biggest wins against the other Six Nations teams have been: *v.* Scotland 43–3, 3 Mar 2001 and 43–22, 19 Mar 2005; *v.* Ireland 50–18, 5 Feb 2000; *v.* France 48–19, 7 Apr 2001.

England has scored 100 points in a game on two more occasions. They beat Uruguay 111–3 at Brisbane in 2003, and in 1998 they beat Netherlands 110–0 at Huddersfield, the first time they scored 100 points in a single game.

MIDDLESEX SEVENS TEAMS

	Team	Wins	Years*
1	Harlequins	14	1926–29, 1933, 1935, 1967, 1978, 1986–90, 2008
2	Richmond	9	1951, 1953, 1955, 1974–5, 1977, 1979–80, 1983
3	London Welsh	8	1930–1, 1956, 1968, 1971–3, 1984
4	London Scottish	7	1937, 1960–3, 1965, 1991
5	London Wasps	5	1948, 1952, 1985, 1993, 2006
=	Loughborough Colleges	5	1959, 1964, 1966, 1970, 1976
=	St Mary's Hospital	5	1940, 1942–4, 1946
8	Rosslyn Park	4	1947, 1950, 1954, 1981

9	Barbarians	3	1934, 1997–8
10	St Luke's College, Exeter	2	1957, 1959
=	Blackheath	2	1932, 1958
=	British Army	2	2001, 2004
=	Penguins	2	1999–2000

* Up to and including 2010

Sevens rugby was first played in Scotland towards the end of the 19th century and it was a Scot, Dr. J A Russell-Cargill, who inaugurated England's most famous Sevens tournament, the Middlesex Sevens, in 1926.

HIGHEST ICC WORLD CUP TEAM TOTALS AT LORDS*

		Date	Team/opponents	Score
1	England *v*. India	7 Jun 1975	334–4
2	Australia *v*. Zimbabwe	9 Jun 1999	303–4
3	West Indies *v*. Australia+	21 Jun 1975	291–8
4	West Indies *v*. England+	23 Jun 1979	286–9
5	West Indies *v*. Australia	18 Jun 1983	276–3
6	Australia *v*. West Indies+	21 Jun 1975	274
7	Australia *v*. West Indies	18 Jun 1983	273–6
8	Zimbabwe *v*. Australia	9 Jun 1999	259–6
9	England *v*. Sri Lanka	14 May 1999	207–2
10	Sri Lanka *v*. England	14 May 1999	204

* Up to and including the 2011 tournament
+ Indicates final

The highest individual World Cup innings at Lord's is 138 not out by Viva Richards for West Indies against England in 1979 (as above). He beat the previous record of 137 set by England's Dennis Amiss against India in 1975.

HIGHEST INDIVIDUAL TEST INNINGS AT LORD'S

	Player	Runs	Match	Date
1	Graham Gooch	333	England *v.* India	26 Jul 1990
2	Graeme Smith	259	South Africa *v.* England	31 Jul 2003
3	Donald Bradman	254	Australia *v.* England	27 Jun 1930
4	Walter Hammond	240	England *v.* Australia	24 Jun 1938
5	Jonathan Trott	226	England *v.* Bangladesh	27 May 2010
6	Robert Key	221	England *v.* West Indies	22 Jul 2004
7	Gordon Greenidge	214*	West Indies *v.* England	28 Jun 1984
8	Jack Hobbs	211	England *v.* South Africa	28 Jun 1924
9	Denis Compton	208	England *v.* South Africa	21 Jun 1947
10	Bill Brown	206*	Australia *v.* England	24 Jun 1938
=	Martin Donnelly	206	New Zealand *v.* England	25 Jun 1949

* Indicates not out

The first Test century at Lord's was by Allan Steel, who scored 148 for England against Australia on 21 July 1884. The first Test double century was scored by Jack Hobbs (as above). As of the start of 2011, there have been 212 Test centuries at Lords.

LATEST WINNERS OF THE MEN'S SINGLES AT WIMBLEDON

Year	Winner	Country	Runner-up	Country
2011	Novak Djokovic	Serbia	Rafael Nadal	Spain
2010	Rafael Nadal	Spain	Tomás Berdych	Czech Republic
2009	Roger Federer	Switzerland	Andy Roddick	USA
2008	Rafael Nadal	Spain	Roger Federer	Switzerland
2007	Roger Federer	Switzerland	Rafael Nadal	Spain
2006	Roger Federer	Switzerland	Rafael Nadal	Spain
2005	Roger Federer	Switzerland	Andy Roddick	USA
2004	Roger Federer	Switzerland	Andy Roddick	USA
2003	Roger Federer	Switzerland	Mark Philippoussis	Australia
2002	Lleyton Hewitt	Australia	David Nalbandian	Argentina

In 2007 Roger Federer became the first man to win five consecutive titles since Björn Borg of Sweden achieved the record in 1976–80.

LATEST WINNERS OF THE
WOMEN'S SINGLES AT WIMBLEDON

Year	Winner	Country	Runner-up	Country
2011	Petra Kvitová	Czech Republic	Maria Sharapova	Russia
2010	Serena Williams	USA	Vera Zvonareva	Russia
2009	Serena Williams	USA	Venus Williams	USA
2008	Venus Williams	USA	Serena Williams	USA
2007	Venus Williams	USA	Marion Bartoli	France
2006	Amélie Mauresmo	France	Justine Henin	Belgium
2005	Venus Williams	USA	Lindsay Davenport	USA
2004	Maria Sharapova	Russia	Serena Williams	USA
2003	Serena Williams	USA	Venus Williams	USA
2002	Serena Williams	USA	Venus Williams	USA

Between 2000 and 2010 the Williams sisters won 9 of the 11 ladies' titles, with Venus leading their own personal rivalry with five wins to four.

LONDON MARATHON MEN'S RACE WINNERS*

	Athlete	Country	Year	Time (hr:min:sec)
1	Emmanuel Mutai	Kenya	2011	2:04:40
2	Samuel Wanjiru	Kenya	2009	2:05:10
3	Martin Lel	Kenya	2008	2:05:15
4	Tsegaye Kebede	Ethiopia	2010	2:05:19
5	Khalid Khannouchi	USA	2002	2:05:38
6	Evans Rutto	Kenya	2004	2:06:18
7	António Pinto	Portugal	2000	2:06:36
8	Felix Limo	Kenya	2006	2:06:39
9	Abdelkader El Mouaziz	Morocco	2001	2:07:11
10	Martin Lel	Kenya	2005	2:07:36

* Up to and including 2011

The first London Marathon was held on 29 March 1981 when Dick Beardsley (USA) and Inge Simonsen (Norway) crossed the line together to share first place. The London Marathon has grown from 7,741 entrants in the first race to around 36,500 people in 2011.

LONDON MARATHON WOMEN'S RACE WINNERS*

	Athlete	Country	Year	Time (hr:min:sec)
1	Paula Radcliffe	UK	2003	2:15:25
2	Paula Radcliffe	UK	2005	2:17:42
3	Paula Radcliffe	UK	2002	2:18:56
4	Mary Keitany	Kenya	2011	2:19:19
5	Deena Kastor	USA	2006	2:19:36
6	Chunxiu Zhou	China	2007	2:20:38
7	Ingrid Kristiansen	Norway	1985	2:21:06
8	Liliya Shobukhova	Russia	2010	2:22:00
9	Irina Mikitenko	Germany	2009	2:22:11
10	Margaret Okayo	Kenya	2004	2:22:35

* Up to and including 2011

Joyce Smith of the UK won the first women's race in 1981, as well as the second race the following year. Norway's Ingrid Kristiansen has won the women's race a record four times (in 1984–5 and 1987–8).

LONDON OLYMPIC 2012 VENUES FURTHEST FROM LONDON

	Stadium	Location	Sport	Distance* (km)	(miles)
1	Hampden Park	Glasgow	Football	552.1	343.1
2	St James' Park	Newcastle upon Tyne	Football	396.8	246.6
3	Old Trafford	Manchester	Football	263.6	163.8
4	Millennium Stadium	Cardiff	Football	219.2	136.2
5	Weymouth & Portland National Sailing Academy	Dorset	Sailing	201.6	125.2
6	City of Coventry Stadium	Coventry	Football	143.1	88.9
7	Hadleigh Farm	Essex	Mountain Bike	46.8	29.1
8	Dorney Lake	Buckinghamshire	Canoeing, Rowing	45.2	28.1
9	Brands Hatch	Kent	Paralympic Road Cycling	28.0	17.4
10	Lee Valley White Water Centre	Hertfordshire	Canoe Slalom	16.8	10.4

* From the Olympic Stadium, as the crow flies

LARGEST VENUES FOR THE 2012 OLYMPIC GAMES

	Stadium	Location	Use	Capacity
1	Wembley Stadium	London	Football	90,000
2	Olympic Stadium	London	Athletics, Opening Closing Ceremonies	80,000
3	Old Trafford	Manchester	Football	75,957
4	Millennium Stadium	Cardiff	Football	74,500
5	St James' Park	Newcastle upon Tyne	Football	52,409
6	Hampden Park	Glasgow	Football	52,103
7	City of Coventry Stadium	Coventry	Football	32,609
8	All England Club	Wimbledon	Lawn Tennis	30,000
=	Dorney Lake	Dorney, Bucks	Canoeing, Rowing	30,000
10	Greenwich Park	London	Equestrian	23,000

* The new 80,000-capacity Olympic Stadium is the third largest stadium in Britain after Wembley and Twickenham. Built in the Stratford district of London, work started on the stadium in May 2008 and was completed in just less than three years at a cost of over £500 million. After the 2012 Olympics and Paralympics, West Ham United are hoping to take over the ground as their new permanent home.

SPORTS FOR BRITISH MEDALS AT THE 1948 OLYMPICS

	Sport	Gold	Silver	Bronze	Total
1	Athletics	0	6	1	7
2	Cycling	0	3	2	5
3	Rowing	2	1	0	3
4	Painting & Graphic Art	1	1	0	2
=	Boxing	0	2	0	2
=	Sculpture	0	1	1	2
=	Weightlifting	0	1	1	2

8	Sailing	1	0	0	1
=	Hockey	0	1	0	1
=	Equestrian	0	0	1	1
=	Swimming	0	0	1	1

London played host to the Olympic games in 1948. These figures include the Art competitions which were officially part of the Summer Olympic programme for the last time that year, having made their debut in 1912. The works were on display at the Victoria and Albert Museum between 15 July and 14 August. In 1948, cyclist Reg Harris was Britain's only double medallist, winning two silver medals.

10
FAMOUS LONDON SPORTING EVENTS

All-England tennis championships at Wimbledon
Ask any tennis player which tournament they would like to win more than any other, and the answer will almost certainly be Wimbledon. It has been one of the sport's most coveted titles since the championship's inauguration in 1877. The Centre Court, with it retractable roof, is one of the great show courts in world tennis and the tradition that surrounds Wimbledon makes it unique in the game.

Boat race
An estimated 250,000 watch the race each year from the banks of the Thames. As of 2011, Cambridge have won 80 races, Oxford 76 and there has been one dead-heat, in 1877.

Christmas dip in the Serpentine
Swimming in the Serpentine on Christmas Day is a tradition going back more than 145 years. Members of the Serpentine Swimming Club take part in a 100-yard race across the lake each year, no matter what the weather – unless ice prevents the race as it did in 2010.

Doggett's coat and badge
The Doggett's Coat and Badge is the oldest rowing race in the world, having been contested on the River Thames every year since 1715.

FA cup final
The very first FA Cup final between Wanderers and Royal Engineers was held at London's Kennington Oval in 1872 and attracted a crowd of just 2,000.

Henley royal regatta
Held on the Thames since 1839 it is an annual event over five days. The main event is the Diamond Sculls, which is regarded as the Blue Riband of amateur sculling

London marathon

One of the world's great sporting institutions, the London Marathon attracts over 35,000 runners to the streets of the capital each Spring, raising around £40 million for charity.

Lord's test match

England beat Australia in the first Test Match played at Lord's in 1884 by an innings and five runs. Over 100 Tests have been held at Lord's and the England versus India match at Lord's in July 2011 was the 2000th Test Match.

Olympic games

In 2012, London will become the first city to host the Summer Olympics on three occasions, having held the 1908 and 1948 competitions.

Six nations rugby

The Six Nations started life as the Home (Four) Nations Tournament in 1883 and in 1910 when France joined, it became the Five Nations. Italy's addition in 2000 led to its renaming in the present style of Six Nations.

FAMOUS SPORTING LONDONERS

DAVID BECKHAM
Born: 2 May 1975, Leytonstone

The former England captain, David Beckham made 115 appearances for the national team, a record for an outfield player.

ERIC BRISTOW
Born: 25 April 1957, Hackney

Probably one of London's best known sportsmen, if only for his nickname, 'The Crafty Cockney', Bristow won the World Darts Championship five times between 1980 and 1986.

SEBASTIAN COE
Born: 29 September 1956, Chiswick

Now Baron Coe of Ranmore, in the 1980s he dominated world middle distance running, winning gold at the 1980 Moscow Olympics in the 1500 metres and silver in the 800 metres.

DENIS COMPTON
Born: 23 May 1918, Hendon

In the 1947 season, Denis Compton scored a staggering 3,816 first-class runs including 18 centuries, a record which still stands today.

HENRY COOPER
Born: 3 May 1934, Southwark

Probably Britain's best-loved boxer, Henry Cooper came close to notoriety at Wembley Stadium in 1963 when he floored Cassius Clay towards the end of the fourth round. Only some dubious corner work from Clay's camp, including mysterious damage to one of his gloves, gave the American time to recover and go on and win the fight.

STEVE DAVIS   Born: 22 August 1957, Plumstead

After winning his first Embassy World title in 1981 Steve was to dominate the sport
throughout the decade, winning the world title five more times, a record only beaten in
the modern era by Stephen Hendry.

BOBBY MOORE   Born: 12 April 1941, Barking

A stylish footballer, Bobby Moore is known as the man who lifted the World Cup for
England in 1966. He played for his country 108 times, and was captain in a record 97
of them.

ZARA PHILLIPS   Born: 15 May 1981, Paddington

One of a small band of sportswomen born in London. Zara Phillips is the daughter of
Princess Anne, and like her mother is a proficient horsewoman and eventer.

DALEY THOMPSON   Born: 30 July 1958, Notting Hill

Britain's most successful decathlete, Daley Thompson won the Olympic gold medal in
1980 and 1984 and broke the world record four times.

JIMMY WHITE   Born: 2 May 1962, Tooting

Jimmy White may never have won the world professional snooker title, but he remained
one of the most popular and charismatic players in the game and rightly earned the
accolade, 'The People's Champion'. Certainly the best player never to win the world title,
he appeared in six world finals, including five consecutive finals between 1990–94.

FAMOUS LONDON SPORTING VENUES

Alexandra Palace
Built in 1873, Alexandra Palace is home of the PDC Darts World Championship and, from 2012, is to be the new home of the Masters Snooker tournament, which is the biggest snooker tournament after the World Championship.

Lord's Cricket Ground
Cricketer Thomas Lord opened his first cricket ground in 1787 on what is now Dorset Square, moving twice before Marylebone Cricked Club (MCC) entertained Hertfordshire in the first match on the current ground in June 1814. The museum at Lord's is the world's oldest sporting museum.

Olympic Stadium
The 80,000-seater stadium at Stratford was purpose built for the 2012 London Olympics at a cost of £500 million.

Queen's Club
Queen's Club in Hammersmith dates to 1886 and is named after Queen Victoria, a patron of the club.

Royal Blackheath Golf Course
Laid out over the Great Park of Eltham Palace, the Royal Blackheath Club was founded in 1608 and is reputed to be the oldest golf club in the world.

The Oval
Situated at Kennington, The Oval is owned by the Duchy of Cornwall. It was the first English ground to host Test Match cricket in 1880.

Twickenham
The Rugby Football Union (RFU) bought a piece of Twickenham market garden land in 1907 with a view to building their own stadium. Two years later Harlequins played Richmond on what because known as Billy Williams' Cabbage Patch.

Wembley Arena
Built for the 1934 Empire Games it originally housed the famous Empire Pool, which was used for the swimming events at the 1948 Olympics.

Wembley Stadium
Wembley first played host to the FA Cup final of 1923 between Bolton Wanderers and West Ham. It was not an all-ticket match, so while the official attendance was given as 126,047, it is estimated that nearly 200,000 were inside the ground.

Wimbledon
The All-England Lawn Tennis and Croquet Club was founded in 1868 as the All-England Croquet Club. Lawn tennis had not been invented at that time, but within a year of its birth, the All-England club added a tennis court alongside its croquet lawns and in 1877 changed its name to its present style.

* Twickenham is named Billy Williams Cabbage Patch after the land on which the stadium was built, was bought in 1907 by RFU committee member William Williams, a former Middlesex cricket who was one of the innovators of leg-break bowling. Because the land was formerly a market garden it acquired the nickname by which it is affectionately known.

WINNING TIMES OF THE BOAT RACE*

	Winning boat	Date	Time (min:sec)
1	Cambridge	28 Mar 1998	16:19
2	Cambridge	3 Apr 1999	16:41
3	Oxford	27 Mar 2005	16:42
4	Oxford	18 Mar 1984	16:45
5	Oxford	30 Mar 2002	16:54
6=	Oxford	20 Mar 1976	16:58
=	Cambridge	6 Apr 1996	16:58
8	Oxford	30 Mar 1991	16:59
9=	Cambridge	27 Mar 1993	17:00
=	Oxford	29 Mar 2009	17:00

* Over the current course on the Thames from Putney to Mortlake and measuring 4 miles 374 yards (6.8 km). Times up to and including 2011.

The first Boat Race was won by Oxford in 1829 over a course from Hambleden Lock to Henley Bridge. Their winning time of 14 minutes 3 seconds is the fastest winning time for the Boat Race, but the course measured only 2 miles 440 yards (3.6 km).

MISCELLANEOUS

OLDEST ITEMS IN THE CROWN JEWELS

	Item	Year made
1	Sword of Mercy	*c.*11th century
=	Sword of Spiritual Justice	*c.*11th century
=	Sword of Temporal Justice	*c.*11th century
4	Golden Anointing Spoon	*c.*12th century
5	Golden Ampulla	1661
=	St Edward's Crown	1661
=	St Edward's Staff	1661
=	St George's Spurs	1661
=	Sceptre with the Dove	1661
=	Sovereign's Orb	1661

The three swords and golden Anointing Spoon are the only pieces to survive the destruction of the pre-civil war Regalia, ordered by Oliver Cromwell following the execution of King Charles I in 1649. Following the theft of items from Westminster Abbey in 1303, the Crown Jewels have been kept under armed guard in the Tower of London.

UNIVERSITIES IN LONDON

		Global rank
1	University College London	4
2	Imperial College London	7
3	Kings College London	21
4	London School of Economics and Political Science	80
5	Queen Mary, University of London	147
6	The School of Oriental and African Studies	258
7	Royal Holloway, University of London	291
8	Brunel University	361
9	Goldsmiths, University of London	386
10	City University London	495

Source – QS World University Rankings 2010/11
Topped by the University of Cambridge, the QS World University Rankings take into account factors including: academic peer and recruiter review, faculty student ratio, citations per faculty and international orientation.

INCIDENTS COVERED BY CCTV AT NIGHT IN THE WEST END

	Type	Incidents (%)
1	Fighting	25.2
2	Drunks	16.5
3	Anti-social behaviour	11.7
4	Assault	9.7
5	Theft	8.3
6	Disturbance	7.3
7	Missing person	5.3
8	Personal injury	4.4
9	Illegal street trading	3.9
10	Drug related	2.4
=	Indecency	2.4

Source – New West End Company

In Westminster, you are never more than 300m (328 yards) away from somewhere that sells alcohol, with the total capacity of all the West End's licensed premises exceeding 125,000.

THE LONGEST HOSPITAL WAITING TIMES

	Trust	People waiting over 4 hours at A&E
1	Barking, Havering and Redbridge	8,502
2	Imperial College Healthcare	5,435
3	North West London Hospitals	5,062
4	South London Healthcare	4,715
5	Whipps Cross University Hospital	3,973
6	Guy's and St Thomas' Foundation	3,664
7	St George's Healthcare	3,265
8	Barts and The London	2,980
9	Barnet and Chase Farm Hospitals	2,580
10	Croydon Healthcare	2,570
	London	*68,068*

Source – Quarterly Monitoring of Accident and Emergency, Department of Health, 2010
The Barking, Havering and Redbridge Hospitals NHS trust treats 323,000 Accident and Emergency patients a year, the most in London. The rate of people waiting over four hours is more than four times that of the best performing trust, University College London Hospitals.

TOP10

OLDEST GENTLEMAN'S CLUBS

	Club	Year founded	Notable members
1	White's	1693	David Cameron, Prince Charles
2	Boodle's	1762	Ian Fleming, Adam Smith
3	Brooks's	1764	William Pitt the Younger
4	Royal Thames Yacht Club	1775	Duke of Cumberland
5	Marylebone Cricket Club	1787	Ian Botham, John Major
6	Cavalry and Guards Club	1810	Prince Philip, D. of E.
7	Portland Club*	1815	Charles Darwin, H.G. Wells
8	Travelers Club	1819	Duke of Wellington, Ranulph Fiennes
9	Oxford and Cambridge Club	1821	Stephen Fry, Edward VII
10	Athenaeum Club	1824	Winston Churchill, Charles Dickens

* Now hosted in the Saville Club, whose former members are Charles Darwin and H.G. Wells.

The most traditional of gentlemen's clubs, White's, still has a 'no women' policy (although the Queen was invited once).

DRINK DRIVING BOROUGHS

	Borough	test arrests	Positive breath Charges
1	Westminster	801	488
2	Brent	688	477
3	Ealing	598	407
4	Southwark	594	395
5	Barnet	557	373
6	Hounslow	519	357
7	Haringey	480	298
8	Lambeth	475	319
9	Newham	462	336
10	Redbridge	436	302
	London	*12,789*	*8,615*

Source – Metropolitan Police
Around 60,000 breath tests are administrated in London each year, of which 20% occur around Christmas time.

10 FIRST UNDERGROUND STATIONS TO CLOSE

	Station	Opened	Closed
1	King William Street	1890	1900
2	City Road	1901	1922
3	South Kentish Road	1907	1924
4	Down Street	1907	1932
5	York Road	1906	1932
6	British Museum	1900	1933
7	Brompton Road	1906	1934
8	St. Mary's	1884	1938
9	Lords	1868	1939
=	Marlborough Road	1868	1939

Many of the platforms of closed stations are easily seen when passed on the Underground, while the station buildings have seen a variety of uses; British Museum was used by the Ministry of Defence in the Second World War and South Kentish Town is now a health club.

NEWEST UNDERGROUND STATIONS

	Station	Opened
1	Wood Lane	12 October 2008
2	Heathrow Terminal 5	27 March 2008
3	Southwark	24 September 1999
4	Bermondsey	17 September 1999
=	Canada Water	17 September 1999
=	Canary Wharf	17 September 1999
7	North Greenwich	14 May 1999
8	Canning Town	28 March 1994
9	Heathrow Terminal 4	12 April 1986
10	Heathrow Terminals 1,2,3	16 September 1977

MOST COMMON TYPES OF MARRIAGE IN LONDON

	Marriage	Number
1	Civil	20,678
2	Church of England	3,335
3	Roman Catholic	1,412
4	Other Christian	578
5	Other bodies	459
6	Jewish	447
7	Baptist	164
8	Methodist	156
9	United Reformed Church	82
10	Congregationalist	19
	London total	*27,333*

Source – Office for National Statistics, 2009

When records began in 1837, fewer than 1% of marriages were with civil ceremonies, and 97% of marriages took place within the Church of England. London currently has over 3,000 buildings of worship in which marriages may be solemnised, including Shakespeare's Globe, The London Dungeon and Tower Bridge.

POSTCODES MOST AT RISK FROM IDENTITY FRAUD

		Risk Index*
1	SW1X 8, Kinnerton Street	408
2	W1K 7, Park Street	407
3	SW1X 7, Knightsbridge	401
4	W1J 5, HIll Street	400
5	SW3 1, Brompton Road	398
6	SW17 6, Macmillan Way	397
7	E14 5, Chancellor Passage	396
8	SW1X 0, Lennox Gardens	396
9	W1K 2, South Audley Street	395
10	E14 2, Blackwall	393

* Relative to UK average of 100

Source – Experian Victims of Fraud Survey
Nineteen of the Top 20 identity fraud hotspots are in London, with 72 fraud attempts made for every 100,000 adults in 2010.

FASTEST GROWING BOROUGHS IN THE 19TH CENTURY

	Borough	Growth	1801	1901
1	Brent	59.00	2000	120000
2	Newham	44.75	8000	366000
3	Haringey	33.83	6000	209000
4	Hammersmith and Fulham	24.00	10000	250000
5	Waltham Forest	23.75	8000	198000
6	Wandsworth	23.54	13000	319000
7	Croydon	16.88	8000	143000
8	Redbridge	15.50	4000	66000
9	Lewisham	13.88	16000	238000
10	Kensington and Chelsea	12.89	18000	250000

BOROUGHS FOR RECYCLING

		Proportion of household waste recycled (%)
1	Bexley	40.0
2	Bromley	31.9
3	Richmond upon Thames	31.7
4	Hilingdon	30.6
5	Sutton	30.3
6	Enfield	29.6
7	Barnet	29.5
8	City of London	28.2
9	Camden	28.1
10	Harrow	27.7

Source – Department for Environment, Food and Rural Affairs
The divergence of recycling rates across boroughs can be partly explained by the differing collection scheme each authority runs (Bexley residents separate five different sources of waste, for example, compared to two in others).

WORST BOROUGHS FOR FLY-TIPPING

	Borough	Incidents
1	Haringey	5,228
2	Camden	2,015
3	Southwark	1,849
4	Lewisham	1,742
5	Lambeth	1,738
6	Croydon	839
7	Hounslow	758
8	Waltham Forest	686
9	Hammersmith & Fulham	676
10	Newham	674

Fly-tipping (the illegal dumping of waste) in London is prevalent, despite carrying a maximum fine of £50,000 and five years in prison. Even littering has a maximum fine of £2,500, though £80 fixed penalty notices are normally issued to offenders.

ENERGY USES IN LONDON

	Use	Gigawatt hours	Petajoules (PJ)*
1	Domestic gas	49,450	178
2	Commercial gas	36,043	130
3	Domestic electricity	18,706	67
4	Petrol	17,503	63
5	Commercial electricity	10,100	36
6	Diesel	9,452	34
7	Commercial oil	4,664	17
8	Air transport	3,635	13
9	Underground electricity	1,095	4
10	Train electricity	690	2
	Total	*151,502*	*545*

* = 1015J

Source – Greater London Authority
London's annual energy requirements would require all the nuclear power plants in the world to work flat out for nearly three weeks. They are equivalent to over twice the energy released by the Tsar Bomba, the most powerful nuclear weapon ever detonated, or 20 times the combined power of all the explosives used in World War II.

10

MOST ENERGY-INEFFICIENT BUILDINGS

Building

1   Buckingham Palace

2   The Department for Energy and Climate Change

3   The Ministry of Defence

4   Horse Guards Barracks

5   Shell Building

6   The Home Office

7   Houses of Parliament

8   The Treasury

9   Portcullis House

10   MI6 Headquarters

Source – Navitron

Buckingham Palace's annual utility bill is £2.2 million, approximately 25 times the price per room than the average London home. The most energy efficient building of the 170 that were surveyed using thermal imaging technology was the HSBC tower block in Canary Wharf.

COMPONENTS OF LONDONERS' WASTE

	Material	Weight (kg)	Proportion of domestic waste* (%)
1	Newspaper and Magazines	112.5	18.2
2	Other organic waste	86.5	14.0
3	Garden organic waste	69.2	11.2
4	Other Paper and Card	53.1	8.6
5	Kitchen organic waste	52.5	8.5
6	Glass	50.1	8.1
7	Dense plastics	37.7	6.1
8	Ferrous metal	28.4	4.6
9	Textiles	15.4	2.5
10	Plastic film	6.8	0.9
	Total	618.0	100.0

* Annual per household

Source – Office for National Statistics
City of London residents produce the most rubbish; over twice as much per head than those living in Camden and Tower Hamlets. Bexley is the best borough, recycling 40% of their waste.

DESTINATIONS FOR LANDFILL WASTE

	Destination	Waste (tonnes)
1	London	2,001,000
2	Buckinghamshire	1,328,000
3	Essex	1,183,000
4	Surrey	851,000
5	Thurrock	381,000
6	Hertfordshire	341,000
7	Kent	334,000
8	Northamptonshire	272,000
9	Oxfordshire	254,000
10	Bedfordshire	236,000
	Total	*7,770,000*

Source – Environment Agency
Of the waste that goes to landfill, over 3 million tonnes is from construction and demolition, 2 million tonnes from commercial and industrial, with the remainder being municipal solid waste. Each year over one million tonnes of whole or unopened food is thrown away in London.

LONGEST RIVERS IN LONDON

River	Length (km)	(miles)
1 Thames	70.4	43.7
2 Lee	31.5	19.6
3 Colne	27.4	17.0
4 Grand Union Canal	24.5	15.2
5 Brent	24.0	14.9
6 Pinn	19.9	12.5
7 Yeading Brook	19.1	11.9
8 Rom/Beam	16.1	10.0
9 Wandle	15.9	9.9
10 Longford	15.7	9.8

Source – Greater London Authority Environment Team
Water covers 3% of the capital, with well over 160 kilometres (100 miles) of canals and navigable rivers in London other than the Thames.

BOROUGHS WITH THE MOST PROPERTIES AT RISK OF FLOODING

	Borough	Properties at significant risk	Properties within floodplain
1	Enfield	9,655	19,261
2	Merton	5,467	10,339
3	Hillingdon	4,209	6,815
4	Waltham Forest	3,887	6,788
5	Richmond upon Thames	3,563	36,726
6	Haringey	3,547	8,238
7	Westminster	3,420	21,952
8	Lewisham	3,263	19,630
9	Bromley	3,133	7,944
10	Wandsworth	3,050	38,604

Source – Environment Agency

The last flood in central London occurred in 1928. The House of Commons and the Underground flooded, 14 people lost their lives and many thousands were left homeless. The Thames barrier, opened in 1984, now protects London from storm surges and exceptionally high tides, and has closed an average of 7 times a year over the last decade.

TYPES OF CHARITY IN
VICTORIAN LONDON

	Cause	Distributed (£)	Charities
1	Foreign mission societies	459,668	14
2	Home mission societies	319,705	43
3	Medical charities	266,925	92
4	Maintenance of children	88,228	15
5	Asylums for the reception of the aged	87,630	126
6	Promotion of schools	72,247	21
7	Professional benevolent funds	53,467	32
8	Maintenance of orphans	45,464	13
9	Reclaiming asylums	39,486	17
10	Preservation of life and public morals	35,717	12
	Total	*1,805,635*	*530*

Source – Charities in London, 1852–3
This list excludes money disbursed by private philanthropic individuals. This was estimated
to be at least as much as distributed by the charities.

TOP10

CHARITIES IN LONDON

Charity	Annual income (£) (2009/10)	Total funds
1 The British Council	706,560,000	227,000,000
2 Cancer Research UK	514,950,000	182,000,000
3 Arts Council for England	461,200,000	126,000,000
4 Anchor Trust	288,760,000	193,000,000
5 Wellcome Trust	230,300,000	1,274,050,000
6 British Heart Foundation	213,760,000	52,000,000
7 The Girls' Day School Trust	203,880,000	238,000,000
8 Action For Children	194,660,000	10,000,000
9 British Red Cross	182,050,000	146,000,000
10 Save The Children	170,910,000	54,000,000

Source – Charities Direct
Despite a large London presence, many large UK charities do not have headquarters in the capital, including Oxfam (Oxford), Barnardo's (Essex), Nuffield Health Trust (Surrey) and The National Trust (Wiltshire).

18TH CENTURY TURNPIKE TRUSTS

Trust

1 Bethnal Green

2 Hackney

3 Hampstead and Highgate

4 Hyde Park

5 Kensington Road

6 Marylebone

7 Old Street

8 Shoreditch

9 Stamford Hill

10 Whitechapel

Prior to the Turnpike Act in 1707, London's roads were the responsibility of each parish. As trade and travellers increased, the main routes used deteriorated faster than parish statute labour could repair them. Local gentlemen were appointed as unpaid 'Turnpike trustees' instead, and given the right to collect tolls to administer and maintain the roads.

BOROUGHS FOR WAR MEMORIALS

	Borough	Memorials
1	Westminster	951
2	City of London	378
3	Bromley	366
4	Croydon	354
5	Harrow	307
6	Wandsworth	237
7	Lambeth	221
8	Redbridge	170
9	Barnet	154
10	Kensington and Chelsea	150

Source – Imperial War Museum
War memorials in London take many forms, from crosses and plaques to gardens, hospitals and windows.

LARGEST SISTER CITIES

	City	City proper population*
1	Moscow	11,551,930
2	Beijing	10,123,000
3	Tokyo	8,887,608
4	New York City	8,363,710
5	Bogota	7,259,597
6	Tehran	7,241,000
7	Berlin	3,426,354
8	Rome	2,754,440
9	Paris	2,193,031
10	Kuala Lumpur	1,627,172
	London	*7,753,600*

* Defined as the area within boundaries of local government, not the metropolitan area

The Greater London Authority is twinned with the above cities, while each borough has its own additional twin towns (of which Barnet has the most, with nine).

LARGEST OTHER LONDONS

	Town	Population
1	London, Ontario, Canada	457,720
2	New London, Connecticut, USA	25,671
3	London, Ohio, USA	8,771
4	London, Kentucky, USA	7,993
5	New London, Minnesota, USA	4,604
6	New London, Iowa, USA	3,180
7	London, California, USA	1,848
8	London, Kiribati	1,829
9	London, Arkansas, USA	925
10	London, West Virginia, USA	305

Situated on the Thames River in Middlesex County and home to the London Beefeaters, London in Ontario was settled as a village in 1826 and a city in 1855. There are 46 other Londons on six continents worldwide.

TOP10

PICTURE CREDITS

D0655430

Everyman, I will go with thee, and be thy guide,
In thy most need to go by thy side.

EVERYMAN'S LIBRARY

Founded 1906 by J. M. Dent (d. 1926)
Edited by Ernest Rhys (d. 1946)

POETRY & THE DRAMA

POEMS AND PLAYS
BY OLIVER GOLDSMITH · INTRODUC-
TION AND NOTES BY AUSTIN DOBSON

OLIVER GOLDSMITH, born at Pallasmore, Co. Longford, Ireland. After a varied and unprofitable life in England and Ireland, tramped through Europe, 1754–6. Arriving penniless in London, he took to journalism. In spite of his success in literature he died in poverty on 4th April 1774.

POEMS AND PLAYS

OLIVER GOLDSMITH

LONDON: J. M. DENT & SONS LTD.
NEW YORK: E. P. DUTTON & CO. INC.

INTRODUCTION

I

THIRTY years of taking-in; fifteen years of giving out; —that, in brief, is Oliver Goldsmith's story. When, in 1758, his failure to pass at Surgeons' Hall finally threw him on letters for a living, the thirty years were finished, and the fifteen years had been begun. What was to come he knew not; but, from his bare-walled lodging in Green-Arbour-Court, he could at least look back upon a sufficiently diversified past. He had been an idle, orchard-robbing schoolboy; a tuneful but intractable sizar of Trinity; a lounging, loitering, fair-haunting, flute-playing Irish "buckeen." He had tried both Law and Divinity, and crossed the threshold of neither. He had started for London and stopped at Dublin; he had set out for America and arrived at Cork. He had been many things:—a medical student, a strolling musician, a corrector of the press, an apothecary, an usher at a Peckham "academy." Judged by ordinary standards, he had wantonly wasted his time. And yet, as things fell out, it is doubtful whether his parti-coloured experiences were not of more service to him than any he could have obtained if his progress had been less erratic. Had he fulfilled the modest expectations of his family, he would probably have remained a simple curate in Westmeath, eking out his "forty pounds a year" by farming a field or two, migrating contentedly at the fitting season from the "blue bed to the brown," and (it may be) subsisting vaguely as a local poet upon the tradition of some youthful couplets to a pretty cousin, who had married a richer man. As it was, if he could not be said "to have seen life steadily, and seen it whole," he had, at all events, inspected it pretty narrowly in parts; and, at a time when he was most impressible, had preserved the impress of many things which, in his turn, he was to re-impress upon his writings. "No man"—says one of his biographers—"ever put so much of himself into his books as Goldsmith." To his last hour he was drawing upon the thoughts and reviving the memories of that "unhallowed time" when, to all appearance, he was hopelessly squandering his opportunities. To do as Goldsmith did, would scarcely enable a man to write a *Vicar of Wakefield* or a *Deserted Village*,—certainly his practice cannot be preached with safety "to those that eddy round and round." But viewing his entire career, it is difficult not to see how one part seems to have been an indispensable preparation for the other, and to marvel once more (with the philosopher Square) at "the eternal Fitness of Things."

II

The events of Goldsmith's life have been too often narrated to need repetition here, and we shall not resort to the well-worn device of repeating them in order to say so. But, in a fresh reprint of his Poems and Plays, some brief preamble to those branches of his work may be excusable, and even useful. And, with regard to both, what strikes one first is the extreme tardiness of that late blossoming to which Johnson referred. When a man succeeds as Goldsmith succeeded, friends and critics speedily discover that he had shown signs of excellence even from his boyish years. But, setting aside those half-mythical ballads for the Dublin street-singers, and some doubtful verses for Jane Contarine, there is no definite evidence that, from a doggerel couplet in his childhood to an epigram not much better than doggerel composed when he was five and twenty, he had written a line of verse of the slightest importance ; and even five years later, although he refers to himself in a private letter as a "poet," it must have been solely upon the strength of the unpublished fragment of *The Traveller*, which in the interval, he had sent to his brother Henry from abroad. It is even more remarkable that—although so skilful a correspondent must have been fully sensible of his gifts—until, under the pressure of circumstances, he drifted into literature, the craft of letters seems never to have been his ambition. He thinks of being a lawyer, a physician, a clergyman,—anything but an author; and when at last he engages in that profession, it is to free himself from a scholastic servitude which he appears to have always regarded with peculiar bitterness, yet to which, after a first unsatisfactory trial of what was to be his true vocation, he unhesitatingly returned. If he went back once more to his pen, it was only to enable him to escape from it more effectually, and he was prepared to go as far as Coromandel. But Literature—"*toute entière à sa proie attachée*"—refused to relinquish him; and, although he continued to make spasmodic efforts to extricate himself, detained him to the day of his death.

If there is no evidence that he had written much when he entered upon what has been called his second period, he had not the less formed his opinions on many literary questions. Much of the matter of the *Polite Learning* is plainly manufactured *ad hoc;* but in its references to the profession of authorship, there is a personal note which is absent elsewhere; and when he speaks of the tyranny of publishers, the sordid standards of criticism, and the forlorn and precarious existence of the hapless writer for bread, he is evidently reproducing a condition of things with which he had become familiar during his brief bondage on the *Monthly Review*. As to his personal views on poetry in particular, it is easy to collect them from this, and later utterances. Against blank verse he protests from the first, as suited only to the sublimest themes—which is a polite way of shelving it altogether; while in favour of rhyme he alleges that the very restriction stimulates the fancy, as a fountain plays higher when the aperture is diminished. Blank verse, too (he asserted), imported into poetry a "disgusting solemnity of manner" which was fatal to "agreeable trifling,"—an objection intimately connected with the feeling which afterwards made him the champion on the stage of character and humour. Among the poets who were his contemporaries and immediate predecessors, his likes and dislikes were strong. He fretted at the fashion which Gray's *Elegy* set in poetry ; he considered it a fine poem, but " overloaded with epithet," and he deplored the remoteness and want of emotion which distinguished the Pindaric Odes. Yet from many indications in his own writings, he seems to have genuinely appreciated the work of Collins. Churchill, and Churchill's satire, he detested. With Young he had some personal acquaintance, and had attentively read his *Night Thoughts*. Of the poets of the last age, he admired Dryden, Pope and Gay, but more than any of these, if imitation is to be regarded as the proof of sympathy, Prior, Addison and Swift. By his inclinations and his training, indeed, he belonged to this school. But he was in advance of it in thinking that poetry, however didactic after the fashion of his own day, should be simple in its utterance and directed at the many rather than the few. This is what he meant when, from the critical elevation of Griffiths' back parlour, he recommended Gray to take the advice of Isocrates, and " study the people." If, with these ideas, he had been able to divest himself of the " warbling groves " and " finny deeps " of the Popesque vocabulary (of much of the more " mechanic art " of that supreme artificer he *did* successfully divest himself), it would have needed but little to make him a prominent pioneer of the new school which was coming with Cowper. As it is, his poetical attitude is a little that intermediate one of Longfellow's maiden—

> " Standing, with reluctant feet,
> Where the brook and river meet."

Most of his minor and earlier pieces are imitative. In *A New Simile*, and *The Logicians Refuted*, Swift is his acknowledged model; in *The Double Transformation* it is Prior, modified by certain theories personal to himself. He was evidently well acquainted with collections like the *Ménagiana*, and with the French minor poets of the

eighteenth century, many of which latter were among his
books at his death.   These he had carefully studied,
probably during his continental wanderings, and from
them he derives, like Prior, much of his grace and
metrical buoyancy.   The *Elegy on the Death of a Mad
Dog*, and *Madame Blaize*, are both more or less con-
structed on the old French popular song of the hero of
Pavia, Jacques de Chabannes, Seigneur de la Palice
(sometimes Galisse), with, in the case of the former, a
tag from an epigram by Voltaire, the original of which is
in the Greek Anthology, though Voltaire simply "con-
veyed" his version from an anonymous French predecessor.   Similarly the lively stanzas *To Iris, in Bow
Street*, the lines to Myra, the quatrain called *A South
American Ode*, and that *On a Beautiful Youth struck
blind with Lightning*, are all confessed or unconfessed
translations.   It is possible that if Goldsmith had lived
to collect his own works, he would have announced the
source of his inspiration in these instances as well as in
one or two other cases—the epitaph on Ned Purdon, for
example,—where it has been reserved to his editors to
discover his obligations.   On the other hand, he might
have contended, with perfect justice, that whatever the
source of his ideas, he had made them his own when he
got them ; and certainly in lilt and lightness, the lines
To Iris are infinitely superior to those of La Monnoye,
on which they are based.   But even a fervent admirer
may admit that, dwelling as he did in this very vitreous
palace of Gallic adaptation, one does not expect to find
him throwing stones at Prior for borrowing from the
French, or commenting solemnly in the life of Parnell
upon the heinousness of plagiarism.   "It was the fashion,"
he says, "with the wits of the last age, to conceal the
places from whence they took their hints or their subjects.
A trifling acknowledgment would have made that lawful
prize, which may now be considered as plunder."   He
might judiciously have added to this latter sentence the
quotation which he struck out of the second issue of the
Polite Learning,—"*Haud inexpertus loquor.*"
    Of his longer pieces, *The Traveller* was apparently

suggested to him by Addison's *Letter from Italy to Lord Halifax*, a poem to which, in his preliminary notes to the *Beauties of English Poesy*, he gives significant praise. "There is in it," he says, "a strain of political thinking that was, at that time, new in our poetry." He obviously intended that *The Traveller* should be admired for the same reason ; and both in that poem and its successor, *The Deserted Village*, he lays stress upon the political import of his work. The one, we are told, is to illustrate the position that the happiness of the subject is independent of the goodness of the Sovereign ; the other, to deplore the increase of luxury and the miseries of depopulation. But, as a crowd of commentators have pointed out, it is hazardous for a poet to meddle with "political thinking," however much, under George the Second, it may have been needful to proclaim a serious purpose. If Goldsmith had depended solely upon the professedly didactic part of his attempt, his work would be as dead as *Freedom*, or *Sympathy*, or any other of Dodsley's forgotten *quartos*. Fortunately he did more than this. Sensibly or insensibly, he suffused his work with that philanthropy which is "not learned by the royal road of tracts, and platform speeches, and monthly magazines," but by personal commerce with poverty and sorrow ; and he made his appeal to that clinging love of country, of old association, of "home-bred happiness," of innocent pleasure, which, with Englishmen, is never made in vain. Employing the couplet of Pope and Johnson, he has added to his measure a suavity that belonged to neither ; but the beauty of his humanity and the tender melancholy of his wistful retrospect hold us more strongly and securely than the studious finish of his style.

" *Vingt fois sur le métier remettez votre ouvrage*"—said the arch-critic whose name, according to Keats, the school of Pope displayed upon their "decrepit standard." Even in *The Traveller* and *The Deserted Village*, there are indications of over-labour ; but in a poem which comes between them—the once famous *Edwin and Angelina*—Goldsmith certainly carried out Boileau's maxim to the full. The first privately-printed version differs considerably from that in the first edition of the *Vicar*; this again is altered in the fourth; and there are other variations in the piece as printed in the *Poems for Young Ladies*. "As to my 'Hermit'," said the poet complacently, "that poem, Cradock, cannot be amended," and undoubtedly it has been skilfully wrought. But it is impossible to look upon it now with the unpurged eyes of those upon whom the *Reliques of Ancient Poetry* had but recently dawned, still less to endorse the verdict of Sir John Hawkins that "it is one of the finest poems of the lyric kind that our language has to boast of." Its over-soft prettiness is too much that of the chromo-lithograph or the Parian bust (the porcelain, not the marble), and its "beautiful simplicity" is in parts perilously close upon that inanity which Johnson, whose sturdy good sense not even friendship could silence, declared to be the characteristic of much of Percy's collection. It is instructive as a study of poetical progress to contrast it with a ballad of our own day in the same measure—the *Talking Oak* of Tennyson.

The remaining poems of Goldsmith, excluding the *Captivity*, and the admittedly occasional *Threnodia Augustalis*, are not open to the charge of fictitious simplicity, or of that hyper-elaboration, which, in the words of the poet just mentioned, makes for the "ripe and rotten." The gallery of kit-cats in *Retaliation*, and the delightful *bonhomie* of *The Haunch of Venison* need no commendation. In kindly humour and not unkindly satire Goldsmith was at his best, and the imperishable portraits of Burke and Garrick and Reynolds, and the inimitable dinner at which Lord Clare's pasty was *not*, are as well known as any of the stock passages of *The Deserted Village* or *The Traveller*, though they have never been babbled "*in extremis vicis*" by successive generations of schoolboys. It is usually said, probably with truth, that in these poems and the delightful *Letter to Mrs. Bunbury*, Goldsmith's metre was suggested by the cantering anapæsts of the *New Bath Guide*, and it is to be observed that "Little Comedy's" letter of invitation is to the same popular tune. But in preparing this edition, some enquiries as to the song of *Ally Croaker* mentioned in *She Stoops to Conquer*, elicited the fact that a line of that once popular lyric—

> "Too dull for a wit, and too grave for a joker"—

has a kind of echo in the—

> "Too nice for a statesman, too proud for a wit"—

of Burke's portrait in *Retaliation*. What is still more remarkable is that Gray's *Sketch of his own Character*, the resemblance of which to Goldsmith has been pointed out by his editors, begins—

> "Too poor for a bribe, and too proud to importune."

Whether Goldsmith was thinking of Anstey or *Ally Croaker*, it is at least worthy of passing notice that an Irish song of no particular literary merit should have succeeded in haunting the two foremost poets of their day.

III

Poetry brought Goldsmith fame, but money only indirectly. Those Saturnian days of the subscription-edition, when Pope and Gay and Prior counted their gains by thousands, were over and gone. He had arrived, it has been well said, too late for the Patron, and too early for the Public. Of his lighter pieces the best were posthumous ; the rest were either paid for at hack prices or not at all. For *The Deserted Village* Griffin gave him a hundred guineas, a sum so unexampled as to have prompted the pleasant legend that he returned it. For *The Traveller* the only payment that can be definitely traced is £21. "I cannot afford to court the draggle-tail Muses," he said laughingly to Lord Lisburn, "they would let me starve; but by my other labours I can make shift to eat, and drink, and have good clothes." It was in his "other labours" that his poems helped him. The booksellers who would not or could not remunerate him adequately for delayed production and minute revision, were willing enough to secure the sanction of his name for humbler journey-work. If he was ill-paid for *The Traveller*, he was not ill-paid for the *Beauties of English Poesy* or the *History of Animated Nature*.

Yet, notwithstanding his ready pen, and his skill as a compiler, his life was a *métier de forçat*. "While you are nibbling about elegant phrases, I am obliged to write half a volume,"—he told his friend Cradock ; and it was but natural that he should desire to escape into walks where he might accomplish something "for his own hand," by which, at the same time, he might exist. Fiction he had already essayed. Nearly two years before *The Traveller* appeared, he had written a story about the length of *Joseph Andrews*, for which he had received little more than a third of the sum paid by Andrew Millar to Fielding for his burlesque of Richardson's *Pamela*. But obscure circumstances delayed the publication of the *Vicar of Wakefield* for four years, and when at last it was issued, its first burst of success—a success, as far as can be ascertained, productive of no further profit to its author—was followed by a long period during which the sales were languid and uncertain. There remained the stage, with its two-fold allurement of fame and fortune, both payable at sight, added to which it was always possible that a popular play, in those days when plays were bought to read, might find a brisk market in book form. The prospect was a tempting one, and it is scarcely surprising that Goldsmith, weary of the "dry drudgery at the desk's dead wood," and conscious of better things within him, should engage in that most tantalizing of all enterprises, the pursuit of dramatic success.

For acting and actors he had always shown a decided partiality.[1] Vague stories, based, in all probability, upon the references to strolling players in his writings, hinted

[1] This is not inconsistent with the splenetic utterances in the letters to Daniel Hodson, first made public in the "Great Writers" *Life of Goldsmith*, where he speaks of the stage as "an abominable resource which neither became a man of honour, nor a man of sense." Those letters were written when the production of *The Good-Natur'd Man* had supplied him with abundant practical evidence of the vexations and difficulties of theatrical ambition.

that he himself had once worn the comic sock as "Scrub" in *The Beaux' Stratagem ;* and it is clear that soon after he arrived in England, he had completed a tragedy, for he read it in manuscript to a friend. That he had been besides an acute and observant playgoer, is plain from his excellent account in *The Bee* of Mademoiselle Clairon, whom he had seen at Paris, and from his sensible notes in the same periodical on "gestic lore" as exhibited on the English stage. In his *Polite Learning in Europe*, he had followed up Ralph's *Case of Authors by Profession*, by protesting against the despotism of managers, and the unenlightened but economical policy of producing only the works of deceased playwrights ; and he was equally opposed to the growing tendency on the part of the public—a tendency dating from Richardson and the French *comédie larmoyante*—to substitute sham sensibility and superficial refinement for that humorous delineation of manners, which, with all their errors of morality and taste, had been the chief aim of Congreve and his contemporaries. To the fact that what was now known as "genteel comedy" had almost wholly supplanted this elder and better manner, must be attributed his deferred entry upon a field so obviously adapted to his gifts. But when, in 1766, the *Clandestine Marriage* of Garrick and Colman, with its evergreen "Lord Ogleby," seemed to herald a return to the side of laughter as opposed to that of tears, he took heart of grace, and, calling to mind something of the old inconsiderate benevolence which had been the Goldsmith family-failing, set about his first comedy, *The Good-Natur'd Man.*

Even without experiment, no one could have known better than Goldsmith, upon what a sea of troubles he had embarked. Those obstacles which, more than thirty years before, had been so graphically described in Fielding's *Pasquin*,—which Goldsmith himself had indicated with equal accuracy in his earliest book, still lay in the way of all dramatic purpose, and he was to avoid none of them. When he submitted his completed work to Garrick, the all-powerful actor, who liked neither piece nor author, blew hot and cold so long, that Goldsmith at last, in despair, transferred it to Colman. But, as if fate was inexorable, Colman, after accepting it effusively, also grew dilatory, and ultimately entered into a tacit league with Garrick not to produce it at Covent Garden until his former rival had brought out at Drury Lane a comedy by Goldsmith's countryman, Hugh Kelly, a sentimentalist of the first water. Upon the heels of the enthusiastic reception which Garrick's administrative tact secured for the superfine *imbroglios* of *False Delicacy*, came limping *The Good-Natur'd Man* of Goldsmith, wet-blanketed beforehand by a sentinous prologue from Johnson. No *début* could have been less favourable. Until it was finally saved in the fourth act by the excellent art of Shuter, its fate hung trembling in the balance, and even then one of its scenes—not afterwards reckoned the worst—had to be withdrawn in deference to the delicate scruples of an audience which could not suffer such inferior beings as bailiffs to come between the wind and its gentility. Yet, in spite of all these disadvantages, *The Good-Natur'd Man* obtained a hearing, besides bringing its author about five hundred pounds, a sum far larger than anything he had ever made by poetry or fiction.

That the superior success of *False Delicacy*, with its mincing morality and jumble of inadequate motive, was wholly temporary and accidental, is evident from the fact that, to use a felicitous phrase, it has now to be disinterred in order to be discussed. But, notwithstanding one's instinctive sympathy for Goldsmith in his struggles with the managers, it is not equally clear that, everything considered, *The Good-Natur'd Man* was unfairly treated by the public. Because Kelly's play was praised too much, it by no means follows that Goldsmith's play was praised too little. With all the advantage of its author's reputation, it has never since passed into the *répertoire*, and, if it had something of the freshness of a first effort, it had also its inexperience. The chief character, Honeywood—the weak and amiable "good-natur'd man"—never stands very firmly on his feet, and the first actor, Garrick's promising young rival, Powell, failed, or disdained to make it a stage creation. On the other hand, "Croaker," an admitted elaboration of Johnson's sketch of "Suspirius" in the *Rambler*, is a first-rate comic character, and the charlatan "Lofty," a sort of "Beau Tibbs above-Stairs," is almost as good. But, as Garrick's keen eye saw, to have a second male figure of greater importance than the central personage was a serious error of judgment, added to which neither "Miss Richland" nor "Mrs. Croaker" ever establish any hold upon the audience. Last of all, the plot, such as it is, cannot be described as either particularly ingenious or particularly novel. In another way, the merit of the piece is, however, incontestable. It is written with all the perspicuous grace of Goldsmith's easy pen, and, in the absence of stage-craft, sparkles with neat and effective epigrams. One of these may be mentioned as illustrating the writer's curious (perhaps unconscious) habit of repeating ideas which had pleased him. He had quoted in his *Polite Learning* the exquisitely rhythmical close of Sir William Temple's prose essay on "Poetry," and in *The Bee* it still seems to haunt him. In *The Good-Natur'd Man* he has absorbed it altogether, for he places it, without inverted commas, in the lips of Croaker.

But, if its lack of constructive power and its errors of conception make it impossible to regard *The Good-Natur'd Man* as a substantial gain to humorous drama, it was undoubtedly a formidable attack upon that "mawkish drab of spurious breed," Sentimental Comedy, and its success was amply sufficient to justify a second trial. That Goldsmith did not forthwith make this renewed effort must be attributed partly to the recollection of his difficulties in getting his first play produced, partly to the fact that, his dramatic gains exhausted, he was almost immediately involved in a sequence of laborious taskwork. Still, he had never abandoned his ambition to restore humour and character to the stage ; and as time went on, the sense of his past discouragements grew fainter, while the success of *The Deserted Village* increased his importance as an author.

Sentimentalism, in the meantime, had still a majority. Kelly, it is true, was now no longer to be feared. His sudden good fortune had swept him into the ranks of the party-writers, with the result that the damning of his next play, *A Word to the Wise*, had been exaggerated into a political necessity. But the school which he represented had been recruited by a much abler man, Richard Cumberland, and it was probably the favourable reception of Cumberland's *West Indian* that stimulated Goldsmith into striking one more blow for legitimate comedy. At all events, in the autumn of the year in which *The West Indian* was produced, he is hard at work in the lanes at Hendon and Edgware, "studying jests with a most tragical countenance" for a successor to *The Good-Natur'd Man.*

To the modern spectator of *She Stoops to Conquer*, with its unflagging humour and bustling action, it must seem almost inconceivable that its stage qualities can ever have been questioned. Yet questioned they undoubtedly were, and Goldsmith was spared none of his former humiliations. Even from the outset, all was against him. His differences with Garrick had long been adjusted, and the Drury Lane manager would now probably have accepted a new play from his pen, especially as that astute observer had already detected signs of a reaction in the public taste. But Goldsmith was morally bound to Colman and Covent Garden; and Colman, in whose hands he placed his manuscript, proved even more disheartening and unmanageable than Garrick had been in the past. Before he had come to his decision, the close of 1772 had arrived. Early in the following year, under the irritation of suspense and suggested amendments combined, Goldsmith hastily transferred his proposal to Garrick; but, by Johnson's advice, as hastily withdrew it. Only by the express interposition of Johnson was Colman at last induced to make a distinct promise to bring out the play at a specific date. To believe in it, he could not be persuaded, and his contagious anticipations of its failure passed insensibly to the actors, who, one after the other, shuffled out of their parts. Even over the

epilogue there were vexatious disputes, and when at last,
in March, 1773, *She Stoops to Conquer* was acted, its *jeune
premier* had previously held no more exalted position than
that of ground-harlequin, while one of its most prominent
characters had simply been a post-boy in *The Good-Natur'd
Man*.   But once fairly upon the boards neither lukewarm
actors nor an adverse manager had any further influence
over it, and the doubts of everyone vanished in the uninterrupted applause of the audience.   When, a few days
later, it was printed with a grateful dedication to its best
friend, Johnson, the world already knew the certainty
that a fresh masterpiece had been added to the roll of
English Dramatic Literature, and that "genteel comedy"
had received a decisive blow.

The effect of this blow, it must be admitted, had been
aided not a little by the appearance, only a week or two
earlier, of Foote's clever puppet-show of *The Handsome
Housemaid; or, Piety in Pattens*, which was openly
directed at Kelly and his following.   But ridicule by
itself, without some sample of a worthier substitute, could
not have sufficed to displace a persistent fashion.   This
timely antidote *She Stoops to Conquer*, in the most un-
mistakable way, afforded.   From end to end of the piece
there is not a sickly or a maudlin word.   Even Sheridan,
writing *The Rivals* two years later, thought it politic to
insert "Faulkland" and "Julia" for the benefit of the
sentimentalists.   Goldsmith made no such concession,
and his wholesome hearty merriment put to flight the
Comedy of Tears,—even as the Coquecigrues vanished
before the large-lunged laugh of Pantagruel.   If, as
Johnson feared, his plot bordered slightly upon farce—
and of what good comedy may this not be said?—at
least it can be urged that its most farcical incident, the
mistaking of a gentleman's house for an inn, had really
happened, since it had happened to the writer himself.
But the superfine objections of Walpole and his friends
are now ancient history,—history so ancient that it is
scarcely credited, while Goldsmith's manly assertion (after
Fielding) of the author's right "to stoop among the low
to copy nature," has been ratified by successive genera-

Introduction xxi

tions of novelists and playwrights. What is beyond dispute is the healthy atmosphere, the skilful setting, the lasting freshness and fidelity to human nature of the persons of the drama. Not content with the finished portraits of the Hardcastles (a Vicar and Mrs. Primrose promoted to the squirearchy),—not content with the incomparable and unapproachable Tony, the author has managed to make attractive what is too often insipid, his heroines and their lovers. Miss Hardcastle and Miss Neville are not only charming young women, but charming characters, while Marlow and Hastings are much more than stage young men. And let it be remembered —it cannot be too often remembered—that in returning to those Farquhars and Vanbrughs "of the last age," who differed so widely from the Kellys and Cumberlands of his own, Goldsmith has brought back no taint of their baser part. Depending solely for its avowed intention to "make an audience merry," upon the simple development of its humorous incident, his play (wonderful to relate!) attains its end without resorting to the aid of equivocal intrigue. Indeed, there is but one married woman in the piece, and she traverses it without a stain upon her character.

She Stoops to Conquer is Goldsmith's last dramatic work, for the trifling sketch of *The Grumbler* had never more than a grateful purpose. When, only a year later, the little funeral procession from 2, Brick Court laid him in his unknown grave in the Temple burying-ground, the new comedy of which he had written so hopefully to Garrick was still non-existent. Would it have been better than its last fortunate predecessor?—would those early reserves of memory and experience have still proved inexhaustible? The question cannot be answered. Through debt, and drudgery, and depression, the writer's genius had still advanced, and these might yet have proved powerless to check his progress. But at least it was given to him to end upon his best, and not to outlive it. For, in that critical sense which estimates the value of a work by its excellence at all points, it can scarcely be contested that *She Stoops to Conquer* is his best production. In spite of their beauty and humanity, the lasting quality of *The Traveller* and *The Deserted Village* is seriously prejudiced by his half-way attitude between the poetry of convention and the poetry of nature—between the gradus epithet of Pope and the direct vocabulary of Wordsworth. With *The Vicar of Wakefield*, again, immortal though it be, it is less his art that holds us, than his charm, his humour and his tenderness which tempt us to forget his inconsistency and his errors of haste. In *She Stoops to Conquer*, neither defect of art nor defect of nature forbids us to give unqualified admiration to a work which lapse of time has shown to be still unrivalled of its kind.

AUSTIN DOBSON.

The following is a list of Oliver Goldsmith's works (1728–1774) :—

Memoirs of a Protestant condemned to the Galleys of France for his Religion (translation), 2 vols., 1758 ; Enquiry into the Present State of Polite Learning in Europe, 1759 ; The Bee, being Essays on the Most Interesting Subjects (eight numbers of a weekly periodical), 1759 ; History of Mecklenburgh, 1762 ; The Mystery Revealed, containing a Series of Transactions and Authentic Testimonials respecting the supposed Cock-Lane Ghost, 1762 ; The Citizen of the World, or Letters from a Chinese Philosopher residing in London to his Friends in the East (from the *Public Ledger*, 1760, 1761), 2 vols., 1762 ; Life of Richard Nash, of Bath, Esquire, 1762 ; A History of England in a Series of Letters from a Nobleman to his Son, 2 vols., 1764 ; The Traveller, 1765 ; Essays, 1765 ; The Vicar of Wakefield, a tale supposed to be written by himself, 2 vols., 1766 ; The Good-Natured Man, a Comedy, 1768 ; The Roman History, from the foundation of the City of Rome to the destruction of the Western Empire, 2 vols., 1769 ; Abridgment by the Author, 1772 ; The Deserted Village, 1770 ; The Life of Thomas Parnell, compiled from original papers and memoirs, 1770 ; Life of Henry St. John, Lord Viscount Bolingbroke, 1770 ; The History of England, from the Earliest Times to the Death of George II., 4 vols., 1771 ; Abridged Edition, 1774 ; Threnodia Augustalis, sacred to the memory of Her Royal Highness the Princess Dowager of Wales, 1772 ; She Stoops to Conquer, or the Mistakes of a Night, 1773 ; Retaliation, a Poem, including Epitaphs on the most distinguished Wits of this Metropolis, 1774 (five editions were published this year ; the fifth edition contains the postscript and epitaph on Caleb Whitefoord) ; The Grecian History, from the Earliest State to the Death of Alexander the

Great, 2 vols., 1774; An History of the Earth and Animated Nature, 8 vols., 1774; The Haunch of Venison, a Poetical Epistle to Lord Clare, 1776; another edition, with additions and corrections, appeared this same year; A Survey of Experimental Philosophy considered in its Present State of Improvement, 2 vols., 1776; The Captivity, an Oratorio, 1836 (first printed in the Trade edition of Goldsmith's Works, 1820. See Anderson's Bibl.).

Goldsmith contributed to the *Monthly Review, Critical Review, Literary Magazine, Busy Body, Public Ledger, British Magazine, Lady's Magazine, Westminster Magazine,* and *Universal Magazine;* he edited Poems for Young Ladies, 1766; Beauties of English Poesy, 1767; to him is attributed The History of Little Goody Two-Shoes, published by Newbery, 3rd ed., 1766; and also A Pretty Book of Pictures for Little Masters and Misses, etc., 1767; and his translations include Formey's Concise History of Philosophy, 1766; Scarron's Comic Romance, 1780. An abridged edition of Plutarch's Lives was undertaken by him in collaboration with Joseph Collyer, 1762; The Grumbler, an adaptation of Brueys and Palaprat's Le Grondeur, was performed once at Covent Garden in 1773, but not printed by the author.

The miscellaneous works of Goldsmith (containing all his Essays and Poems) were published in 1775, 1792, and in 1801 with the Percy Memoir; Poems and Plays, 1777; Poetical and Dramatic Works, 1780.

Among later editions are those by Prior, 4 vols., 1837; Cunningham, 4 vols., 1854; J. F. Waller, 1864, etc.; J. W. M. Gibbs, 1884–6; the Globe Edition, 1869; Bohn's Standard Library has also included Goldsmith's miscellaneous works. Many smaller collections have been published.

The complete Poetical works were edited by Austin Dobson (Oxford Edition), 1906.

The Vicar of Wakefield has appeared in innumerable editions, has been frequently illustrated, and translated into nearly every European language.

A bibliography of Goldsmith's works is appended to the Life by Austin Dobson.

Life: The life known as the " Percy Memoir " (see above), 1801, and later editions; by James Prior, 1837; John Forster, Life and Adventures of Oliver Goldsmith, 1848, 1854, 1855, 1903; Washington Irving (founded on two previous biographies), with selections, 1844, 1849, 1850; W. Black (English Men of Letters), 1878; Austin Dobson (Great Writers), 1888, 1899; Macaulay (Encyclopædia Britannica), ed. H. B. Cotterill, 1904, and published in Blackie's English Classics, 1901; Oliver Goldsmith (Cameo Classics, No. 4), 1905.

CONTENTS

THE TRAVELLER

OR

A PROSPECT OF SOCIETY

A POEM

[*The Traveller, or a Prospect of Society. A Poem. Inscribed to the Rev. Henry Goldsmith. By Oliver Goldsmith, M.B.*—was first published by John Newbery of St. Paul's Church-yard, in a 4to. of thirty pages, on the 19th December, 1764. The title-page of the book (as given above) was dated 1765, and the price was 1s. 6d. Up to the sixth edition of 1770 numerous alterations were made in the text by the author. The poem is here reprinted from the ninth edition, issued in 1774, the year of Goldsmith's death.]

DEDICATION

DEAR SIR,

I am sensible that the friendship between us can acquire no new force from the ceremonies of a Dedication; and perhaps it demands an excuse thus to prefix your name to my attempts, which you decline giving with your own. But as a part of this Poem was formerly written to you from Switzerland, the whole can now, with propriety, be only inscribed to you. It will also throw a light upon many parts of it, when the reader understands, that it is addressed to a man, who, despising Fame and Fortune, has retired early to Happiness and Obscurity, with an income of forty pounds a year.

I now perceive, my dear brother, the wisdom of your humble choice. You have entered upon a sacred office, where the harvest is great, and the labourers are but few; while you have left the field of Ambition, where the labourers are many, and the harvest not worth carrying away. But of all kinds of ambition, what from the refinement of the times, from different systems of criticism, and from the divisions of party, that which pursues poetical fame is the wildest.

Poetry makes a principal amusement among unpolished nations; but in a country verging to the extremes of refinement, Painting and Music come in for a share. As these offer the feeble mind a less laborious entertainment, they at first rival Poetry, and at length supplant her; they engross all that favour once shown to her, and though but younger sisters, seize upon the elder's birthright.

Yet, however this art may be neglected by the powerful, it is still in greater danger from the mistaken efforts of

[1 Goldsmith's eldest brother. He died in May, 1768, being then curate of Kilkenny West.]

3

the learned to improve it. What criticisms have we not heard of late in favour of blank verse, and Pindaric odes, choruses, anapests and iambics, alliterative care and happy negligence ! Every absurdity has now a champion to defend it; and as he is generally much in the wrong, so he has always much to say; for error is ever talkative.

But there is an enemy to this art still more dangerous, I mean Party. Party entirely distorts the judgment, and destroys the taste. When the mind is once infected with this disease, it can only find pleasure in what contributes to increase the distemper. Like the tiger, that seldom desists from pursuing man after having once preyed upon human flesh, the reader, who has once gratified his appetite with calumny, makes, ever after, the most agreeable feast upon murdered reputation. Such readers generally admire some half-witted thing, who wants to be thought a bold man, having lost the character of a wise one. Him they dignify with the name of poet; his tawdry lampoons are called satires, his turbulence is said to be force, and his phrensy fire.[1]

What reception a Poem may find, which has neither abuse, party, nor blank verse to support it, I cannot tell, nor am I solicitous to know. My aims are right. Without espousing the cause of any party, I have attempted to moderate the rage of all. I have endeavoured to show, that there may be equal happiness in states that are differently governed from our own; that every state has a particular principle of happiness, and that this principle in each may be carried to a mischievous excess. There are few can judge, better than yourself, how far these positions are illustrated in this Poem.

I am, dear Sir,
Your most affectionate Brother,
OLIVER GOLDSMITH.

[1 Charles Churchill, the satirist (1731–64), is undoubtedly intended here.]

THE TRAVELLER

OR

A PROSPECT OF SOCIETY

REMOTE, unfriended, melancholy, slow,
Or by the lazy Scheldt, or wandering Po;
Or onward, where the rude Carinthian boor,
Against the houseless stranger shuts the door;
Or where Campania's plain forsaken lies,
A weary waste expanding to the skies:
Where'er I roam, whatever realms to see,
My heart untravell'd fondly turns to thee;
Still to my Brother turns, with ceaseless pain,
And drags at each remove a lengthening chain.[1]

Eternal blessings crown my earliest friend,
And round his dwelling guardian saints attend:
Bless'd be that spot, where cheerful guests retire
To pause from toil, and trim their ev'ning fire;
Bless'd that abode, where want and pain repair,
And every stranger finds a ready chair;
Bless'd be those feasts with simple plenty crown'd,
Where all the ruddy family around
Laugh at the jests or pranks that never fail,
Or sigh with pity at some mournful tale,
Or press the bashful stranger to his food,
And learn the luxury of doing good.

But me, not destin'd such delights to share,
My prime of life in wand'ring spent and care,
Impell'd, with steps unceasing, to pursue
Some fleeting good, that mocks me with the view;
That, like the circle bounding earth and skies,
Allures from far, yet, as I follow, flies;[2]
My fortune leads to traverse realms alone,
And find no spot of all the world my own.

[1 Cf. *The Citizen of the World*, 1762, i. 5. (Letter iii.)]
[2 Cf. *The Vicar of Wakefield*, 1766, ii. 160-1 (ch. x.).]

Even now, where Alpine solitudes ascend,
I sit me down a pensive hour to spend;
And, plac'd on high above the storm's career,
Look downward where an hundred realms appear;
Lakes, forests, cities, plains, extending wide,
The pomp of kings, the shepherd's humbler pride.

When thus Creation's charms around combine,
Amidst the store, should thankless pride repine?
Say, should the philosophic mind disdain
That good, which makes each humbler bosom vain?
Let school-taught pride dissemble all it can,
These little things are great to little man;
And wiser he, whose sympathetic mind
Exults in all the good of all mankind.
Ye glitt'ring towns, with wealth and splendour crown'd,
Ye fields, where summer spreads profusion round,
Ye lakes, whose vessels catch the busy gale,
Ye bending swains, that dress the flow'ry vale,
For me your tributary stores combine;
Creation's heir, the world, the world is mine!

As some lone miser visiting his store,
Bends at his treasure, counts, re-counts it o'er;
Hoards after hoards his rising raptures fill,
Yet still he sighs, for hoards are wanting still:
Thus to my breast alternate passions rise,
Pleas'd with each good that heaven to man supplies:
Yet oft a sigh prevails, and sorrows fall,
To see the hoard of human bliss so small;
And oft I wish, amidst the scene, to find
Some spot to real happiness consign'd,
Where my worn soul, each wand'ring hope at rest,
May gather bliss to see my fellows bless'd.

But where to find that happiest spot below,
Who can direct, when all pretend to know?
The shudd'ring tenant of the frigid zone
Boldly proclaims that happiest spot his own,
Extols the treasures of his stormy seas,
And his long nights of revelry and ease;

The naked negro, panting at the line,
Boasts of his golden sands and palmy wine,
Basks in the glare, or stems the tepid wave,
And thanks his Gods for all the good they gave
Such is the patriot's boast, where'er we roam,
His first, best country ever is, at home.
And yet, perhaps, if countries we compare,
And estimate the blessings which they share,
Though patriots flatter, still shall wisdom find
An equal portion dealt to all mankind,
As different good, by Art or Nature given,
To different nations makes their blessings even.

Nature, a mother kind alike to all,
Still grants her bliss at Labour's earnest call;
With food as well the peasant is supplied
On Idra's [1] cliffs as Arno's shelvy side;
And though the rocky-crested summits frown,
These rocks, by custom, turn to beds of down.
From Art more various are the blessings sent;
Wealth, commerce, honour, liberty, content.
Yet these each other's power so strong contest,
That either seems destructive of the rest.
Where wealth and freedom reign contentment fails,
And honour sinks where commerce long prevails.
Hence every state to one lov'd blessing prone,
Conforms and models life to that alone.
Each to the favourite happiness attends,
And spurns the plan that aims at other ends;
Till, carried to excess in each domain,
This favourite good begets peculiar pain.

But let us try these truths with closer eyes,
And trace them through the prospect as it lies:
Here for a while my proper cares resign'd,
Here let me sit in sorrow for mankind,
Like yon neglected shrub at random cast,
That shades the steep, and sighs at every blast.

[1 Bolton Corney thought Idria in Carniola intended. Birkbeck
Hill suggests Lake Idro in North Italy, which has rocky shores.]

Far to the right where Appenine ascends,
Bright as the summer, Italy extends ;
Its uplands sloping deck the mountain's side,
Woods over woods in gay theatric pride ;
While oft some temple's mould'ring tops between
With venerable grandeur mark the scene.

Could Nature's bounty satisfy the breast,
The sons of Italy were surely blest.
Whatever fruits in different climes were found,
That proudly rise, or humbly court the ground ;
Whatever blooms in torrid tracts appear,
Whose bright succession decks the varied year ;
Whatever sweets salute the northern sky
With vernal lives that blossom but to die ;
These here disporting own the kindred soil,
Nor ask luxuriance from the planter's toil ;
While sea-born gales their gelid wings expand
To winnow fragrance round the smiling land.

But small the bliss that sense alone bestows,
And sensual bliss is all the nation knows.
In florid beauty groves and fields appear,
Man seems the only growth that dwindles here.
Contrasted faults through all his manners reign,
Though poor, luxurious, though submissive, vain,
Though grave, yet trifling, zealous, yet untrue ;
And e'en in penance planning sins anew.
All evils here contaminate the mind,
That opulence departed leaves behind ;
For wealth was theirs, not far remov'd the date,
When commerce proudly flourish'd through the state ;
At her command the palace learn'd to rise,
Again the long-fall'n column sought the skies ;
The canvas glow'd beyond e'en Nature warm,
The pregnant quarry teem'd with human form ;
Till, more unsteady than the southern gale,
Commerce on other shores display'd her sail ;
While nought remain'd of all that riches gave,
But towns unmann'd, and lords without a slave ;

And late the nation found with fruitless skill
Its former strength was but plethoric ill.[1]

Yet still the loss of wealth is here supplied
By arts, the splendid wrecks of former pride ;
From these the feeble heart and long-fall'n mind
An easy compensation seem to find.
Here may be seen, in bloodless pomp array'd,
The paste-board triumph and the cavalcade ;
Processions form'd for piety and love,
A mistress or a saint in every grove.
By sports like these are all their cares beguil'd,
The sports of children satisfy the child ;[2]
Each nobler aim, represt by long control,
Now sinks at last, or feebly mans the soul ;
While low delights, succeeding fast behind,
In happier meanness occupy the mind :
As in those domes, where Caesars once bore sway,
Defaced by time and tottering in decay,
There in the ruin, heedless of the dead,
The shelter-seeking peasant builds his shed.
And, wond'ring man could want the larger pile,
Exults, and owns his cottage with a smile.

My soul, turn from them, turn we to survey
Where rougher climes a nobler race display,
Where the bleak Swiss their stormy mansions tread,
And force a churlish soil for scanty bread ;
No product here the barren hills afford,
But man and steel, the soldier and his sword.
No vernal blooms their torpid rocks array.
But winter ling'ring chills the lap of May ;
No Zephyr fondly sues the mountain's breast,
But meteors glare, and stormy glooms invest.

Yet still, even here, content can spread a charm,
Redress the clime, and all its rage disarm.
Though poor the peasant's hut, his feasts though small,
He sees his little lot the lot of all ;

[1 Cf. *The Citizen of the World*, 1762, i. 98. (Letter xxv.)]
[2 A pretty anecdote *à propos* of this couplet is related in Forster's
Life, 1871, i. pp. 347-8.]

Sees no contiguous palace rear its head
To shame the meanness of his humble shed;
No costly lord the sumptuous banquet deal,
To make him loathe his vegetable meal;
But calm, and bred in ignorance and toil,
Each wish contracting, fits him to the soil.
Cheerful at morn he wakes from short repose,
Breasts the keen air, and carols as he goes;
With patient angle trolls the finny deep,
Or drives his venturous ploughshare to the steep;
Or seeks the den where snow-tracks mark the way,
And drags the struggling savage [1] into day.
At night returning, every labour sped,
He sits him down the monarch of a shed;
Smiles by his cheerful fire, and round surveys
His children's looks, that brighten at the blaze;
While his lov'd partner, boastful of her hoard,
Displays her cleanly platter on the board;
And haply too some pilgrim, thither led,
With many a tale repays the nightly bed.

Thus every good his native wilds impart,
Imprints the patriot passion on his heart,
And even those ills, that round his mansion rise,
Enhance the bliss his scanty fund supplies.
Dear is that shed to which his soul conforms,
And dear that hill which lifts him to the storms;
And as a child, when scaring sounds molest,
Clings close and closer to the mother's breast,
So the loud torrent, and the whirlwind's roar,
But bind him to his native mountains more.

Such are the charms to barren states assign'd;
Their wants but few, their wishes all confin'd.
Yet let them only share the praises due,
If few their wants, their pleasures are but few;
For every want that stimulates the breast
Becomes a source of pleasure when redrest.

[1 *i. e.* wolf or bear. Pope uses the word several times in this
sense.]

Whence from such lands each pleasing science flies,
That first excites desire, and then supplies ;
Unknown to them, when sensual pleasures cloy,
To fill the languid pause with finer joy ;
Unknown those powers that raise the soul to flame,
Catch every nerve, and vibrate through the frame.
Their level life is but a smould'ring fire,
Unquench'd by want, unfann'd by strong desire ;
Unfit for raptures, or, if raptures cheer
On some high festival of once a year,
In wild excess the vulgar breast takes fire,
Till, buried in debauch, the bliss expire.

But not their joys alone thus coarsely flow :
Their morals, like their pleasures, are but low,
For, as refinement stops, from sire to son
Unalter'd, unimprov'd, the manners run ;
And love's and friendship's finely-pointed dart
Fall blunted from each indurated heart.
Some sterner virtues o'er the mountain's breast
May sit, like falcons cow'ring on the nest ;
But all the gentler morals, such as play
Through life's more cultur'd walks and charm the way,
These far dispers'd, on timorous pinions fly,
To sport and flutter in a kinder sky.

To kinder skies, where gentler manners reign,
I turn ; and France displays her bright domain.
Gay sprightly land of mirth and social ease,
Pleas'd with thyself, whom all the world can please,
How often have I led thy sportive choir,
With tuneless pipe, beside the murmuring Loire ? [1]
Where shading elms along the margin grew,
And freshen'd from the wave the Zephyr flew ;
And haply, though my harsh touch faltering still,
But mock'd all tune, and marr'd the dancer's skill ;
Yet would the village praise my wondrous power,
And dance, forgetful of the noon-tide hour.

[1 A reference to the author's pedestrian travels on the Continent
in 1755-6. Cf. *The Vicar of Wakefield*, 1766, ii. 24-5 (ch. i.).]

Alike all ages.   Dames of ancient days
Have led their children through the mirthful maze,
And the gay grandsire, skill'd in gestic lore,[1]
Has frisk'd beneath the burthen of threescore.

So bless'd a life these thoughtless realms display,
Thus idly busy rolls their world away :
Theirs are those arts that mind to mind endear,
For honour forms the social temper here :
Honour, that praise which real merit gains,
Or even imaginary worth obtains,
Here passes current ; paid from hand to hand,
It shifts in splendid traffic round the land :
From courts, to camps, to cottages it strays,
And all are taught an avarice of praise ;
They please, are pleas'd, they give to get esteem,
Till, seeming bless'd, they grow to what they seem.

But while this softer art their bliss supplies,
It gives their follies also room to rise ;
For praise too dearly lov'd, or warmly sought,
Enfeebles all internal strength of thought ;
And the weak soul, within itself unblest,
Leans for all pleasure on another's breast.
Hence ostentation here, with tawdry art,
Pants for the vulgar praise which fools impart ;
Here vanity assumes her pert grimace,
And trims her robes of frieze with copper lace ;
Here beggar pride defrauds her daily cheer,
To boast one splendid banquet once a year ;
The mind still turns where shifting fashion draws,
Nor weights the solid worth of self-applause.

To men of other minds my fancy flies,
Embosom'd in the deep where Holland lies.
Methinks her patient sons before me stand,
Where the broad ocean leans against the land,
And, sedulous to stop the coming tide,
Lift the tall rampire's artificial pride.

[¹ *i. e.* traditional gestures or action.]

Onward, methinks, and diligently slow,
The firm-connected bulwark seems to grow;
Spreads its long arms amidst the wat'ry roar,
Scoops out an empire, and usurps the shore.
While the pent ocean rising o'er the pile,
Sees an amphibious world beneath him smile;
The slow canal, the yellow-blossom'd vale,
The willow-tufted bank, the gliding sail,
The crowded mart, the cultivated plain,
A new creation rescu'd from his reign.

    Thus, while around the wave-subjected soil
Impels the native to repeated toil,
Industrious habits in each bosom reign,
And industry begets a love of gain.
Hence all the good from opulence that springs,
With all those ills superfluous treasure brings,
Are here displayed.   Their much-lov'd wealth imparts
Convenience, plenty, elegance, and arts;
But view them closer, craft and fraud appear,
Even liberty itself is bartered here.
At gold's superior charms all freedom flies,
The needy sell it, and the rich man buys;
A land of tyrants, and a den of slaves,[1]
Here wretches seek dishonourable graves,[2]
And calmly bent, to servitude conform,
Dull as their lakes that slumber in the storm.

    Heavens! how unlike their Belgic sires of old!
Rough, poor, content, ungovernably bold;
War in each breast, and freedom on each brow;
How much unlike the sons of Britain now!

    Fir'd at the sound, my genius spreads her wing,
And flies where Britain courts the western spring;
Where lawns extend that scorn Arcadian pride,
And brighter streams than fam'd Hydaspes[3] glide.

[1 This line occurs as prose in *The Citizen of the World*, 1762, i.
147.   (Letter xxxiv.)]
[2 *Julius Cæsar*, Act i. Sc. 2.]
[3 *Fabulosus Hydaspes*, Hor. Bk. i., Ode 22.]

There all around the gentle breezes stray,
There gentle music melts on every spray;
Creation's mildest charms are there combin'd,
Extremes are only in the master's mind!
Stern o'er each bosom reason holds her state,
With daring aims irregularly great,
Pride in their port, defiance in their eye,
I see the lords of human kind pass by,
Intent on high designs, a thoughtful band,
By forms unfashion'd, fresh from Nature's hand;
Fierce in their native hardiness of soul,
True to imagin'd right, above control,
While even the peasant boasts these rights to scan,
And learns to venerate himself as man.

Thine, Freedom, thine the blessings pictur'd here,
Thine are those charms that dazzle and endear;
Too bless'd, indeed, were such without alloy,
But foster'd even by Freedom ills annoy:
That independence Britons prize too high,
Keeps man from man, and breaks the social tie;
The self-dependent lordlings stand alone,
All claims that bind and sweeten life unknown;
Here by the bonds of nature feebly held,
Minds combat minds, repelling and repell'd.
Ferments arise, imprison'd factions roar,
Repress'd ambition struggles round her shore,
Till over-wrought, the general system feels
Its motions stop, or phrenzy fire the wheels.

Nor this the worst.   As nature's ties decay,
As duty, love, and honour fail to sway,
Fictitious bonds, the bonds of wealth and law,
Still gather strength, and force unwilling awe.
Hence all obedience bows to these alone,
And talent sinks, and merit weeps unknown;
Till time may come, when stripp'd of all her charms,
The land of scholars, and the nurse of arms,
Where noble stems transmit the patriot flame,
Where kings have toil'd, and poets wrote for fame,

One sink of level avarice shall lie,
And scholars, soldiers, kings, unhonour'd die.

Yet think not, thus when Freedom's ills I state,
I mean to flatter kings, or court the great;
Ye powers of truth, that bid my soul aspire,
Far from my bosom drive the low desire;
And thou, fair Freedom, taught alike to feel
The rabble's rage, and tyrant's angry steel;
Thou transitory flower, alike undone
By proud contempt, or favour's fostering sun,
Still may thy blooms the changeful clime endure,
I only would repress them to secure:
For just experience tells, in every soil,
That those who think must govern those that toil;
And all that freedom's highest aims can reach,
Is but to lay proportion'd loads on each.
Hence, should one order disproportion'd grow,
Its double weight must ruin all below.

O then how blind to all that truth requires,
Who think it freedom when a part aspires!
Calm is my soul, nor apt to rise in arms,
Except when fast-approaching danger warms:
But when contending chiefs blockade the throne,
Contracting regal power to stretch their own,[1]
When I behold a factious band agree
To call it freedom when themselves are free;
Each wanton judge new penal statutes draw,
Laws grind the poor, and rich men rule the law;[2]
The wealth of climes, where savage nations roam,
Pillag'd from slaves to purchase slaves at home;
Fear, pity, justice, indignation start,
Tear off reserve, and bare my swelling heart;
Till half a patriot, half a coward grown,
I fly from petty tyrants to the throne.[3]

[1 Cf. *The Vicar of Wakefield*, 1766, i. 202 (ch. xix.).]
[2 *Ibid.*, i. 206 (ch. xix.).]
[3 *Ibid.*, i. 201 (ch. xix.).]

    Yes, brother, curse with me that baleful hour,
When first ambition struck at regal power;
And thus polluting honour in its source,
Gave wealth to sway the mind with double force.
Have we not seen, round Britain's peopled shore,[1]
Her useful sons exchanged for useless ore?
Seen all her triumphs but destruction haste,
Like flaring tapers brightening as they waste;
Seen opulence, her grandeur to maintain,
Lead stern depopulation in her train,
And over fields where scatter'd hamlets rose,
In barren solitary pomp repose?
Have we not seen at pleasure's lordly call,
The smiling long-frequented village fall?
Beheld the duteous son, the sire decay'd,
The modest matron, and the blushing maid,
Forc'd from their homes, a melancholy train,
To traverse climbs beyond the western main;
Where wild Oswego spreads her swamps around,
And Niagara stuns with thund'ring sound?
Even now, perhaps, as there some pilgrim strays
Through tangled forests, and through dangerous ways;
Where beasts with man divided empire claim,
And the brown Indian marks with murderous aim;
There, while above the giddy tempest flies,
And all around distressful yells arise,
The pensive exile, bending with his woe,
To stop too fearful, and too faint to go,[2]
Casts a long look where England's glories shine,
And bids his bosom sympathise with mine.

    Vain, very vain, my weary search to find
That bliss which only centres in the mind:
Why have I stray'd from pleasure and repose,
To seek a good each government bestows?
In every government, though terrors reign,
Though tyrant kings, or tyrant laws restrain,

[1 This and the lines that follow contain the germ of *The Deserted Village*.]

[2 Johnson contributed this line. (Birkbeck Hill's *Boswell*, 1887, ii. 6.)]

How small, of all that human hearts endure,[1]
That part which laws or kings can cause or cure.
Still to ourselves in every place consign'd,
Our own felicity we make or find:
With secret course, which no loud storms annoy,
Glides the smooth current of domestic joy.
The lifted axe, the agonising wheel,
Luke's iron crown,[2] and Damiens' bed of steel,[3]
To men remote from power but rarely known,
Leave reason, faith, and conscience, all our own.

[1] Johnson wrote these last lines, the penultimate couplet excepted. (*Boswell, ut supra.*)]

[2] George (not Luke) Dosa, a Hungarian patriot, suffered in 1514 the penalty of the red-hot iron crown. Cf. H. Morley's *Montaigne*, 1886, xvi.]

[3] Robert-François Damiens was executed in 1757 after horrible tortures for an attempt to assassinate Louis XV. When in the Conciergerie, he is said to have been chained to an iron bed. (Smollett's *History of England*, 1823, bk. iii. ch. 7, § xxv.).]

THE DESERTED VILLAGE

A POEM

[*The Deserted Village, a Poem. By Dr. Goldsmith,*—was published by W. Griffin, at Garrick's Head, in Catherine-street, Strand, in a 4to. of thirty-two pages, on the 26th May, 1770. The price was two shillings. It is here reprinted from the fourth edition, issued in the same year as the first, but considerably revised.]

DEDICATION

TO SIR JOSHUA REYNOLDS

DEAR SIR,

I can have no expectations in an address of this kind, either to add to your reputation, or to establish my own. You can gain nothing from my admiration, as I am ignorant of that art in which you are said to excel; and I may lose much by the severity of your judgment, as few have a juster taste in poetry than you. Setting interest therefore aside, to which I never paid much attention, I must be indulged at present in following my affections. The only dedication I ever made was to my brother, because I loved him better than most other men. He is since dead.[1] Permit me to inscribe this Poem to you.

How far you may be pleased with the versification and mere mechanical parts of this attempt, I don't pretend to enquire: but I know you will object (and indeed several of our best and wisest friends concur in the opinion) that the depopulation it deplores is no where to be seen, and the disorders it laments are only to be found in the poet's own imagination. To this I can scarce make any other answer than that I sincerely believe what I have written; that I have taken all possible pains, in my country excursions, for these four or five years past, to be certain of what I allege; and that all my views and enquiries have led me to believe those miseries real, which I here attempt to display. But this is not the place to enter into an enquiry, whether the country be depopulating, or not; the discussion would take up much room, and I should prove myself, at best, an indifferent politician, to tire the reader with a long preface when I want his unfatigued attention to a long poem.

In regretting the depopulation of the country, I inveigh

[1 See p. 3, and note.]

21

against the increase of our luxuries; and here also I
expect the shout of modern politicians against me. For
twenty or thirty years past, it has been the fashion to
consider luxury as one of the greatest national advantages; and all the wisdom of antiquity in that particular,
as erroneous. Still, however, I must remain a professed
ancient on that head, and continue to think those
luxuries prejudicial to states, by which so many vices are
introduced, and so many kingdoms have been undone.[1]
Indeed so much has been poured out of late on the
other side of the question, that, merely for the sake of
novelty and variety, one would sometimes wish to be in
the right.

I am, Dear Sir,
Your sincere friend, and ardent admirer,
OLIVER GOLDSMITH.

[1 The increase of luxury was a favourite topic with Goldsmith.
Cf. Birkbeck Hill's *Boswell*, 1887, ii. 217-8.)]

THE DESERTED VILLAGE

Sweet Auburn ! loveliest village of the plain,
Where health and plenty cheer'd the labouring swain,
Where smiling spring its earliest visit paid,
And parting summer's lingering blooms delay'd :
Dear lovely bowers of innocence and ease,
Seats of my youth,[1] when every sport could please,
How often have I loiter'd o'er thy green,
Where humble happiness endear'd each scene ;
How often have I paus'd on every charm,
The shelter'd cot, the cultivated farm,
The never-failing brook, the busy mill,
The decent church that topp'd the neighbouring hill,
The hawthorn bush, with seats beneath the shade,
For talking age and whispering lovers made ;
How often have I bless'd the coming day,
When toil remitting lent its turn to play,
And all the village train, from labour free,
Led up their sports beneath the spreading tree :
While many a pastime circled in the shade,
The young contending as the old survey'd ;
And many a gambol frolick'd o'er the ground,
And sleights of art and feats of strength went round ;
And still as each repeated pleasure tir'd,
Succeeding sports the mirthful band inspir'd ;
The dancing pair that simply sought renown,
By holding out to tire each other down !
The swain mistrustless of his smutted face,
While secret laughter titter'd round the place ;
The bashful virgin's side-long looks of love,
The matron's glance that would those looks reprove :
These were thy charms, sweet village ; sports like these,
With sweet succession, taught even toil to please ;

[1 Some of the details of the picture are borrowed from Lissoy,
the little hamlet in Westmeath where the author spent his younger
days.]

These round thy bowers their cheerful influence shed,
These were thy charms—But all these charms are fled.

Sweet smiling village, loveliest of the lawn,
Thy sports are fled, and all thy charms withdrawn;
Amidst thy bowers the tyrant's hand is seen,
And desolation saddens all thy green:
One only master grasps the whole domain,
And half a tillage stints thy smiling plain:
No more thy glassy brook reflects the day,
But chok'd with sedges, works its weedy way.
Along thy glades, a solitary guest,
The hollow-sounding bittern guards its nest;[1]
Amidst thy desert walks the lapwing flies,
And tires their echoes with unvaried cries.
Sunk are thy bowers, in shapeless ruin all,
And the long grass o'ertops the mouldering wall;
And, trembling, shrinking from the spoiler's hand,
Far, far away, thy children leave the land.

Ill fares the land, to hastening ills a prey,
Where wealth accumulates, and men decay:
Princes and lords may flourish, or may fade;
A breath can make them, as a breath has made;
But a bold peasantry, their country's pride,
When once destroy'd, can never be supplied.

A time there was, ere England's griefs began,
When every rood of ground maintain'd its man;
For him light labour spread her wholesome store,
Just gave what life requir'd, but gave no more:
His best companions, innocence and health;
And his best riches, ignorance of wealth.

But times are alter'd; trade's unfeeling train
Usurp the land and dispossess the swain;
Along the lawn, where scatter'd hamlets rose,
Unwieldy wealth, and cumbrous pomp repose;
And every want to opulence allied,
And every pang that folly pays to pride.

[1 Cf. Bewick's *Water Birds*, 1847, p. 49.]

Those gentle hours that plenty bade to bloom,
Those calm desires that ask'd but little room,
Those healthful sports that grac'd the peaceful scene,
Liv'd in each look, and brighten'd all the green;
These, far departing, seek a kinder shore,
And rural mirth and manners are no more.

Sweet AUBURN! parent of the blissful hour,
Thy glades forlorn confess the tyrant's power.
Here as I take my solitary rounds,
Amidst thy tangling walks, and ruin'd grounds,
And, many a year elaps'd, return to view
Where once the cottage stood, the hawthorn grew,
Remembrance wakes with all her busy train,
Swells at my breast, and turns the past to pain.[1]

In all my wanderings round this world of care,
In all my griefs—and GOD has given my share—
I still had hopes my latest hours to crown,
Amidst these humble bowers to lay me down;
To husband out life's taper at the close,
And keep the flame from wasting by repose.
I still had hopes, for pride attends us still,
Amidst the swains to show my book-learn'd skill,
Around my fire an evening group to draw,
And tell of all I felt, and all I saw;
And, as an hare, whom hounds and horns pursue,
Pants to the place from whence at first she flew,
I still had hopes, my long vexations pass'd,
Here to return—and die at home at last.[2]

O blest retirement, friend to life's decline,
Retreats from care, that never must be mine,
How happy he who crowns in shades like these,
A youth of labour with an age of ease;
Who quits a world where strong temptations try,
And, since 'tis hard to combat, learns to fly!
For him no wretches, born to work and weep,
Explore the mine, or tempt the dangerous deep;

[1 There is no satisfactory evidence that Goldsmith ever revisited
Ireland after he left it in 1752.]
[2 Cf. *The Citizen of the World*, 1762, ii. 153. (Letter C.)]

No surly porter stands in guilty state
To spurn imploring famine from the gate;
But on he moves to meet his latter end,
Angels around befriending Virtue's friend;
Bends to the grave with unperceiv'd decay,
While Resignation gently slopes the way;
And, all his prospects brightening to the last,
His Heaven commences ere the world be pass'd:[1]

Sweet was the sound, when oft at evening's close
Up yonder hill the village murmur rose;
There, as I pass'd with careless steps and slow,
The mingling notes came soften'd from below;
The swain responsive as the milkmaid sung,
The sober herd that low'd to meet their young;
The noisy geese that gabbled o'er the pool,
The playful children just let loose from school;
The watchdog's voice that bay'd the whisp'ring wind,
And the loud laugh that spoke the vacant mind;
These all in sweet confusion sought the shade,
And fill'd each pause the nightingale had made.
But now the sounds of population fail,
No cheerful murmurs fluctuate in the gale,
No busy steps the grass-grown footway tread,
For all the bloomy flush of life is fled.
All but yon widow'd, solitary thing,
That feebly bends beside the plashy spring;
She, wretched matron, forc'd in age, for bread,
To strip the brook with mantling cresses spread,
To pick her wintry faggot from the thorn,
To seek her nightly shed, and weep till morn;
She only left of all the harmless train,
The sad historian of the pensive plain.[2]

Near yonder copse, where once the garden smil'd,
And still where many a garden flower grows wild;

[1 Under the title of *Resignation*, Reynolds in 1771 dedicated a print of an old man to Goldsmith as "expressing the character" sketched in this paragraph.]

[2 This has been identified with Catherine Geraghty, a familiar personage at Lissoy in Goldsmith's boyhood.]

There, where a few torn shrubs the place disclose,
The village preacher's modest mansion rose.[1]
A man he was to all the country dear,
And passing rich with forty pounds a year;[2]
Remote from towns he ran his godly race,
Nor e'er had chang'd, nor wished to change his place;
Unpractis'd he to fawn, or seek for power,
By doctrines fashion'd to the varying hour;
Far other aims his heart had learn'd to prize,
More skill'd to raise the wretched than to rise.
His house was known to all the vagrant train,
He chid their wanderings, but reliev'd their pain;
The long remember'd beggar was his guest,
Whose beard descending swept his aged breast;
The ruin'd spendthrift, now no longer proud,
Claim'd kindred there, and had his claims allow'd;
The broken soldier, kindly bade to stay,
Sat by his fire, and talk'd the night away;
Wept o'er his wounds, or tales of sorrow done,
Shoulder'd his crutch, and show'd how fields were won.
Pleas'd with his guests, the good man learned to glow,
And quite forgot their vices in their woe;
Careless their merits, or their faults to scan,
His pity gave ere charity began.

Thus to relieve the wretched was his pride,
And e'en his failings lean'd to Virtue's side;
But in his duty prompt at every call,
He watch'd and wept, he pray'd and felt, for all.
And, as a bird each fond endearment tries
To tempt its new-fledg'd offspring to the skies,
He tried each art, reprov'd each dull delay,
Allur'd to brighter worlds, and led the way.

Beside the bed where parting life was laid,
And sorrow, guilt, and pain, by turns dismay'd,
The reverend champion stood.   At his control
Despair and anguish fled the struggling soul;

[1 The character that follows is probably combined from the author's father, his brother Henry, and his uncle Contarine, all clergymen.]

[2 See p. 3.]

Comfort came down the trembling wretch to raise,
And his last faltering accents whisper'd praise.

At church with meek and unaffected grace,
His looks adorn'd the venerable place;
Truth from his lips prevail'd with double sway,
And fools, who came to scoff, remain'd to pray.
The service pass'd, around the pious man,
With steady zeal, each honest rustic ran;
Even children follow'd with endearing wile,
And pluck'd his gown, to share the good man's smile.
His ready smile a parent's warmth express'd,
Their welfare pleas'd him, and their cares distress'd;
To them his heart, his love, his griefs were given,
But all his serious thoughts had rest in Heaven.
As some tall cliff, that lifts its awful form,
Swells from the vale, and midway leaves the storm,
Though round its breast the rolling clouds are spread,
Eternal sunshine settles on its head.[1]

Beside yon straggling fence that skirts the way,
With blossom'd furze unprofitably gay,
There, in his noisy mansion, skill'd to rule,
The village master taught his little school;[2]
A man severe he was, and stern to view;
I knew him well, and every truant knew;
Well had the boding tremblers learn'd to trace
The day's disasters in his morning face;
Full well they laugh'd, with counterfeited glee,
At all his jokes, for many a joke had he;
Full well the busy whisper, circling round,
Convey'd the dismal tidings when he frown'd;
Yet he was kind: or if severe in aught,
The love he bore to learning was in fault;
The village all declar'd how much he knew;
'Twas certain he could write, and cypher too;

[1 Chaulieu, Chapelain, and several "ancients" have been
credited with the suggestion of this simile. But perhaps Goldsmith
went no farther than the character of "Philander" in Young's
Complaint (*Night the Second*, 1740, p. 42).]

[2 Some of the traits of this portrait correspond with those of
Goldsmith's master at Lissoy, one Byrne.]

Lands he could measure, terms and tides presage,
And even the story ran that he could gauge.
In arguing too, the parson own'd his skill,
For e'en though vanquish'd, he could argue still;
While words of learned length and thundering sound
Amaz'd the gazing rustics rang'd around,
And still they gaz'd, and still the wonder grew,
That one small head could carry all he knew.

But past is all his fame. The very spot
Where many a time he triumph'd, is forgot.
Near yonder thorn, that lifts its head on high,
Where once the sign-post caught the passing eye,
Low lies that house where nut-brown draughts inspir'd,
Where grey-beard mirth and smiling toil retir'd,
Where village statesmen talk'd with looks profound,
And news much older than their ale went round.
Imagination fondly stoops to trace
The parlour splendours of that festive place;
The white-wash'd wall, the nicely sanded floor,
The varnish'd clock that click'd behind the door;
The chest contriv'd a double debt to pay,
A bed by night, a chest of drawers by day;
The pictures plac'd for ornament and use,
The twelve good rules,[1] the royal game of goose;[2]
The hearth, except when winter chill'd the day,
With aspen boughs, and flowers, and fennel gay;
While broken tea-cups, wisely kept for show,
Rang'd o'er the chimney, glisten'd in a row.

Vain transitory splendours! could not all
Reprieve the tottering mansion from its fall!
Obscure it sinks, nor shall it more impart
An hour's importance to the poor man's heart;
Thither no more the peasant shall repair
To sweet oblivion of his daily care;
No more the farmer's news, the barber's tale,
No more the wood-man's ballad shall prevail;

[1 The well-known maxims "found in the study of King Charles
the First, of Blessed Memory," and common in Goldsmith's day as
a broadside. Her late Majesty had a copy of them in the servants'
hall at Windsor Castle.]

[2 See Strutt's *Sports and Pastimes*, Bk. iv. ch. 2, § xxv.]

No more the smith his dusky brow shall clear,
Relax his ponderous strength, and lean to hear;
The host himself no longer shall be found
Careful to see the mantling bliss go round;
Nor the coy maid, half willing to be press'd,
Shall kiss the cup to pass it to the rest.

Yes! let the rich deride, the proud disdain,
These simple blessings of the lowly train;
To me more dear, congenial to my heart,
One native charm, than all the gloss of art;
Spontaneous joys, where Nature has its play,
The soul adopts, and owns their first-born sway;
Lightly they frolic o'er the vacant mind,
Unenvied, unmolested, unconfin'd:
But the long pomp, the midnight masquerade,
With all the freaks of wanton wealth array'd,
In these, ere triflers half their wish obtain,
The toiling pleasure sickens into pain;
And, even while fashion's brightest arts decoy,
The heart distrusting asks, if this be joy.

Ye friends to truth, ye statesmen, who survey
The rich man's joys increase, the poor's decay,
'Tis yours to judge, how wide the limits stand
Between a splendid and a happy land.
Proud swells the tide with loads of freighted ore,
And shouting Folly hails them from her shore;
Hoards, even beyond the miser's wish abound,
And rich men flock from all the world around.
Yet count our gains. This wealth is but a name
That leaves our useful products still the same.
Not so the loss. The man of wealth and pride
Takes up a space that many poor supplied;
Space for his lake, his park's extended bounds,
Space for his horses, equipage, and hounds;
The robe that wraps his limbs in silken sloth
Has robb'd the neighbouring fields of half their growth,
His seat, where solitary sports are seen,
Indignant spurns the cottage from the green;

Around the world each needful product flies,
For all the luxuries the world supplies :
While thus the land adorn'd for pleasure, all
In barren splendour feebly waits the fall.

As some fair female unadorn'd and plain,
Secure to please while youth confirms her reign,
Slights every borrow'd charm that dress supplies,
Nor shares with art the triumph of her eyes :
But when those charms are pass'd, for charms are frail,
When time advances and when lovers fail,
She then shines forth, solicitous to bless,
In all the glaring impotence of dress.
Thus fares the land, by luxury betray'd,
In nature's simplest charms at first array'd,
But verging to decline, its splendours rise,
Its vistas strike, its palaces surprise ;
While, scourg'd by famine, from the smiling land
The mournful peasant leads his humble band ;
And while he sinks, without one arm to save,
The country blooms—a garden, and a grave.

Where then, ah ! where, shall poverty reside,
To 'scape the pressure of contiguous pride ?
If to some common's fenceless limits stray'd,
He drives his flock to pick the scanty blade,
Those fenceless fields the sons of wealth divide,
And even the bare-worn common is denied.

If to the city sped—What waits him there ?
To see profusion that he must not share ;
To see ten thousand baneful arts combin'd
To pamper luxury, and thin mankind ;
To see those joys the sons of pleasure know
Extorted from his fellow creature's woe.
Here, while the courtier glitters in brocade,
There the pale artist plies the sickly trade ;
Here, while the proud their long-drawn pomps display,
There the black gibbet glooms beside the way.
The dome where Pleasure holds her midnight reign
Here, richly deck'd, admits the gorgeous train ;

Tumultuous grandeur crowds the blazing square,
The rattling chariots clash, the torches glare.
Sure scenes like these no troubles e'er annoy !
Sure these denote one universal joy !
Are these thy serious thoughts ?—Ah, turn thine eyes
Where the poor houseless shivering female lies.[1]
She once, perhaps, in village plenty bless'd,
Has wept at tales of innocence distress'd ;
Her modest looks the cottage might adorn,
Sweet as the primrose peeps beneath the thorn ;
Now lost to all ; her friends, her virtue fled,
Near her betrayer's door she lays her head,
And, pinch'd with cold, and shrinking from the shower,
With heavy heart deplores that luckless hour,
When idly first, ambitious of the town,
She left her wheel and robes of country brown.

Do thine, sweet AUBURN, thine, the loveliest train,
Do thy fair tribes participate her pain ?
E'en now, perhaps, by cold and hunger led,
At proud men's doors they ask a little bread !

Ah, no.   To distant climes, a dreary scene,
Where half the convex world intrudes between,
Through torrid tracts with fainting steps they go,
Where wild Altama[2] murmurs to their woe.
Far different there from all that charm'd before,
The various terrors of that horrid shore ;
Those blazing suns that dart a downward ray,
And fiercely shed intolerable day ;
Those matted woods where birds forget to sing,
But silent bats in drowsy clusters cling,
Those poisonous fields with rank luxuriance crown'd,
Where the dark scorpion gathers death around ;
Where at each step the stranger fears to wake
The rattling terrors of the vengeful snake ;
Where crouching tigers wait their hapless prey,
And savage men more murderous still than they ;

[1 Cf. *The Bee*, 27th October, 1759 (*A City Night-Piece*).]
[2 Alatamaha, in Georgia, North America.]

The Deserted Village

While oft in whirls the mad tornado flies,
Mingling the ravag'd landscape with the skies.
Far different these from every former scene,
The cooling brook, the grassy-vested green,
The breezy covert of the warbling grove,
That only shelter'd thefts of harmless love.

Good Heaven! what sorrows gloom'd that parting
    day,
That call'd them from their native walks away;
When the poor exiles, every pleasure pass'd,
Hung round their bowers, and fondly look'd their last,
And took a long farewell, and wish'd in vain
For seats like these beyond the western main;
And shuddering still to face the distant deep,
Return'd and wept, and still returned to weep.
The good old sire, the first prepar'd to go
To new-found worlds, and wept for others' woe;
But for himself, in conscious virtue brave,
He only wish'd for worlds beyond the grave.
His lovely daughter, lovelier in her tears,
The fond companion of her helpless years,
Silent went next, neglectful of her charms,
And left a lover's for a father's arms.
With louder plaints the mother spoke her woes,
And bless'd the cot where every pleasure rose;
And kiss'd her thoughtless babes with many a tear,
And clasp'd them close, in sorrow doubly dear;
Whilst her fond husband strove to lend relief
In all the silent manliness of grief.

O luxury! thou curs'd by Heaven's decree,
How ill exchang'd are things like these for thee!
How do thy potions, with insidious joy
Diffuse their pleasures only to destroy!
Kingdoms, by thee, to sickly greatness grown,
Boast of a florid vigour not their own;
At every draught more large and large they grow,
A bloated mass of rank unwieldy woe;
Till sapp'd their strength, and every part unsound,
Down, down they sink, and spread a ruin round.

Even now the devastation is begun,
And half the business of destruction done;
Even now, methinks, as pondering here I stand,
I see the rural virtues leave the land:
Down where yon anchoring vessel spreads the sail,
That idly waiting flaps with every gale,
Downward they move, a melancholy band,
Pass from the shore, and darken all the strand.
Contented toil, and hospitable care,
And kind connubial tenderness, are there;
And piety with wishes plac'd above,
And steady loyalty, and faithful love.
And thou, sweet Poetry, thou loveliest maid,
Still first to fly where sensual joys invade;
Unfit in these degenerate times of shame,
To catch the heart, or strike for honest fame:
Dear charming nymph, neglected and decried,
My shame in crowds, my solitary pride;
Thou source of all my bliss, and all my woe,
That found'st me poor at first, and keep'st me so;
Thou guide by which the nobler arts excel,
Thou nurse of every virtue, fare thee well!
Farewell, and Oh! where'er thy voice be tried,
On Torno's [1] cliffs, or Pambamarca's [2] side,
Whether where equinoctial fervours glow,
Or winter wraps the polar world in snow,
Still let thy voice, prevailing over time,
Redress the rigours of th' inclement clime;
Aid slighted truth; with thy persuasive strain
Teach erring man to spurn the rage of gain;
Teach him, that states of native strength possess'd,
Though very poor, may still be very bless'd;
That trade's proud empire hastes to swift decay,
As ocean sweeps the labour'd mole away;
While self-dependent power can time defy,
As rocks resist the billows and the sky. [3]

[1 Tornea, a river falling into the Gulf of Bothnia.]
[2 A mountain near Quito, South America.]
[3 Johnson wrote the last four lines. (Birkbeck Hill's *Boswell*, 1887, ii. 7.)]

RETALIATION

A POEM

[*Retaliation : A Poem. By Dr. Goldsmith. Including Epitaphs on the Most Distinguished Wits of the Metropolis*—was first published on the 18th or 19th April, 1774, as a 4to of twenty pages, by G. Kearsly of No. 46 Fleet Street. Under the title was a vignette-head of Goldsmith etched by Basire after Reynolds. To the second edition, which followed almost immediately, and the text of which is here printed, were added four pages of " Explanatory Notes and Observations, etc."

The poem originated in a contest of epitaphs which took place after a club dinner at the St. James's Coffee-house. Garrick led off with his well-known epigram :—

" Here lies NOLLY Goldsmith, for shortness called Noll,
    Who wrote like an angel, but talked like poor Poll,"

and several more were written by the company. Goldsmith reserved his "retaliation," and shortly afterwards set about the annexed poem, left incomplete at his death.]

RETALIATION

A POEM

OF old, when Scarron [1] his companions invited,
Each guest brought his dish, and the feast was united;
If our landlord supplies us with beef, and with fish,
Let each guest bring himself, and he brings the best
    dish:
Our Dean [2] shall be venison, just fresh from the plains;
Our Burke [3] shall be tongue with a garnish of brains;
Our Will [4] shall be wild-fowl, of excellent flavour,
And Dick [5] with his pepper shall heighten their savour;
Our Cumberland's [6] sweet-bread its place shall obtain,
And Douglas [7] is pudding, substantial and plain:
Our Garrick's [8] a salad; for in him we see
Oil, vinegar, sugar, and saltness agree:
To make out the dinner, full certain I am,
That Ridge [9] is anchovy, and Reynolds [10] is lamb;
That Hickey's [11] a capon, and by the same rule,
Magnanimous Goldsmith a gooseberry fool.
At a dinner so various, at such a repast,
Who'd not be a glutton, and stick to the last?
Here, waiter! more wine, let me sit while I'm able,
Till all my companions sink under the table;
Then, with chaos and blunders encircling my head,
Let me ponder, and tell what I think of the dead.

[1 Paul Scarron (1610–60), author of the *Roman Comique*, to
whose pic-nic dinners "*chacun apportait son plat.*" (*Œuvres*, 1877,
i., viii.)]
  [2 Thomas Barnard, Dean of Derry, d. 1806.]
  [3 Edmund Burke, 1729–97.]
  [4 William Burke (his relation), d. 1798.]
  [5 Richard Burke (Edmund Burke's brother), d. 1794.]
  [6 Richard Cumberland, the dramatist, 1732–1811.]
  [7 Dr. Douglas, afterwards Bishop of Salisbury, d. 1807.]
  [8 David Garrick, the actor, 1716–79.]
  [9 John Ridge, an Irish barrister.]
  [10 Sir Joshua Reynolds, 1723–92.]
  [11 Joseph Hickey, d. 1794, the legal adviser of Reynolds.]

Here lies the good Dean, re-united to earth,
Who mix'd reason with pleasure, and wisdom with mirth:
If he had any faults, he has left us in doubt,
At least, in six weeks, I could not find 'em out;
Yet some have declar'd, and it can't be denied 'em,
That sly-boots was cursedly cunning to hide 'em.

Here lies our good Edmund, whose genius was such,
We scarcely can praise it, or blame it too much;
Who, born for the Universe, narrow'd his mind,
And to party gave up what was meant for mankind.
Though fraught with all learning, yet straining his throat
To persuade Tommy Townshend [1] to lend him a vote;
Who, too deep for his hearers, still went on refining,
And thought of convincing, while they thought of dining;
Though equal to all things, for all things unfit,
Too nice for a statesman, too proud for a wit:
For a patriot, too cool; for a drudge, disobedient;
And too fond of the *right* to pursue the *expedient*.
In short, 'twas his fate, unemploy'd, or in place, Sir,
To eat mutton cold, and cut blocks with a razor.

Here lies honest William, whose heart was a mint,
While the owner ne'er knew half the good that was in't;
The pupil of impulse, it forced him along,
His conduct still right, with his argument wrong;
Still aiming at honour, yet fearing to roam,
The coachman was tipsy, the chariot drove home;
Would you ask for his merits? alas! he had none;
What was good was spontaneous, his faults were his own.

Here lies honest Richard, whose fate I must sigh at;
Alas, that such frolic should now be so quiet;
What spirits were his! what wit and what whim!
Now breaking a jest, and now breaking a limb; [2]

[1 M.P. for Whitchurch, afterwards Lord Sydney.]
[2 "The above Gentleman (Richard Burke) having slightly frac-
tured one of his arms and legs, at different times, the Doctor (*i. e.*
Goldsmith) has rallied him on those accidents, as a kind of *retribu-*
tive justice for breaking his jests on other people." (*Note to Second*
Edition.)]

Now wrangling and grumbling to keep up the ball,
Now teasing and vexing, yet laughing at all !
In short, so provoking a devil was Dick,
That we wish'd him full ten times a day at Old Nick
But, missing his mirth and agreeable vein,
As often we wish'd to have Dick back again.

Here Cumberland lies, having acted his parts,
The Terence of England, the mender of hearts ;
A flattering painter, who made it his care
To draw men as they ought to be, not as they are.
His gallants are all faultless, his women divine,
And comedy wonders at being so fine ;
Like a tragedy queen he has dizen'd her out,
Or rather like tragedy giving a rout.
His fools have their follies so lost in a crowd
Of virtues and feelings, that folly grows proud ;
And coxcombs, alike in their failings alone,
Adopting his portraits, are pleas'd with their own.
Say, where has our poet this malady caught ?
Or, wherefore his characters thus without fault
Say, was it that vainly directing his view
To find out men's virtues, and finding them few,
Quite sick of pursuing each troublesome elf,
He grew lazy at last, and drew from himself ?[1]

Here Douglas retires, from his toils to relax,
The scourge of impostors, the terror of quacks :[2]
Come, all ye quack bards, and ye quacking divines,
Come, and dance on the spot where your tyrant reclines :
When Satire and Censure encircl'd his throne,
I fear'd for your safety, I fear'd for my own ;
But now he is gone, and we want a detector,
Our Dodds[3] shall be pious, our Kenricks[4] shall lecture ;

[1 Cumberland is said to have fancied that this epitaph was *not* ironical.]

[2 Douglas exposed two literary impostors—Archibald Bower, author of a *History of the Popes*, and William Lauder, who fabricated a charge of plagiarism against Milton.]

[3 The Rev. William Dodd, executed for forgery in June, 1777.]

[4 Dr. Kenrick, who lectured on Shakespeare at the Devil Tavern in 1774.]

Macpherson [1] write bombast, and call it a style,
Our Townshend make speeches, and I shall compile;
New Lauders and Bowers [2] the Tweed shall cross over,
No countryman living their tricks to discover;
Detection her taper shall quench to a spark,
And Scotchmen meet Scotchmen, and cheat in the dark.

Here lies David Garrick, describe me, who can,
An abridgment of all that was pleasant in man;
As an actor, confessed without rival to shine:
As a wit, if not first, in the very first line:
Yet, with talents like these, and an excellent heart,
The man had his failings, a dupe to his art.
Like an ill-judging beauty, his colours he spread,
And beplaster'd with rouge his own natural red.
On the stage he was natural, simple, affecting;
'Twas only that when he was off he was acting.
With no reason on earth to go out of his way,
He turn'd and he varied full ten times a day.
Though secure of our hearts, yet confoundedly sick
If they were not his own by finessing and trick;
He cast off his friends, as a huntsman his pack,
For he knew when he pleas'd he could whistle them
    back.
Of praise a mere glutton, he swallowed what came,
And the puff of a dunce he mistook it for fame;
Till his relish grown callous, almost to disease,
Who pepper'd the highest was surest to please.
But let us be candid, and speak out our mind,
If dunces applauded, he paid them in kind.
Ye Kenricks, ye Kellys, [3] and Woodfalls [4] so grave,
What a commerce was yours, while you got and you
    gave!
How did Grub-street re-echo the shouts that you rais'd,
While he was be-Roscius'd, and you were be-prais'd!

[1] James Macpherson (1728–96) of *Ossian* notoriety. He had recently (1773) published a prose Translation of Homer.]
[2] *Vide* note 2, p. 39.]
[3] Hugh Kelly, the dramatist (1739–77), author of *False Delicacy, A Word to the Wise*, etc.]
[4] William Woodfall, d. 1803, editor of *The Morning Chronicle*.}

But peace to his spirit, wherever it flies,
To act as an angel, and mix with the skies:
Those poets, who owe their best fame to his skill,
Shall still be his flatterers, go where he will.
Old Shakespeare, receive him, with praise and with love,
And Beaumonts and Bens be his Kellys above.

Here Hickey reclines, a most blunt, pleasant creature,
And slander itself must allow him good nature:
He cherish'd his friend, and he relish'd a bumper;
Yet one fault he had, and that one was a thumper.
Perhaps you may ask if the man was a miser?
I answer, no, no, for he always was wiser:
Too courteous, perhaps, or obligingly flat?
His very worst foe can't accuse him of that:
Perhaps he confided in men as they go,
And so was too foolishly honest? Ah no!
Then what was his failing? come tell it, and burn ye!
He was, could he help it?—a special attorney.

Here Reynolds is laid, and to tell you my mind,
He has not left a better or wiser behind:
His pencil was striking, resistless, and grand;
His manners were gentle, complying, and bland;
Still born to improve us in every part,
His pencil our faces, his manners our heart:
To coxcombs averse, yet most civilly steering,
When they judg'd without skill he was still hard of
      hearing:
When they talked of their Raphaels, Correggios, and
      stuff,
He shifted his trumpet, and only took snuff . . .[1]

POSTSCRIPT.

[*First printed in the Fifth Edition*, 1774.]

After the Fourth Edition of this Poem was printed, the Publisher
received an Epitaph on Mr. Whiteford, from a friend of the late

---

[1 Prior (*Life of Goldsmith*, 1837, ii. 499) says half a line more
had been written. It was, " By flattery unspoiled "—and remained
unaltered in the MS.]

Doctor Goldsmith, inclosed in a letter, of which the following is
an abstract:—

"I have in my possession a sheet of paper, containing near forty
lines in the Doctor's own handwriting: there are many scattered,
broken verses, on Sir Jos. Reynolds, Counsellor Ridge, Mr. Beau-
clerk, and Mr. Whitefoord. The Epitaph on the last-mentioned
gentleman is the only one that is finished, and therefore I have
copied it, that you may add it to the next edition. It is a striking
proof of Doctor Goldsmith's good-nature. I saw this sheet of
paper in the Doctor's room, five or six days before he died; and,
as I had got all the other Epitaphs, I asked him if I might take it.
'*In truth you may, my Boy*,' (replied he) '*for it will be of no use to
me where I am going.*'"

HERE Whitefoord[1] reclines, and deny it who can,
Though he *merrily* liv'd, he is now a *grave* man;
Rare compound of oddity, frolic, and fun!
Who relish'd a joke, and rejoic'd in a pun;
Whose temper was generous, open, sincere;
A stranger to flatt'ry, a stranger to fear;
Who scatter'd around wit and humour at will;
Whose daily *bon mots* half a column might fill;
A Scotchman, from pride and from prejudice free;
A scholar, yet surely no pedant was he.
What pity, alas! that so lib'ral a mind
Should so long be to news-paper essays confin'd;
Who perhaps to the summit of science could soar,
Yet content "if the table he set on a roar;"
Whose talents to fill any station were fit,
Yet happy if Woodfall[2] confess'd him a wit.
Ye news-paper witlings! ye pert scribbling folks!
Who copied his squibs, and re-echoed his jokes;
Ye tame imitators, ye servile herd, come,
Still follow your master, and visit his tomb:
To deck it bring with you festoons of the vine,
And copious libations bestow on his shrine:
Then strew all around it (you can do no less)
Cross-readings, Ship-news, and *Mistakes of the Press.*

[1 Caleb Whitefoord, d. 1810, an inveterate punster, and author
of the once-popular "Cross Readings," for an account of which see
Smith's *Life of Nollekens*, 1828, i. 336-7.]

[2 H. S. Woodfall, d. 1805, printer of the *Public Advertiser*, in
which the "Cross Readings" appeared.]

Merry Whitefoord, farewell! for *thy* sake I admit
That a Scot may have humour, I had almost said wit:
This debt to thy mem'ry I cannot refuse,
"Thou best humour'd man with the worst humour'd
    muse." [1]

[1 An adaptation of Rochester on Lord Buckhurst. It is half
suspected that Whitefoord wrote this "Postscript" himself. The
recently published *Whitefoord Papers* (1898) throw no light on the
subject.]

THE HAUNCH OF VENISON

A POETICAL EPISTLE TO LORD CLARE

[*The Haunch of Venison, a Poetical Epistle to Lord Clare. By the late Dr. Goldsmith. With a Head of the Author, Drawn by Henry Bunbury, Esq.; and Etched by* [James] *Bretherton*,—was first published in 1776 by J. Ridley, in St. James's Street, and G. Kearsly, in Fleet Street. It is supposed to have been written early in 1771. The present version is printed from the second edition "taken from the author's *last* Transcript," and issued in the same year as the first.]

THE HAUNCH OF VENISON

A POETICAL EPISTLE TO LORD CLARE [1]

THANKS, my Lord, for your venison, for finer or fatter
Never rang'd in a forest, or smok'd in a platter;
The haunch was a picture for painters to study,
The fat was so white, and the lean was so ruddy.
Though my stomach was sharp, I could scarce help
    regretting
To spoil such a delicate picture by eating;
I had thoughts, in my chambers, to place it in view,
To be shown to my friends as a piece of *virtù*;
As in some Irish houses, where things are so so,
One gammon of bacon hangs up for a show:
But for eating a rasher of what they take pride in,
They'd as soon think of eating the pan it is fried in.
But hold—let me pause—Don't I hear you pronounce
This tale of the bacon a damnable bounce?
Well, suppose it a bounce—sure a poet may try,
By a bounce now and then, to get courage to fly.

But, my Lord, it's no bounce: I protest in my turn,
It's a truth—and your Lordship may ask Mr. Byrne. [2]
To go on with my tale—as I gaz'd on the haunch,
I thought of a friend that was trusty and staunch;
So I cut it, and sent it to Reynolds undress'd,
To paint it, or eat it, just as he lik'd best.
Of the neck and the breast I had next to dispose;
'Twas a neck and a breast—that might rival M[on]-
    r[oe]'s :—[3]
But in parting with these I was puzzled again,
With the how, and the who, and the where, and the
    when.

[1 Robert Nugent of Carlanstown, Westmeath; created Viscount
Clare in 1766; in 1796 Earl Nugent. A Memoir of Earl Nugent
was published in 1898 by Mr. Claud Nugent.]
[2 Lord Clare's nephew.]
[3 Dorothy Monroe, a celebrated beauty.]

There's H[*owar*]d, and C[*oie*]y, and H—rth, and H[*i*]ff,[1]
I think they love venison—I know they love beef ;
There's my countryman H[*i*]gg[*i*]ns—Oh ! let him alone,
For making a blunder, or picking a bone.
But hang it—to poets who seldom can eat,
Your very good mutton's a very good treat ;
Such dainties to them, their health it might hurt,
It's like sending them ruffles, when wanting a shirt.
While thus I debated, in reverie centred,
An acquaintance, a friend as he call'd himself, enter'd ;
An under-bred, fine-spoken fellow was he,
And he smil'd as he look'd at the venison and me.
"What have we got here?—Why this is good eating !
Your own, I suppose—or is it in waiting ?"
"Why, whose should it be ?" cried I with a flounce,
"I get these things often ; "—but that was a bounce :
"Some lords, my acquaintance, that settle the nation,
Are pleas'd to be kind—but I hate ostentation."

"If that be the case, then," cried he, very gay,
"I'm glad I have taken this house in my way.
To-morrow you take a poor dinner with me ;
No words—I insist on't—precisely at three :
We'll have Johnson, and Burke ; all the wits will be
    there ;[2]
My acquaintance is slight, or I'd ask my Lord Clare.
And now that I think on't, as I am a sinner !
We wanted this venison to make out the dinner.
What say you—a pasty ? it shall, and it must,
And my wife, little Kitty, is famous for crust.
Here, porter !—this venison with me to Mile-end ;
No stirring—I beg—my dear friend—my dear friend !"
Thus snatching his hat, he brush'd off like the wind,
And the porter and eatables follow'd behind.

Left alone to reflect, having emptied my shelf,
"And nobody with me at sea but myself ; "[3]

[1 Paul Hifferman, M.D., a Grub Street writer.]
[2 Cf. Boileau, *Sat.*, iii. ll. 25-6, which Goldsmith had in mind.]
[3 A textual quotation from the love-letters of Henry Frederick,
Duke of Cumberland, to Lady Grosvenor.]

Though I could not help thinking my gentleman hasty,
Yet Johnson, and Burke, and a good venison pasty,
Were things that I never dislik'd in my life,
Though clogg'd with a coxcomb, and Kitty his wife.
So next day, in due splendour to make my approach,
I drove to his door in my own hackney-coach.

When come to the place where we all were to dine,
(A chair-lumber'd closet just twelve feet by nine :)
My friend bade me welcome, but struck me quite dumb,
With tidings that Johnson and Burke would not come ;[1]
"For I knew it," he cried, "both eternally fail,
The one with his speeches, and t'other with Thrale ;[2]
But no matter, I'll warrant we'll make up the party
With two full as clever, and ten times as hearty.
The one is a Scotchman, the other a Jew,
They['re] both of them merry and authors like you ;
The one writes the *Snarler*, the other the *Scourge ;*
Some think he writes *Cinna*—he owns to *Panurge.*"[3]
While thus he describ'd them by trade and by name,
They enter'd, and dinner was serv'd as they came.

At the top a fried liver and bacon were seen,
At the bottom was tripe in a swingeing tureen ;
At the sides there was spinach and pudding made hot ;
In the middle a place where the pasty—was not.
Now, my Lord, as for tripe, it's my utter aversion,
And your bacon I hate like a Turk or a Persian ;
So there I sat stuck, like a horse in a pound,
While the bacon and liver went merrily round.
But what vex'd me most was that d—'d Scottish rogue,
With his long-winded speeches, his smiles and his brogue ;
And, "Madam," quoth he, "may this bit be my poison,[4]
A prettier dinner I never set eyes on ;
Pray a slice of your liver, though may I be curs'd,
But I've eat of your tripe till I'm ready to burst."

[1 Cf. Boileau, *ut supra*, ll. 31–4.]
[2 Henry Thrale, the Southwark brewer, Johnson's close friend from 1765.]
[3 These were *noms de guerre* of Dr. W. Scott, Lord Sandwich's chaplain, an active supporter of the Government.]
[4 Cf. *She Stoops to Conquer*, Act i. Sc. 2.]

"The tripe," quoth the Jew, with his chocolate cheek,
"I could dine on this tripe seven days in the week:
I like these here dinners so pretty and small;
But your friend there, the Doctor, eats nothing at all."
"O—Oh!" quoth my friend, "he'll come on in a trice,
He's keeping a corner for something that's nice:
There's a pasty"—"A pasty!" repeated the Jew,
"I don't care if I keep a corner for't too."
"What the de'il, mon, a pasty!" re-echoed the Scot,
"Though splitting, I'll still keep a corner for thot."
"We'll all keep a corner," the lady cried out;
"We'll all keep a corner," was echoed about.
While thus we resolv'd, and the pasty delay'd,
With looks that quite petrified, enter'd the maid;
A visage so sad, and so pale with affright,
Wak'd Priam in drawing his curtains by night.[1]
But we quickly found out, for who could mistake her?
That she came with some terrible news from the baker:
And so it fell out, for that negligent sloven
Had shut out the pasty on shutting his oven.
Sad Philomel thus—but let similes drop—
And now that I think on't, the story may stop.
To be plain, my good Lord, it's but labour misplaced
To send such good verses to one of your taste;
You've got an odd something—a kind of discerning—
A relish—a taste—sicken'd over by learning;
At least it's your temper, as very well known,
That you think very slightly of all that's your own:
So, perhaps, in your habits of thinking amiss,
You may make a mistake, and think slightly of this.

[1 Cf. 2 *Henry IV*. Act i. Sc. 1.]

MISCELLANEOUS PIECES

PART OF A PROLOGUE WRITTEN AND SPOKEN BY THE POET LABERIUS

A ROMAN KNIGHT WHOM CAESAR FORCED UPON THE STAGE

PRESERVED BY MACROBIUS [1]

What! no way left to shun th' inglorious stage,
And save from infamy my sinking age!
Scarce half alive, oppress'd with many a year,
What in the name of dotage drives me here?
A time there was, when glory was my guide,
Nor force nor fraud could turn my steps aside;
Unaw'd by pow'r, and unappall'd by fear,
With honest thrift I held my honour dear:
But this vile hour disperses all my store,
And all my hoard of honour is no more.
For ah! too partial to my life's decline,
Caesar persuades, submission must be mine;
Him I obey, whom heaven itself obeys,
Hopeless of pleasing, yet inclin'd to please.
Here then at once, I welcome every shame,
And cancel at threescore a line of fame;
No more my titles shall my children tell,
The old buffoon will fit my name as well;
This day beyond its term my fate extends,
For life is ended when our honour ends.

[1 First printed at pp. 176-7 of Goldsmith's *Enquiry into the Present State of Polite Learning*, 1759 (ch. xii.—"Of the Stage"). The original lines are to be found in the *Saturnalia* of Macrobius, lib. ii. cap. vii. ed. Zeunii, pp. 369-70.]

ON A BEAUTIFUL YOUTH STRUCK BLIND WITH LIGHTNING [1]

(Imitated from the Spanish)

SURE 'twas by Providence design'd,
   Rather in pity, than in hate,
That he should be, like Cupid, blind,
   To save him from Narcissus' fate.

THE GIFT

TO IRIS, IN BOW-STREET, COVENT GARDEN [2]

SAY, cruel IRIS, pretty rake,
   Dear mercenary beauty,
What annual offering shall I make,
   Expressive of my duty?

My heart, a victim to thine eyes,
   Should I at once deliver,
Say would the angry fair one prize
   The gift, who slights the giver?

A bill, a jewel, watch, or toy,
   My rivals give—and let 'em:
If gems, or gold, impart a joy,
   I'll give them—when I get 'em.

I'll give—but not the full-blown rose,
   Or rose-bud more in fashion;
Such short-liv'd offerings but disclose
   A transitory passion.

I'll give thee something yet unpaid,
   Not less sincere than civil:
I'll give thee—Ah! too charming maid,
   I'll give thee—To the Devil.

[1] First printed in *The Bee*, 6th October, 1759.]
[2] First printed in *The Bee*, 13th October, 1759. It is an adaptation of some lines headed *Etrene à Iris* in Part iii. of the *Ménagiana*.]

THE LOGICIANS REFUTED

IN IMITATION OF DEAN SWIFT [1]

LOGICIANS have but ill defin'd
As rational the human kind ;
Reason, they say, belongs to man,
But let them prove it if they can.
Wise Aristotle and Smiglecius,
By ratiocinations specious,
Have strove to prove with great precision,
With definition and division,
Homo est ratione praeditum,—
But for my soul I cannot credit 'em ;
And must in spite of them maintain,
That man and all his ways are vain ;
And that this boasted lord of nature
Is both a weak and erring creature ;
That instinct is a surer guide
Than reason-boasting mortal's pride ;
And that brute beasts are far before 'em
Deus est anima brutorum.
Who ever knew an honest brute
At law his neighbour prosecute,
Bring action for assault and battery,
Or friends beguile with lies and flattery?
O'er plains they ramble unconfin'd,
No politics disturb their mind ;
They eat their meals, and take their sport,
Nor know who's in or out at court ;
They never to the levee go
To treat as dearest friend, a foe ;
They never importune his Grace,
Nor ever cringe to men in place ;

[1 First printed in *The Busy Body*, 18th October, 1759, with the heading :—" The following poem, written by Dr. SWIFT, is communicated to the Public by the BUSY BODY, to whom it was presented by a Nobleman of distinguished Learning and Taste." But tradition, and the early editors, ascribe the lines to Goldsmith.]

Nor undertake a dirty job,
Nor draw the quill to write for B—b.[1]
Fraught with invective they ne'er go,
To folks at Paternoster Row;
No judges, fiddlers, dancing-masters,
No pickpockets, or poetasters,
Are known to honest quadrupeds;
No single brute his fellow leads.
Brutes never meet in bloody fray,
Nor cut each other's throats, for pay.
Of beasts, it is confessed, the ape
Comes nearest us in human shape;
Like man he imitates each fashion,
And malice is his ruling passion;
But both in malice and grimaces
A courtier any ape surpasses.
Behold him humbly cringing wait
Upon a minister of state;
View him soon after to inferiors,
Aping the conduct of superiors;
He promises with equal air;
And to perform takes equal care.
He in his turn finds imitators;
At court, the porters, lacqueys, waiters,
Their master's manners still contract,
And footmen, lords and dukes can act.
Thus at the court both great and small
Behave alike, for all ape all.

A SONNET [2]

WEEPING, murmuring, complaining,
Lost to every gay delight;
MYRA, too sincere for feigning,
Fears th' approaching bridal night.

[1 Sir Robert Walpole.]
[2 First printed in *The Bee*, 20th October, 1759. It is said to be an imitation of Denis Sanguin de St. Pavin, d. 1670.]

Yet, why impair thy bright perfection?
  Or dim thy beauty with a tear?
Had MYRA follow'd my direction,
  She long had wanted cause of fear.

STANZAS

ON THE TAKING OF QUEBEC, AND DEATH OF GENERAL WOLFE [1]

AMIDST the clamour of exulting joys,
  Which triumph forces from the patriot heart,
Grief dares to mingle her soul-piercing voice,
  And quells the raptures which from pleasures start.

O Wolfe! to thee a streaming flood of woe,
  Sighing we pay, and think e'en conquest dear;
Quebec in vain shall teach our breast to glow,
  Whilst thy sad fate exhorts the heart-wrung tear.

Alive, the foe thy dreadful vigour fled,
  And saw thee fall with joy-pronouncing eyes:
Yet they shall know thou conquerest, though dead—
  Since from thy tomb a thousand heroes rise!

AN ELEGY ON THAT GLORY OF HER SEX, MRS. MARY BLAIZE [2]

GOOD people all, with one accord,
  Lament for Madam BLAIZE,
Who never wanted a good word—
  From those who spoke her praise.

[1 First printed in *The Busy Body*, 20th October, 1759, a week after the news of Wolfe's death (on 13th September previous) had reached England.]
[2 First printed in *The Bee*, 27th October, 1759. It is modelled on the old song of M. de la Palice, a version of which is to be found in Part iii. of the *Ménagiana*.]

The needy seldom pass'd her door,
  And always found her kind ;
She freely lent to all the poor,—
  Who left a pledge behind.

She strove the neighbourhood to please,
  With manners wond'rous winning,
And never followed wicked ways,—
  Unless when she was sinning.

At church, in silks and satins new,
  With hoop of monstrous size,
She never slumber'd in her pew,—
  But when she shut her eyes.

Her love was sought, I do aver,
  By twenty beaux and more ;
The king himself has follow'd her,—
  When she has walk'd before.

But now her wealth and finery fled,
  Her hangers-on cut short all ;
The doctors found, when she was dead,—
  Her last disorder mortal.

Let us lament, in sorrow sore,
  For Kent-street well may say,
That had she lived a twelve-month more,—
  She had not died to-day.

DESCRIPTION OF AN AUTHOR'S BEDCHAMBER [1]

WHERE the Red Lion flaring o'er the way,
Invites each passing stranger that can pay ;
Where Calvert's butt, and Parson's black champagne, [2]
Regale the drabs and bloods of Drury-lane ;

[1 First printed in a Chinese Letter in *The Public Ledger*, 2nd May, 1760, afterwards Letter xxix. of *The Citizen of the World*, 1762, i. 121.]
[2 *i. e.* "entire butt beer" or porter.]

There in a lonely room, from bailiffs snug,
The Muse found Scroggen stretch'd beneath a rug;
A window, patch'd with paper, lent a ray,
That dimly show'd the state in which he lay;
The sanded floor that grits beneath the tread;
The humid wall with paltry pictures spread:
The royal game of goose was there in view,
And the twelve rules the royal martyr drew; [1]
The seasons, fram'd with listing, found a place,
And brave prince William show'd his lamp-black face; [2]
The morn was cold, he views with keen desire
The rusty grate unconscious of a fire;
With beer and milk arrears the frieze was scor'd,
And five crack'd teacups dress'd the chimney board;
A nightcap deck'd his brows instead of bay,
A cap by night—a stocking all the day! [3]

ON SEEING MRS. * * PERFORM IN THE CHARACTER OF * * * * [4]

FOR you, bright fair, the Nine address their lays,
And tune my feeble voice to sing thy praise.
The heartfelt power of every charm divine,
Who can withstand their all commanding shine?
She how she moves along with every grace,
While soul-brought tears steal down each shining face.
She speaks! 'tis rapture all, and nameless bliss,
Ye gods! what transport e'er compared to this?
As when in Paphian groves the Queen of Love
With fond complaint address'd the listening Jove;

[1] *Vide* note 1, p. 29.]
[2] William Augustus, Duke of Cumberland, 1721-65,—probably a silhouette.]
[3] Cf. *The Deserted Village*, p. 29:—
    " A bed by night, a chest of drawers by day."]
[4] From Letter lxxxii. of *The Citizen of the World*, 1762, ii. 87, first printed in *The Public Ledger*, 21st October, 1760. The verses are intended as a specimen of the newspaper muse.]

'Twas joy and endless blisses all around,
And rocks forgot their hardness at the sound.
Then first, at last even Jove was taken in,
And felt her charms, without disguise, within.

OF THE DEATH OF THE RIGHT
HON. * * *[1]

YE muses, pour the pitying tear
   For Pollio snatch'd away;
O! had he liv'd another year!
   He had not died to-day.

O! were he born to bless mankind
   In virtuous times of yore,
Heroes themselves had fallen behind
   Whene'er he went before.

How sad the groves and plains appear,
   And sympathetic sheep;
Even pitying hills would drop a tear
   If hills could learn to weep.

His bounty in exalted strain
   Each bard might well display:
Since none implor'd relief in vain
   That went reliev'd away.

And hark! I hear the tuneful throng
   His obsequies forbid,
He still shall live, shall live as long
   As ever dead man did.

[¹ From Letter ciii. of *The Citizen of the World*, 1762, ii. 164, first printed in *The Public Ledger*, 4th March, 1761. The verses are given as "a specimen of a poem on the decease of a great man." Cf. the *Elegy on Mrs. Mary Blaize*, p. 57.]

AN EPIGRAM

ADDRESSED TO THE GENTLEMEN REFLECTED ON IN THE
ROSCIAD, A POEM, BY THE AUTHOR [1]

LET not the *hungry* Bavius' angry stroke
Awake resentment, or your rage provoke—
But pitying his distress, let virtue [2] shine,
And giving each your bounty,[3] *let him dine.*
For thus retain'd, as learned counsel can,
Each case, however bad, he'll new japan;
And by a quick transition, plainly show
'Twas no defect of yours, but *pocket low,*
That caus'd his *putrid kennel* to o'erflow.

TO G. C. AND R. L.[4]

'TWAS you, or I, or he, or all together,
'Twas one, both, three of them, they know not whether;
This, I believe, between us great or small,
You, I, he, wrote it not—'twas Churchill's all.

[1 From Letter cx. of *The Citizen of the World*, 1762, ii. 193, first printed in *The Public Ledger*, 14th April, 1761. The epigram, however, had been printed in the *Ledger* for 4th April, and so was only revived in the letter of ten days later. It is one of Goldsmith's doubtful pieces, but his animosity to Churchill is notorious.]

[2 Charity (*Author's note*).]

[3 Settled at one shilling, the price of the poem (*Author's note*).]

[4 From the same letter as the preceding epigram. George Colman (G. C.) and Robert Lloyd (R. L.) were supposed to have assisted Churchill in the *Rosciad*, the " it " of the epigram.]

TRANSLATION OF A SOUTH AMERICAN ODE [1]

In all my Enna's beauties blest,
Amidst profusion still I pine;
For though she gives me up her breast,
Its panting tenant is not mine.

THE DOUBLE TRANSFORMATION

A TALE [2]

Secluded from domestic strife,
Jack Book-worm led a college life;
A fellowship at twenty-five
Made him the happiest man alive;
He drank his glass and cracked his joke,
And Freshmen wondered as he spoke.

Such pleasures unalloy'd with care,
Could any accident impair?
Could Cupid's shaft at length transfix
Our swain, arriv'd at thirty-six?
O had the archer ne'er come down
To ravage in a country town!
Or Flavia been content to stop
At triumphs in a Fleet-street shop.
O had her eyes forgot to blaze!
Or Jack had wanted eyes to gaze.
O!——But let exclamation cease,
Her presence banish'd all his peace.
So with decorum all things carried;
Miss frown'd, and blushed, and then was—married.

[1 From Letter cxiii. of *The Citizen of the World*, 1762, ii. 209,
first printed in *The Public Ledger*, 13th May, 1762.]
[2 First printed in *Essays, by Mr. Goldsmith*, 1765, p. 229. The
version here followed is that of the second edition of 1766, which
was revised.]

Need we expose to vulgar sight
The raptures of the bridal night?
Need we intrude on hallow'd ground,
Or draw the curtains clos'd around?
Let it suffice, that each had charms;
He clasp'd a goddess in his arms;
And, though she felt his usage rough,
Yet in a man 'twas well enough.

The honey-moon like lightning flew,
The second brought its transports too.
A third, a fourth, were not amiss,
The fifth was friendship mix'd with bliss:
But, when a twelvemonth pass'd away,
Jack found his goddess made of clay;
Found half the charms that deck'd her face
Arose from powder, shreds, or lace;
But still the worst remain'd behind,
That very face had robb'd her mind.

Skill'd in no other arts was she,
But dressing, patching, repartee;
And, just as humour rose or fell,
By turns a slattern or a belle;
'Tis true she dress'd with modern grace,
Half naked at a ball or race;
But when at home, at board or bed,
Five greasy nightcaps wrapp'd her head.
Could so much beauty condescend
To be a dull domestic friend?
Could any curtain-lectures bring
To decency so fine a thing?
In short, by night, 'twas fits or fretting;
By day, 'twas gadding or coquetting.
Fond to be seen, she kept a bevy
Of powder'd coxcombs at her levy;
The 'squire and captain took their stations,
And twenty other near relations;
Jack suck'd his pipe, and often broke
A sigh in suffocating smoke;

While all their hours were passed between
Insulting repartee or spleen.

Thus as her faults each day were known,
He thinks her features coarser grown;
He fancies every vice she shows,
Or thins her lip, or points her nose:
Whenever rage or envy rise,
How wide her mouth, how wild her eyes!
He knows not how, but so it is,
Her face is grown a knowing phiz;
And, though her fops are wond'rous civil,
He thinks her ugly as the devil.

Now, to perplex the ravell'd noose,
As each a different way pursues,
While sullen or loquacious strife,
Promis'd to hold them on for life,
That dire disease, whose ruthless power
Withers the beauty's transient flower:
Lo! the small-pox, whose horrid glare
Levell'd its terrors at the fair:
And, rifling ev'ry youthful grace,
Left but the remnant of a face.

The glass, grown hateful to her sight,
Reflected now a perfect fright:
Each former art she vainly tries
To bring back lustre to her eyes.
In vain she tries her paste and creams,
To smooth her skin, or hide its seams;
Her country beaux and city cousins,
Lovers no more, flew off by dozens:
The 'squire himself was seen to yield,
And even the captain quit the field.

Poor Madam, now condemn'd to hack
The rest of life with anxious Jack,
Perceiving others fairly flown,
Attempted pleasing him alone.
Jack soon was dazzl'd to behold
Her present face surpass the old;

With modesty her cheeks are dy'd,
Humility displaces pride;
For tawdry finery is seen
A person ever neatly clean:
No more presuming on her sway,
She learns good-nature every day;
Serenely gay, and strict in duty,
Jack finds his wife a perfect beauty.

A NEW SIMILE

IN THE MANNER OF SWIFT [1]

LONG had I sought in vain to find
A likeness for the scribbling kind;
The modern scribbling kind, who write
In wit, and sense, and nature's spite:
Till reading, I forgot what day on,
A chapter out of Tooke's Pantheon,
I think I met with something there,
To suit my purpose to a hair;
But let us not proceed too furious,
First please to turn to god Mercurius;
You'll find him pictur'd at full length
In book the second, page the tenth:
The stress of all my proofs on him I lay,
And now proceed we to our simile.

Imprimis, pray observe his hat,
Wings upon either side—mark that.
Well! what is it from thence we gather?
Why these denote a brain of feather.
A brain of feather! very right,
With wit that's flighty, learning light;
Such as to modern bards decreed:
A just comparison,—proceed.

[1 First printed in *Essays, by Mr. Goldsmith*, 1765, p. 234. The version here followed is that of the second edition of 1766, which was slightly revised.]

In the next place, his feet peruse,
Wings grow again from both his shoes;
Design'd, no doubt, their part to bear,
And waft his godship through the air:
And here my simile unites,
For in a modern poet's flights,
I'm sure it may be justly said,
His feet are useful as his head.

Lastly, vouchsafe t' observe his hand,
Filled with a snake-encircl'd wand;
By classic authors term'd caduceus,
And highly fam'd for several uses.
To wit—most wond'rously endu'd,
No poppy water [1] half so good;
For let folks only get a touch,
Its soporific virtue's such,
Though ne'er so much awake before,
That quickly they begin to snore.
Add too, what certain writers tell,
With this he drives men's souls to hell.

Now to apply, begin we then;
His wand's a modern author's pen;
The serpents round about it twin'd
Denote him of the reptile kind;
Denote the rage with which he writes,
His frothy slaver, venom'd bites;
An equal semblance still to keep,
Alike too both conduce to sleep.
This diff'rence only, as the god
Drove souls to Tart'rus with his rod,
With his goosequill the scribbling elf,
Instead of others, damns himself.

And here my simile almost tript,
Yet grant a word by way of postscript.
Moreover, Merc'ry had a failing:
Well! what of that? out with it—stealing;

[1 A favourite sleeping-draught. "Juno shall give her peacock *poppy-water*." (Congreve's *Love for Love*, 1695, Act iv. Sc. 3.)]

In which all modern bards agree,
Being each as great a thief as he :
But ev'n this deity's existence
Shall lend my simile assistance.
Our modern bards ! why what a pox
Are they but senseless stones and blocks?

EDWIN AND ANGELINA

A BALLAD [1]

" TURN, gentle Hermit of the dale,
     And guide my lonely way,
To where yon taper cheers the vale,
     With hospitable ray.

" For here, forlorn and lost I tread,
     With fainting steps and slow ;
Where wilds, immeasurably spread,
     Seem lengthening as I go."

" Forbear, my son," the Hermit cries,
     " To tempt the dangerous gloom ;
For yonder faithless phantom [2] flies
     To lure thee to thy doom.

" Here to the houseless child of want
     My door is open still ;
And though my portion is but scant,
     I give it with good will.

[1 Written in or before 1765, when it was printed privately " for
the amusement of the Countess of Northumberland," under the
title of *Edwin and Angelina. A Ballad. By Mr. Goldsmith.* A
copy in this form was sold at Heber's sale for 3*s.* It was first
published in *The Vicar of Wakefield*, 1766, i. 70 (ch. viii.) ; and
again in *Poems for Young Ladies*, 1767, p. 91. The version here
followed is that in the fifth edition of the *Vicar*, 1773 [4], pp. 78–85.]

[2 *i. e.*, Will o' the Wisp.]

"Then turn to-night, and freely share
    Whate'er my cell bestows ;
My rushy couch, and frugal fare,
    My blessing and repose.

"No flocks that range the valley free
    To slaughter I condemn ;
Taught by that Power that pities me,
    I learn to pity them.

"But from the mountain's grassy side
    A guiltless feast I bring ;
A scrip with herbs and fruits supplied,
    And water from the spring.

"Then, pilgrim, turn, thy cares forego ;
    All earth-born cares are wrong :
Man wants but little here below,
    Nor wants that little long." [1]

Soft as the dew from heav'n descends,
    His gentle accents fell :
The modest stranger lowly bends,
    And follows to the cell.

Far in a wilderness obscure
    The lonely mansion lay ;
A refuge to the neighbouring poor
    And strangers led astray.

No stores beneath its humble thatch
    Requir'd a master's care ;
The wicket, opening with a latch,
    Receiv'd the harmless pair.

And now, when busy crowds retire
    To take their evening rest,
The Hermit trimm'd his little fire,
    And cheer'd his pensive guest :

And spread his vegetable store,
    And gaily press'd, and smil'd ;
And, skill'd in legendary lore,
    The lingering hours beguil'd.

[1] A quotation from Young's *Complaint* (*Night the Fourth*, 1743, p. 9).]

Around in sympathetic mirth
   Its tricks the kitten tries;
The cricket chirrups in the hearth;
   The crackling faggot flies.

But nothing could a charm impart
   To soothe the stranger's woe;
For grief was heavy at his heart,
   And tears began to flow.

His rising cares the Hermit spied,
   With answering care oppress'd;
"And whence, unhappy youth," he cried,
   "The sorrows of thy breast?

'From better habitations spurn'd,
   Reluctant dost thou rove;
Or grieve for friendship unreturn'd,
   Or unregarded love?

"Alas! the joys that fortune brings
   Are trifling and decay;
And those who prize the paltry things,
   More trifling still than they.

"And what is friendship but a name,
   A charm that lulls to sleep;
A shade that follows wealth or fame,
   But leaves the wretch to weep?

"And love is still an emptier sound,
   The modern fair one's jest:
On earth unseen, or only found
   To warm the turtle's nest.

"For shame, fond youth, thy sorrows hush
   And spurn the sex," he said:
But, while he spoke, a rising blush
   His love-lorn guest betray'd.

Surpris'd, he sees new beauties rise,
   Swift mantling to the view;
Like colours o'er the morning skies,
   As bright, as transient too.

The bashful look, the rising breast,
   Alternate spread alarms :
The lovely stranger stands confess'd
   A maid in all her charms.

"And, ah! forgive a stranger rude,
   A wretch forlorn," she cried ;
"Whose feet unhallow'd thus intrude
   Where heaven and you reside.

"But let a maid thy pity share,
   Whom love has taught to stray ;
Who seeks for rest, but finds despair
   Companion of her way.

"My father liv'd beside the Tyne,
   A wealthy lord was he ;
And all his wealth was mark'd as mine,
   He had but only me.

"To win me from his tender arms
   Unnumber'd suitors came ;
Who prais'd me for imputed charms,
   And felt or feign'd a flame.

"Each hour a mercenary crowd
   With richest proffers strove :
Amongst the rest young Edwin bow'd,
   But never talk'd of love.

"In humble, simplest habit clad,
   No wealth nor power had he ;
Wisdom and worth were all he had,
   But these were all to me.

["And when beside me in the dale
   He caroll'd lays of love ;
His breath lent fragrance to the gale,
   And music to the grove.[1]]

[1 This stanza, which is not in the contemporary versions, was
given to Bishop Percy, for his edition of the *Works* (1801), by
Richard Archdal, Esq., who had received it from the author.]

" The blossom opening to the day,
  The dews of heaven refin'd,
Could nought of purity display,
  To emulate his mind.

" The dew, the blossom on the tree,
  With charms inconstant shine ;
Their charms were his, but woe to me !
  Their constancy was mine.

" For still I tried each fickle art,
  Importunate and vain :
And while his passion touch'd my heart,
  I triumph'd in his pain.

" Till quite dejected with my scorn,
  He left me to my pride ;
And sought a solitude forlorn,
  In secret, where he died.

" But mine the sorrow, mine the fault,
  And well my life shall pay ;
I'll seek the solitude he sought,
  And stretch me where he lay.

" And there forlorn, despairing, hid,
  I'll lay me down and die ;
'Twas so for me that Edwin did,
  And so for him will I."

" Forbid it, Heaven ! " the Hermit cried,
  And clasp'd her to his breast :
The wondering fair one turned to chide,
  'Twas Edwin's self that prest.

" Turn, Angelina, ever dear,
  My charmer, turn to see
Thy own, thy long-lost Edwin here,
  Restor'd to love and thee.

" Thus let me hold thee to my heart,
  And ev'ry care resign ;
And shall we never, never part,
  My life—my all that's mine ?

"No, never from this hour to part,
    We'll live and love so true;
The sigh that rends thy constant heart
    Shall break thy Edwin's too."

ELEGY ON THE DEATH OF A MAD DOG [1]

GOOD people all, of every sort,
    Give ear unto my song;
And if you find it wond'rous short,
    It cannot hold you long.

In Islington there was a man,
    Of whom the world might say,
That still a godly race he ran,
    Whene'er he went to pray. [2]

A kind and gentle heart he had,
    To comfort friends and foes;
The naked every day he clad,
    When he put on his clothes. [2]

And in that town a dog was found,
    As many dogs there be,
Both mongrel, puppy, whelp, and hound,
    And curs of low degree.

This dog and man at first were friends;
    But when a pique began,
The dog, to gain some private ends,
    Went mad and bit the man.

Around from all the neighbouring streets
    The wond'ring neighbours ran,
And swore the dog had lost his wits,
    To bite so good a man.

[1 First printed in *The Vicar of Wakefield*, 1766, i. 175.]
[2 Cf. *An Elegy on Mrs. Mary Blaize*, p. 57 *ante*.]

The wound it seem'd both sore and sad
    To every Christian eye;
And while they swore the dog was mad,
    They swore the man would die.

But soon a wonder came to light,
    That show'd the rogues they lied:
The man recover'd of the bite,
    The dog it was that died.[1]

SONG

FROM "THE VICAR OF WAKEFIELD"[2]

WHEN lovely Woman stoops to folly,
    And finds too late that men betray,
What charm can soothe her melancholy,
    What art can wash her guilt away?

The only art her guilt to cover,
    To hide her shame from every eye,
To give repentance to her lover,
    And wring his bosom, is—to die.

EPILOGUE TO "THE SISTER"[3]

WHAT! five long acts—and all to make us wiser!
Our authoress sure has wanted an adviser.
Had she consulted *me*, she should have made
Her moral play a speaking masquerade;

[1 This termination is based upon an epigram in the *Greek Anthology*, or perhaps upon an adaptation by Voltaire:

    "L'autre jour, au fond d'un vallon
      Un serpent mordit Jean Fréron.
      Devinez ce qu'il arriva?
      Ce fut le serpent qui creva."]

[2 Sung, very inappropriately, by Olivia in chap. v. of *The Vicar of Wakefield*, 1766, ii. 78, where it was first printed.]

[3 *The Sister*, 1769, in which this Epilogue was first printed, was a comedy by Mrs. Charlotte Lenox (1720–1804), produced at Covent Garden, 18th February, 1769.]

Warm'd up each bustling scene, and in her rage
Have emptied all the green-room on the stage.
My life on't, this had kept her play from sinking;
Have pleas'd our eyes, and sav'd the pain of thinking.
Well! since she thus has shown her want of skill,
What if I give a masquerade?—I will.
But how? ay, there's the rub! [*pausing*]—I've got my
        cue:
The world's a masquerade! the maskers, you, you, you.
                    (*To Boxes, Pit, and Gallery.*)
Lud! what a group the motley scene discloses!
False wits, false wives, false virgins, and false spouses!
Statesmen with bridles on; and, close beside 'em,
Patriots, in party-coloured suits, that ride 'em.
There Hebes, turn'd of fifty, try once more
To raise a flame in Cupids of threescore.
These in their turn, with appetites as keen,
Deserting fifty, fasten on fifteen,
Miss, not yet full fifteen, with fire uncommon,
Flings down her sampler, and takes up the woman:
The little urchin smiles, and spreads her lure,
And tries to kill, ere she's got power to cure.
Thus 'tis with all—their chief and constant care
Is to seem everything but what they are.
Yon broad, bold, angry spark, I fix my eye on,
Who seems to have robb'd his vizor from the lion;
Who frowns, and talks, and swears with round parade,
Looking, as who should say, Dam'me! who's afraid?
                                (*mimicking.*)
Strip but his vizor off, and sure I am
You'll find his lionship a very lamb.
Yon politician, famous in debate,
Perhaps, to vulgar eyes, bestrides the state;
Yet, when he deigns his real shape t' assume,
He turns old woman, and bestrides a broom.
Yon patriot, too, who presses on your sight,
And seems to every gazer all in white,
If with a bribe his candour you attack,
He bows, turns round, and whip—the man's a black!
Yon critic, too—but whither do I run?

If I proceed, our bard will be undone!
Well then a truce, since she requests it too:
Do you spare her, and I'll for once spare you.

PROLOGUE TO "ZOBEIDE"[1]

SPOKEN BY QUICK IN THE CHARACTER OF A SAILOR

In these bold times,[2] when Learning's sons explore
The distant climate and the savage shore;
When wise Astronomers to India steer,
And quit for Venus, many a brighter here;
While Botanists, all cold to smiles and dimpling,
Forsake the fair, and patiently—go simpling;
When every bosom swells with wond'rous scenes,
Priests, cannibals, and hoity-toity queens:
Our bard into the general spirit enters,
And fits his little frigate for adventures:
With Scythian stores, and trinkets deeply laden,
He this way steers his course, in hopes of trading—
Yet ere he lands he'as ordered me before,
To make an observation on the shore.
Where are we driven? our reck'ning sure is lost!
This seems a barren and a dangerous coast.
Lord, what a sultry climate am I under!
Yon ill foreboding cloud seems big with thunder.

(*Upper Gallery.*)

There Mangroves spread, and larger than I've seen 'em—

(*Pit.*)

Here trees of stately size—and turtles in 'em—

(*Balconies.*)

[1 *Zobeide* was a play by Joseph Cradock of Gumley, in Leicester-
shire, a friend of Goldsmith's latter days. It was translated from
Les Scythes of Voltaire, and produced at Covent Garden, 11th
December, 1771. Goldsmith's Prologue is here printed from
Cradock's *Memoirs*, 1828, iii. 8.]

[2 A reference to Cook's just concluded voyage to Otaheite to
observe the transit of Venus.]

Here ill-condition'd oranges abound——   (*Stage.*)
And apples (*takes up one and tastes it*), bitter apples strew
    the ground.
The place is uninhabited, I fear!
I heard a hissing—there are serpents here!
O there the natives are—a dreadful race!
The men have tails, the women paint their face!
No doubt they're all barbarians.—Yes, 'tis so;
I'll try to make palaver[1] with them though;
                        (*making signs.*)

'Tis best, however, keeping at a distance.
Good Savages, our Captain craves assistance;
Our ship's well stor'd;—in yonder creek we've laid her;
His honour is no mercenary trader;[2]
This is his first adventure; lend him aid,
Or you may chance to spoil a thriving trade.
His goods, he hopes, are prime, and brought from far,
Equally fit for gallantry and war.
What! no reply to promises so ample?
I'd best step back—and order up a sample.

THRENODIA AUGUSTALIS:

SACRED TO THE MEMORY OF HER LATE ROYAL HIGHNESS THE PRINCESS DOWAGER OF WALES [3]

ADVERTISEMENT

THE following may more properly be termed a compilation than a poem. It was prepared for the composer in little more than two days: and may therefore rather

[1 *i. e.* to hold a parley.]

[2 Cradock gave his profits to "Zobeide,"—Mrs. Yates, the actress of the part.]

[3 Augusta, mother of George the Third, who died at Carlton House, 8th February 1772. This piece was spoken and sung in Mrs. Teresa Cornelys' Great Room in Soho Square on Thursday, the 20th following, being sold at the door as a 4to. pamphlet. The publisher was W. Woodfall. The author's name was not given; but the advertisement here reproduced preceded the verses, with the list of performers.]

be considered as an industrious effort of gratitude than of genius.

In justice to the composer it may likewise be right to inform the public, that the music was adapted in a period of time equally short.

SPEAKERS

Mr. Lee and Mrs. Bellamy

SINGERS

Mr. Champnes, Mr. Dine, and Miss Jameson. The music prepared and adapted by Signor Vento

---

PART I

OVERTURE—A SOLEMN DIRGE.   AIR—TRIO

ARISE, ye sons of worth, arise,
And waken every note of woe;
When truth and virtue reach the skies,
'Tis ours to weep the want below!

CHORUS

When truth and virtue, &c.

MAN SPEAKER

The praise attending pomp and power,
The incense given to kings,
Are but the trappings of an hour,
Mere transitory things.
The base bestow them: but the good agree
To spurn the venal gifts as flattery.
But when to pomp and power are joined
An equal dignity of mind;
When titles are the smallest claim:
When wealth, and rank, and noble blood,
But aid the power of doing good,
Then all their trophies last,—and flattery turns to fame.
  Blest spirit thou, whose fame, just born to bloom,
Shall spread and flourish from the tomb,
How hast thou left mankind for Heaven!
Even now reproach and faction mourn,
And, wondering how their rage was born,

Request to be forgiven!
Alas! they never had thy hate:
Unmov'd in conscious rectitude,
Thy towering mind self-centred stood,
Nor wanted man's opinion to be great.
In vain, to charm thy ravish'd sight,
A thousand gifts would fortune send;
In vain, to drive thee from the right,
A thousand sorrows urg'd thy end:
Like some well-fashion'd arch thy patience stood,
And purchas'd strength from its increasing load.
Pain met thee like a friend to set thee free,
Affliction still is virtue's opportunity!
Virtue, on herself relying,
Every passion hushed to rest,
Loses every pain of dying
In the hopes of being blest.
Every added pang she suffers
Some increasing good bestows,
And every shock that malice offers
Only rocks her to repose.

SONG.   BY A MAN—AFFETTUOSO

Virtue, on herself relying,
Every passion hushed to rest,
Loses every pain of dying
In the hopes of being blest.
Every added pang she suffers
Some increasing good bestows,
And every shock that malice offers
Only rocks her to repose.

WOMAN SPEAKER

Yet ah! what terrors frowned upon her fate,
Death with its formidable band,
Fever, and pain, and pale consumptive care,
Determin'd took their stand.
Nor did the cruel ravagers design
To finish all their efforts at a blow:
But, mischievously slow,
They robb'd the relic and defac'd the shrine.

With unavailing grief,
Despairing of relief,
Her weeping children round,
Beheld each hour
Death's growing power,
And trembled as he frown'd.

As helpless friends who view from shore
The labouring ship, and hear the tempest roar,
While winds and waves their wishes cross :
They stood, while hope and comfort fail,
Not to assist, but to bewail
The inevitable loss.
Relentless tyrant, at thy call
How do the good, the virtuous fall !
Truth, beauty, worth, and all that most engage,
But wake thy vengeance and provoke thy rage.

SONG. BY A MAN—BASSO, STACCATO, SPIRITOSO

When vice my dart and scythe supply
How great a king of terrors I !
If folly, fraud, your hearts engage,
Tremble, ye mortals, at my rage !
Fall, round me fall, ye little things,
Ye statesmen, warriors, poets, kings !
   If virtue fail her counsel sage,
   Tremble, ye mortals, at my rage !

MAN SPEAKER

Yet let that wisdom, urged by her example,
Teach us to estimate what all must suffer ;
Let us prize death as the best gift of nature,
As a safe inn, where weary travellers,
When they have journey'd through a world of cares,
May put off life and be at rest for ever.
Groans, weeping friends, indeed, and gloomy sables,
May oft distract us with their sad solemnity.
The preparation is the executioner.
Death, when unmask'd, shows me a friendly face,
And is a terror only at a distance :
For as the line of life conducts me on

To death's great court, the prospect seems more fair,
'Tis nature's kind retreat, that's always open
To take us in when we have drained the cup
Of life, or worn our days to wretchedness.
In that secure, serene retreat,
Where all the humble, all the great,
Promiscuously recline :
Where wildly huddled to the eye,
The beggar's pouch and prince's purple lie,
May every bliss be thine.
And ah ! blest spirit, wheresoe'er thy flight,
Through rolling worlds, or fields of liquid light,
May cherubs welcome their expected guest,
May saints with songs receive thee to their rest,
May peace that claim'd while here thy warmest love,
May blissful endless peace be thine above !

SONG.   BY A WOMAN—AMOROSO

Lovely lasting Peace below,
Comforter of every woe,
Heavenly born and bred on high,
To crown the favourites of the sky ;
Lovely lasting Peace, appear,
This world itself, if thou art here,
Is once again with Eden blest,
And man contains it in his breast.

WOMAN SPEAKER

Our vows are heard !   Long, long to mortal eyes,
Her soul was fitting to its kindred skies :
Celestial-like her bounty fell,
Where modest want and patient sorrow dwell,
Want pass'd for merit at her door,
Unseen the modest were supplied,
Her constant pity fed the poor,
Then only poor, indeed, the day she died.
And oh ! for this ! while sculpture decks thy shrine,
And art exhausts profusion round,
The tribute of a tear be mine,
A simple song, a sigh profound.

There Faith shall come, a pilgrim gray,[1]
To bless the tomb that wraps thy clay:
And calm Religion shall repair
To dwell a weeping hermit there.
Truth, Fortitude, and Friendship, shall agree
To blend their virtues while they think of thee.

AIR. CHORUS—POMPOSO

Let us, let all the world agree,
To profit by resembling thee.

PART II

OVERTURE—PASTORALE

MAN SPEAKER

Fast by that shore where Thames' translucent stream
Reflects new glories on his breast,
Where, splendid as the youthful poet's dream,
He forms a scene beyond Elysium blest:
Where sculptur'd elegance and native grace
Unite to stamp the beauties of the place:
While, sweetly blending, still are seen
The wavy lawn, the sloping green:
While novelty, with cautious cunning.
Through every maze of fancy running,
From China borrows aid to deck the scene:
There sorrowing by the river's glassy bed,
Forlorn, a rural band complain'd,
All whom Augusta's bounty fed,
All whom her clemency sustain'd;
The good old sire, unconscious of decay,
The modest matron, clad in homespun gray,
The military boy, the orphan'd maid,
The shatter'd veteran, now first dismay'd;
These sadly join beside the murmuring deep,

[1 These four lines, with some alteration, are taken from Collins's *Ode written in the year* 1746.]

*D 4¹5

And as they view
The towers of Kew,[1]
Call on their mistress, now no more, and weep.

CHORUS—AFFETTUOSO, LARGO

Ye shady walks, ye waving greens,
Ye nodding towers, ye fairy scenes,
Let all your echoes now deplore,
That she who form'd your beauties is no more.

MAN SPEAKER

First of the train the patient rustic came,
Whose callous hand had form'd the scene,
Bending at once with sorrow and with age,
With many a tear, and many a sigh between,
"And where," he cried, "shall now my babes have bread,
Or how shall age support its feeble fire?
No lord will take me now, my vigour fled,
Nor can my strength perform what they require:
Each grudging master keeps the labourer bare,
A sleek and idle race is all their care:
My noble mistress thought not so!
Her bounty, like the morning dew,
Unseen, though constant, used to flow,
And as my strength decay'd, her bounty grew."

WOMAN SPEAKER

In decent dress, and coarsely clean,
The pious matron next was seen,
Clasp'd in her hand a godly book was borne,
By use and daily meditation worn;
That decent dress, this holy guide,
Augusta's care had well supplied.
"And ah!" she cries, all woe-begone,
"What now remains for me?
Oh! where shall weeping want repair,
To ask for charity?

[1 "The embellishment of Kew Palace and garden, under the direction of [Sir William] Chambers and others, was the favourite object of her [Royal Highness's] widowhood." (Bolton Corney.)]

Too late in life for me to ask,
And shame prevents the deed,
And tardy, tardy are the times
To succour, should I need.
But all my wants, before I spoke,
Were to my Mistress known;
She still reliev'd, nor sought my praise,
Contented with her own.
But every day her name I'll bless,
My morning prayer, my evening song,
I'll praise her while my life shall last
A life that cannot last me long."

SONG. BY A WOMAN

Each day, each hour, her name I'll bless,
My morning and my evening song,
And when in death my vows shall cease,
My children shall the note prolong.

MAN SPEAKER

The hardy veteran after struck the sight,
Scarr'd, mangled, maim'd in every part,
Lopp'd of his limbs in many a gallant fight,
In nought entire—except his heart:
Mute for a while, and sullenly distress'd,
At last the impetuous sorrow fired his breast.
"Wild is the whirlwind rolling
O'er Afric's sandy plain,
And wild the tempest howling
Along the billowed main: [1]
But every danger felt before,
The raging deep, the whirlwind's roar,
Less dreadful struck me with dismay,
Than what I feel this fatal day.
Oh, let me fly a land that spurns the brave,
Oswego's dreary shores shall be my grave; [2]
I'll seek that less inhospitable coast,
And lay my body where my limbs were lost."

[1 Cf. *The Captivity*, p. 98.]
[2 Cf. *The Traveller*, p. 16.]

SONG.   BY A MAN—BASSO, SPIRITOSO

Old Edward's sons, unknown to yield,
Shall crowd from Cressy's laurell'd field,
To do thy memory right :
For thine and Britain's wrongs they feel,
Again they snatch the gleamy steel,
And wish the avenging fight.[1]

WOMAN SPEAKER

In innocence and youth complaining,
Next appear'd a lovely maid,
Affliction o'er each feature reigning
Kindly came in beauty's aid ;
Every grace that grief dispenses,
Every glance that warms the soul,
In sweet succession charm'd the senses,
While pity harmoniz'd the whole.
" The garland of beauty " ('tis thus she would say,)
" No more shall my crook or my temples adorn,
I'll not wear a garland, Augusta's away,
I'll not wear a garland until she return :
But alas ! that return I never shall see :
The echoes of Thames shall my sorrows proclaim,
There promis'd a lover to come, but, Oh me !
'Twas death,—'twas the death of my mistress that came.
But ever, for ever, her image shall last,
I'll strip all the spring of its earliest bloom ;
On her grave shall the cowslip and primrose be cast,
And the new-blossom'd thorn shall whiten her tomb."

SONG.   BY A WOMAN—PASTORALE

With garlands of beauty the queen of the May,
No more will her crook or her temples adorn :
For who'd wear a garland when she is away,
When she is remov'd, and shall never return.

On the grave of Augusta these garlands be plac'd,
We'll rifle the spring of its earliest bloom,[2]

[1 Varied from Collins's *Ode on the Death of Colonel Charles Ross at Fontenoy.*]
[2 Cf. Collins's *Dirge in Cymbeline.*]

And there shall the cowslip and primrose be cast,
And the new-blossom'd thorn shall whiten her tomb.

CHORUS—ALTRO MODO

On the grave of Augusta this garland be plac'd,
We'll rifle the spring of its earliest bloom ;
And there shall the cowslip and primrose be cast,
And the tears of her country shall water her tomb.

SONG

INTENDED TO HAVE BEEN SUNG IN "SHE STOOPS TO
CONQUER"[1]

AH, me ! when shall I marry me?
    Lovers are plenty; but fail to relieve me :
He, fond youth, that could carry me,
    Offers to love, but means to deceive me.

But I will rally, and combat the ruiner :
    Not a look, not a smile shall my passion discover :
She that gives all to the false one pursuing her,
    Makes but a penitent, loses a lover.

TRANSLATION [2]

Addison, in some beautiful Latin lines inserted in the *Spectator*,
is entirely of opinion that birds observe a strict chastity of manners,
and never admit the caresses of a different tribe.—(*v. Spectator*,
No. 412.)

CHASTE are their instincts, faithful is their fire,
No foreign beauty tempts to false desire ;
The snow-white vesture, and the glittering crown,
The simple plumage, or the glossy down

[[1] This was first printed by Boswell in the *London Magazine* for
June, 1774. It had been intended for the part of "Miss Hardcastle,"
but Mrs. Bulkley, who played that part, was no vocalist. Goldsmith himself sang it very agreeably to an Irish air, *The Humours of
Balamagairy*. (See Birkbeck Hill's *Boswell*, 1887, ii. 219.)]

[[2] From Goldsmith's *History of the Earth and Animated Nature*,
1774, v. 312.]

Prompt not their love :—the patriot bird pursues
His well acquainted tints, and kindred hues.
Hence through their tribes no mix'd polluted flame,
No monster-breed to mark the groves with shame ;
But the chaste blackbird, to its partner true,
Thinks black alone is beauty's favourite hue.
The nightingale, with mutual passion blest,
Sings to its mate, and nightly charms the nest :
While the dark owl to court its partner flies,
And owns its offspring in their yellow eyes.

EPITAPH ON THOMAS PARNELL [1]

THIS tomb, inscrib'd to gentle Parnell's name,
May speak our gratitude, but not his fame.
What heart but feels his sweetly-moral lay,
That leads to truth through pleasure's flowery way !
Celestial themes confess'd his tuneful aid ;
And Heaven, that lent him genius, was repaid.
Needless to him the tribute we bestow—
The transitory breath of fame below :
More lasting rapture from his works shall rise,
While converts thank their poet in the skies.

THE CLOWN'S REPLY [2]

JOHN TROTT was desired by two witty peers
To tell them the reason why asses had ears.
"An't please you," quoth John, "I'm not given to letters,
Nor dare I pretend to know more than my betters ;
Howe'er from this time I shall ne'er see your graces,
As I hope to be saved! without thinking on asses."

[[1] This epitaph was first printed with *The Haunch of Venison*,
1776.   Parnell died in 1718.   In 1770 Goldsmith wrote his life.]
  [[2] First printed at p. 79 of *Poems and Plays. By Oliver
Goldsmith, M.B.* Dublin, 1777.   It is there dated " Edinburgh,
1753."]

EPITAPH ON EDWARD PURDON[1]

HERE lies poor Ned Purdon, from misery freed,
Who long was a bookseller's hack ;
He led such a damnable life in this world,—
I don't think he'll wish to come back.

EPILOGUE FOR MR. LEE LEWES[2]

HOLD ! Prompter, hold ! a word before your nonsense ;
I'd speak a word or two to ease my conscience.
My pride forbids it ever should be said,
My heels eclips'd the honours of my head ;
That I found humour in a piebald vest,
Or ever thought that jumping was a jest.

(Takes off his mask.)

Whence, and what art thou, visionary birth ?
Nature disowns, and reason scorns thy mirth,
In thy black aspect every passion sleeps,
The joy that dimples, and the woe that weeps.
How hast thou fill'd the scene with all thy brood,
Of fools pursuing, and of fools pursu'd !
Whose ins and outs no ray of sense discloses,
Whose only plot it is to break our noses ;
Whilst from below the trap-door Demons rise,
And from above the dangling deities ;
And shall I mix in this unhallow'd crew ?
May rosin'd lightning blast me, if I do !

[1 First printed as Goldsmith's in *Poems and Plays*, 1777, p. 79. Purdon had been at Trinity College, Dublin, with Goldsmith. Swift wrote a somewhat similar epigram ; but Goldsmith's model was probably *La Mort du Sieur Etienne*. (Forster's *Life*, 1871, ii. 39.)]

[2 Charles Lee Lewes (1740-1803) was the original " Young Marlow " of *She Stoops to Conquer*. He had previously been Harlequin of the theatre, but he thoroughly succeeded in his new part, and the grateful author wrote him this *Epilogue* for his Benefit, May 7, 1773.]

No—I will act, I'll vindicate the stage :
Shakespeare himself shall feel my tragic rage.
Off ! off ! vile trappings ! a new passion reigns !
The madd'ning monarch revels in my veins.
Oh ! for a Richard's voice to catch the theme :
"Give me another horse ! bind up my wounds !—soft—
      'twas but a dream."
Ay, 'twas but a dream, for now there's no retreating :
If I cease Harlequin, I cease from eating.
'Twas thus that Aesop's stag, a creature blameless,
Yet something vain, like one that shall be nameless,
Once on the margin of a fountain stood,
And cavill'd at his image in the flood.
"The deuce confound," he cries, "these drumstick
      shanks,
They never have my gratitude nor thanks ;
They're perfectly disgraceful ! strike me dead !
But for a head, yes, yes, I have a head.
How piercing is that eye ! how sleek that brow !
My horns ! I'm told horns are the fashion now."
Whilst thus he spoke, astonish'd, to his view,
Near, and more near, the hounds and huntsmen drew.
"Hoicks ! hark forward ! " came thund'ring from behind,
He bounds aloft, outstrips the fleeting wind :
He quits the woods, and tries the beaten ways ;
He starts, he pants, he takes the circling maze.
At length his silly head, so priz'd before,
Is taught his former folly to deplore ;
Whilst his strong limbs conspire to set him free,
And at one bound he saves himself,—like me.

(Taking a jump through the stage door.)

EPILOGUE

INTENDED TO HAVE BEEN SPOKEN FOR "SHE STOOPS TO CONQUER"[1]

Enter MRS. BULKLEY, *who curtsies very low as beginning to speak. Then enter* MISS CATLEY, *who stands full before her, and curtsies to the audience.*

MRS. BULKLEY

HOLD, Ma'am, your pardon. What's **your** business here?

MISS CATLEY

The Epilogue.

MRS. BULKLEY

The Epilogue?

MISS CATLEY

Yes, the Epilogue, my dear.

MRS. BULKLEY

Sure you mistake, Ma'am. The Epilogue, *I* bring it.

MISS CATLEY

Excuse me, Ma'am. The Author bid *me* sing it.

Recitative

Ye beaux and belles, that form this splendid ring,
Suspend your conversation while I sing.

MRS. BULKLEY

Why, sure the girl's beside herself: an Epilogue of singing,
A hopeful end indeed to such a blest beginning.
Besides, a singer in a comic set!—
Excuse me, Ma'am, I know the etiquette.

[1 This Epilogue, given to Bishop Percy by Goldsmith, was first printed at p. 82, vol. ii. of the *Miscellaneous Works* of 1801. It was written with intent to conciliate the rival claims of Mrs. Bulkley and Miss Catley, the former of whom wished to speak, the latter to sing, the Epilogue. (See Cradock's *Memoirs*, 1826, i. 225.)]

MISS CATLEY

What if we leave it to the House?

MRS. BULKLEY

                     The House !—Agreed.

MISS CATLEY

                            Agreed.

MRS. BULKLEY

And she, whose party's largest, shall proceed.
And first, I hope you'll readily agree
I've all the critics and the wits for me.
They, I am sure, will answer my commands ;
Ye candid judging few, hold up your hands.
What ! no return ? I find too late, I fear,
That modern judges seldom enter here.

MISS CATLEY

I'm for a different set.—Old men, whose trade is
Still to gallant and dangle with the ladies ;—

Recitative

Who mump their passion, and who, grimly smiling,
Still thus address the fair with voice beguiling :—

Air—Cotillon

Turn, my fairest, turn, if ever
     Strephon caught thy ravish'd eye ;
Pity take on your swain so clever,
     Who without your aid must die.
         Yes, I shall die, hu, hu, hu, hu !
         Yes, I must die, ho, ho, ho, ho !
                          (*Da capo.*)

MRS. BULKLEY

Let all the old pay homage to your merit ;
Give me the young, the gay, the men of spirit.
Ye travell'd tribe, ye macaroni [1] train,

[1 A name derived from the Italian dish first patronized by the "Macaroni Club," and afterwards extended to "the younger and gayer part of our nobility and gentry, who, at the same time they gave in to the luxuries of eating, went equally into the extravagancies of dress." (*Macaroni and Theatrical Magazine*, October, 1770.) See note to the *Dullissimo Macaroni* in *She Stoops to Conquer*.]

Of French friseurs, and nosegays, justly vain,
Who take a trip to Paris once a year
To dress, and look like awkward Frenchmen here,
Lend me your hands.—Oh ! fatal news to tell :
Their hands are only lent to the Heinel.[1]

MISS CATLEY

Ay, take your travellers, travellers indeed !
Give me my bonny Scot, that travels from the Tweed,
Where are the chiels ?   Ah ! Ah, I well discern
The smiling looks of each bewitching bairn.

Air—A bonny young lad is my Jockey

I'll sing to amuse you by night and by day,
And be unco merry when you are but gay ;
When you with your bagpipes are ready to play,
My voice shall be ready to carol away
        With Sandy, and Sawney, and Jockey.
        With Sawney, and Jarvie, and Jockey.

MRS. BULKLEY

Ye gamesters, who, so eager in pursuit,
Make but of all your fortune one *va toute :*
Ye jockey tribe, whose stock of words are few,
" I hold the odds.—Done, done, with you, with you."
Ye barristers, so fluent with grimace,
" My Lord,—your Lordship misconceives the case."
Doctors, who cough and answer every misfortuner,
" I wish I'd been call'd in a little sooner,"
Assist my cause with hands and voices hearty,
Come end the contest here, and aid my party.

MISS CATLEY
Air—Ballinamony

Ye brave Irish lads, hark away to the crack,
Assist me, I pray, in this woful attack ;

[1 Mlle. Anna-Frederica Heinel, a beautiful Prussian *danseuse* at this time in London, afterwards the wife of the elder Vestris. " 1771.   June 22nd.   Mr. William Hanger bets Mr. Lee Twenty Guineas to 25 that Mlle. Heinel does not dance in England at the Opera House next Month."—(Extract from the Betting Book at Brooks's Club, printed by Mr. G. S. Street in the *North American Review* for July 15, 1901.)

For sure I don't wrong you, you seldom are slack,
When the ladies are calling, to blush, and hang back.
  For you're always polite and attentive,
  Still to amuse us inventive,
  And death is your only preventive:
    Your hands and your voices for me.

MRS. BULKLEY

Well, Madam, what if, after all this sparring,
We both agree, like friends, to end our jarring?

MISS CATLEY

And that our friendship may remain unbroken,
What if we leave the Epilogue unspoken?

MRS. BULKLEY

Agreed.

MISS CATLEY

  Agreed.

MRS. BULKLEY

      And now with late repentance,
Un-epilogued the Poet waits his sentence.
Condemn the stubborn fool who can't submit
To thrive by flattery, though he starves by wit.

  (*Exeunt.*)

EPILOGUE

INTENDED TO HAVE BEEN SPOKEN BY MRS. BULKLEY
FOR "SHE STOOPS TO CONQUER"[1]

THERE is a place, so Ariosto sings,[2]
A treasury for lost and missing things;
Lost human wits have places there assign'd them,
And they, who lose their senses, there may find them.
But where's this place, this storehouse of the age?
The Moon, says he:—but *I* affirm the Stage:

[1 This Epilogue, also given to Bishop Percy by Goldsmith in MS., was first printed in the *Miscellaneous Works* of 1801, ii. 87. Colman, the Manager, thought it "too bad to be spoken," and the author accordingly wrote that printed with *She Stoops to Conquer*. (See Cradock's *Memoirs*, 1826, i. 225.)]

[2 *Orlando Furioso*, Canto xxxiv.]

Epilogue

At least in many things, I think, I see
His lunar, and our mimic world agree.
Both shine at night, for, but at Foote's alone,[1]
We scarce exhibit till the sun goes down.
Both prone to change, no settled limits fix,
And sure the folks of both are lunatics.
But in this parallel my best pretence is,
That mortals visit both to find their senses.
To this strange spot, Rakes, Macaronies, Cits,
Come thronging to collect their scatter'd wits.
The gay coquette, who ogles all the day,
Comes here at night, and goes a prude away.
Hither the affected city dame advancing,
Who sighs for operas, and dotes on dancing,
Taught by our art her ridicule to pause on,
Quits the *Ballet*, and calls for *Nancy Dawson*.[2]
The Gamester too, whose wit's all high or low,
Oft risks his fortune on one desperate throw,
Comes here to saunter, having made his bets,
Finds his lost senses out, and pay his debts.
The Mohawk too, with angry phrases stored,
As " Dam'me, Sir," and " Sir, I wear a sword ; "
Here lesson'd for a while, and hence retreating,
Goes out, affronts his man, and takes a beating.
Here comes the son of scandal and of news,
But finds no sense—for they had none to lose.
Of all the tribe here wanting an adviser
Our Author's the least likely to grow wiser ;
Has he not seen how you your favour place,
On sentimental Queens and Lords in lace ?
Without a star, a coronet or garter,
How can the piece expect or hope for quarter ?
No high-life scenes, no sentiment :—the creature
Still stoops among the low to copy nature.[3]
Yes, he's far gone :—and yet some pity fix,
The English laws forbid to punish lunatics.

[1 Foote gave *matinées* at the Haymarket.]
[2 A popular song bearing the name of a famous hornpipe dancer
and "toast" who died at Hampstead in 1767.]
[3 An obvious reference to the title of the play.]

THE CAPTIVITY : AN ORATORIO [1]

[THE PERSONS

First Jewish Prophet.   *First Chaldean Priest.*
Second Jewish Prophet.   *Second Chaldean Priest.*
Israelitish Woman.   *Chaldean Woman.*
           Chorus of Youths and Virgins.
SCENE—*The banks of the River Euphrates, near Babylon.*]

ACT I

SCENE—*Israelites sitting on the banks of the Euphrates*

FIRST PROPHET

RECITATIVE

YE captive tribes, that hourly work and weep
Where flows Euphrates murmuring to the deep,
Suspend awhile the task, the tear suspend,
And turn to God, your Father and your Friend.
Insulted, chain'd, and all the world a foe,
Our God alone is all we boast below.

CHORUS OF ISRAELITES

Our God is all we boast below,
    To Him we turn our eyes;
And every added weight of woe
    Shall make our homage rise.

And though no temple richly drest,
    Nor sacrifice is here;
We'll make His temple in our breast,
    And offer up a tear.

[1 *The Captivity* was set to music, but never performed. It was first printed in the *Miscellaneous Works* (Trade edition), 1820. In 1837, Prior printed it again from another MS. (*Miscellaneous Works*, 1837). It is here given mainly as reproduced by Mr. Bolton Corney from the second version, Author's MS. Two of the songs, with variations, were published with *The Haunch of Venison*, 1776.]

SECOND PROPHET

RECITATIVE

That strain once more ; it bids remembrance rise,
And calls my long-lost country to mine eyes.
Ye fields of Sharon, drest in flowery pride,
Ye plains where Jordan rolls its glassy tide,
Ye hills of Lebanon, with cedars crown'd,
Ye Gilead groves, that fling perfumes around,
These hills how sweet, those plains how wondrous fair,
But sweeter still when Heaven was with us there !

AIR

O Memory ! thou fond deceiver,
    Still importunate and vain ;
To former joys recurring ever,
    And turning all the past to pain :

Hence, deceiver most distressing !
    Seek the happy and the free :
The wretch who wants each other blessing,
    Ever wants a friend in thee.

FIRST PROPHET

RECITATIVE

Yet why repine ?   What though by bonds confin'd,
Should bonds enslave the vigour of the mind ?
Have we not cause for triumph when we see
Ourselves alone from idol-worship free ?
Are not this very day those rites begun
Where prostrate folly hails the rising sun ?
Do not our tyrant lords this day ordain
For superstitious rites and mirth profane ?
And should we mourn ? should coward virtue fly,
When impious folly rears her front on high ?
No ; rather let us triumph still the more,
And as our fortune sinks, our wishes soar.

AIR

The triumphs that on vice attend
Shall ever in confusion end ;
The good man suffers but to gain,
And every virtue springs from pain :

As aromatic plants bestow
No spicy fragrance while they grow;
But crush'd, or trodden to the ground,
Diffuse their balmy sweets around.

SECOND PROPHET

RECITATIVE

But hush, my sons, our tyrant lords are near,
The sound of barbarous mirth offends mine ear;
Triumphant music floats along the vale,
Near, nearer still, it gathers on the gale;
The growing note their near approach declares!
Desist, my sons, nor mix the strain with theirs.

Enter Chaldean Priests attended

FIRST PRIEST

AIR

Come on, my companions, the triumph display,
    Let rapture the minutes employ;
The sun calls us out on this festival day,
    And our monarch partakes of our joy.

Like the sun, our great monarch all pleasure supplies,
    Both similar blessings bestow;
The sun with his splendour illumines the skies,
    And our monarch enlivens below.

AIR

CHALDEAN WOMAN

Haste, ye sprightly sons of pleasure,
Love presents its brightest treasure,
    Leave all other sports for me.

A CHALDEAN ATTENDANT

Or rather, love's delights despising,
Haste to raptures ever rising,
    Wine shall bless the brave and free.

SECOND PRIEST

Wine and beauty thus inviting,
Each to different joys exciting,
    Whither shall my choice incline?

FIRST PRIEST

I'll waste no longer thought in choosing,
But, neither love nor wine refusing,
　　I'll make them both together mine.

RECITATIVE

But whence, when joys should brighten o'er the land,
This sullen gloom in Judah's captive band?
Ye sons of Judah, why the lute unstrung?
Or why those harps on yonder willows hung?
Come, leave your griefs, and join our tuneful choir,
For who like you can wake the sleeping lyre?

SECOND PROPHET

Bow'd down with chains, the scorn of all mankind,
To want, to toil, and every ill consign'd,
Is this a time to bid us raise the strain,
And mix in rites that Heaven regards with pain?
No, never.　May this hand forget each art
That speeds the powers of music to the heart,
Ere I forget the land that gave me birth,
Or join with sounds profane its sacred mirth!

FIRST PRIEST

Insulting slaves! if gentler methods fail,
The whip and angry tortures shall prevail.
　　　　　　　　　　　　[Exeunt Chaldeans.

FIRST PROPHET

Why, let them come, one good remains to cheer—
We fear the Lord, and know no other fear.

CHORUS

Can whips or tortures hurt the mind
On God's supporting breast reclin'd?
Stand fast, and let our tyrants see
That fortitude is victory.

End of the First Act

ACT II
SCENE—*As before*

CHORUS OF ISRAELITES

O PEACE of mind, thou lovely guest !
Thou softest soother of the breast !
   Dispense thy balmy store !
Wing all our thoughts to reach the skies
Till earth, diminish'd to our eyes,
   Shall vanish as we soar.

FIRST PRIEST
RECITATIVE

No more !   Too long has justice been delay'd,
The king's commands must fully be obey'd ;
Compliance with his will your peace secures,
Praise but our gods, and every good is yours.
But if, rebellious to his high command,
You spurn the favours offer'd at his hand,
Think, timely think, what ills remain behind ;
Reflect, nor tempt to rage the royal mind.

SECOND PRIEST
AIR

Fierce is the whirlwind howling,
   O'er Afric's sandy plain,
And fierce the tempest rolling
   Along the furrow'd main.
     But storms that fly,
     To rend the sky,
   Every ill presaging,
     Less dreadful show
     To worlds below,
   Than angry monarch's raging.

ISRAELITISH WOMAN
RECITATIVE

Ah me ! what angry terrors round us grow,
How shrinks my soul to meet the threaten'd blow !

Ye prophets, skill'd in Heaven's eternal truth,
Forgive my sex's fears, forgive my youth !
If shrinking thus, when frowning power appears
I wish for life, and yield me to my fears :
Let us one hour, one little hour obey ;
To-morrow's tears may wash our stains away.

AIR

To the last moment of his breath
  On hope the wretch relies ;
And e'en the pang preceding death
  Bids expectation rise.

Hope, like the gleaming taper's light,
  Adorns and cheers our way ;
And still, as darker grows the night,
  Emits a brighter ray.

SECOND PRIEST

RECITATIVE

Why this delay ? at length for joy prepare.
I read your looks, and see compliance there.
Come, raise the strain, and grasp the full-ton'd lyre—
The time, the theme, the place, and all conspire.

CHALDEAN WOMAN

AIR

See the ruddy morning smiling,
Hear the grove to bliss beguiling ;
Zephyrs through the valley playing,
Streams along the meadow straying.

FIRST PRIEST

While these a constant revel keep,
Shall reason only bid me weep ?
Hence, intruder ! we'll pursue
Nature, a better guide than you.

SECOND PRIEST

Every moment, as it flows,
Some peculiar pleasure owes ;

Then let us providently wise,
Seize the debtor as it flies.
Think not to-morrow can repay
The pleasures that we lose to-day;
To-morrow's most unbounded store
Can but pay its proper score.

FIRST PRIEST

RECITATIVE

But hush! see, foremost of the captive choir,
The master-prophet grasps his full-toned lyre.
Mark where he sits with executing art,
Feels for each tone and speeds it to the heart;
See inspiration fills his rising form,
Awful as clouds that nurse the growing storm.
And now his voice, accordant to the string,
Prepares our monarch's victories to sing.

FIRST PROPHET

AIR

From north, from south, from east, from west,
    Conspiring foes shall come;
Tremble, thou vice-polluted breast;
    Blasphemers, all be dumb.

The tempest gathers all around,
    On Babylon it lies;
Down with her! down, down to the ground;
    She sinks, she groans, she dies.

SECOND PROPHET

Down with her, Lord, to lick the dust,
    Ere yonder setting sun;
Serve her as she hath serv'd the just!
    'Tis fix'd—It shall be done.

FIRST PRIEST

RECITATIVE

Enough! when slaves thus insolent presume,
The king himself shall judge, and fix their doom.

Short-sighted wretches! have not you, and all,
Beheld our power in Zedekiah's fall?
To yonder gloomy dungeon turn your eyes;
Mark where dethron'd your captive monarch lies,
Depriv'd of sight, and rankling in his chain;
He calls on death to terminate his pain.
Yet know, ye slaves, that still remain behind
More ponderous chains, and dungeons more confined.

CHORUS

Arise, All-potent Ruler, rise,
    And vindicate Thy people's cause,
Till every tongue in every land
    Shall offer up unfeign'd applause.

End of the Second Act

ACT III
Scene—*As before*

FIRST PRIEST

RECITATIVE

YES, my companions, Heaven's decrees are past,
And our fix'd empire shall for ever last:
In vain the madd'ning prophet threatens woe,
In vain rebellion aims her secret blow;
Still shall our fame and growing power be spread,
And still our vengeance crush the guilty head.

AIR

Coeval with man
Our empire began,
And never shall fall
Till ruin shakes all.
With the ruin of all,
Shall Babylon fall.

SECOND [FIRST] PROPHET

RECITATIVE

'Tis thus that pride triumphant rears the head,
A little while, and all their power is fled.
But ha! what means yon sadly plaintive train,
That this way slowly bends along the plain?
And now, methinks, a pallid corse they bear
To yonder bank, and rest the body there.
Alas! too well mine eyes observant trace
The last remains of Judah's royal race.
Our monarch falls, and now our fears are o'er,
The wretched Zedekiah is no more.

AIR

Ye wretches who by fortune's hate
    In want and sorrow groan,
Come ponder his severer fate
    And learn to bless your own.

Ye sons, from fortune's lap supplied,
    Awhile the bliss suspend;
Like yours, his life began in pride,
    Like his, your lives may end.

SECOND PROPHET

RECITATIVE

Behold his squalid corse with sorrow worn,
His wretched limbs with ponderous fetters torn;
Those eyeless orbs that shock with ghastly glare,
These ill-becoming robes, and matted hair!
And shall not Heaven for this its terror show,
And deal its angry vengeance on the foe?
How long, how long, Almighty Lord of all,
Shall wrath vindictive threaten ere it fall!

ISRAELITISH WOMAN

AIR

As panting flies the hunted hind,
    Where brooks refreshing stray;

And rivers through the valley wind,
    That stop the hunter's way;

Thus we, O Lord, alike distress'd,
    For streams of mercy long;
Those streams that cheer the sore oppress'd,
    And overwhelm the strong.

FIRST PROPHET

RECITATIVE

But whence that shout? Good heavens! amazement all!
See yonder tower just nodding to the fall:
See where an army covers all the ground,
Saps the strong wall and pours destruction round;—
The ruin smokes, destruction pours along—
How low the great, how feeble are the strong!
The foe prevails, the lofty walls recline—
Oh, God of hosts, the victory is Thine!

CHORUS OF ISRAELITES

Down with her, Lord, to lick the dust;
    Let vengeance be begun;
Serve her as she hath serv'd the just,
    And let Thy Will be done.

FIRST PRIEST

RECITATIVE

All, all is lost. The Syrian army fails,
Cyrus, the conqueror of the world, prevails!
Save us, O Lord! to Thee, though late, we pray;
And give repentance but an hour's delay.

SECOND PRIEST

AIR

Thrice happy, who in happy hour
    To Heaven their praise bestow,
And own His all-consuming power
    Before they feel the blow!

FIRST PROPHET

RECITATIVE

Now, now's your time ! ye wretches bold and blind,
Brave but to God, and cowards to mankind,
Too late you seek that power unsought before,
Your wealth, your pride, your empire, are no more.

AIR

O Lucifer ! thou son of morn,
Alike of Heaven and man the foe ;
  Heaven, men, and all,
  Now press thy fall,
And sink thee lowest of the low.

SECOND PRIEST [PROPHET ?]

O Babylon, how art thou fallen—
Thy fall more dreadful from delay ;
  Thy streets forlorn
  To wilds shall turn,
Where toads shall pant, and vultures prey !

FIRST PROPHET

RECITATIVE

Such be their fate.   But listen ! from afar
The clarion's note proclaims the finished **war** !
Cyrus, our great restorer, is at hand,
And this way leads his formidable band.
Now give your songs of Zion to the wind,
And hail the benefactor of mankind :
He comes pursuant to divine decree,
To chain the strong, and set the captive free.

CHORUS OF YOUTHS

Rise to raptures past expressing,
  Sweeter from remember'd woes ;
Cyrus comes, our wrongs redressing,
  Comes to give the world repose.

CHORUS OF VIRGINS

Cyrus comes, the world redressing,
  Love and pleasure in his train ;
Comes to heighten every blessing,
  Comes to soften every pain.

CHORUS OF YOUTHS AND VIRGINS

Hail to him with mercy reigning,
  Skill'd in every peaceful art ;
Who, from bonds our limbs unchaining,
  Only binds the willing heart.

LAST CHORUS

But chief to Thee, our God, our Father, Friend,
  Let praise be given to all eternity ;
O Thou, without beginning, without end—
  Let us, and all, begin and end in Thee !

VERSES IN REPLY TO AN INVITATION TO DINNER AT DR. BAKER'S[1]

" This is a poem !   This is a copy of verses ! "

YOUR mandate I got,
You may all go to pot ;
Had your senses been right,
You'd have sent before night ;
As I hope to be saved,
I put off being shaved ;
For I could not make bold,
While the matter was cold,
To meddle in suds,
Or to put on my duds ;

[1 **Prior** first printed this in the *Miscellaneous Works* of 1837, iv. 132, having obtained it from Major-General Sir H. E. Bunbury, Bart., son of H. W. Bunbury, the artist.   (See note 2 to p. 107.)]

So tell Horneck [1] and Nesbitt, [2]
And Baker [3] and his bit,
And Kauffman [4] beside,
And the Jessamy Bride, [5]
With the rest of the crew,
The Reynoldses two, [6]
Little Comedy's face, [7]
And the Captain in lace, [8]
(By-the-bye you may tell him,
I have something to sell him;
Of use I insist,
When he comes to enlist.
Your worships must know
That a few days ago,
An order went out,
For the foot-guards so stout
To wear tails in high taste,
Twelve inches at least:
Now I've got him a scale
To measure each tail,
To lengthen a short tail,
And a long one to curtail.)—
Yet how can I when vext,
Thus stray from my text?
Tell each other to rue
Your Devonshire crew,
For sending so late
To one of my state.
But 'tis Reynolds's way
From wisdom to stray,
And Angelica's whim
To be frolick like him,

[1 Mrs. Horneck, widow of Captain Kane Horneck.]
[2 Mr. Thrale's brother-in-law.]
[3 Dr. (afterwards Sir) George Baker, Reynolds's doctor.]
[4 Angelica Kauffmann, the artist, 1740–1807.]
[5 Mrs. Horneck's younger daughter, Mary.]
[6 Sir Joshua and his sister.]
[7 Mrs. Horneck's elder daughter, Catherine. (See notes, p. 107.)]
[8 Captain Charles Horneck, Mrs. Horneck's son.]

But alas ! your good worships, how could they be wiser,
When both have been spoil'd in to-day's *Advertiser ?*[1]

OLIVER GOLDSMITH.

LETTER IN PROSE AND VERSE TO MRS. BUNBURY[2]

MADAM,

I read your letter with all that allowance which critical candour could require, but after all find so much to object to, and so much to raise my indignation, that I cannot help giving it a serious answer.

I am not so ignorant, Madam, as not to see there are many sarcasms contained in it, and solecisms also. (Solecism is a word that comes from the town of Soleis in Attica, among the Greeks, built by Solon, and applied as we use the word Kidderminster for curtains from a town also of that name ;—but this is learning you have no taste for !)—I say, Madam, there are sarcasms in it, and solecisms also. But, not to seem an ill-natured critic, I'll take leave to quote your own words, and give you my remarks upon them as they occur. You begin as follows :—

"I hope, my good Doctor, you soon will be here,
And your spring-velvet coat very smart will appear,
To open our ball the first day of the year."[3]

Pray, Madam, where did you ever find the epithet "good," applied to the title of Doctor ? Had you called me "learned Doctor," or "grave Doctor," or "noble Doctor," it might be allowable, because they belong to the profession. But, not to cavil at trifles, you talk of

[1 An allusion to some complimentary verses which appeared in that paper.]
[2 This letter, "probably written in 1773 or 1774," was first printed by Prior in the *Miscellaneous Works*, 1837, iv. 148. It was addressed to the "Little Comedy" of p. 106, by this time married to H. W. Bunbury, the artist.]
[3 Mrs. Bunbury had apparently invited the poet (in rhyme) to spend Christmas at the family seat of Great Barton in Suffolk.]

my "spring-velvet coat," and advise me to wear it the
first day in the year,—that is, in the middle of winter !—
a spring-velvet in the middle of winter ! ! ! That would
be a solecism indeed ! and yet, to increase the incon-
sistence, in another part of your letter you call me a
beau. Now, on one side or other, you must be wrong.
If I am a beau, I can never think of wearing a spring-
velvet in winter : and if I am not a beau, why then, that
explains itself. But let me go on to your two next
strange lines :—

> "And bring with you a wig, that is modish and gay,
> To dance with the girls that are makers of hay."

The absurdity of making hay at Christmas you yourself seem sensible of : you say your sister will laugh ;
and so indeed she well may ! The Latins have an
expression for a contemptuous sort of laughter, " Naso
contemnere adunco"; that is, to laugh with a crooked
nose. She may laugh at you in a manner of the ancients
if she thinks fit. But now I come to the most extraordinary of all extraordinary propositions, which is, to
take your and your sister's advice in playing at loo. The
presumption of the offer raises my indignation beyond the
bounds of prose ; it inspires me at once with verse and
resentment.   I take advice ! and from whom ?   You shall
hear.

First let me suppose, what may shortly be true,
The company set, and the word to be, Loo ;
All smirking, and pleasant, and big with adventure,
And ogling the stake which is fix'd in the centre.
Round and round go the cards, while I inwardly damn
At never once finding a visit from Pam.
I lay down my stake, apparently cool,
While the harpies about me all pocket the pool.
I fret in my gizzard, yet, cautious and sly,
I wish all my friends may be bolder than I :
Yet still they sit snug, not a creature will aim
By losing their money to venture at fame.
'Tis in vain that at niggardly caution I scold,
'Tis in vain that I flatter the brave and the bold :

All play their own way, and they think me an ass,—
"What does Mrs. Bunbury?"   "I, Sir? I pass."
"Pray what does Miss Horneck?[1] take courage, come
    do,"—
"Who, I? let me see, Sir, why I must pass too."
Mr. Bunbury frets, and I fret like the devil,
To see them so cowardly, lucky, and civil.
Yet still I sit snug, and continue to sigh on,
Till made by my losses as bold as a lion,
I venture at all,—while my avarice regards
The whole pool as my own—"Come, give me five cards."
"Well done!" cry the ladies; "Ah, Doctor, that's good!
The pool's very rich—ah! the Doctor is loo'd!"
Thus foil'd in my courage, on all sides perplex'd,
I ask for advice from the lady that's next:
"Pray, Ma'am, be so good as to give your advice;
Don't you think the best way is to venture for't twice?"
"I advise," cries the lady, "to try it, I own.—
Ah! the Doctor is loo'd! Come, Doctor, put down."
Thus, playing, and playing, I still grow more eager,
And so bold, and so bold, I'm at last a bold beggar.
Now, ladies, I ask, if law-matters you're skill'd in,
Whether crimes such as yours should not come before
    Fielding?[2]
For giving advice that is not worth a straw,
May well be call'd picking of pockets in law;
And picking of pockets, with which I now charge ye,
Is, by quinto Elizabeth, Death without Clergy.
What justice, when both to the Old Bailey brought!
By the gods, I'll enjoy it; though 'tis but in thought!
Both are plac'd at the bar, with all proper decorum,
With bunches of fennel, and nosegays before 'em;[3]
Both cover their faces with mobs and all that;
But the judge bids them, angrily, take off their hat.

[1 Mary Horneck, see p. 106 and note. She ultimately married
Colonel Gwyn, and survived until 1840. Reynolds and Hoppner
both painted her.]

[2 Sir John Fielding, d. 1780, Henry Fielding's blind half-brother
and successor at Bow Street.]

[3 To prevent infection,—a practice dating from the gaol-fever of
1750.]

When uncover'd, a buzz of enquiry runs round,—

"Pray what are their crimes?"—"They've been pilfering found."

"But, pray, whom have they pilfer'd?"—"A Doctor, I hear."

"What, yon solemn-faced, odd-looking man that stands near!"

"The same."—"What a pity! how does it surprise one!

Two handsomer culprits I never set eyes on!"

Then their friends all come round me with cringing and leering,

To melt me to pity, and soften my swearing.

First Sir Charles [1] advances with phrases well strung,

"Consider, dear Doctor, the girls are but young."

"The younger the worse," I return him again,

"It shows that their habits are all dyed in grain."

"But then they're so handsome, one's bosom it grieves."

"What signifies *handsome*, when people are thieves?"

"But where is your justice? their cases are hard."

"What signifies *justice?* I want the *reward*.

There's the parish of Edmonton offers forty pounds; there's the parish of St. Leonard, Shoreditch, offers forty pounds; there's the parish of Tyburn, from the Hog-in-the-Pound to St. Giles's watchhouse, offers forty pounds, —I shall have all that if I convict them!"—

"But consider their case,—it may yet be your own!

And see how they kneel! Is your heart made of stone?"

This moves:—so at last I agree to relent,

For ten pounds in hand, and ten pounds to be spent.

I challenge you all to answer this: I tell you, you cannot. It cuts deep;—but now for the rest of the letter: and next—but I want room—so I believe I shall battle the rest out at Barton some day next week.

I don't value you all!

O. G.

[1 Sir Charles Bunbury, H. W. Bunbury's elder brother, died s.p. 1821.]

VIDA'S GAME OF CHESS

TRANSLATED [1]

ARMIES of box that sportively engage
And mimic real battles in their rage,
Pleas'd I recount; how, smit with glory's charms,
Two mighty Monarchs met in adverse arms,
Sable and white; assist me to explore,
Ye Serian Nymphs, what ne'er was sung before.
No path appears: yet resolute I stray
Where youth undaunted bids me force my way.
O'er rocks and cliffs while I the task pursue,
Guide me, ye Nymphs, with your unerring clue.
For you the rise of this diversion know,
You first were pleas'd in Italy to show
This studious sport; from Scacchis was its name,
The pleasing record of your Sister's fame.

When Jove through Ethiopia's parch'd extent
To grace the nuptials of old Ocean went,
Each god was there; and mirth and joy around
To shores remote diffus'd their happy sound.
Then when their hunger and their thirst no more
Claim'd their attention, and the feast was o'er;
Ocean, with pastime to divert the thought,
Commands a painted table to be brought.
Sixty-four spaces fill the chequer'd square;
Eight in each rank eight equal limits share.
Alike their form, but different are their dyes,
They fade alternate, and alternate rise,
White after black; such various stains as those
The shelving backs of tortoises disclose.
Then to the Gods that mute and wondering sate,
You see (says he) the field prepared for fate.

[1 This translation of Marco Vida's *Scacchia Ludus* was first
printed by Mr. Peter Cunningham in 1854, from a manuscript in
Goldsmith's handwriting then in the possession of Mr. Bolton
Corney, who, with Mr. Forster, believed it to be by Goldsmith.]

Here will the little armies please your sight,
With adverse colours hurrying to the fight :
On which so oft, with silent sweet surprise,
The Nymphs and Nereids used to feast their eyes,
And all the neighbours of the hoary deep,
When calm the sea, and winds were lull'd asleep.
But see, the mimic heroes tread the board ;
He said, and straightway from an urn he pour'd
The sculptur'd box, that neatly seem'd to ape
The graceful figure of a human shape :—
Equal the strength and number of each foe,
Sixteen appeared like jet, sixteen like snow.
As their shape varies various is the name,
Different their posts, nor is their strength the same.
There might you see two Kings with equal pride
Gird on their arms, their Consorts by their side ;
Here the Foot-warriors glowing after fame,
There prancing Knights and dexterous Archers came
And Elephants, that on their backs sustain
Vast towers of war, and fill and shake the plain.
And now both hosts, preparing for the storm
Of adverse battle, their encampments form.
In the fourth space, and on the farthest line,
Directly opposite the Monarchs shine ;
The swarthy on white ground, on sable stands
The silver King ; and thence they send commands.
Nearest to these the Queens exert their might ;
One the left side, and t'other guards the right :
Where each, by her respective armour known,
Chooses the colour that is like her own.
Then the young Archers, two that snowy-white
Bend the tough yew, and two as black as night ;
(Greece called them Mars's favourites heretofore,
From their delight in war, and thirst of gore).
These on each side the Monarch and his Queen
Surround obedient ; next to these are seen
The crested Knights in golden armour gay ;
Their steeds by turns curvet, or snort or neigh.
In either army on each distant wing
Two mighty Elephants their castles bring,

Bulwarks immense! and then at last combine
Eight of the Foot to form the second line,
The vanguard to the King and Queen; from far
Prepared to open all the fate of war.
So moved the boxen hosts, each double-lined,
Their different colours floating in the wind:
As if an army of the Gauls should go,
With their white standards, o'er the Alpine snow
To meet in rigid fight on scorching sands
The sun-burnt Moors and Memnon's swarthy bands.

 Then Father Ocean thus; you see them here,
Celestial Powers, what troops, what camps appear.
Learn now the sev'ral orders of the fray,
For ev'n these arms their stated laws obey.
To lead the fight, the Kings from all their bands
Choose whom they please to bear their great commands.
Should a black hero first to battle go,
Instant a white one guards against the blow;
But only one at once can charge or shun the foe.
Their gen'ral purpose on one scheme is bent,
So to besiege the King within the tent,
That there remains no place by subtle flight
From danger free; and that decides the fight.
Meanwhile, howe'er, the sooner to destroy
Th' imperial Prince, remorseless they employ
Their swords in blood; and whosoever dare
Oppose their vengeance, in the ruin share.
Fate thins their camp; the parti-colour'd field
Widens apace, as they o'ercome or yield,
But the proud victor takes the captive's post;
There fronts the fury of th' avenging host
One single shock: and (should he ward the blow),
May then retire at pleasure from the foe.
The Foot alone (so their harsh laws ordain)
When they proceed can ne'er return again.

 But neither all rush on alike to prove
The terror of their arms: the Foot must move
Directly on, and but a single square;
Yet may these heroes, when they first prepare
To mix in combat on the bloody mead,

Double their sally, and two steps proceed ;
But when they wound, their swords they subtly guide
With aim oblique, and slanting pierce his side.
But the great Indian beasts, whose backs sustain
Vast turrets arm'd, when on the redd'ning plain
They join in all the terror of the fight,
Forward or backward, to the left or right,
Run furious, and impatient of confine
Scour through the field, and threat the farthest line.
Yet must they ne'er obliquely aim their blows ;
That only manner is allow'd to those
Whom Mars has favour'd most, who bend the stubborn
　　　bows.
These glancing sideways in a straight career,
Yet each confin'd to their respective sphere,
Or white or black, can send th' unerring dart
Wing'd with swift death to pierce through ev'ry part.
The fiery steed, regardless of the reins,
Comes prancing on ; but sullenly disdains
The path direct, and boldly wheeling round,
Leaps o'er a double space at ev'ry bound :
And shifts from white or black to diff'rent colour'd
　　　ground.
But the fierce Queen, whom dangers ne'er dismay,
The strength and terror of the bloody day,
In a straight line spreads her destruction wide,
To left or right, before, behind, aside.
Yet may she never with a circling course
Sweep to the battle like the fretful Horse ;
But unconfin'd may at her pleasure stray,
If neither friend nor foe block up the way ;
For to o'erleap a warrior, 'tis decreed
Those only dare who curb the snorting steed.
With greater caution and majestic state
The warlike Monarchs in the scene of fate
Direct their motions, since for these appear
Zealous each hope, and anxious ev'ry fear.
While the King's safe, with resolution stern
They clasp their arms ; but should a sudden turn
Make him a captive, instantly they yield,

Resolv'd to share his fortune in the field.
He moves on slow ; with reverence profound
His faithful troops encompass him around,
And oft, to break some instant fatal scheme,
Rush to their fates, their sov'reign to redeem ;
While he, unanxious where to wound the foe,
Need only shift and guard against a blow.
But none, however, can presume t' appear
Within his reach, but must his vengeance fear ;
For he on ev'ry side his terror throws ;
But when he changes from his first repose,
Moves but one step, most awfully sedate,
Or idly roving, or intent on fate.
These are the sev'ral and establish'd laws :
Now see how each maintains his bloody cause.

Here paused the God, but (since whene'er they wage
War here on earth the Gods themselves engage
In mutual battle as they hate or love,
And the most stubborn war is oft above)
Almighty Jove commands the circling train
Of Gods from fav'ring either to abstain,
And let the fight be silently survey'd ;
And added solemn threats if disobey'd.
Then call'd he Phœbus from among the Powers
And subtle Hermes, whom in softer hours
Fair Maia bore : youth wanton'd in their face ;
Both in life's bloom, both shone with equal grace.
Hermes as yet had never wing'd his feet ;
As yet Apollo in his radiant seat
Had never driv'n his chariot through the air,
Known by his bow alone and golden hair.
These Jove commission'd to attempt the fray,
And rule the sportive military day ;
Bid them agree which party each maintains,
And promis'd a reward that's worth their pains.
The greater took their seats ; on either hand
Respectful the less Gods in order stand,
But careful not to interrupt their play,
By hinting when t' advance or run away.
Then they examine, who shall first proceed

To try their courage, and their army lead.
Chance gave it for the White, that he should go
First with a brave defiance to the foe.
Awhile he ponder'd which of all his train
Should bear his first commission o'er the plain ;
And then determin'd to begin the scene
With him that stood before to guard the Queen.
He took a double step : with instant care
Does the black Monarch in his turn prepare
The adverse champion, and with stern command
Bid him repel the charge with equal hand.
There front to front, the midst of all the field,
With furious threats their shining arms they wield ;
Yet vain the conflict, neither can prevail
While in one path each other they assail.
On ev'ry side to their assistance fly
Their fellow soldiers, and with strong supply
Crowd to the battle, but no bloody stain
Tinctures their armour ; sportive in the plain
Mars plays awhile, and in excursion slight
Harmless they sally forth, or wait the fight.
    But now the swarthy Foot, that first appear'd
To front the foe, his pond'rous jav'lin rear'd
Leftward aslant, and a pale warrior slays,
Spurns him aside, and boldly takes his place.
Unhappy youth, his danger not to spy !
Instant he fell, and triumph'd but to die.
At this the sable King with prudent care
Remov'd his station from the middle square,
And slow retiring to the farthest ground,
There safely lurk'd, with troops entrench'd around.
Then from each quarter to the war advance
The furious Knights, and poise the trembling lance :
By turns they rush, by turns the victors yield,
Heaps of dead Foot choke up the crimson'd field :
They fall unable to retreat ; around
The clang of arms and iron hoofs resound.
    But while young Phœbus pleas'd himself to view
His furious Knight destroy the vulgar crew,
Sly Hermes long'd t' attempt with secret aim

Some noble act of more exalted fame.
For this, he inoffensive pass'd along
Through ranks of Foot, and 'midst the trembling throng
Sent his left Horse, that free without confine
Rov'd o'er the plain, upon some great design
Against the King himself. At length he stood,
And having fix'd his station as he would,
Threaten'd at once with instant fate the King
And th' Indian beast that guarded the right wing.
Apollo sigh'd, and hast'ning to relieve
The straiten'd Monarch, griev'd that he must leave
His martial Elephant exposed to fate,
And view'd with pitying eyes his dang'rous state.
First in his thoughts however was his care
To save his King, whom to the neighbouring square
On the right hand, he snatch'd with trembling flight;
At this with fury springs the sable Knight,
Drew his keen sword, and rising to the blow,
Sent the great Indian brute to shades below.
O fatal loss! for none except the Queen
Spreads such a terror through the bloody scene.
Yet shall you ne'er unpunish'd boast your prize,
The Delian God with stern resentment cries;
And wedg'd him round with Foot, and pour'd in fresh
    supplies.
Thus close besieg'd trembling he cast his eye
Around the plain, but saw no shelter nigh,
No way for flight; for here the Queen oppos'd,
The Foot in phalanx there the passage clos'd:
At length he fell; yet not unpleas'd with fate,
Since victim to a Queen's vindictive hate.
With grief and fury burns the whiten'd host,
One of their Tow'rs thus immaturely lost.
As when a bull has in contention stern
Lost his right horn, with double vengeance burn
His thoughts for war, with blood he's cover'd o'er,
And the woods echo to his dismal roar,
So look'd the flaxen host, when angry fate
O'erturn'd the Indian bulwark of their state.
Fir'd at this great success, with double rage

Apolio hurries on his troops t' engage,
For blood and havoc wild; and, while he leads
His troops thus careless, loses both his steeds:
For if some adverse warriors were o'erthrown,
He little thought what dangers threat his own.
But slyer Hermes with observant eyes
March'd slowly cautious, and at distance spies
What moves must next succeed, what dangers next arise.
Often would he, the stately Queen to snare,
The slender Foot to front her arms prepare,
And to conceal his scheme he sighs and feigns
Such a wrong step would frustrate all his pains.
Just then an Archer, from the right-hand view,
At the pale Queen his arrow boldly drew,
Unseen by Phœbus, who, with studious thought,
From the left side a vulgar hero brought.
But tender Venus, with a pitying eye,
Viewing the sad destruction that was nigh,
Wink'd upon Phœbus (for the Goddess sat
By chance directly opposite); at that
Rous'd in an instant, young Apollo threw
His eyes around the field his troops to view;
Perceived the danger, and with sudden fright
Withdrew the Foot that he had sent to fight,
And sav'd his trembling Queen by seasonable flight.
But Maia's son with shouts filled all the coast:
The Queen, he cried, the important Queen is lost.
Phœbus, howe'er, resolving to maintain
What he had done, bespoke the heavenly train.

What mighty harm, in sportive mimic fight,
Is it to set a little blunder right,
When no preliminary rule debarr'd?
If you henceforward, Mercury, would guard
Against such practice, let us make the law:
And whosoe'er shall first to battle draw,
Or white, or black, remorseless let him go
At all events, and dare the angry foe.

He said, and this opinion pleas'd around:
Jove turn'd aside, and on his daughter frown'd,
Unmark'd by Hermes, who, with strange surprise,

Fretted and foam'd, and roll'd his ferret eyes,
And but with great reluctance could refrain
From dashing at a blow all off the plain.
Then he resolv'd to interweave deceits,—
To carry on the war by tricks and cheats.
Instant he call'd an Archer from the throng,
And bid him like the courser wheel along:
Bounding he springs, and threats the pallid Queen.
The fraud, however, was by Phœbus seen;
He smil'd, and, turning to the Gods, he said:
Though, Hermes, you are perfect in your trade,
And you can trick and cheat to great surprise, ⎫
These little sleights no more shall blind my eyes; ⎬
Correct them if you please, the more you thus disguise. ⎭
The circle laugh'd aloud; and Maia's son
(As if it had but by mistake been done)
Recall'd his Archer, and with motion due,
Bid him advance, the combat to renew.
But Phœbus watch'd him with a jealous eye,
Fearing some trick was ever lurking nigh,
For he would oft, with sudden sly design,
Send forth at once two combatants to join
His warring troops, against the law of arms,
Unless the wary foe was ever in alarms.
   Now the white Archer with his utmost force
Bent the tough bow against the sable Horse,
And drove him from the Queen, where he had stood
Hoping to glut his vengeance with her blood.
Then the right Elephant with martial pride
Rov'd here and there, and spread his terrors wide:
Glittering in arms from far a courser came,
Threaten'd at once the King and Royal Dame;
Thought himself safe when he the post had seiz'd,
And with the future spoils his fancy pleas'd.
Fir'd at the danger a young Archer came,
Rush'd on the foe, and levell'd sure his aim;
(And though a Pawn his sword in vengeance draws,
Gladly he'd lose his life in glory's cause).
The whistling arrow to his bowels flew,
And the sharp steel his blood profusely drew;

He drops the reins, he totters to the ground,
And his life issu'd murm'ring through the wound.
Pierc'd by the Foot, this Archer bit the plain ;
The Foot himself was by another slain ;
And with inflam'd revenge, the battle burns again.
Towers, Archers, Knights, meet on the crimson ground,
And the field echoes to the martial sound.
Their thoughts are heated, and their courage fir'd,
Thick they rush on with double zeal inspir'd ;
Generals and Foot, with different colour'd mien,
Confus'dly warring in the camps are seen,—
Valour and Fortune meet in one promiscuous scene.
Now these victorious, lord it o'er the field ;
Now the foe rallies, the triumphant yield :
Just as the tide of battle ebbs or flows.
As when the conflict more tempestuous grows
Between the winds, with strong and boisterous sweep
They plough th' Ionian or Atlantic deep !
By turns prevails the mutual blustering roar,
And the big waves alternate lash the shore.

But in the midst of all the battle rag'd
The snowy Queen, with troops at once engag'd ;
She fell'd an Archer as she sought the plain,—
As she retir'd an Elephant was slain :
To right and left her fatal spears she sent,
Burst through the ranks, and triumph'd as she went ;
Through arms and blood she seeks a glorious fate,
Pierces the farthest lines, and nobly great
Leads on her army with a gallant show,
Breaks the battalions, and cuts through the foe.
At length the sable King his fears betray'd,
And begged his military consort's aid :
With cheerful speed she flew to his relief,
And met in equal arms the female chief.

Who first, great Queen, and who at last did bleed ?
How many Whites lay gasping on the mead ?
Half dead, and floating in a bloody tide,
Foot, Knights, and Archer lie on every side.
Who can recount the slaughter of the day ?
How many leaders threw their lives away ?

The chequer'd plain is fill'd with dying box,
Havoc ensues, and with tumultuous shocks
The different colour'd ranks in blood engage,
And Foot and Horse promiscuously rage.
With nobler courage and superior might
The dreadful Amazons sustain the fight,
Resolv'd alike to mix in glorious strife,
Till to imperious fate they yield their life.

    Meanwhile each Monarch, in a neighbouring cell,
Confin'd the warriors that in battle fell,
There watch'd the captives with a jealous eye,
Lest, slipping out again, to arms they fly.
But Thracian Mars, in steadfast friendship join'd
To Hermes, as near Phœbus he reclin'd,
Observ'd each chance, how all their motions bend,
Reso v'd if possible to serve his friend.
He a Foot-soldier and a Knight purloin'd
Out from the prison that the dead confin'd ;
And slyly push'd 'em forward on the plain ;
Th' enliven'd combatants their arms regain,
Mix in the bloody scene, and boldly war again.

    So the foul hag, in screaming wild alarms,
O'er a dead carcase muttering her charms
(And with her frequent and tremendous yell
Forcing great Hecate from out of hell),
Shoots in the corpse a new fictitious soul ;
With instant glare the supple eyeballs roll,
Again it moves and speaks, and life informs the whole.

    Vulcan alone discern'd the subtle cheat ;
And wisely scorning such a base deceit,
Call'd out to Phœbus.   Grief and rage assail
Phœbus by turns ; detected Mars turns pale.
Then awful Jove with sullen eye reprov'd
Mars, and the captives order'd to be mov'd
To their dark caves ; bid each fictitious spear
Be straight recall'd, and all be as they were.

    And now both Monarchs with redoubl'd rage
Led on their Queens, the mutual war to wage.
O'er all the field their thirsty spears they send,
Then front to front their Monarchs they defend.

But lo! the female White rush'd in unseen,
And slew with fatal haste the swarthy Queen;
Yet soon, alas! resign'd her royal spoils,
Snatch'd by a shaft from her successful toils.
Struck at the sight, both hosts in wild surprise
Pour'd forth their tears, and fill'd the air with cries;
They wept and sigh'd, as passed the fun'ral train,
As if both armies had at once been slain.

And now each troop surrounds its mourning chief,
To guard his person, or assuage his grief.
One is their common fear; one stormy blast
Has equally made havoc as it pass'd.
Not all, however, of their youth are slain;
Some champions yet the vig'rous war maintain.
Three Foot, an Archer, and a stately Tower,
For Phœbus still exert their utmost power.
Just the same number Mercury can boast,
Except the Tower, who lately in his post
Unarm'd inglorious fell, in peace profound,
Pierced by an Archer with a distant wound;
But his right Horse retain'd its mettled pride,—
The rest were swept away by war's strong tide.

But fretful Hermes, with despairing moan,
Griev'd that so many champions were o'erthrown,
Yet reassumes the fight; and summons round
The little straggling army that he found,—
All that had 'scap'd from fierce Apollo's rage,—
Resolv'd with greater caution to engage
In future strife, by subtle wiles (if fate
Should give him leave) to save his sinking state,
The sable troops advance with prudence slow,
Bent on all hazards to distress the foe.
More cheerful Phœbus, with unequal pace,
Rallies his arms to lessen his disgrace.
But what strange havoc everywhere has been! ⎫
A straggling champion here and there is seen; ⎬
And many are the tents, yet few are left within. ⎭

Th' afflicted Kings bewail their consorts dead,
And loathe thoughts of a deserted bed;
And though each Monarch studies to improve

The tender mem'ry of his former love,
Their state requires a second nuptial tie.
Hence the pale ruler with a love-sick eye
Surveys th' attendants of his former wife,
And offers one of them a royal life.
These, when their martial mistress had been slain,
Weak and despairing tried their arms in vain;
Willing, howe'er, amidst the Black to go,
They thirst for speedy vengeance on the foe.
Then he resolves to see who merits best,
By strength and courage, the imperial vest;
Points out the foe, bids each with bold design
Pierce through the ranks, and reach the deepest line:
For none must hope with Monarchs to repose
But who can first, through thick surrounding foes,
Through arms and wiles, with hazardous essay,
Safe to the farthest quarters force their way.
Fir'd at the thought, with sudden, joyful pace
They hurry on; but first of all the race
Runs the third right-hand warrior for the prize,—
The glitt'ring crown already charms her eyes.
Her dear associates cheerfully give o'er
The nuptial chase; and swift she flies before, ⎫
And Glory lent her wings, and the reward in store. ⎭
Nor would the sable King her hopes prevent,
For he himself was on a Queen intent,
Alternate, therefore, through the field they go.
Hermes led on, but by a step too slow,
His fourth left Pawn: and now th' advent'rous White
Had marched through all, and gain'd the wish'd-for site.
Then the pleas'd King gives orders to prepare
The crown, the sceptre, and the royal chair,
And owns her for his Queen; around exult
The snowy troops, and o'er the Black insult.
    Hermes burst into tears,—with fretful roar
Fill'd the wide air, and his gay vesture tore.
The swarthy Foot had only to advance
One single step; but oh! malignant chance!
A tower'd Elephant, with fatal aim,
Stood ready to destroy her when she came:

He keeps a watchful eye upon the whole,
Threatens her entrance, and protects the goal.
Meanwhile the royal new-created bride,
Pleas'd with her pomp, spread death and terror wide ;
Like lightning through the sable troops she flies,
Clashes her arms, and seems to threat the skies.
The sable troops are sunk in wild affright,
And wish th' earth op'ning snatch'd 'em from her sight.
In burst the Queen, with vast impetuous swing : ⎫
The trembling foes come swarming round the King, ⎬
Where in the midst he stood, and form a valiant ring. ⎭
So the poor cows, straggling o'er pastureland,
When they perceive the prowling wolf at hand,
Crowd close together in a circle full,
And beg the succour of the lordly bull ;
They clash their horns, they low with dreadful sound,
And the remotest groves re-echo round.

But the bold Queen, victorious, from behind
Pierces the foe ; yet chiefly she design'd
Against the King himself some fatal aim,
And full of war to his pavilion came.
Now here she rush'd, now there ; and had she been
But duly prudent, she had slipp'd between,
With course oblique, into the fourth white square,
And the long toil of war had ended there,
The King had fall'n, and all his sable state ;
And vanquish'd Hermes curs'd his partial fate.
For thence with ease the championess might go,
Murder the King, and none could ward the blow.

With silence, Hermes, and with panting heart,
Perceiv'd the danger, but with subtle art
(Lest he should see the place) spurs on the foe,
Confounds his thoughts, and blames his being slow.
For shame ! move on ; would you for ever stay ?
What sloth is this, what strange perverse delay ?—
How could you e'er my little pausing blame ?—
What ! you would wait till night shall end the game ?
Phœbus, thus nettled, with imprudence slew
A vulgar Pawn, but lost his nobler view.
Young Hermes leap'd, with sudden joy elate ;

And then, to save the Monarch from his fate,
Led on his martial Knight, who stepp'd between,
Pleas'd that his charge was to oppose the Queen—
Then, pondering how the Indian beast to slay,
That stopp'd the Foot from making farther way,—
From being made a Queen; with slanting aim
An Archer struck him; down the monster came,
And dying shook the earth: while Phœbus tries
Without success the Monarch to surprise,
The Foot, then uncontroll'd with instant pride,
Seiz'd the last spot, and mov'd a royal bride.
And now with equal strength both war again,
And bring their second wives upon the plain;
Then, though with equal views each hop'd and fear'd,
Yet, as if every doubt had disappear'd,
As if he had the palm, young Hermes flies
Into excess of joy; with deep disguise,
Extols his own Black troops, with frequent spite
And with invective taunts disdains the White.
Whom Phœbus thus reprov'd with quick return—
As yet we cannot the decision learn
Of this dispute, and do you triumph now?
Then your big words and vauntings I'll allow,
When you the battle shall completely gain;
At present I shall make your boasting vain.
He said, and forward led the daring Queen;
Instant the fury of the bloody scene
Rises tumultuous, swift the warriors fly
From either side to conquer or to die.
They front the storm of war; around 'em Fear,
Terror, and Death, perpetually appear.
All meet in arms, and man to man oppose,
Each from their camp attempts to drive their foes;
Each tries by turns to force the hostile lines;
Chance and impatience blast their best designs.
The sable Queen spread terror as she went
Through the mid ranks: with more reserv'd intent
The adverse dame declin'd the open fray,
And to the King in private stole away:
Then took the royal guard, and bursting in,

With fatal menace close besieg'd the King.
Alarm'd at this, the swarthy Queen, in haste,
From all her havoc and destructive waste
Broke off, and her contempt of death to show,
Leap'd in between the monarch and the foe,
To save the King and state from this impending blow,
But Phœbus met a worse misfortune here :
For Hermes now led forward, void of fear,
His furious Horse into the open plain,
That onward chaf'd, and pranc'd, and paw'd amain.
Nor ceas'd from his attempts until he stood
On the long-wish'd-for spot, from whence he could
Slay King or Queen.   O'erwhelm'd with sudden fears,
Apollo saw, and could not keep from tears.
Now all seem'd ready to be overthrown ;
His strength was wither'd, ev'ry hope was flown.
Hermes, exulting at this great surprise,
Shouted for joy, and fill'd the air with cries ;
Instant he sent the Queen to shades below,
And of her spoils made a triumphant show.
But in return, and in his mid career,
Fell his brave Knight, beneath the Monarch's spear.
    Phœbus, however, did not yet despair,
But still fought on with courage and with care.
He had but two poor common men to show,
And Mars's favourite with his iv'ry bow.
The thoughts of ruin made 'em dare their best
To save their King, so fatally distress'd.
But the sad hour requir'd not such an aid ;
And Hermes breath'd revenge where'er he stray'd.
Fierce comes the sable Queen with fatal threat,
Surrounds the Monarch in his royal seat :
Rush'd here and there, nor rested till she slew
The last remainder of the whiten'd crew.
Sole stood the King, the midst of all the plain,
Weak and defenceless, his companions slain,
As when the ruddy morn ascending high
Has chas'd the twinkling stars from all the sky,
Your star, fair Venus, still retains its light,
And, loveliest, goes the latest out of sight.

No safety's left, no gleams of hope remain;
Yet did he not as vanquish'd quit the plain,
But tried to shut himself between the foe,—
Unhurt through swords and spears he hoped to go,
Until no room was left to shun the fatal blow.
For if none threaten'd his immediate fate,
And his next move must ruin all his state,
All their past toil and labour is in vain,
Vain all the bloody carnage of the plain,—
Neither would triumph then, the laurel neither gain.
Therefore through each void space and desert tent,
By different moves his various course he bent:
The Black King watch'd him with observant eye,
Follow'd him close, but left him room to fly.
Then when he saw him take the farthest line,
He sent the Queen his motions to confine,
And guard the second rank, that he could go
No farther now than to that distant row.
The sable monarch then with cheerful mien
Approach'd, but always with one space between.
But as the King stood o'er against him there,
Helpless, forlorn, and sunk in his despair,
The martial Queen her lucky moment knew,
Seized on the farthest seat with fatal view,
Nor left th' unhappy King a place to flee unto.
At length in vengeance her keen sword she draws,
Slew him, and ended thus the bloody cause:
And all the gods around approv'd it with applause.
　　The victor could not from his insults keep,
But laugh'd and sneer'd to see Apollo weep.
Jove call'd him near, and gave him in his hand
The powerful, happy, and mysterious wand
By which the Shades are call'd to purer day,
When penal fire has purged their sins away;
By which the guilty are condemn'd to dwell
In the dark mansions of the deepest hell;
By which he gives us sleep, or sleep denies,
And closes at the last the dying eyes.
Soon after this, the heavenly victor brought
The game on earth, and first th' Italians taught.

For (as they say) fair Scacchis he espied
Feeding her cygnets in the silver tide
(Scacchis, the loveliest Seriad of the place),
And as she stray'd, took her to his embrace.
Then, to reward her for her virtue lost,
Gave her the men and chequer'd board, emboss'd
With gold and silver curiously inlay'd ;
And taught her how the game was to be play'd.
Ev'n now 'tis honour'd with her happy name ;
And Rome and all the world admire the game.
All which the Seriads told me heretofore,
When my boy-notes amus'd the Serian shore.

THE GOOD-NATUR'D MAN:

A COMEDY

[*The Good-Natur'd Man* was produced on Friday, the 29th January, 1768. It was played for ten nights in succession, the fifth representation being "commanded by Their Majesties." On the 5th February it was published in *octavo* by W. Griffin of Catherine-Street, Strand, with the following title :— *The Good-Natur'd Man : A Comedy. As Performed at the Theatre-Royal in Covent Garden. By Mr. Goldsmith.* The price was one shilling and sixpence. The present reprint is from the fifth edition, which appeared in the same year as the first.]

PREFACE

WHEN I undertook to write a comedy, I confess I was strongly prepossessed in favour of the poets of the last age, and strove to imitate them. The term, *genteel comedy*, was then unknown amongst us, and little more was desired by an audience, than nature and humour, in whatever walks of life they were most conspicuous. The author of the following scenes never imagined that more would be expected of him, and therefore to delineate character has been his principal aim. Those who know anything of composition, are sensible that in pursuing humour, it will sometimes lead us into the recesses of the mean; I was even tempted to look for it in the master of a spunging-house: but in deference to the public taste, grown of late, perhaps, too delicate, the scene of the bailiffs was retrenched in the representation.[1] In deference also to the judgment of a few friends, who think in a particular way, the scene is here restored. The author submits it to the reader in his closet; and hopes that too much refinement will not banish humour and character from ours, as it has already done from the French theatre. Indeed the French comedy is now become so very elevated and sentimental, that it has not only banished humour and *Molière* from the stage, but it has banished all spectators too.

Upon the whole, the author returns his thanks to the public for the favourable reception which the "Good-Natur'd Man" has met with: and to Mr. Colman in particular, for his kindness to it.[2] It may not also be improper to assure any, who shall hereafter write for the theatre, that merit, or supposed merit, will ever be a sufficient passport to his protection.

[1 *Vide* Act iii. pp. 165–171.]
[2 This was the gratitude of success. Colman had not been particularly kind to *The Good-Natur'd Man*.]

PREFACE

When I undertook to write a comedy, I confess I was
supposedly prepossessed in favour of the . . . of the heroine, and shove to polish them. The term, genteel
. . . , was then unknown amongst us, and little more
. . . desired by an audience . . . than nature and humour, in
whatever walks of life they were most conspicuous. The
author of the following scenes never imagined that more
would be expected of him, and therefore to delineate
character has been his principal aim. Those who know
anything of composition, are sensible that, in pursuing
humour, it will sometimes lead us into the recesses of
the mean; I was even tempted to look for it in the
masses of a springing nature: but in deference to the
public taste, grown of late, perhaps, too delicate, the
scene of the beggar was retrenched in the representation.
In deference also to the judgment of a few friends, who
think in a particular way, the scene is here restored. The
author submits it to the reader in his closet; and hopes
that, too much refinement will not banish humour and
character from ours, as it has already done from the
French theatre. Indeed the French comedy is now
become so very elevated and sentimental, that it has not
only banished humour and Molière from the stage, but it
has banished all spectators too.

Upon the whole, the author returns his thanks to the
public for the favourable reception which the "Good
Natur'd Man" has met with: and to Mr. Colman in
particular, for his kindness to it.[1] It may not also be
improper to assure any, who shall hereafter write for the
theatre, that merit, or supposed merit, will ever be a
sufficient passport to his protection.

[1] First Act iii. pp. 185-191.]

[2 This was the gratitude of success. Colman had not been
particularly kind to The Good Natur'd Man.]

PROLOGUE

WRITTEN BY DR. JOHNSON

SPOKEN BY MR. BENSLEY

PREST by the load of life, the weary mind
Surveys the general toil of human kind;
With cool submission joins the labouring train,
And social sorrow loses half its pain:
Our anxious Bard,[1] without complaint, may share
This bustling season's epidemic care,
Like Cæsar's pilot, dignified by fate,
Tost in one common storm with all the great;
Distrest alike, the statesman and the wit,
When one a Borough courts, and one the Pit.
The busy candidates for power and fame,
Have hopes, and fears, and wishes, just the same;
Disabled both to combat, or to fly,
Must hear all taunts, and hear without reply.
Uncheck'd on both, loud rabbles vent their rage,
As mongrels bay the lion in a cage.
Th' offended burgess hoards his angry tale,
For that blest year when all that vote may rail;
Their schemes of spite the poet's foes dismiss,
Till that glad night, when all that hate may hiss.
This day the powder'd curls and golden coat,
Says swelling Crispin, begg'd a cobbler's vote.
This night, our wit, the pert apprentice cries,
Lies at my feet, I hiss him, and he dies.

[1 This Prologue, as spoken, and as published in the *Public Advertiser* for February, 3, 1768, differs somewhat from the version here printed. In particular "Our anxious Bard" was originally "Our *little* Bard"—an epithet which could scarcely have gratified the sensitive author of the Play.]

The great, 'tis true, can charm th' electing tribe;
The bard may supplicate, but cannot bribe.
Yet judg'd by those, whose voices ne'er were sold,
He feels no want of ill-persuading gold;
But, confident of praise, if praise be due,
Trusts without fear, to merit, and to you.

DRAMATIS PERSONÆ[1]

MEN

Mr. Honeywood,	Mr. Powell.
Croaker,	Mr. Shuter.
Lofty,	Mr. Woodward.
Sir William Honeywood,	Mr. Clarke.
Leontine,	Mr. Bensley.
Jarvis,	Mr. Dunstall.
Butler,	Mr. Cushing.
Bailiff,	Mr. R. Smith.
Dubardieu,	Mr. Holton.
Postboy,	Mr. Quick.

WOMEN

Miss Richland,	Mrs. Bulkley.
Olivia,	Mrs. Mattocks.
Mrs. Croaker,	Mrs. Pitt.
Garnet,	Mrs. Green.
Landlady,	Mrs. White.

Scene—LONDON

[1 The cast given is that of the piece as first acted.]

455

THE GOOD-NATUR'D MAN[1]

ACT THE FIRST

SCENE—*An Apartment in* YOUNG HONEYWOOD'S *House*

Enter SIR WILLIAM HONEYWOOD, JARVIS

Sir Will. Good Jarvis, make no apologies for this honest bluntness. Fidelity, like yours, is the best excuse for every freedom.

Jarvis. I can't help being blunt, and being very angry too, when I hear you talk of disinheriting so good, so worthy a young gentleman as your nephew, my master. All the world loves him.

Sir Will. Say rather, that he loves all the world ; that is his fault.

Jarvis. I'm sure there is no part of it more dear to him than you are, though he has not seen you since he was a child.

Sir Will. What signifies his affection to me, or how can I be proud of a place in a heart where every sharper and coxcomb find an easy entrance ?

Jarvis. I grant you that he's rather too good-natured ; that he's too much every man's man ; that he laughs this minute with one, and cries the next with another ; but whose instructions may he thank for all this ?

Sir Will. Not mine, sure ? My letters to him during my employment in Italy, taught him only that philosophy which might prevent, not defend his errors.

Jarvis. Faith, begging your honour's pardon, I'm sorry they taught him any philosophy at all ; it has only served to spoil him. This same philosophy is a good horse in the stable, but an arrant jade on a journey. For my own

[1 A personage known as "The good-natured man" is described at p. 85 of Goldsmith's *Life of Richard Nash, of Bath, Esq.*, 1762, and may have suggested this title.]

part, whenever I hear him mention the name on't, I'm always sure he's going to play the fool.

Sir Will. Don't let us ascribe his faults to his philosophy, I entreat you. No, Jarvis, his good nature arises rather from his fears of offending the importunate, than his desire of making the deserving happy.

Jarvis. What it rises from, I don't know. But, to be sure, everybody has it, that asks it.

Sir Will. Ay, or that does not ask it. I have been now for some time a concealed spectator of his follies, and find them as boundless as his dissipation.

Jarvis. And yet, faith, he has some fine name or other for them all. He calls his extravagance, generosity; and his trusting everybody, universal benevolence. It was but last week he went security for a fellow whose face he scarce knew, and that he called an act of exalted mu—mu—munificence; ay, that was the name he gave it.

Sir Will. And upon that I proceed, as my last effort, though with very little hopes to reclaim him. That very fellow has just absconded, and I have taken up the security. Now, my intention is to involve him in fictitious distress, before he has plunged himself into real calamity. To arrest him for that very debt, to clap an officer upon him, and then let him see which of his friends will come to his relief.

Jarvis. Well, if I could but any way see him thoroughly vexed, every groan of his would be music to me; yet, faith, I believe it impossible. I have tried to fret him myself every morning these three years; but instead of being angry, he sits as calmly to hear me scold, as he does to his hairdresser.

Sir Will. We must try him once more, however, and I'll go this instant to put my scheme into execution; and I don't despair of succeeding, as, by your means, I can have frequent opportunities of being about him, without being known. What a pity it is, Jarvis, that any man's good-will to others should produce so much neglect of himself, as to require correction. Yet, we must touch his weaknesses with a delicate hand. There are some faults so nearly allied to excellence, that we can scarce weed out the vice without eradicating the virtue.   [*Exit.*

Jarvis. Well, go thy ways, Sir William Honeywood. It is not without reason that the world allows thee to be the best of men.   But here comes his hopeful nephew; the strange good-natur'd, foolish, open-hearted—And yet, all his faults were such that one loves him still the better for them.

Enter HONEYWOOD

Honeyw. Well, Jarvis, what messages from my friends this morning?

Jarvis. You have no friends.

Honeyw. Well; from my acquaintance then?

Jarvis. (*Pulling out bills.*) A few of our usual cards of compliment, that's all.   This bill from your tailor; this from your mercer; and this from the little broker in Crooked-lane.[1]   He says he has been at a great deal of trouble to get back the money you borrowed.

Honeyw. That I don't know; but I'm sure we were at a great deal of trouble in getting him to lend it.

Jarvis. He has lost all patience.

Honeyw. Then he has lost a very good thing.

Jarvis. There's that ten guineas you were sending to the poor gentleman and his children in the Fleet.   I believe that would stop his mouth, for a while at least.

Honeyw. Ay, Jarvis, but what will fill their mouths in the mean time?   Must I be cruel because he happens to be importunate; and, to relieve his avarice, leave them to insupportable distress?

Jarvis. 'Sdeath! Sir, the question now is how to relieve yourself.   Yourself—Haven't I reason to be out of my senses, when I see things going on at sixes and sevens?

Honeyw. Whatever reason you may have for being out of your senses, I hope you'll allow that I'm not quite unreasonable for continuing in mine.

[1 Perhaps, but not necessarily, Crooked-lane, Cannon Street, City.]

Jarvis. You're the only man alive in your present situation that could do so—Everything upon the waste. There's Miss Richland and her fine fortune gone already, and upon the point of being given to your rival.

Honeyw. I'm no man's rival.

Jarvis. Your uncle in Italy preparing to disinherit you ; your own fortune almost spent ; and nothing but pressing creditors, false friends, and a pack of drunken servants that your kindness has made unfit for any other family.

Honeyw. Then they have the more occasion for being in mine.

Jarvis. Soh ! What will you have done with him that I caught stealing your plate in the pantry ?   In the fact ; I caught him in the fact.

Honeyw. In the fact ! If so, I really think that we should pay him his wages, and turn him off.

Jarvis. He shall be turn'd off at Tyburn, the dog ; we'll hang him, if it only be to frighten the rest of the family.

Honeyw. No, Jarvis : it's enough that we have lost what he has stolen, let us not add to it the loss of a fellow-creature !

Jarvis. Very fine ; well, here was the footman just now, to complain of the butler ; he says he does most work, and ought to have most wages..

Honeyw. That's but just ; though perhaps, here comes the butler to complain of the footman.

Jarvis. Ay, it's the way with them all, from the scullion to the privy-counsellor.   If they have a bad master, they keep quarrelling with him ; if they have a good master, they keep quarrelling with one another.

Enter BUTLER, *drunk*

Butler. Sir, I'll not stay in the family with Jonathan ; you must part with him, or part with me, that's the ex-ex-exposition of the matter, sir.

Honeyw. Full and explicit enough. But what's his fault, good Philip ?

Butler. Sir, he's given to drinking, sir, and I shall have my morals corrupted, by keeping such company.

Honeyw. Ha! Ha! He has such a diverting way—

Jarvis. O quite amusing!

Butler. I find my wines a-going, sir; and liquors don't go without mouths, sir; I hate a drunkard, sir!

Honeyw. Well, well, Philip, I'll hear you upon that another time, so go to bed now.

Jarvis. To bed! Let him go to the devil!

Butler. Begging your honour's pardon, and begging your pardon, master Jarvis, I'll not go to bed, nor to the devil neither. I have enough to do to mind my cellar. I forgot, your honour, Mr. Croaker is below. I came on purpose to tell you.

Honeyw. Why didn't you show him up, blockhead?

Butler. Show him up, sir? With all my heart, sir. Up or down, all's one to me. [*Exit.*

Jarvis. Ay, we have one or other of that family in this house from morning till night. He comes on the old affair, I suppose. The match between his son, that's just returned from Paris, and Miss Richland, the young lady he's guardian to.

Honeyw. Perhaps so. Mr. Croaker, knowing my friendship for the young lady, has got it into his head that I can persuade her to what I please.

Jarvis. Ah! If you loved yourself but half as well as she loves you, we should soon see a marriage that would set all things to rights again.

Honeyw. Love me! Sure, Jarvis, you dream. No, no; her intimacy with me never amounted to more than friendship—mere friendship. That she is the most lovely woman that ever warmed the human heart with desire, I own. But never let me harbour a thought of making her unhappy, by a connection with one so unworthy her merits as I am. No, Jarvis, it shall be my study to serve her, even in spite of my wishes; and to secure her happiness, though it destroys my own.

Jarvis. Was ever the like! I want patience.

Honeyw. Besides, Jarvis, though I could obtain Miss Richland's consent, do you think I could succeed with her guardian, or Mrs. Croaker his wife; who, though both very fine in their way, are yet a little opposite in their dispositions, you know.

Jarvis. Opposite enough, Heaven knows; the very reverse of each other; she all laugh and no joke; he always complaining, and never sorrowful; a fretful poor soul that has a new distress for every hour in the four-and-twenty—

Honeyw. Hush, hush, he's coming up, he'll hear you.

Jarvis. One whose voice is a passing bell—

Honeyw. Well, well, go, do.

Jarvis. A raven that bodes nothing but mischief; a coffin and cross bones; a bundle of rue; a sprig of deadly night shade; a—(*Honeywood stopping his mouth at last, pushes him off.*)   [*Exit* Jarvis.

Honeyw. I must own my old monitor is not entirely wrong. There is something in my friend Croaker's conversation that quite depresses me. His very mirth is an antidote to all gaiety, and his appearance has a stronger effect on my spirits than an undertaker's shop. —Mr. Croaker, this is such a satisfaction—

Enter CROAKER [1]

Croaker. A pleasant morning to Mr. Honeywood, and many of them. How is this! You look most shockingly to-day, my dear friend. I hope this weather does not affect your spirits. To be sure, if this weather continues—I say nothing—But God send we be all better this day three months.

Honeyw. I heartily concur in the wish, though I own not in your apprehensions.

Croaker. May be not! Indeed what signifies what weather we have in a country going to ruin like ours? Taxes rising and trade falling. Money flying out of the kingdom and Jesuits swarming into it. I know at this time no less than a hundred and twenty-seven Jesuits between Charing-cross and Temple-bar.

[1 The character of Croaker is admitted to have been based on Johnson's " Suspirius," *Rambler*, No. 59.]

Honeyw. The Jesuits will scarce pervert you or me, I should hope.

Croaker. May be not. Indeed what signifies whom they pervert in a country that has scarce any religion to lose? I'm only afraid for our wives and daughters.

Honeyw. I have no apprehensions for the ladies, I assure you.

Croaker. May be not. Indeed what signifies whether they be perverted or no? The women in my time were good for something. I have seen a lady dressed from top to toe in her own manufactures formerly. But now-a-days, the devil a thing of their own manufactures about them, except their faces.

Honeyw. But, however these faults may be practised abroad, you don't find them at home, either with Mrs. Croaker, Olivia or Miss Richland.

Croaker. The best of them will never be canoniz'd for a saint when she's dead. By the bye, my dear friend, I don't find this match between Miss Richland and my son much relish'd, either by one side or t'other.

Honeyw. I thought otherwise.

Croaker. Ah, Mr. Honeywood, a little of your fine serious advice to the young lady might go far: I know she has a very exalted opinion of your understanding.

Honeyw. But would not that be usurping an authority that more properly belongs to yourself?

Croaker. My dear friend, you know but little of my authority at home. People think, indeed, because they see me come out in a morning thus, with a pleasant face, and to make my friends merry, that all's well within. But I have cares that would break a heart of stone. My wife has so encroach'd upon every one of my privileges, that I'm now no more than a mere lodger in my own house!

Honeyw. But a little spirit exerted on your side might perhaps restore your authority.

Croaker. No, though I had the spirit of a lion! I do rouse sometimes. But what then! Always haggling and haggling. A man is tired of getting the better before his wife is tired of losing the victory.

Honeyw. It's a melancholy consideration indeed, that our chief comforts often produce our greatest anxieties, and that an increase of our possessions is but an inlet to new disquietudes.

Croaker. Ah, my dear friend, these were the very words of poor Dick Doleful to me not a week before he made away with himself. Indeed, Mr. Honeywood, I never see you but you put me in mind of poor—Dick. Ah, there was merit neglected for you ! and so true a friend ! we lov'd each other for thirty years, and yet he never asked me to lend him a single farthing !

Honeyw. Pray what could induce him to commit so rash an action at last ?

Croaker. I don't know, some people were malicious enough to say it was keeping company with me ; because we used to meet now and then and open our hearts to each other. To be sure I lov'd to hear him talk, and he lov'd to hear me talk ; poor dear Dick. He used to say that Croaker rhymed to joker ; and so we used to laugh —Poor Dick. (*Going to cry.*)

Honeyw. His fate affects me.

Croaker. Ay, he grew sick of this miserable life, where we do nothing but eat and grow hungry, dress and undress, get up and lie down ; while reason, that should watch like a nurse by our side, falls as fast asleep as we do.

Honeyw. To say truth, if we compare that part of life which is to come, by that which we have past, the prospect is hideous.

Croaker. Life at the greatest and best is but a froward child, that must be humour'd and coax'd a little till it falls asleep, and then all the care is over.[1]

Honeyw. Very true, sir, nothing can exceed the vanity of our existence, but the folly of our pursuits. We wept when we came into the world, and every day tells us why.

[1 An unacknowledged quotation from Sir William Temple's essay on Poetry (*Works*, 1720, i. 249). Goldsmith had already used it in the *Enquiry into the Present State of Polite Learning*, 1759, p. 196.]

Croaker. Ah, my dear friend, it is a perfect satisfaction to be miserable with you. My son Leontine shan't lose the benefit of such fine conversation. I'll just step home for him. I am willing to shew him so much seriousness in one scarce older than himself—And what if I bring my last letter to the Gazetteer on the increase and progress of earthquakes? It will amuse us, I promise you. I there prove how the late earthquake is coming round to pay us another visit from London to Lisbon, from Lisbon to the Canary Islands, from the Canary Islands to Palmyra, from Palmyra to Constantinople, and so from Constantinople back to London again.   [*Exit.*

Honeyw. Poor Croaker! His situation deserves the utmost pity. I shall scarce recover my spirits these three days. Sure, to live upon such terms is worse than death itself. And yet, when I consider my own situation, a broken fortune, a hopeless passion, friends in distress; the wish but not the power to serve them—(*pausing and sighing.*)

Enter BUTLER

Butler. More company below, sir; Mrs. Croaker and Miss Richland; shall I show them up? But they're showing up themselves.   [*Exit.*

Enter Mrs. CROAKER and Miss RICHLAND

Miss Rich. You're always in such spirits.

Mrs. Croaker. We have just come, my dear Honeywood, from the auction. There was the old deaf dowager, as usual, bidding like a fury against herself. And then so curious in antiques! Herself the most genuine piece of antiquity in the whole collection!

Honeyw. Excuse me, ladies, if some uneasiness from friendship makes me unfit to share in this good humour: I know you'll pardon me.

Mrs. Croaker. I vow he seems as melancholy as if he had taken a dose of my husband this morning. Well, if Richland here can pardon you, I must.

Miss Rich. You would seem to insinuate, madam, that I have particular reasons for being dispos'd to refuse it.

Mrs. Croaker. Whatever I insinuate, my dear, don't be so ready to wish an explanation.

Miss Rich. I own I should be sorry Mr. Honeywood's long friendship and mine should be misunderstood.

Honeyw. There's no answering for others, madam. But I hope you'll never find me presuming to offer more than the most delicate friendship may readily allow.

Miss Rich. And I shall be prouder of such a tribute from you than the most passionate professions from others.

Honeyw. My own sentiments, madam : friendship is a disinterested commerce between equals ; love, an abject intercourse between tyrants and slaves.

Miss Rich. And without a compliment, I know none more disinterested or more capable of friendship than Mr. Honeywood.

Mrs. Croaker. And indeed I know nobody that has more friends, at least among the ladies. Miss Fruzz, Miss Oddbody and Miss Winterbottom, praise him in all companies. As for Miss Biddy Bundle, she's his professed admirer.

Miss Rich. Indeed ! an admirer ! I did not know, sir, you were such a favourite there. But is she seriously so handsome ? Is she the mighty thing talk'd of ?

Honeyw. The town, madam, seldom begins to praise a lady's beauty, till she's beginning to lose it ! (*Smiling.*)

Mrs. Croaker. But she's resolved never to lose it, it seems. For as her natural face decays, her skill improves in making the artificial one. Well, nothing diverts me more than one of those fine old dressy things, who thinks to conceal her age, by everywhere exposing her person ; sticking herself up in the front of a side-box ;[1] trailing through a minuet at Almack's ; and then, in the public gardens ; looking for all the world like one of the painted ruins of the place.[2]

[1 In Pope's time the gentlemen sat in the *side*-boxes, and it was from the front row of a *side*-box that, according to Cumberland (*Memoirs*, 1807, i. 368), Johnson and his friends witnessed the first representation of *She Stoops to Conquer*.]

[2 *E.g.* the Ruins of Palmyra (popularized by Wood's book), and other painted scenes in the walks at old Vauxhall Gardens.]

Honeyw. Every age has its admirers, ladies. While you, perhaps, are trading among the warmer climates of youth, there ought to be some to carry on a useful commerce in the frozen latitudes beyond fifty.

Miss Rich. But then the mortifications they must suffer before they can be fitted out for traffic. I have seen one of them fret a whole morning at her hair-dresser, when all the fault was her face.

Honeyw. And yet I'll engage has carried that face at last to a very good market. This good-natur'd town, madam, has husbands, like spectacles, to fit every age, from fifteen to fourscore.

Mrs. Croaker. Well, you're a dear good-natur'd creature. But you know you're engaged with us this morning upon a strolling party. I want to shew Olivia the town, and the things; I believe I shall have business for you for the whole day.

Honeyw. I am sorry, madam, I have an appointment with Mr. Croaker, which it is impossible to put off.

Mrs. Croaker. What! with my husband! Then I'm resolved to take no refusal. Nay, I protest you must. You know I never laugh so much as with you.

Honeyw. Why, if I must, I must. I'll swear you have put me into such spirits. Well, do you find jest, and I'll find laugh, I promise you. We'll wait for the chariot in the next room. [*Exeunt.*

Enter LEONTINE and OLIVIA

Leont. There they go, thoughtless and happy. My dearest Olivia, what would I give to see you capable of sharing in their amusements, and as cheerful as they are.

Olivia. How, my Leontine, how can I be cheerful, when I have so many terrors to oppress me? The fear of being detected by this family, and the apprehensions of a censuring world, when I must be detected—

Leont. The world! my love, what can it say? At worst it can only say that, being compelled by a mercenary guardian to embrace a life you disliked, you formed a resolution of flying with the man of your choice; that you confided in his honour, and took refuge in my father's house; the only one where your's could remain without censure.

Olivia. But consider, Leontine, your disobedience and my indiscretion: your being sent to France to bring home a sister; and, instead of a sister, bringing home—

Leont. One dearer than a thousand sisters. One that I am convinc'd will be equally dear to the rest of the family, when she comes to be known.

Olivia. And that, I fear, will shortly be.

Leont. Impossible, till we ourselves think proper to make the discovery. My sister, you know, has been with her aunt, at Lyons, since she was a child, and you find every creature in the family takes you for her.

Olivia. But mayn't she write, mayn't her aunt write?

Leont. Her aunt scarce ever writes, and all my sister's letters are directed to me.

Olivia. But won't your refusing Miss Richland, for whom you know the old gentleman intends you, create a suspicion?

Leont. There, there's my master-stroke. I have resolved not to refuse her; nay, an hour hence I have consented to go with my father, to make her an offer of my heart and fortune.

Olivia. Your heart and fortune!

Leont. Don't be alarmed, my dearest. Can Olivia think so meanly of my honour, or my love, as to suppose I could ever hope for happiness from any but her? No, my Olivia, neither the force, nor, permit me to add, the delicacy of my passion, leave any room to suspect me. I only offer Miss Richland a heart I am convinced she will refuse; as I am confidant that, without knowing it, her affections are fixed upon Mr. Honeywood.

Olivia. Mr. Honeywood! You'll excuse my apprehensions; but when your merits come to be put in the balance—

Leont. You view them with too much partiality. However, by making this offer, I show a seeming compliance with my father's commands; and perhaps, upon her refusal, I may have his consent to choose for myself.

Olivia. Well, I submit. And yet, my Leontine, I own, I shall envy her even your pretended addresses. I consider every look, every expression of your esteem, as due only to me. This is folly, perhaps: I allow it; but it is natural to suppose, that merit which has made an impression on one's own heart, may be powerful over that of another.

Leont. Don't, my life's treasure, don't let us make imaginary evils, when you know we have so many real ones to encounter. At worst, you know, if Miss Richland should consent, or my father refuse his pardon, it can but end in a trip to Scotland; and———

Enter CROAKER

Croaker. Where have you been, boy? I have been seeking you. My friend Honeywood here, has been saying such comfortable things. Ah! he's an example indeed. Where is he? I left him here.

Leont. Sir, I believe you may see him, and hear him, too, in the next room: he's preparing to go out with the ladies.

Croaker. Good gracious, can I believe my eyes or my ears! I'm struck dumb with his vivacity, and stunn'd with the loudness of his laugh. Was there ever such a transformation! (*A laugh behind the scenes, Croaker mimics it.*) Ha! ha! ha! there it goes: a plague take their balderdash; yet I could expect nothing less, when my precious wife was of the party. On my conscience, I believe she could spread a horse-laugh through the pews of a tabernacle.

Leont. Since you find so many objections to a wife, sir, how can you be so earnest in recommending one to me?

Croaker. I have told you, and tell you again, boy, that Miss Richland's fortune must not go out of the family; one may find comfort in the money, whatever one does in the wife.

Leont. But, sir, though, in obedience to your desire, I

am ready to marry her, it may be possible she has no inclination to me.

Croaker. I'll tell you once for all how it stands. A good part of Miss Richland's large fortune consists in a claim upon government, which my good friend Mr. Lofty, assures me the Treasury will allow. One half of this she is to forfeit, by her father's will, in case she refuses to marry you. So, if she rejects you, we seize half her fortune; if she accepts you, we seize the whole, and a fine girl into the bargain.

Leont. But, sir, if you will but listen to reason—

Croaker. Come, then, produce your reasons. I tell you I'm fixed, determined, so now produce your reasons. When I'm determined, I always listen to reason, because it can then do no harm.

Leont. You have alleged that a mutual choice was the first requisite in matrimonial happiness.

Croaker. Well, and you have both of you a mutual choice. She has her choice—to marry you, or lose half her fortune; and you have your choice—to marry her, or pack out of doors without any fortune at all.

Leont. An only son, sir, might expect more indulgence.

Croaker. An only father, sir, might expect more obedience; besides, has not your sister here, that never disobliged me in her life, as good a right as you? He's a sad dog, Livy, my dear, and would take all from you. But he shan't, I tell you he shan't, for you shall have your share.

Olivia. Dear sir, I wish you'd be convinced that I can never be happy in any addition to my fortune, which is taken from his.

Croaker. Well, well, it's a good child, so say no more, but come with me, and we shall see something that will give us a great deal of pleasure, I promise you; old Ruggins, the curry-comb-maker, lying in state;[1] I'm told he makes a very handsome corpse, and becomes his

[1 Lying in state for several days, with a "fitting environment" of wax candles and velvet hangings, was a common practice in the last century, even among merchants and tradesmen. Cf. *The Citizen of the World*, 1762, i. 39.]

coffin prodigiously.   He was an intimate friend of mine, and these are friendly things we ought to do for each other.   [*Exeunt.*

END OF THE FIRST ACT

ACT THE SECOND

SCENE—*Croaker's House*

Miss RICHLAND, GARNET

Miss Rich. Olivia not his sister? Olivia not Leontine's sister? You amaze me!

Gar. No more his sister than I am; I had it all from his own servant; I can get anything from that quarter.

Miss Rich. But how? Tell me again, Garnet.

Gar. Why, madam, as I told you before, instead of going to Lyons to bring home his sister, who has been there with her aunt these ten years, he never went further than Paris; there he saw and fell in love with this young lady; by the bye, of a prodigious family.

Miss Rich. And brought her home to my guardian, as his daughter?

Gar. Yes, and daughter she will be.   If he don't consent to their marriage, they talk of trying what a Scotch parson can do.

Miss Rich. Well, I own they have deceived me—And so demurely as Olivia carried it, too!—Would you believe it, Garnet, I told her all my secrets; and yet the sly cheat concealed all this from me?

Gar. And, upon my word, madam, I don't much blame her; she was loath to trust one with her secrets, that was so very bad at keeping her own.

Miss Rich. But, to add to their deceit, the young gentleman, it seems, pretends to make me serious proposals.   My guardian and he are to be here presently, to open the affair in form.   You know I am to lose half my fortune if I refuse him.

Gar. Yet, what can you do?   For being, as you are, in love with Mr. Honeywood, madam—

Miss Rich. How! idiot! what do you mean?   In love with Mr. Honeywood!   Is this to provoke me?

Gar. That is, madam, in friendship with him; I meant nothing more than friendship, as I hope to be married; nothing more.

Miss Rich. Well, no more of this!   As to my guardian, and his son, they shall find me prepared to receive them; I'm resolved to accept their proposal with seeming pleasure, to mortify them by compliance, and so throw the refusal at last upon them.

Gar. Delicious! and that will secure your whole fortune to yourself.   Well, who could have thought so innocent a face could cover so much cuteness!

Miss Rich. Why, girl, I only oppose my prudence to their cunning, and practise a lesson they have taught me against themselves.

Gar. Then you're likely not long to want employment, for here they come, and in close conference!

Enter CROAKER, LEONTINE

Leont. Excuse me, sir, if I seem to hesitate upon the point of putting the lady so important a question.

Croaker. Lord! good sir, moderate your fears; you're so plaguy shy, that one would think you had changed sexes.   I tell you we must have the half or the whole. Come, let me see with what spirit you begin?   Well, why don't you?   Eh!   What?   Well then—I must, it seems—Miss Richland, my dear, I believe you guess at our business; an affair which my son here comes to open, that nearly concerns your happiness.

Miss Rich. Sir, I should be ungrateful not to be pleased with anything that comes recommended by you.

Croaker. How, boy, could you desire a finer opening? Why don't you begin, I say?   (*To Leont.*)

Leont. 'Tis true, madam, my father, madam, has some

intentions—hem—of explaining an affair—which—himself—can best explain, madam.

Croaker. Yes, my dear; it comes entirely from my son; it's all a request of his own, madam. And I will permit him to make the best of it.

Leont. The whole affair is only this, madam; my father has a proposal to make, which he insists none but himself shall deliver.

Croaker. My mind misgives me, the fellow will never be brought on. (*Aside.*)—In short, madam, you see before you one that loves you; one whose whole happiness is all in you.

Miss Rich. I never had any doubts of your regard, sir, and I hope you can have none of my duty.

Croaker. That's not the thing, my little sweeting, my love! No, no, another guess[1] lover than I; there he stands, madam; his very looks declare the force of his passion!—Call up a look, you dog—But then, had you seen him, as I have, weeping, speaking soliloquies and blank verse, sometimes melancholy, and sometimes absent—

Miss Rich. I fear, sir, he's absent now; or such a declaration would have come most properly from himself.

Croaker. Himself! madam! he would die before he could make such a confession; and if he had not a channel, for his passion through me, it would ere now have drowned his understanding.

Miss Rich. I must grant, sir, there are attractions in modest diffidence, above the force of words. A silent address is the genuine eloquence of sincerity.

Croaker. Madam, he has forgot to speak any other language: silence is become his mother tongue.

Miss Rich. And it must be confessed, sir, it speaks very powerfully in his favour. And yet, I shall be thought too forward in making such a confession; shan't I, Mr. Leontine?

Leont. Confusion! my reserve will undo me. But, if modesty attracts her, impudence may disgust her. I'll

[1 Of another sort, fashion, guise.]

try. (*Aside.*)—Don't imagine from my silence, madam, that I want a due sense of the honour and happiness intended me. My father, madam, tells me your humble servant is not totally indifferent to you. He admires you; I adore you; and when we come together, upon my soul I believe we shall be the happiest couple in all St. James's!

Miss Rich. If I could flatter myself you thought as you speak, sir——

Leont. Doubt my sincerity, madam? By your dear self I swear. Ask the brave if they desire glory; ask cowards if they covet safety——

Croaker. Well, well, no more questions about it.

Leont. Ask the sick if they long for health, ask misers if they love money, ask——

Croaker. Ask a fool if he can talk nonsense! What's come over the boy? What signifies asking, when there's not a soul to give you an answer? If you would ask to the purpose, ask this lady's consent to make you happy.

Miss Rich. Why, indeed, sir, his uncommon ardour almost compels me, forces me, to comply. And yet I'm afraid he'll despise a conquest gained with too much ease; won't you, Mr. Leontine?

Leont. Confusion! (*Aside.*)—O, by no means, madam, by no means. And yet, madam, you talked of force. There is nothing I would avoid so much as compulsion in a thing of this kind. No, madam, I will still be generous, and leave you at liberty to refuse.

Croaker. But I tell you, sir, the lady is not at liberty. It's a match. You see she says nothing. Silence gives consent.

Leont. But, sir, she talked of force. Consider, sir, the cruelty of constraining her inclinations.

Croaker. But I say there's no cruelty. Don't you know, blockhead, that girls have always a roundabout way of saying yes before company? So get you both gone together into the next room, and hang him that interrupts the tender explanation. Get you gone, I say; I'll not hear a word.

Leont. But, sir, I must beg leave to insist——

Croaker. Get off, you puppy, or I'll beg leave to insist upon knocking you down. Stupid whelp! But I don't wonder, the boy takes entirely after his mother!

[*Exeunt Miss* RICH. *and* LEONT.

Enter Mrs. CROAKER

Mrs. Croaker. Mr. Croaker, I bring you something, my dear, that I believe will make you smile.

Croaker. I'll hold you a guinea of that, my dear.

Mrs. Croaker. A letter; and, as I knew the hand, I ventured to open it!

Croaker. And how can you expect your breaking open my letters should give me pleasure!

Mrs. Croaker. Poo, it's from your sister at Lyons, and contains good news: read it.

Croaker. What a Frenchified cover is here! That sister of mine has some good qualities, but I could never teach her to fold a letter.

Mrs. Croaker. Fold a fiddlestick! Read what it contains.

Croaker, (*reading.*)

DEAR NICK,

An English gentleman, of large fortune, has for some time made private, though honourable proposals to your daughter Olivia. They love each other tenderly, and I find she has consented, without letting any of the family know, to crown his addresses. As such good offers don't come every day, your own good sense, his large fortune, and family considerations, will induce you to forgive her.

Yours ever,

RACHEL CROAKER.

My daughter, Olivia, privately contracted to a man of large fortune! This is good news indeed! My heart never foretold me of this. And yet, how slily the little baggage has carried it since she came home. Not a word on't to the old ones for the world. Yet, I thought I saw something she wanted to conceal.

Mrs. Croaker. Well, if they have concealed their

amour, they shan't conceal their wedding ; that shall be public, I'm resolved.

Croaker. I tell thee, woman, the wedding is the most foolish part of the ceremony. I can never get this woman to think of the more serious part of nuptial engagement.

Mrs. Croaker. What, would you have me think of their funeral? But come, tell me, my dear, don't you owe more to me than you care to confess? Would you have ever been known to Mr. Lofty, who has undertaken Miss Richland's claim at the Treasury, but for me? Who was it first made him an acquaintance at Lady Shabbaroon's rout? Who got him to promise us his interest? Is not he a backstairs favourite, one that can do what he pleases with those that do what they please? Isn't he an acquaintance that all your groaning and lamentations could never have got us?

Croaker. He is a man of importance, I grant you. And yet, what amazes me is, that while he is giving away places to all the world, he can't get one for himself.

Mrs. Croaker. That perhaps may be owing to his nicety. Great men are not easily satisfied!

Enter FRENCH SERVANT

Servant. An expresse from Monsieur Lofty. He vil be vait upon your honours instammant. He be only giving four five instruction, read two tree memorial, call upon von ambassadeur! He vil be vid you in one tree minutes.

Mrs. Croaker. You see now, my dear. What an extensive department! Well, friend, let your master know, that we are extremely honoured by this honour. Was there anything ever in a higher style of breeding! All messages among the great are now done by express.

Croaker. To be sure, no man does little things with more solemnity, or claims more respect than he. But he's in the right on't. In our bad world, respect is given, where respect is claimed.

Mrs. Croaker. Never mind the world, my dear ; you were never in a pleasanter place in your life. Let us now think of receiving him with proper respect (*a loud rapping at the door*), and there he is, by the thundering rap.

Croaker. Ay, verily, there he is; as close upon the heels of his own express, as an endorsement upon the back of a bill. Well, I'll leave you to receive him, whilst I go to chide my little Olivia for intending to steal a marriage without mine or her aunt's consent. I must seem to be angry, or she, too, may begin to despise my authority.   [*Exit.*

Enter LOFTY,[1] *speaking to his servant*

Lofty. And if the Venetian Ambassador, or that teasing creature the Marquis, should call, I'm not at home. Dam'me, I'll be pack-horse to none of them! My dear madam, I have just snatched a moment—And if the expresses to his Grace be ready, let them be sent off; they're of importance. Madam, I ask a thousand pardons!

Mrs. Croaker. Sir, this honour——

Lofty. And, Dubardieu! If the person calls about the commission, let him know that it is made out. As for Lord Cumbercourt's stale request, it can keep cold: you understand me. Madam, I ask ten thousand pardons!

Mrs. Croaker. Sir, this honour——

Lofty. And, Dubardieu! If the man comes from the Cornish borough, you must do him; you must do him, I say! Madam I ask ten thousand pardons! And if the Russian—Ambassador calls: but he will scarce call to-day, I believe. And now, madam, I have just got time to express my happiness in having the honour of being permitted to profess myself your most obedient humble servant!

Mrs. Croaker. Sir, the happiness and honour are all mine; and yet, I'm only robbing the public while I detain you.

Lofty. Sink the public, madam, when the fair are to

[1 Lofty, in some respects, is a variation upon "Beau Tibbs" in *The Citizen of the World*.]

be attended. Ah, could all my hours be so charmingly devoted! Sincerely, don't you pity us poor creatures in affairs? Thus it is eternally; solicited for places here, teased for pensions there, and courted everywhere. I know you pity me. Yes, I see you do!

Mrs. Croaker. Excuse me, sir. Toils of empires pleasures are, as Waller says.

Lofty. Waller, Waller; is he of the House?

Mrs. Croaker. The modern poet of that name, sir.

Lofty. Oh, a modern! We men of business despise the moderns; and as for the ancients, we have no time to read them. Poetry is a pretty thing enough for our wives and daughters; but not for us. Why now, here I stand that know nothing of books. I say, madam, I know nothing of books; and yet, I believe, upon a land carriage fishery, a stamp act, or a jag-hire, I can talk my two hours without feeling the want of them!

Mrs. Croaker. The world is no stranger to Mr. Lofty's eminence in every capacity!

Lofty. I vow to Gad, madam, you make me blush. I'm nothing, nothing, nothing in the world; a mere obscure gentleman! To be sure, indeed, one or two of the present ministers are pleased to represent me as a formidable man. I know they are pleased to bespatter me at all their little dirty levées. Yet, upon my soul, I wonder what they see in me to treat me so! Measures, not men,[1] have always been my mark; and I vow, by all that's honourable, my resentment has never done the men, as mere men, any manner of harm—That is, as mere men.

Mrs. Croaker. What importance, and yet what modesty!

Lofty. Oh, if you talk of modesty, madam! There, I own, I'm accessible to praise: modesty is my foible: it was so the Duke of Brentford used to say of me. I love Jack Lofty, he used to say: no man has a finer knowledge of things; quite a man of information; and

[1 Goldsmith is generally credited with this sentiment; but from a sentence in Burke's *Thoughts on the Causes of the Present Discontents*, 1770, it would seem to have been a cant political phrase.]

when he speaks upon his legs, by the lord, he's prodigious, he scouts them ; and yet all men have their faults ; too much modesty is his, says his Grace.

Mrs. Croaker. And yet, I dare say, you don't want assurance when you come to solicit for your friends.

Lofty. O, there indeed I'm in bronze. A-propos, I have just been mentioning Miss Richland's case to a certain personage ; we must name no names. When I ask, I am not to be put off, madam ! No, no, I take my friend by the button. A fine girl, sir ; great justice in her case. A friend of mine. Borough interest. Business must be done, Mr. Secretary. I say, Mr. Secretary, her business must be done, sir. That's my way, madam !

Mrs. Croaker. Bless me ! you said all this to the Secretary of State, did you ?

Lofty. I did not say the Secretary, did I ? Well, curse it, since you have found me out, I will not deny it. It was to the Secretary !

Mrs. Croaker. This was going to the fountain-head at once, not applying to the understrappers, as Mr. Honeywood would have had us.

Lofty. Honeywood ! he ! he ! He was, indeed, a fine solicitor. I suppose you have heard what has just happened to him ?

Mrs. Croaker. Poor dear man ! no accident, I hope !

Lofty. Undone, madam, that's all. His creditors have taken him into custody. A prisoner in his own house !

Mrs. Croaker. A prisoner in his own house ! How ! At this very time ! I'm quite unhappy for him.

Lofty. Why, so am I ! The man, to be sure, was immensely good-natur'd. But then, I could never find that he had anything in him.

Mrs. Croaker. His manner, to be sure, was excessive harmless ; some, indeed, thought it a little dull. For my part, I always concealed my opinion.

Lofty. It can't be concealed, madam ; the man was dull, dull as the last new comedy![1] A poor impracticable

---

[1 The " last new comedy" was the *False Delicacy* of Goldsmith's Rival, Hugh Kelly, just produced at Drury Lane. But Goldsmith could scarcely have intended this "palpable hit."]

creature! I tried once or twice to know if he was fit for business; but he had scarce talents to be groom-porter to an orange barrow!

Mrs. Croaker. How differently does Miss Richland think of him! For, I believe, with all his faults, she loves him.

Lofty. Loves him! Does she? You should cure her of that, by all means. Let me see, what if she were sent to him this instant, in his present doleful situation? My life for it, that works her cure! Distress is a perfect antidote to love. Suppose we join her in the next room? Miss Richland is a fine girl, has a fine fortune, and must not be thrown away. Upon my honour, madam, I have a regard for Miss Richland; and, rather than she should be thrown away, I should think it no indignity to marry her myself! [*Exeunt.*

Enter Olivia *and* Leontine

Leont. And yet, trust me, Olivia, I had every reason to expect Miss Richland's refusal, as I did everything in my power to deserve it. Her indelicacy surprises me!

Olivia. Sure, Leontine, there's nothing so indelicate in being sensible of your merit. If so, I fear, I shall be the most guilty thing alive!

Leont. But you mistake, my dear. The same attention I used to advance my merit with you, I practised to lessen it with her. What more could I do?

Olivia. Let us now rather consider what's to be done. We have both dissembled too long—I have always been asham'd—I am now quite weary of it. Sure, I could never have undergone so much for any other but you.

Leont. And you shall find my gratitude equal to your kindest compliance. Though our friends should totally forsake us, Olivia, we can draw upon content for the deficiencies of fortune.

Olivia. Then why should we defer our scheme of humble happiness, when it is now in our power? I may be the favourite of your father, it is true; but can it ever be thought, that his present kindness to a supposed child, will continue to a known deceiver?

Leont. I have many reasons to believe it will. As his attachments are but few, they are lasting. His own marriage was a private one, as ours may be. Besides, I have sounded him already at a distance, and find all his answers exactly to our wish. Nay, by an expression or two that dropped from him, I am induced to think he knows of this affair.

Olivia. Indeed! But that would be an happiness too great to be expected.

Leont. However it be, I'm certain you have power over him; and am persuaded, if you informed him of our situation, that he would be disposed to pardon it.

Olivia. You had equal expectations, Leontine, from your last scheme with Miss Richland, which you find has succeeded most wretchedly.

Leont. And that's the best reason for trying another.

Olivia. If it must be so, I submit.

Leont. As we could wish, he comes this way. Now, my dearest Olivia, be resolute. I'll just retire within hearing, to come in at a proper time, either to share your danger, or confirm your victory. [*Exit.*

Enter CROAKER

Croaker. Yes, I must forgive her; and yet not too easily, neither. It will be proper to keep up the decorums of resentment a little, if it be only to impress her with an idea of my authority.

Olivia. How I tremble to approach him!—Might I presume, sir—if I interrupt you—

Croaker. No, child, where I have an affection, it is not a little thing can interrupt me. Affection gets over little things.

Olivia. Sir, you're too kind! I'm sensible how ill I deserve this partiality. Yet, Heaven knows, there is nothing I would not do to gain it.

Croaker. And you have but too well succeeded, you little hussy, you! With those endearing ways of yours, on my conscience, I could be brought to forgive anything, unless it were a very great offence indeed.

Olivia. But mine is such an offence—when you know my guilt—yes, you shall know it, though I feel the greatest pain in the confession.

Croaker. Why, then, if it be so very great a pain, you may spare yourself the trouble, for I know every syllable of the matter before you begin.

Olivia. Indeed! Then I'm undone!

Croaker. Ay, miss, you wanted to steal a match, without letting me know it, did you! But I'm not worth being consulted, I suppose, when there's to be a marriage in my own family! No, I'm to have no hand in the disposal of my own children! No, I'm nobody! I'm to be a mere article of family lumber; a piece of cracked china to be stuck up in a corner!

Olivia. Dear sir, nothing but the dread of your authority could induce us to conceal it from you.

Croaker. No, no, my consequence is no more; I'm as little minded as a dead Russian in winter, just stuck up with a pipe in his mouth till there comes a thaw—it goes to my heart to vex her.

Olivia. I was prepared, sir, for your anger, and despaired of pardon, even while I presumed to ask it. But your severity shall never abate my affection, as my punishment is but justice.

Croaker. And yet you should not despair neither, Livy. We ought to hope all for the best.

Olivia. And do you permit me to hope, sir! Can I ever expect to be forgiven? But hope has too long deceived me!

Croaker. Why then, child, it shan't deceive you now, for I forgive you this very moment. I forgive you all; and now you are indeed my daughter.

Olivia. O transport! This kindness overpowers me!

Croaker. I was always against severity to our children. We have been young and giddy ourselves, and we can't expect boys and girls to be old before their time.

Olivia. What generosity! But can you forget the many falsehoods, the dissimulation——

Croaker. You did indeed dissemble, you urchin, you; but where's the girl that won't dissemble for a husband!

My wife and I had never been married, if we had not dissembled a little beforehand!

Olivia. It shall be my future care never to put such generosity to a second trial. And as for the partner of my offence and folly, from his native honour, and the just sense he has of his duty, I can answer for him that——

Enter LEONTINE

Leont. Permit him thus to answer for himself. (*Kneeling.*) Thus, sir, let me speak my gratitude for this unmerited forgiveness. Yes, sir, this even exceeds all your former tenderness : I now can boast the most indulgent of fathers. The life, he gave, compared to this, was but a trifling blessing!

Croaker. And, good sir, who sent for you, with that fine tragedy face, and flourishing manner ? I don't know what we have to do with your gratitude upon this occasion !

Leont. How, sir ! is it possible to be silent when so much obliged ? Would you refuse me the pleasure of being grateful ? Of adding my thanks to my Olivia's ! Of sharing in the transports that you have thus occasioned ?

Croaker. Lord, sir, we can be happy enough, without your coming in to make up the party. I don't know what's the matter with the boy all this day ; he has got into such a rhodomontade manner all the morning !

Leont. But, sir, I that have so large a part in the benefit, is it not my duty to show my joy ? Is the being admitted to your favour so slight an obligation ? Is the happiness of marrying my Olivia so small a blessing ?

Croaker. Marrying Olivia ! marrying Olivia ! marrying his own sister ! Sure the boy is out of his senses. His own sister !

Leont. My sister !

Olivia. Sister ! How have I been mistaken ! (*aside.*)

Leont. Some cursed mistake in this I find. (*aside.*)

Croaker. What does the booby mean, or has he any meaning. Eh, what do you mean, you blockhead, you ?

Leont. Mean, sir—why, sir—only when my sister is to

be married, that I have the pleasure of marrying her, sir; that is, of giving her away, sir—I have made a point of it.

Croaker. O, is that all? Give her away. You have made a point of it. Then you had as good make a point of first giving away yourself, as I'm going to prepare the writings between you and Miss Richland this very minute. What a fuss is here about nothing! Why, what's the matter now? I thought I had made you at least as happy as you could wish.

Olivia. O! yes, sir, very happy.

Croaker. Do you foresee anything, child? You look as if you did. I think if anything was to be foreseen, I have as sharp a look out as another: and yet I foresee nothing.   [*Exit.*

Leontine, Olivia

Olivia. What can it mean?

Leont. He knows something, and yet for my life, I can't tell what.

Olivia. It can't be the connection between us, I'm pretty certain.

Leont. Whatever it be, my dearest, I'm resolved to put it out of fortune's power to repeat our mortification. I'll haste, and prepare for our journey to Scotland this very evening. My friend Honeywood has promised me his advice and assistance. I'll go to him, and repose our distresses on his friendly bosom: and I know so much of his honest heart, that if he can't relieve our uneasinesses, he will at least share them.   [*Exeunt.*

END OF THE SECOND ACT

ACT THE THIRD

SCENE— *Young Honeywood's House*

BAILIFF, HONEYWOOD, FOLLOWER

Bailiff. Looky, sir, I have arrested as good men as you in my time : no disparagement of you neither. Men that would go forty guineas on a game of cribbage. I challenge the town to shew a man in more genteeler practice than myself !

Honeyw. Without all question, Mr.——I forget your name, sir ?

Bailiff. How can you forget what you never knew ? he, he, he !

Honeyw. May I beg leave to ask your name ?

Bailiff. Yes, you may.

Honeyw. Then, pray, sir, what is your name, sir ?

Bailiff. That I didn't promise to tell you. He, he, he ! A joke breaks no bones, as we say among us that practise the law.

Honeyw. You may have reason for keeping it a secret, perhaps ?

Bailiff. The law does nothing without reason. I'm ashamed to tell my name to no man, sir. If you can shew cause, as why, upon a special capus, that I should prove my name—But, come, Timothy Twitch is my name. And, now you know my name, what have you to say to that ?

Honeyw. Nothing in the world, good Mr. Twitch, but that I have a favour to ask, that's all.

Bailiff. Ay, favours are more easily asked than granted, as we say among us that practise the law. I have taken an oath against granting favours. Would you have me perjure myself ?

Honeyw. But my request will come recommended in

so strong a manner, as I believe you'll have no scruple (*pulling out his purse*). The thing is only this : I believe I shall be able to discharge this trifle in two or three days at farthest ; but as I would not have the affair known for the world, I have thoughts of keeping you, and your good friend here, about me, till the debt is discharged ; for which I shall be properly grateful.[1]

Bailiff. Oh ! that's another maxum, and altogether within my oath. For certain, if an honest man is to get anything by a thing, there's no reason why all things should not be done in civility.

Honeyw. Doubtless, all trades must live, Mr. Twitch ; and yours is a necessary one.   [*Gives him money.*

Bailiff. Oh ! your honour ; I hope your honour takes nothing amiss as I does, as I does nothing but my duty in so doing. I'm sure no man can say I ever give a gentleman, that was a gentleman, ill usage. If I saw that a gentleman was a gentleman, I have taken money not to see him for ten weeks together.

Honeyw. Tenderness is a virtue, Mr. Twitch.

Bailiff. Ay, sir, it's a perfect treasure. I love to see a gentleman with a tender heart. I don't know, but I think I have a tender heart myself. If all that I have lost by my heart was put together, it would make a—but no matter for that.

Honeyw. Don't account it lost, Mr. Twitch. The ingratitude of the world can never deprive us of the conscious happiness of having acted with humanity ourselves.

Bailiff. Humanity, sir, is a jewel. It's better than gold. I love humanity. People may say that we in our way have no humanity ; but I'll show you my humanity this moment. There's my follower here, little Flanigan, with a wife and four children, a guinea or two would be more to him, than twice as much to another. Now, as I can't shew him any humanity myself, I must beg leave you'll do it for me.

[1 The elaboration of this expedient was perhaps suggested by an anecdote of Steele, who is said to have put his bailiffs into livery. See *Steele* (*English Worthies*), 1886, p. 222.]

Honeyw. I assure you, Mr. Twitch, yours is a most powerful recommendation.

[Giving money to the follower.

Bailiff. Sir, you're a gentleman. I see you know what to do with your money. But, to business : we are to be with you here as your friends, I suppose. But set in case company comes.—Little Flanigan here, to be sure, has a good face, a very good face : but then, he is a little seedy, as we say among us that practise the law. Not well in clothes. Smoke [1] the pocket holes.

Honeyw. Well, that shall be remedied without delay.

Enter SERVANT

Servant. Sir, Miss Richland is below.

Honeyw. How unlucky! Detain her a moment. We must improve, my good friend, little Mr. Flanigan's appearance first. Here, let Mr. Flanigan have a suit of my clothes—quick—the brown and silver—Do you hear?

Servant. That your honour gave away to the begging gentleman that makes verses, because it was as good as new.

Honeyw. The white and gold, then.

Servant. That, your honour, I made bold to sell, because it was good for nothing.

Honeyw. Well, the first that comes to hand, then. The blue and gold. I believe Mr. Flanigan will look best in blue.   *[Exit* FLANIGAN.

Bailiff. Rabbit me, but little Flanigan will look well in anything. Ah, if your honour knew that bit of flesh as well as I do, you'd be perfectly in love with him. There's not a prettier scout in the four counties after a shy-cock than he. Scents like a hound; sticks like a weazel. He was master of the ceremonies to the black queen of Morocco when I took him to follow me. *(Re-enter* FLANIGAN.) Heh, ecod, I think he looks so well, that I don't care if I have a suit from the same place for myself.

---

[1] Observe or take note of.   Nowadays Mr. Twitch would say "twig."]

Honeyw. Well, well, I hear the lady coming. Dear Mr. Twitch, I beg you'll give your friend directions not to speak. As for yourself, I know you will say nothing without being directed.

Bailiff. Never you fear me, I'll shew the lady that I have something to say for myself as well as another. One man has one way of talking, and another man has another, that's all the difference between them.

Enter Miss RICHLAND and her MAID

Miss Rich. You'll be surprised, sir, with this visit. But you know I'm yet to thank you for choosing my little library.

Honeyw. Thanks, madam, are unnecessary, as it was I that was obliged by your commands. Chairs here. Two of my very good friends, Mr. Twitch and Mr. Flanigan. Pray, gentlemen, sit without ceremony.

Miss Rich. (*aside.*) Who can these odd-looking men be? I fear it is as I was informed. It must be so.

Bailiff (*after a pause*). Pretty weather, very pretty weather for the time of the year, madam.

Follower. Very good circuit weather in the country.

Honeyw. You officers are generally favourites among the ladies. My friends, madam, have been upon very disagreeable duty, I assure you. The fair should, in some measure, recompense the toils of the brave.

Miss Rich. Our officers do indeed deserve every favour. The gentlemen are in the marine service, I presume, sir?

Honeyw. Why, madam, they do—occasionally serve in the Fleet, madam! A dangerous service!

Miss Rich. I'm told so. And I own, it has often surprised me, that, while we have had so many instances of bravery there, we have had so few of wit at home to praise it.

Honeyw. I grant, madam, that our poets have not written as our soldiers have fought; but they have done all they could, and Hawke or Amherst could do no more.

Miss Rich. I'm quite displeased when I see a fine subject spoiled by a dull writer.

Honeyw. We should not be so severe against dull writers, madam. It is ten to one, but the dullest writer exceeds the most rigid French critic who presumes to despise him.

Follower. Damn the French, the parle-vous, and all that belongs to them!

Miss Rich. Sir!

Honeyw. Ha, ha, ha, honest Mr. Flanigan! A true English officer, madam; he's not contented with beating the French, but he will scold them too.

Miss Rich. Yet, Mr. Honeywood, this does not convince me but that severity in criticism is necessary. It was our first adopting the severity of French taste that was brought them in turn to taste us.

Bailiff. Taste us! By the Lord, madam, they devour us! Give Monseers but a taste, and I'll be damned, but they come in for a bellyful!

Miss Rich. Very extraordinary, this!

Follower. But very true. What makes the bread rising: the parle-vous that devour us. What makes the mutton fivepence a pound: the parle-vous that eat it up. What makes the beer three pence half-penny a pot——

Honeyw. Ah! the vulgar rogues, all will be out! Right, gentlemen, very right, upon my word, and quite to the purpose. They draw a parallel, madam, between the mental taste, and that of our senses. We are injured as much by French severity in the one, as by French rapacity in the other. That's their meaning.

Miss Rich. Though I don't see the force of the parallel, yet, I'll own, that we should sometimes pardon books, as we do our friends, that have now and then agreeable absurdities to recommend them.

Bailiff. That's all my eye! The King only can pardon, as the law says; for set in case——

Honeyw. I am quite of your opinion, sir! I see the whole drift of your argument. Yes, certainly, our presuming to pardon any work, is arrogating a power that belongs to another. If all have power to condemn, what writer can be free?

Bailiff. By his habus corpus. His habus corpus can set him free at any time. For set in case——

Honeyw. I'm obliged to you, sir, for the hint. If, madam, as my friend observes, our laws are so careful of a gentleman's person, sure we ought to be equally careful of his dearer part, his fame.

Follower. Ay, but if so be a man's nabbed, you know——

Honeyw. Mr. Flanigan, if you spoke for ever, you could not improve the last observation. For my own part, I think it conclusive.

Bailiff. As for the matter of that, mayhap——

Honeyw. Nay, give me leave in this instance to be positive. For where is the necessity of censuring works without genius, which must shortly sink of themselves: what is it, but aiming our unnecessary blow against a victim already under the hands of justice?

Bailiff. Justice! Oh, by the elevens, if you talk about justice, I think I am at home there; for, in a course of law——

Honeyw. My dear Mr. Twitch, I discern what you'd be at perfectly, and I believe the lady must be sensible of the art with which it is introduced. I suppose you perceive the meaning, madam, of his course of law?

Miss Rich. I protest, sir, I do not. I perceive only that you answer one gentleman before he has finished, and the other before he has well begun!

Bailiff. Madam, you are a gentlewoman, and I will make the matter out. This here question is about severity and justice, and pardon, and the like of they. Now, to explain the thing——

Honeyw. (*aside.*) O! curse your explanations.

Enter Servant

Servant. Mr. Leontine, sir, below, desires to speak with you upon earnest business.

Honeyw. That's lucky (*Aside*).—Dear madam, you'll excuse me, and my good friends here, for a few minutes.

There are books, madam, to amuse you. Come, gentlemen, you know I make no ceremony with such friends. After you, sir. Excuse me. Well, if I must. But I know your natural politeness!

Bailiff. Before and behind, you know.

Follower. Aye, aye, before and behind, before and behind!

[*Exeunt* HONEYWOOD, BAILIFF, *and* FOLLOWER.

Miss Rich. What can all this mean, Garnet?

Gar. Mean, madam? why, what should it mean, but what Mr. Lofty sent you here to see? These people he calls officers, are officers sure enough: sheriff's officers; bailiffs, madam!

Miss Rich. Ay, it is certainly so. Well, though his perplexities are far from giving me pleasure, yet, I own, there's something very ridiculous in them, and a just punishment for his dissimulation.

Gar. And so they are. But I wonder, madam, that the lawyer you just employed to pay his debts, and set him free, has not done it by this time. He ought at least to have been here before now. But lawyers are always more ready to get a man into troubles, than out of them!

Enter SIR WILLIAM

Sir Will. For Miss Richland to undertake setting him free, I own, was quite unexpected. It has totally unhinged my schemes to reclaim him. Yet, it gives me pleasure to find, that, among a number of worthless friendships, he has made one acquisition of real value; for there must be some softer passion on her side that prompts this generosity. Ha! here before me: I'll endeavour to sound her affections. Madam, as I am the person that have had some demands upon the gentleman of this house, I hope you'll excuse me, if, before I enlarged him, I wanted to see yourself!

Miss Rich. The precaution was very unnecessary, sir! I suppose your wants were only such as my agent had power to satisfy.

Sir Will. Partly, madam. But I was also willing you

should be fully apprized of the character of the gentleman you intended to serve.

Miss Rich. It must come, sir, with a very ill grace from you. To censure it, after what you have done, would look like malice; and to speak favourably of a character you have oppressed, would be impeaching your own. And, sure, his tenderness, his humanity, his universal friendship, may atone for many faults!

Sir Will. That friendship, madam, which is exerted in too wide a sphere, becomes totally useless. Our bounty, like a drop of water, disappears when diffused too widely. They, who pretend most to this universal benevolence, are either deceivers, or dupes. Men who desire to cover their private ill-nature, by a pretended regard for all; or, men who, reasoning themselves into false feelings, are more earnest in pursuit of splendid, than of useful virtues.

Miss Rich. I am surprised, sir, to hear one who has probably been a gainer by the folly of others, so severe in his censure of it.

Sir Will. Whatever I may have gained by folly, madam, you see I am willing to prevent your losing by it.

Miss Rich. Your cares for me, sir, are unnecessary! I always suspect those services which are denied where they are wanted, and offered, perhaps in hopes of a refusal. No, sir, my directions have been given, and I insist upon their being complied with.

Sir Will. Thou amiable woman! I can no longer contain the expressions of my gratitude: my pleasure. You see before you, one who has been equally careful of his interest: one who has for some time been a concealed spectator of his follies, and only punished in hopes to reclaim them—His uncle!

Miss Rich. Sir William Honeywood! You amaze me. How shall I conceal my confusion? I fear, sir, you'll think I have been too forward in my services, I confess I——

Sir Will. Don't make any apologies, madam. I only find myself unable to repay the obligation. And yet, I have been trying my interest of late to serve you. Having learnt, madam, that you had some demands upon government, I have, though unasked, been your solicitor there.

Miss Rich. Sir, I'm infinitely obliged to your intentions. But my guardian has employed another gentleman who assures him of success.

Sir Will. Who, the important little man who visits here! Trust me, madam, he's quite contemptible among men in power, and utterly unable to serve you. Mr. Lofty's promises are much better known to people of fashion than his person, I assure you.

Miss Rich. How have we been deceived! As sure as can be, here he comes.

Sir Will. Does he? Remember I'm to continue unknown. My return to England has not as yet been made public. With what impudence he enters!

Enter LOFTY

Lofty. Let the chariot—let my chariot drive off, I'll visit to his Grace's in a chair. Miss Richland here before me! Punctual, as usual, to the calls of humanity. I'm very sorry, madam, things of this kind should happen, especially to a man I have shewn everywhere, and carried amongst us as a particular acquaintance.

Miss Rich. I find, sir, you have the art of making the misfortunes of others your own.

Lofty. My dear madam, what can a private man like me, do? One man can't do everything; and then, I do so much in this way every day: Let me see, something considerable might be done for him by subscription; it could not fail if I carried the list. I'll undertake to set down a brace of dukes, two dozen lords, and half the lower house, at my own peril!

Sir Will. And after all, it's more than probable, sir, he might reject the offer of such powerful patronage.

Lofty. Then, madam, what can we do? You know I never make promises. In truth, I once or twice tried to do something with him in the way of business; but, as I often told his uncle, Sir William Honeywood, the man was utterly impracticable.

Sir Will. His uncle! Then that gentleman, I suppose, is a particular friend of yours.

Lofty. Meaning me, sir?—Yes, madam, as I often said, my dear Sir William, you are sensible I would do anything as far as my poor interest goes, to serve your family; but what can be done? there's no procuring first-rate places for ninth-rate abilities.

Miss Rich. I have heard of Sir William Honeywood; he's abroad in employment; he confided in your judgment, I suppose.

Lofty. Why, yes, madam; I believe Sir William has some reason to confide in my judgment; one little reason, perhaps.

Miss Rich. Pray, sir, what was it?

Lofty. Why, madam—but let it go no further—it was I procured him his place.

Sir Will. Did you, sir?

Lofty. Either you or I, sir.

Miss Rich. This, Mr. Lofty, was very kind, indeed.

Lofty. I did love him, to be sure; he had some amusing qualities; no man was fitter to be toast-master to a club, or had a better head.

Miss Rich. A better head?

Lofty. Ay, at a bottle. To be sure, he was as dull as a choice spirit; but hang it, he was grateful, very grateful; and gratitude hides a multitude of faults!

Sir Will. He might have reason, perhaps. His place is pretty considerable, I'm told.

Lofty. A trifle, a mere trifle, among us men of business. The truth is, he wanted dignity to fill up a greater.

Sir Will. Dignity of person, do you mean, sir? I'm told he's much about my size and figure, sir.

Lofty. Ay, tall enough for a marching regiment; but then he wanted a something—a consequence of form—a kind of a—I believe the lady perceives my meaning.

Miss Rich. O perfectly! you courtiers can do anything, I see!

Lofty. My dear madam, all this is but a mere exchange; we do greater things for one another every day. Why, as thus, now: let me suppose you the first lord of the

Treasury, you have an employment in you that I want; I have a place in me that you want; do me here, do you there: interest of both sides, few words, flat, done and done, and it's over.

Sir Will. A thought strikes me. (*Aside.*)—Now you mention Sir William Honeywood, madam; and as he seems, sir, an acquaintance of yours; you'll be glad to hear he's arrived from Italy; I had it from a friend who knows him as well as he does me, and you may depend on my information.

Lofty. The devil he is!—If I had known that, we should not have been quite so well acquainted. (*Aside.*)

Sir Will. He is certainly returned; and as this gentleman is a friend of yours, he can be of signal service to us, by introducing me to him; there are some papers relative to your affairs, that require dispatch and his inspection.

Miss Rich. This gentleman, Mr. Lofty, is a person employed in my affairs: I know you'll serve us!

Lofty. My dear madam, I live but to serve you. Sir William shall even wait upon him, if you think proper to command it.

Sir Will. That would be quite unnecessary.

Lofty. Well, we must introduce you, then. Call upon me—let me see—ay, in two days.

Sir Will. Now, or the opportunity will be lost for ever.

Lofty. Well, if it must be now, now let it be. But, damn it, that's unfortunate; my lord Grig's cursed Pensacola business comes on this very hour, and I'm engaged to attend—another time——

Sir Will. A short letter to Sir William will do.

Lofty. You shall have it; yet, in my opinion, a letter is a very bad way of going to work; face to face, that's my way.

Sir Will. The letter, sir, will do quite as well.

Lofty. Zounds, sir, do you pretend to direct me; direct me in the business of office? Do you know me, sir? who am I?

Miss Rich. Dear Mr. Lofty, this request is not so

much his as mine; if my commands—but you despise my power.

Lofty. Delicate creature! your commands could even control a debate at midnight; to a power so constitutional, I am all obedience and tranquillity. He shall have a letter; where is my secretary? Dubardieu! And yet I protest I don't like this way of doing business. I think if I spoke first to Sir William—But you will have it so.

[*Exit with Miss* RICH.

Sir WILLIAM *alone*

Sir Will. Ha, ha, ha! This, too, is one of my nephew's hopeful associates. O vanity, thou constant deceiver, how do all thy efforts to exalt, serve but to sink us. Thy false colourings, like those employed to heighten beauty, only seem to mend that bloom which they contribute to destroy. I'm not displeased at this interview; exposing this fellow's impudence to the contempt it deserves, may be of use to my design; at least, if he can reflect, it will be of use to himself.

Enter JARVIS

Sir Will. How now, Jarvis, where's your master, my nephew?

Jarvis. At his wit's end, I believe; he's scarce gotten out of one scrape, but he's running his head into another.

Sir Will. How so?

Jarvis. The house has but just been cleared of the bailiffs, and now he's again engaging tooth and nail in assisting old Croaker's son to patch up a clandestine match with the young lady that passes in the house for his sister!

Sir Will. Ever busy to serve others.

Jarvis. Ay, anybody but himself. The young couple, it seems, are just setting out for Scotland, and he supplies them with money for the journey.

Sir Will. Money! how is he able to supply others, who has scarce any for himself?

Jarvis. Why, there it is; he has no money, that's true; but then, as he never said no to any request in his life, he has given them a bill drawn by a friend of his upon a merchant in the city, which I am to get changed; for you must know that I am to go with them to Scotland myself.

Sir Will. How!

Jarvis. It seems the young gentleman is obliged to take a different road from his mistress, as he is to call upon an uncle of his that lives out of the way, in order to prepare a place for their reception, when they return; so they have borrowed me from my master, as the properest person to attend the young lady down.

Sir Will. To the land of matrimony! A pleasant journey, Jarvis.

Jarvis. Ay, but I'm only to have all the fatigues on't.

Sir Will. Well, it may be shorter, and less fatiguing than you imagine. I know but too much of the young lady's family and connections, whom I have seen abroad. I have also discovered that Miss Richland is not indifferent to my thoughtless nephew: and will endeavour, though I fear, in vain, to establish that connection. But, come, the letter I wait for must be almost finished; I'll let you further into my intentions, in the next room.   [*Exeunt.*

END OF THE THIRD ACT

ACT THE FOURTH

SCENE—*Croaker's House*

LOFTY

Lofty. Well, sure the devil's in me of late, for running my head into such defiles, as nothing but a genius like my own could draw me from. I was formerly contented to husband out my places and pensions with some degree of frugality; but, curse it, of late I have given away the whole Court Register in less time than they could print the title page; yet, hang it, why scruple a lie or two to come at a fine girl, when I every day tell a thousand for nothing. Ha! Honeywood here before me. Could Miss Richland have set him at liberty?

Enter HONEYWOOD

Mr. Honeywood, I'm glad to see you abroad again. I find my concurrence was not necessary in your unfortunate affairs. I had put things in a train to do your business; but it is not for me to say what I intended doing.

Honeyw. It was unfortunate, indeed, sir. But what adds to my uneasiness is, that while you seem to be acquainted with my misfortune, I, myself, continue still a stranger to my benefactor.

Lofty. How! not know the friend that served you?

Honeyw. Can't guess at the person.

Lofty. Enquire.

Honeyw. I have, but all I can learn is, that he chooses to remain concealed, and that all enquiry must be fruitless.

Lofty. Must be fruitless?

Honeyw. Absolutely fruitless.

Lofty. Sure of that?

Honeyw. Very sure.

Lofty. Then I'll be damned if you shall ever know it from me.

Honeyw. How, sir!

Lofty. I suppose, now, Mr. Honeywood, you think my rent-roll very considerable, and that I have vast sums of money to throw away; I know you do. The world, to be sure, says such things of me.

Honeyw. The world, by what I learn, is no stranger to your generosity. But where does this tend?

Lofty. To nothing; nothing in the world. The town, to be sure, when it makes such a thing as me the subject of conversation, has asserted, that I never yet patronized a man of merit.

Honeyw. I have heard instances to the contrary, even from yourself.

Lofty. Yes, Honeywood, and there are instances to the contrary that you shall never hear from myself.

Honeyw. Ha, dear sir, permit me to ask you but one question.

Lofty. Sir, ask me no questions: I say, sir, ask me no questions; I'll be damned if I answer them!

Honeyw. I will ask no further. My friend, my bene-factor, it must be here, that I am indebted for freedom, for honour. Yes, thou worthiest of men, from the beginning I suspected it, but was afraid to return thanks; which, if undeserved, might seem reproaches.

Lofty. I protest I don't understand all this, Mr. Honeywood! You treat me very cavalierly. I do assure you, sir.—Blood, sir, can't a man be permitted to enjoy the luxury of his own feelings without all this parade?

Honeyw. Nay, do not attempt to conceal an action that adds to your honour. Your looks, your air, your manner, all confess it.

Lofty. Confess it, sir! Torture itself, sir, shall never bring me to confess it. Mr. Honeywood, I have admitted you upon terms of friendship. Don't let us fall out: make me happy, and let this be buried in oblivion. You know I hate ostentation; you know I do. Come, come, Honeywood, you know I always loved to be a friend, and not a patron. I beg this may make no kind of distance between us. Come, come, you and I must be more familiar—Indeed we must.

Honeyw. Heavens! Can I ever repay such friend-ship! Is there any way! Thou best of men, can I ever return the obligation?

Lofty. A bagatelle, a mere bagatelle. But I see your heart is labouring to be grateful. You shall be grateful. It would be cruel to disappoint you.

Honeyw. How! Teach me the manner. Is there any way?

Lofty. From this moment you're mine. Yes, my friend, you shall know it—I'm in love!

Honeyw. And can I assist you?

Lofty. Nobody so well.

Honeyw. In what manner? I'm all impatience.

Lofty. You shall make love for me.

Honeyw. And to whom shall I speak in your favour?

Lofty. To a lady with whom you have great interest, I assure you.   Miss Richland!

Honeyw. Miss Richland!

Lofty. Yes, Miss Richland.   She has struck the blow up to the hilt in my bosom, by Jupiter!

Honeyw. Heavens! was ever anything more unfortunate!   It is too much to be endured.

Lofty. Unfortunate, indeed!   And yet I can endure it, till you have opened the affair to her for me.   Between ourselves, I think she likes me.   I'm not apt to boast, but I think she does.

Honeyw. Indeed!   But do you know the person you apply to?

Lofty. Yes, I know you are her friend and mine : that's enough.   To you, therefore, I commit the success of my passion.   I'll say no more, let friendship do the rest.   I have only to add, that if at any time my little interest can be of service—but, hang it, I'll make no promises—you know my interest is yours at any time.   No apologies, my friend, I'll not be answered, it shall be so.   [*Exit.*

Honeyw. Open, generous, unsuspecting man! He little thinks that I love her too ; and with such an ardent passion!—But then it was ever but a vain and hopeless one ; my torment, my persecution!   What shall I do!   Love, friendship, a hopeless passion, a deserving friend!   Love, that has been my tormentor ; a friend, that has, perhaps, distressed himself to serve me.   It shall be so.   Yes, I will discard the fondling hope from my bosom, and exert all my influence in his favour.   And yet to see her in the possession of another!—Insupportable.   But then to betray a generous, trusting friend!—Worse, worse.   Yes, I'm resolved.   Let me but be the instrument of their happiness, and then quit a country, where I must for ever despair of finding my own.   [*Exit.*

Enter OLIVIA *and* GARNET, *who carries a Milliner's Box*

Olivia. Dear me, I wish this journey were over.   No

news of Jarvis yet? I believe the old peevish creature delays purely to vex me.

Gar. Why, to be sure, madam, I did hear him say a little snubbing before marriage would teach you to bear it the better afterwards.

Olivia. To be gone a full hour, though he had only to get a bill changed in the city! How provoking!

Gar. I'll lay my life, Mr. Leontine, that had twice as much to do, is setting off by this time from his inn: and here you are left behind.

Olivia. Well, let us be prepared for his coming, however. Are you sure you have omitted nothing, Garnet?

Gar. Not a stick, madam—all's here. Yet I wish you could take the white and silver to be married in. It's the worst luck in the world, in anything but white. I knew one Bet Stubbs, of our town, that was married in red; and, as sure as eggs is eggs, the bridegroom and she had a miff before morning.

Olivia. No matter. I'm all impatience till we are out of the house.

Gar. Bless me, madam, I had almost forgot the wedding-ring!—The sweet little thing—I don't think it would go on my little finger. And what if I put in a gentleman's night-cap, in case of necessity, madam? But here's Jarvis.

Enter JARVIS

Olivia. O, Jarvis, are you come at last? We have been ready this half hour. Now let's be going. Let us fly!

Jarvis. Aye, to Jericho! for we shall have no going to Scotland this bout, I fancy.

Olivia. How! What's the matter?

Jarvis. Money, money, is the matter, madam. We have got no money. What the plague do you send me of your fool's errand for? My master's bill upon the city is not worth a rush. Here it is; Mrs. Garnet may pin up her hair with it.

Olivia. Undone! How could Honeywood serve us so! What shall we do? Can't we go without it?

Jarvis. Go to Scotland without money! To Scotland

without money! Lord how some people understand geography! We might as well set sail for Patagonia upon a cork jacket.

Olivia. Such a disappointment! What a base insincere man was your master, to serve us in this manner. Is this his good nature?

Jarvis. Nay, don't talk ill of my master, madam. I won't bear to hear anybody talk ill of him but myself.

Gar. Bless us! now I think on't, madam, you need not be under any uneasiness: I saw Mr. Leontine receive forty guineas from his father just before he set out, and he can't yet have left the inn. A short letter will reach him there.

Olivia. Well remembered, Garnet; I'll write immediately. How's this! Bless me, my hand trembles so, I can't write a word. Do you write, Garnet; and, upon second thought, it will be better from you.

Gar. Truly, madam, I write and indite but poorly. I never was kute in my larning. But I'll do what I can to please you. Let me see. All out of my own head, I suppose?

Olivia. Whatever you please.

Gar. (*Writing.*) Muster Croaker—Twenty guineas, madam?

Olivia. Ay, twenty will do.

Gar. At the bar of the Talbot till called for. Expedition—will be blown up—all of a flame—Quick, dispatch—Cupid, the little God of Love—I conclude it, madam, with Cupid; I love to see a love-letter end like poetry.[1]

Olivia. Well, well, what you please, anything. But how shall we send it? I can trust none of the servants of this family.

Gar. Odso, madam, Mr. Honeywood's butler is in the next room; he's a dear, sweet man; he'll do anything for me.

Jarvis. He! the dog, he'll certainly commit some blunder. He's drunk and sober ten times a day!

Olivia. No matter. Fly, Garnet; anybody we can

[1 Sam Weller's opinion. Cf. *Pickwick Papers*, ch. xxxiii.]

trust will do. [*Exit* GARNET.] Well, Jarvis, now we can have nothing more to interrupt us. You may take up the things, and carry them on to the inn. Have you no hands, Jarvis?

Jarvis. Soft and fair, young lady. You, that are going to be married, think things can never be done too fast: but we that are old, and know what we are about, must elope methodically, madam.

Olivia. Well, sure, if my indiscretions were to be done over again——

Jarvis. My life for it you would do them ten times over.

Olivia. Why will you talk so? If you knew how unhappy they make me——

Jarvis. Very unhappy, no doubt: I was once just as unhappy when I was going to be married myself. I'll tell you a story about that——

Olivia. A story! when I'm all impatience to be away. Was there ever such a dilatory creature!——

Jarvis. Well, madam, if we must march, why we will march; that's all. Though, odds bobs we have still forgot one thing we should never travel without—a case of good razors, and a box of shaving-powder. But no matter, I believe we shall be pretty well shaved by the way. [*Going.*

Enter GARNET

Garnet. Undone, undone, madam! Ah, Mr. Jarvis, you said right enough. As sure as death Mr. Honeywood's rogue of a drunken butler dropped the letter before he went ten yards from the door. There's old Croaker has just picked it up, and is this moment reading it to himself in the hall!

Olivia. Unfortunate! We shall be discovered!

Gar. No, madam; don't be uneasy, he can make neither head nor tail of it. To be sure he looks as if he was broke loose from Bedlam about it, but he can't find what it means for all that. O Lud, he is coming this way all in the horrors!

Olivia. Then let us leave the house this instant, for

fear he should ask further questions. In the mean time, Garnet, do you write and send off just such another.　　　　　　　　　　　　　　　　[*Exeunt.*

Enter CROAKER

Croaker. Death and destruction! Are all the horrors of air, fire and water to be levelled only at me! Am I only to be singled out for gunpowder-plots, combustibles, and conflagration! Here it is—An incendiary letter dropped at my door. *To Muster Croaker, these, with speed.* Ay, ay, plain enough the direction: all in the genuine incendiary spelling, and as cramp as the devil. *With speed.* O, confound your speed. But let me read it once more. (*Reads.*)

Mustar Croakar as sone as yoew see this leve twenty gunnes at the bar of the Talboot tell caled for or yowe and yower experetion will be al blown up! Ah, but too plain! Blood and gunpowder in every line of it. Blown up! murderous dog! All blown up! Heavens! what have I and my poor family done, to be all blown up? (*Reads.*) *Our pockets are low, and money we must have.* Ay, there's the reason; they'll blow us up, because they have got low pockets. (*Reads.*) *It is but a short time you have to consider; for if this takes wind, the house will quickly be all of a flame.* Inhuman monsters! blow us up, and then burn us. The earthquake at Lisbon was but a bonfire to it! (*Reads.*) *Make quick dispatch, and so no more at present. But may Cupid, the little God of Love, go with you wherever you go.* The little God of Love! Cupid, the little God of Love go with me! Go you to the devil, you and your little Cupid together; I'm so frightened, I scarce know whether I sit, stand, or go. Perhaps this moment I'm treading on lighted matches, blazing brimstone and barrels of gunpowder. They are preparing to blow me up into the clouds. Murder! We shall be all burnt in our beds; we shall be all burnt in our beds.[1]

[1 Shuter's reading of this letter is said to have decided the success of the play.]

Enter MISS RICHLAND

Miss Rich. Lord, sir, what's the matter?

Croaker. Murder's the matter. We shall be all blown up in our beds before morning!

Miss Rich. I hope not, sir.

Croaker. What signifies what you hope, madam, when I have a certificate of it here in my hand? Will nothing alarm my family? Sleeping and eating, sleeping and eating is the only work from morning till night in my house. My insensible crew could sleep, though rocked by an earthquake, and fry beef steaks at a volcano!

Miss Rich. But, sir, you have alarmed them so often already, we have nothing but earthquakes, famines, plagues, and mad dogs from year's end to year's end. You remember, sir, it is not above a month ago, that you assured us of a conspiracy among the bakers, to poison us in our bread; and so kept the whole family a week upon potatoes.

Croaker. And potatoes were too good for them. But why do I stand talking here with a girl, when I should be facing the enemy without? Here, John, Nicodemus, search the house. Look into the cellars, to see if there be any combustibles below; and above, in the apartments, that no matches be thrown in at the windows. Let all the fires be put out, and let the engine be drawn out in the yard, to play upon the house in case of necessity.   [*Exit.*

MISS RICHLAND *alone*

Miss Rich. What can he mean by all this? Yet, why should I enquire, when he alarms us in this manner almost every day? But Honeywood has desired an interview with me in private. What can he mean; or, rather, what means this palpitation at his approach? It is the first time he ever shewed anything in his conduct that seemed particular. Sure he cannot mean to —— but he's here.

Enter HONEYWOOD

Honeyw. I presumed to solicit this interview, madam, before I left town, to be permitted—

Miss Rich. Indeed ! Leaving town, sir ?—

Honeyw. Yes, madam ; perhaps the kingdom. I have presumed, I say, to desire the favour of this interview— in order to disclose something which our long friendship prompts. And yet my fears—

Miss Rich. His fears ! What are his fears to mine ? (*Aside.*)—We have indeed been long acquainted, sir ; very long. If I remember, our first meeting was at the French Ambassador's.—Do you recollect how you were pleased to rally me upon my complexion there ?

Honeyw. Perfectly, madam ; I presumed to reprove you for painting : but your warmer blushes soon convinced the company that the colouring was all from nature.

Miss Rich. And yet you only meant it, in your good-natur'd way, to make me pay a compliment to myself. In the same manner you danced that night with the most awkward woman in company, because you saw nobody else would take her out.

Honeyw. Yes ; and was rewarded the next night, by dancing with the finest woman in company, whom everybody wished to take out.

Miss Rich. Well, sir, if you thought so then, I fear your judgment has since corrected the errors of a first impression. We generally show to most advantage at first. Our sex are like poor tradesmen, that put all their best goods to be seen at the windows.

Honeyw. The first impression, madam, did indeed deceive me. I expected to find a woman with all the faults of conscious flattered beauty. I expected to find her vain and insolent. But every day has since taught me that it is possible to possess sense without pride, and beauty without affectation.

Miss Rich. This, sir, is a style unusual with Mr. Honeywood ; and I shall be glad to know why he thus attempts to increase that vanity, which his own lessons have taught me to despise.

Honeyw. I ask pardon, madam. Yet, from our long friendship, I presumed I might have some right to offer, without offence, what you may refuse without offending.

Miss Rich. Sir! I beg you'd reflect; though, I fear, I shall scarce have any power to refuse a request of yours; yet, you may be precipitate: consider, sir.

Honeyw. I own my rashness; but, as I plead the cause of friendship, of one who loves—Don't be alarmed, madam —Who loves you with the most ardent passion; whose whole happiness is placed in you—

Miss Rich. I fear, sir, I shall never find whom you mean, by this description of him.

Honeyw. Ah, madam, it but too plainly points him out; though he should be too humble himself to urge his pretensions, or you too modest to understand them.

Miss Rich. Well; it would be affectation any longer to pretend ignorance; and, I will own, sir, I have long been prejudiced in his favour. It was but natural to wish to make his heart mine, as he seemed himself ignorant of its value.

Honeyw. I see she always loved him! (*Aside.*)—I find, madam, you're already sensible of his worth, his passion. How happy is my friend, to be the favourite of one with such sense to distinguish merit, and such beauty to reward it!

Miss Rich. Your friend! sir. What friend?

Honeyw. My best friend—My friend Mr. Lofty, madam.

Miss Rich. He, sir!

Honeyw. Yes, he, madam! He is, indeed, what your warmest wishes might have formed him. And to his other qualities, he adds that of the most passionate regard for you.

Miss Rich. Amazement!—No more of this, I beg you, sir.

Honeyw. I see your confusion, madam, and know how to interpret it. And since I so plainly read the language of your heart, shall I make my friend happy, by communicating your sentiments?

Miss Rich. By no means.

Honeyw. Excuse me; I must; I know you desire it.

Miss Rich. Mr. Honeywood, let me tell you, that you wrong my sentiments and yourself. When I first applied to your friendship, I expected advice and assistance; but now, sir, I see that it is vain to expect happiness from him, who has been so bad an economist of his own; and that I must disclaim his friendship, who ceases to be a friend to himself.   [*Exit.*

Honeyw. How is this! she has confessed she loved him, and yet she seemed to part in displeasure. Can I have done anything to reproach myself with? No; I believe not; yet, after all, these things should not be done by a third person; I should have spared her confusion. My friendship carried me a little too far.

Enter CROAKER, *with the Letter in his Hand, and* MRS. CROAKER

Mrs. Croaker. Ha, ha, ha! And so, my dear, it's your supreme wish that I should be quite wretched upon this occasion? Ha, ha.

Croaker. (*Mimicking*) Ha, ha, ha! and so, my dear, it's your supreme pleasure to give me no better consolation?

Mrs. Croaker. Positively, my dear, what is this incendiary stuff and trumpery to me? Our house may travel through the air like the house of Loretto,[1] for aught I care, if I'm to be miserable in it.

Croaker. Would to Heaven it were converted into a house of correction for your benefit. Have we not everything to alarm us? Perhaps, this very moment, the tragedy is beginning.

Mrs. Croaker. Then let us reserve our distress till the rising of the curtain, or give them the money they want and have done with them.

Croaker. Give them my money!—And pray, what right have they to my money?

Mrs. Croaker. And pray, what right then have you to my good humour?

Croaker. And so your good humour advises me to part with my money? Why, then, to tell your good

[1 The Santa Casa, or House of the Virgin, is said to have been miraculously transported into various towns until it settled finally at Loretto. Cf. Swift's *Tale of a Tub*, 1704, Section iv.

humour a piece of my mind, I'd sooner part with my wife! Here's Mr. Honeywood, see what he'll say to it. My dear Honeywood, look at this incendiary letter dropped at my door. It will freeze you with terror; and yet lovey here can read it—can read it, and laugh!

Mrs. Croaker. Yes, and so will Mr. Honeywood.

Croaker. If he does, I'll suffer to be hanged the next minute in the rogue's place, that's all!

Mrs. Croaker. Speak, Mr. Honeywood! is their anything more foolish than my husband's fright upon this occasion?

Honeyw. It would not become me to decide, madam; but doubtless, the greatness of his terrors now, will but invite them to renew their villainy another time.

Mrs. Croaker. I told you, he'd be of my opinion.

Croaker. How, sir! do you maintain that I should lie down under such an injury, and show, neither by my tears, or complaints, that I have something of the spirit of a man in me?

Honeyw. Pardon me, sir. You ought to make the loudest complaints, if you desire redress. The surest way to have redress, is to be earnest in the pursuit of it.

Croaker. Ay, whose opinion is he of now?

Mrs. Croaker. But don't you think that laughing off our fears is the best way?

Honeyw. What is the best, madam, few can say; but I'll maintain it to be a very wise way.

Croaker. But we're talking of the best. Surely the best way is to face the enemy in the field, and not wait till he plunders us in our very bed-chamber.

Honeyw. Why, sir, as to the best, that—that's a very wise way too.

Mrs. Croaker. But can anything be more absurd, than to double our distresses by our apprehensions, and put it in the power of every low fellow, that can scrawl ten words of wretched spelling, to torment us?

Honeyw. Without doubt, nothing more absurd.

Croaker. How! would it not be more absurd to despise the rattle till we are bit by the snake?

Honeyw. Without doubt, perfectly absurd.

Croaker. Then you are of my opinion?

Honeyw. Entirely.

Mrs. Croaker. And you reject mine?

Honeyw. Heaven forbid, madam. No, sure, no reasoning can be more just than yours. We ought certainly to despise malice if we cannot oppose it, and not make the incendiary's pen as fatal to our repose as the highwayman's pistol.

Mrs. Croaker. O! then you think I'm quite right?

Honeyw. Perfectly right!

Croaker. A plague of plagues, we can't be both right. I ought to be sorry, or I ought to be glad. My hat must be on my head, or my hat must be off.

Mrs. Croaker. Certainly, in two opposite opinions, if one be perfectly reasonable, the other can't be perfectly right.

Honeyw. And why may not both be right, madam? Mr. Croaker in earnestly seeking redress, and you in waiting the event with good humour? Pray let me see the letter again. I have it. This letter requires twenty guineas to be left at the bar of the Talbot inn. If it be indeed an incendiary letter, what if you and I, sir, go there; and, when the writer comes to be paid his expected booty, seize him?

Croaker. My dear friend, it's the very thing; the very thing. While I walk by the door, you shall plant yourself in ambush near the bar; burst out upon the miscreant like a masked battery; extort a confession at once, and so hang him up by surprise.

Honeyw. Yes; but I would not choose to exercise too much severity. It is my maxim, sir, that crimes generally punish themselves.

Croaker. Well, but we may upbraid him a little, I suppose? (*Ironically.*)

Honeyw. Ay, but not punish him too rigidly.

Croaker. Well, well, leave that to my own benevolence.

Honeyw. Well, I do: but remember that universal benevolence is the first law of nature.

[*Exeunt* HONEYWOOD *and* Mrs. CROAKER.

Croaker. Yes; and my universal benevolence will hang the dog, if he had as many necks as a hydra!

END OF THE FOURTH ACT

ACT THE FIFTH

Scene—*An Inn*

Enter OLIVIA, JARVIS

Olivia. Well, we have got safe to the inn, however. Now, if the post-chaise were ready—

Jarvis. The horses are just finishing their oats; and, as they are not going to be married, they choose to take their own time.

Olivia. You are for ever giving wrong motives to my impatience.

Jarvis. Be as impatient as you will, the horses must take their own time; besides, you don't consider, we have got no answer from our fellow-traveller yet. If we hear nothing from Mr. Leontine, we have only one way left us.

Olivia. What way?

Jarvis. The way home again.

Olivia. Not so. I have made a resolution to go, and nothing shall induce me to break it.

Jarvis. Ay; resolutions are well kept when they jump with inclination. However, I'll go hasten things without. And I'll call too at the bar to see if anything should be left for us there. Don't be in such a plaguy hurry, madam, and we shall go the faster, I promise you.

[*Exit* JARVIS.

Enter LANDLADY

Landlady. What! Solomon; why don't you move? Pipes and tobacco for the Lamb there.—Will nobody answer? To the Dolphin; quick. The Angel has been outrageous this half hour. Did your ladyship call, madam?

Olivia. No, madam.

Landlady. I find, as you're for Scotland, madam—But, that's no business of mine; married, or not married, I ask no questions. To be sure, we had a sweet little couple set off from this two days ago for the same place. The gentleman, for a tailor, was, to be sure, as fine a spoken tailor, as ever blew froth from a full pot. And the young lady so bashful, it was near half an hour before we could get her to finish a pint of raspberry between us.

Olivia. But this gentleman and I are not going to be married, I assure you.

Landlady. May be not. That's no business of mine; for certain, Scotch marriages seldom turn out well. There was, of my knowledge, Miss Macfag, that married her father's footman.—Alack-a-day, she and her husband soon parted, and now keep separate cellars in Hedge Lane.[1]

Olivia. (*aside.*) A very pretty picture of what lies before me.

Enter LEONTINE

Leont. My dear Olivia, my anxiety till you were out of danger, was too great to be resisted. I could not help coming to see you set out, though it exposes us to a discovery.

Olivia. May everything you do prove as fortunate. Indeed, Leontine, we have been most cruelly disappointed. Mr. Honeywood's bill upon the city, has, it seems, been protested, and we have been utterly at a loss how to proceed.

Leont. How! An offer of his own too. Sure, he could not mean to deceive us.

Olivia. Depend upon his sincerity; he only mistook the desire for the power of serving us. But let us think no more of it. I believe the post-chaise is ready by this.

Landlady. Not quite yet: and, begging your ladyship's

[1 Cf. Goldsmith's essay entitled *A Register of Scotch Marriages*, in the *Westminster Magazine*, February, 1773.]

pardon, I don't think your ladyship quite ready for the post-chaise. The north road is a cold place, madam. I have a drop in the house of as pretty raspberry as ever was tipt over tongue. Just a thimbleful to keep the wind off your stomach. To be sure, the last couple we had here, they said it was a perfect nosegay. Ecod, I sent them both away as good-natur'd—Up went the blinds, round went the wheels, and drive away post-boy, was the word.

Enter CROAKER

Croaker. Well, while my friend Honeywood is upon the post of danger at the bar, it must be my business to have an eye about me here. I think I know an incendiary's look; for, wherever the devil makes a purchase, he never fails to set his mark. Ha! who have we here? My son and daughter! What can they be doing here?

Landlady. I tell you, madam, it will do you good; I think I know by this time what's good for the north road. It's a raw night, madam—sir—

Leont. Not a drop more, good madam. I should now take it as a greater favour, if you hasten the horses, for I am afraid to be seen myself.

Landlady. That shall be done. Wha, Solomon! are you all dead there? Wha, Solomon, I say.

                    [Exit bawling.

Olivia. Well; I dread lest an expedition begun in fear should end in repentance.—Every moment we stay increases our danger, and adds to my apprehensions.

Leont. There's no danger, trust me, my dear; there can be none: if Honeywood has acted with honour, and kept my father, as he promised, in employment, till we are out of danger, nothing can interrupt our journey.

Olivia. I have no doubt of Mr. Honeywood's sincerity, and even his desires to serve us. My fears are from your father's suspicions. A mind so disposed to be alarmed without a cause, will be but too ready when there's a reason.

Leont. Why, let him, when we are out of his power. But, believe me, Olivia, you have no great reason to dread his resentment. His repining temper, as it does no manner of injury to himself, so will it never do harm to others. He only frets to keep himself employed, and scolds for his private amusement.

Olivia. I don't know that; but, I'm sure, on some occasions, it makes him look most shockingly.

Croaker. (*Discovering himself.*) How does he look now?—How does he look now?

Olivia. Ah!

Leont. Undone!

Croaker. How do I look now? Sir, I am your very humble servant. Madam, I am yours. What, you are going off, are you? Then, first, if you please, take a word or two from me with you before you go. Tell me first where you are going, and when you have told me that, perhaps I shall know as little as I did before.

Leont. If that be so, our answer might but increase your displeasure, without adding to your information.

Croaker. I want no information from you, puppy; and you, too, good madam, what answer have you got? Eh! (*A cry without, stop him.*) I think I heard a noise. My friend, Honeywood, without—has he seized the incendiary? Ah, no, for now I hear no more on't.

Leont. Honeywood, without! Then, sir, it was Mr. Honeywood that directed you hither.

Croaker. No, sir, it was Mr. Honeywood conducted me hither.

Leont. Is it possible!

Croaker. Possible! Why, he's in the house now, sir. More anxious about me, than my own son, sir.

Leont. Then, sir, he's a villain!

Croaker. How, sirrah! a villain, because he takes most care of your father? I'll not bear it. I tell you I'll not bear it. Honeywood is a friend to the family, and I'll have him treated as such.

Leont. I shall study to repay his friendship as it deserves.

Croaker. Ah, rogue, if you knew how earnestly he entered into my griefs, and pointed out the means to detect them, you would love him as I do. (*A cry with-*

out, stop him.) Fire and fury; they have seized the incendiary: they have the villain, the incendiary in view. Stop him, stop an incendiary, a murderer; stop him!

[*Exit.*

Olivia. Oh, my terrors! What can this new tumult mean?

Leont. Some new mark, I suppose, of Mr. Honeywood's sincerity. But we shall have satisfaction: he shall give me instant satisfaction.

Olivia. It must not be, my Leontine, if you value my esteem, or my happiness. Whatever be our fate, let us not add guilt to our misfortunes—Consider that our innocence will shortly be all we have left us. You must forgive him.

Leont. Forgive him! Has he not in every instance betrayed us? Forced me to borrow money from him, which appears a mere trick to delay us: promised to keep my father engaged till we were out of danger, and here brought him to the very scene of our escape?

Olivia. Don't be precipitate. We may yet be mistaken.

Enter POSTBOY, *dragging in* JARVIS: HONEYWOOD
entering soon after

Postboy. Ay, master, we have him fast enough. Here is the incendiary dog. I'm entitled to the reward; I'll take my oath I saw him ask for the money at the bar, and then run for it.

Honeyw. Come, bring him along. Let us see him. Let him learn to blush for his crimes. (*Discovering his mistake.*) Death! what's here! Jarvis, Leontine, Olivia! What can all this mean?

Jarvis. Why, I'll tell you what it means: that I was an old fool, and that you are my master—that's all.

Honeyw. Confusion!

Leont. Yes, sir, I find you have kept your word with me. After such baseness, I wonder how you can venture to see the man you have injured.

Honeyw. My dear Leontine, by my life, my honour——

Leont. Peace, peace, for shame; and do not continue

to aggravate baseness by hypocrisy. I know you, sir, I know you.

Honeyw. Why, won't you hear me! By all that's just, I knew not——

Leont. Hear you, sir! to what purpose? I now see through all your low arts; your ever complying with every opinion; your never refusing any request; your friendship as common as a prostitute's favours, and as fallacious; all these, sir, have long been contemptible to the world, and are now perfectly so to me.

Honeyw. (*aside*). Ha! contemptible to the world! That reaches me.

Leont. All the seeming sincerity of your professions I now find were only allurements to betray; and all your seeming regret for their consequences, only calculated to cover the cowardice of your heart. Draw, villain!

Enter CROAKER *out of breath*

Croaker. Where is the villain? Where is the incendiary? (*Seizing the post-boy.*) Hold him fast, the dog; he has the gallows in his face. Come, you dog, confess; confess all, and hang yourself.

Post-Boy. Zounds! master, what do you throttle me for?

Croaker. (*Beating him*). Dog, do you resist; do you resist?

Post-Boy. Zounds! master, I'm not he; there's the man that we thought was the rogue, and turns out to be one of the company.

Croaker. How!

Honeyw. Mr. Croaker, we have all been under a strange mistake here; I find there is nobody guilty; it was all an error; entirely an error of our own.

Croaker. And I say, sir, that you're in an error: for there's guilt and double guilt, a plot, a damn'd Jesuitical pestilential plot, and I must have proof of it.

Honeyw. Do but hear me.

Croaker. What, you intend to bring 'em off, I suppose; I'll hear nothing.

Honeyw. Madam, you seem at least calm enough to hear reason.

Olivia. Excuse me.

Honeyw. Good Jarvis, let me then explain it to you.

Jarvis. What signifies explanation when the thing is done?

Honeyw. Will nobody hear me? Was there ever such a set, so blinded by passion and prejudice! (*To the Post-Boy.*) My good friend, I believe you'll be surprised when I assure you——

Post-Boy. Sure me nothing—I'm sure of nothing but a good beating.

Croaker. Come then, you, madam, if you ever hope for any favour or forgiveness, tell me sincerely all you know of this affair.

Olivia. Unhappily, sir, I'm but too much the cause of your suspicions: you see before you, sir, one that with false pretences has stept into your family to betray it: not your daughter——

Croaker. Not my daughter!

Olivia. Not your daughter—but a mean deceiver—who—support me, I cannot——

Honeyw. Help, she's going, give her air.

Croaker. Ay, ay, take the young woman to the air; I would not hurt a hair of her head, whose ever daughter she may be—not so bad as that neither.

[*Exeunt all but* CROAKER.

Croaker. Yes, yes, all's out; I now see the whole affair; my son is either married, or going to be so, to this lady, whom he imposed upon me as his sister. Ay, certainly so; and yet I don't find it afflicts me so much as one might think. There's the advantage of fretting away our misfortunes beforehand, we never feel them when they come.

Enter *Miss* RICHLAND *and Sir* WILLIAM

Sir Will. But how do you know, madam, that my nephew intends setting off from this place?

Miss Rich. My maid assured me he was come to this

inn, and my own knowledge of his intending to leave the kingdom, suggested the rest. But what do I see, my guardian here before us! Who, my dear sir, could have expected meeting you here; to what accident do we owe this pleasure?

Croaker. To a fool, I believe.

Miss Rich. But to what purpose did you come?

Croaker. To play the fool.

Miss Rich. But with whom?

Croaker. With greater fools than myself.

Miss Rich. Explain.

Croaker. Why, Mr. Honeywood brought me here, to do nothing now I am here; and my son is going to be married to I don't know who that is here; so now you are as wise as I am.

Miss Rich. Married! to whom, sir?

Croaker. To Olivia; my daughter, as I took her to be; but who the devil she is, or whose daughter she is, I know no more than the man in the moon.

Sir Will. Then, sir, I can inform you; and, though a stranger, yet you shall find me a friend to your family: it will be enough at present, to assure you, that, both in point of birth and fortune, the young lady is at least your son's equal. Being left by her father, Sir James Woodville—

Croaker. Sir James Woodville! What, of the West?

Sir Will. Being left by him, I say, to the care of a mercenary wretch, whose only aim was to secure her fortune to himself, she was sent into France, under pretence of education; and there every art was tried to fix her for life in a convent, contrary to her inclinations. Of this I was informed upon my arrival in Paris; and, as I had been once her father's friend, I did all in my power to frustrate her guardian's base intentions. I had even meditated to rescue her from his authority, when your son stept in with more pleasing violence, gave her liberty, and you a daughter.

Croaker. But I intend to have a daughter of my own choosing, sir. A young lady, sir, whose fortune, by my interest with those that have interest, will be double what my son has a right to expect ! Do you know Mr. Lofty, sir ?

Sir Will. Yes, sir ; and know that you are deceived in him. But step this way, and I'll convince you.

[CROAKER *and Sir* WILLIAM *seem to confer.*

Enter HONEYWOOD

Honeyw. Obstinate man, still to persist in his outrage ! Insulted by him, despised by all, I now begin to grow contemptible, even to myself. How have I sunk by too great an assiduity to please ! How have I overtaxed all my abilities, lest the approbation of a single fool should escape me ! But all is now over ; I have survived my reputation, my fortune, my friendships, and nothing remains henceforward for me but solitude and repentance.

Miss Rich. Is it true, Mr. Honeywood, that you are setting off, without taking leave of your friends ? The report is, that you are quitting England. Can it be ?

Honeyw. Yes, madam ; and though I am so unhappy as to have fallen under your displeasure, yet, thank Heaven, I leave you to happiness : to one who loves you, and deserves your love ; to one who has power to procure you affluence, and generosity to improve your enjoyment of it.

Miss Rich. And are you sure, sir, that the gentleman you mean is what you describe him ?

Honeyw. I have the best assurances of it, his serving me. He does indeed deserve the highest happiness, and that is in your power to confer As for me, weak and wavering as I have been, obliged by all, and incapable of serving any, what happiness can I find but in solitude ? What hope but in being forgotten ?

Miss Rich. A thousand ! to live among friends that esteem you, whose happiness it will be to be permitted to oblige you.

Honeyw. No, madam ; my resolution is fixed. Inferiority among strangers is easy ; but among those that once were equals, insupportable. Nay, to show you how far my resolution can go, I can now speak with calmness of my former follies, my vanity, my dissipation, my weakness. I will even confess, that, among the number of my other presumptions, I had the insolence to think of loving you. Yes, madam, while I was pleading the passion of another, my heart was tortured with its own. But it is over, it was unworthy our friendship, and let it be forgotten.

Miss Rich. You amaze me!

Honeyw. But you'll forgive it, I know you will; since the confession should not have come from me even now, but to convince you of the sincerity of my intention of— never mentioning it more.   [*Going.*

Miss Rich. Stay, sir, one moment—Ha! he here—

Enter LOFTY

Lofty. Is the coast clear? None but friends. I have followed you here with a trifling piece of intelligence: but it goes no farther, things are not yet ripe for a discovery. I have spirits working at a certain board; your affair at the Treasury will be done in less than—a thousand years. Mum!

Miss Rich. Sooner, sir, I should hope!

Lofty. Why, yes, I believe it may, if it falls into proper hands, that know where to push and where to parry; that know how the land lies—eh, Honeywood?

Miss Rich. It is fallen into yours.

Lofty. Well, to keep you no longer in suspense, your thing is done. It is done, I say—that's all. I have just had assurances from Lord Neverout, that the claim has been examined, and found admissible. *Quietus* is the word, madam.

Honeyw. But how! his lordship has been at New-market these ten days!

Lofty. Indeed! Then Sir Gilbert Goose must have been most damnably mistaken. I had it of him.

Miss Rich. He! why Sir Gilbert and his family have been in the country this month!

Lofty. This month! It must certainly be so—Sir Gilbert's letter did come to me from Newmarket, so that he must have met his lordship there; and so it came

about. I have his letter about me, I'll read it to you. (*Taking out a large bundle.*) That's from Paoli of Corsica,[1] that from the Marquis of Squilachi.—Have you a mind to see a letter from Count Poniatowski, now King of Poland—Honest Pon——   [*Searching.*
O, sir, what are you here too? I'll tell you what, honest friend, if you have not absolutely delivered my letter to Sir William Honeywood, you may return it. The thing will do without him.

Sir Will. Sir, I have delivered it, and must inform you it was received with the most mortifying contempt.

Croaker. Contempt! Mr. Lofty, what can that mean?

Lofty. Let him go on, let him go on, I say. You'll find it come to something presently.

Sir Will. Yes, sir, I believe you'll be amazed, if, after waiting some time in the ante-chamber, after being surveyed with insolent curiosity by the passing servants, I was at last assured, that Sir William Honeywood knew no such person, and I must certainly have been imposed upon.

Lofty. Good; let me die, very good. Ha! ha! ha!

Croaker. Now, for my life, I can't find out half the goodness of it.

Lofty. You can't? Ha! ha!

Croaker. No, for the soul of me; I think it was as confounded a bad answer as ever was sent from one private gentleman to another.

Lofty. And so you can't find out the force of the message? Why I was in the house at that very time. Ha! ha! It was I that sent that very answer to my own letter. Ha! ha!

Croaker. Indeed! How! why!

Lofty. In one word, things between Sir William and me must be behind the curtain. A party has many eyes. He sides with Lord Buzzard, I side with Sir Gilbert Goose. So that unriddles the mystery.

Croaker. And so it does indeed, and all my suspicions are over.

[1 Pascal Paoli, the Corsican patriot. He came to England in 1769. Squillaci, an Italian, was Prime Minister at Madrid.]

Lofty. Your suspicions! What then, you have been suspecting, you have been suspecting, have you? Mr. Croaker, you and I were friends, we are friends no longer. Never talk to me. It's over; I say, it's over!

Croaker. As I hope for your favour, I did not mean to offend. It escaped me. Don't be discomposed.

Lofty. Zounds, sir, but I am discomposed, and will be discomposed. To be treated thus! Who am I? Was it for this I have been dreaded both by ins and outs? Have I been libelled in the Gazetteer, and praised in the St. James's;[1] have I been chaired at Wildman's, and a speaker at Merchant Tailor's Hall; have I had my hand to addresses, and my head in the print-shops, and talk to me of suspects!

Croaker. My dear sir, be pacified. What can you have but asking pardon?

Lofty. Sir, I will not be pacified—Suspects! Who am I? To be used thus, have I paid court to men in favour to serve my friends, the Lords of the Treasury. Sir William Honeywood, and the rest of the gang, and talk to me of suspects! Who am I, I say, who am I?

Sir Will. Since, sir, you're so pressing for an answer, I'll tell you who you are. A gentleman, as well acquainted with politics, as with men in power; as well acquainted with persons of fashion, as with modesty; with Lords of the Treasury, as with truth; and with all, as you are with Sir William Honeywood. I am Sir William Honeywood!

[*Discovering his ensigns of the Bath.*

Croaker. Sir William Honeywood!

Honeyw. Astonishment! my uncle! (*aside.*)

Lofty. So then my confounded genius has been all this time only leading me up to the garret, in order to fling me out of the window.

Croaker. What, Mr. Importance, and are these your works? Suspect you! You, who have been dreaded by the ins and outs: you, who have had your hand to addresses, and your head stuck up in print-shops. If you were served right, you should have your head stuck up in the pillory.

Lofty. Ay, stick it where you will, for, by the Lord, it cuts but a very poor figure where it sticks at present.

Sir Will. Well, Mr. Croaker, I hope you now see how incapable this gentleman is of serving you, and how little Miss Richland has to expect from his influence.

Croaker. Ay, sir, too well I see it, and I can't but say I have had some boding of it these ten days. So I'm resolved, since my son has placed his affections on a lady of moderate fortune to be satisfied with his choice, and not run the hazard of another Mr. Lofty, in helping him to a better.

Sir Will. I approve your resolution, and here they come, to receive a confirmation of your pardon and consent.

Enter Mrs. CROAKER, JARVIS, LEONTINE, OLIVIA

Mrs. Croaker. Where's my husband? Come, come, lovey, you must forgive them. Jarvis here has been to tell me the whole affair: and, I say, you must forgive them. Our own was a stolen match, you know, my dear; and we never had any reason to repent of it.

Croaker. I wish we could both say so; however, this gentleman, Sir William Honeywood, has been before-hand with you, in obtaining their pardon. So, if the two poor fools have a mind to marry, I think we can tack them together without crossing the Tweed for it.

[Joining their hands.

Leont. How blest, and unexpected! What, what can we say to such goodness! But our future obedience shall be the best reply. And, as for this gentleman, to whom we owe—

Sir Will. Excuse me, sir, if I interrupt your thanks, as I have here an interest that calls me. (*Turning to Honeywood.*) Yes, sir, you are surprised to see me; and I own that a desire of correcting your follies led me hither. I saw, with indignation, the errors of a mind that only sought applause from others; that easiness of disposition. which, though inclined to the right, had not courage to condemn the wrong. I saw with regret those splendid errors, that still took name from some neighbouring duty. Your charity, that was but injustice; your benevolence, that was but weakness; and your friendship but credulity. I say, with regret, great talents and extensive learning only employed to add sprightliness to error, and increase your perplexities. I saw your mind with a thousand natural charms; but the greatness of its beauty served only to heighten my pity for its prostitution.

Honeyw. Cease to upbraid me, sir; I have for some time but too strongly felt the justice of your reproaches. But there is one way still left me. Yes, sir, I have determined, this very hour, to quit forever a place where I have made myself the voluntary slave of all; and to seek among strangers that fortitude which may give strength to the mind, and marshal all its dissipated virtues. Yet, ere I depart, permit me to solicit favour for this gentleman; who, notwithstanding what has happened, has laid me under the most signal obligations. Mr. Lofty—

Lofty. Mr. Honeywood, I'm resolved upon a reformation, as well as you. I now begin to find that the man who first invented the art of speaking truth was a much cunninger fellow than I thought him. And to prove that I design to speak truth for the future, I must now assure you that you owe your late enlargement to another; as, upon my soul, I had no hand in the matter. So now, if any of the company has a mind for preferment, he may take my place. I'm determined to resign.

[*Exit.*

Honeyw. How have I been deceived!

Sir Will. No, sir, you have been obliged to a kinder, fairer friend for that favour. To Miss Richland. Would she complete our joy, and make the man she has honoured by her friendship happy in her love, I should then forget all, and be as blest as the welfare of my dearest kinsman can make me.

Miss Rich. After what is past, it would be but affectation to pretend to indifference. Yes, I will own an attachment, which I find, was more than friendship. And if my entreaties cannot alter his resolution to quit the country, I will even try if my hand has not power to detain him.   [*Giving her hand.*

Honeyw. Heavens! how can I have deserved all this? How express my happiness, my gratitude? A moment like this over-pays an age of apprehension!

Croaker. Well, now I see content in every face; but Heaven send we be all better this day three months.

Sir Will. Henceforth, nephew, learn to respect yourself. He who seeks only for applause from without, has all his happiness in another's keeping.

Honeyw. Yes, sir, I now too plainly perceive my errors. My vanity, in attempting to please all, by fearing to offend any. My meanness in approving folly, lest fools should disapprove. Henceforth, therefore, it shall be my study to reserve my pity for real distress; my friendship for true merit, and my love for her, who first taught me what it is to be happy.

EPILOGUE [1]

SPOKEN BY MRS. BULKLEY

As puffing quacks some caitiff wretch procure
To swear the pill, or drop, has wrought a cure:
Thus on the stage, our playrights still depend
For Epilogues and Prologues on some friend,
Who knows each art of coaxing up the town,
And makes full many a bitter pill go down.
Conscious of this, our bard has gone about,
And teas'd each rhyming friend to help him out.
An Epilogue, things can't go on without it;
It could not fail, would you but set about it.
Young man, cries one (a bard laid up in clover)
Alas, young man, my writing days are over;
Let boys play tricks, and kick the straw, not I;
Your brother Doctor there, perhaps may try.
What I! dear sir, the Doctor interposes,
What, plant my thistle, sir, among his roses?
No, no, I've other contests to maintain;
To-night I head our troops at Warwick Lane. [2]
Go, ask your manager [3]—Who, me? Your pardon;
Those things are not our forte at Covent Garden.
Our Author's friends, thus plac'd at happy distance,
Give him good words indeed, but no assistance.
As some unhappy wight, at some new play,
At the Pit door stands elbowing away,
While oft, with many a smile, and many a shrug,

[1 "The Author, in expectation of an Epilogue from a friend at Oxford, deferred writing one himself till the very last hour. What is here offered, owes all its success to the graceful manner of the Actress [Mrs. Bulkley] who spoke it" [Goldsmith's note.]

[2 A reference to the pending quarrel between the Fellows and Licentiates of the College of Physicians in Warwick Lane, respecting the exclusion of some of the Licentiates from Fellowships.]

[3 George Colman, the elder.]

He eyes the centre, where his friends sit snug,
His simpering friends with pleasure in their eyes,
Sink as he sinks, and as he rises rise :
He nods, they nod ; he cringes, they grimace ;
But not a soul will budge to give him place.
Since then, unhelp'd, our bard must now conform
To 'bide the pelting of this pitiless storm,[1]
Blame where you must, be candid where you can,
And be each critic the Good-Natur'd Man.

[1 *King Lear*, Act III. Sc. 4.]

SHE STOOPS TO CONQUER:

OR,

THE MISTAKES OF A NIGHT

A COMEDY

[*She Stoops to Conquer* was produced at Covent Garden, Monday, the 15th March, 1773. It was played twelve times before the conclusion of the season (31st May), the tenth representation (5th May) being commanded by the King and Queen. On the 26th March it was published in *octavo* by Francis Newbery, at the corner of St. Paul's Churchyard, with the following title:— *She Stoops to Conquer: or, The Mistakes of a Night. A Comedy. As it is acted at the Theatre-Royal in Covent Garden. Written by Docter Goldsmith.* The price was one shilling and sixpence. The present reprint is from the fourth edition which appeared in the same year as the first.]

TO SAMUEL JOHNSON, LL.D.

Dear Sir,

By inscribing this slight performance to you, I do not mean so much to compliment you as myself. It may do me some honour to inform the public, that I have lived many years in intimacy with you. It may serve the interests of mankind also to inform them, that the greatest wit may be found in a character, without impairing the most unaffected piety.

I have, particularly, reason to thank you for your partiality to this performance.[1] The undertaking a comedy, not merely sentimental, was very dangerous[2]; and Mr. Colman, who saw this piece in its various stages, always thought it so. However, I ventured to trust it to the public; and, though it was necessarily delayed till late in the season,[3] I have every reason to be grateful.

I am, dear sir,
Your most sincere friend
And admirer,
OLIVER GOLDSMITH.

[1 Johnson had throughout befriended the play, and had been mainly instrumental in inducing Colman to produce it.]

[2 Because of the popularity of genteel or sentimental comedy.

[3 *I.e.*, when, owing to holidays and actors' benefits, there could not be many representations.]

PROLOGUE

BY DAVID GARRICK, ESQ.

Enter Mr. WOODWARD,[1] *dressed in black, and holding a Handkerchief to his Eyes*

EXCUSE me, sirs, I pray—I can't yet speak—
I'm crying now—and have been all the week!
'Tis not alone this mourning suit, good masters;[2]
I've that within—for which there are no plasters!
Pray would you know the reason why I'm crying?
The Comic muse, long sick, is now a-dying!
And if she goes, my tears will never stop:
For as a player, I can't squeeze out one drop:
I am undone, that's all—shall lose my bread—
I'd rather, but that's nothing—lose my head.
When the sweet maid is laid upon the bier,
Shuter and *I* shall be chief mourners here.
To *her* a mawkish drab of spurious breed,
Who deals in *sentimentals* will succeed!
Poor *Ned* and *I* are dead to all intents,
We can as soon speak *Greek* as *sentiments!*
Both nervous grown, to keep our spirits up,
We now and then take down a hearty cup.
What shall we do?—If Comedy forsake us!
They'll turn us out, and no one else will take us,
But why can't I be moral?—Let me try—
My heart thus pressing—fix'd my face and eye—
With a sententious look, that nothing means
(Faces are blocks, in sentimental scenes),
Thus I begin—*All is not gold that glitters,*
Pleasure seems sweet, but proves a glass of bitters.
When ignorance enters, folly is at hand;

[1 Woodward had no part in the piece. He refused "Tony Lumpkin," which fell to Quick, who had played the "Postboy" in *The Good-Natur'd Man.*]

[2 *Hamlet*, Act I. Sc. 2.]

Learning is better far than house and land.
Let not your virtue trip, who trips may stumble,
And virtue is not virtue, if she tumble.

I give it up—morals won't do for me;
To make you laugh I must play tragedy.
One hope remains—hearing the maid was ill,
A *doctor* comes this night to show his skill.
To cheer her heart, and give your muscles motion,
He in *five draughts* prepar'd, presents a potion:
A kind of magic charm—for be assur'd,
If you will *swallow* it, the maid is cur'd.
But desperate the Doctor, and her case is,
If you reject the dose, and make wry faces!
This truth he boasts, will boast it while he lives,
No *poisonous drugs* are mix'd in what he gives;
Should he succeed, you'll give him his degree;
If not, within he will receive no fee!
The college *you*, must his pretentions back,
Pronounce him *regular*, or dub him *quack*.

DRAMATIS PERSONÆ[1]

MEN

Sir Charles Marlow,	Mr. Gardner.
Young Marlow (his Son)	Mr. Lewes.
Hardcastle,	Mr. Shuter.
Hastings,	Mr. Dubellamy.
Tony Lumpkin,	Mr. Quick.
Diggory,	Mr. Saunders.

WOMEN

Mrs. Hardcastle,	Mrs. Green.
Miss Hardcastle,	Mrs. Bulkley.
Miss Neville,	Mrs. Kniveton.
Maid,	Miss Willems.

Landlords, Servants, &c., &c.

[1 The cast given is that of the piece as first acted.]

SHE STOOPS TO CONQUER:

OR,

THE MISTAKES OF A NIGHT[1]

ACT I

SCENE—*A Chamber in an old-fashioned House*

Enter Mrs. HARDCASTLE *and* Mr. HARDCASTLE

Mrs. Hardcastle. I vow, Mr. Hardcastle, you're very particular. Is there a creature in the whole country, but ourselves, that does not take a trip to town now and then, to rub off the rust a little? There's the two Miss Hoggs, and our neighbour, Mrs. Grigsby, go to take a month's polishing every winter.

Hard. Ay, and bring back vanity and affectation to last them the whole year. I wonder why London cannot keep its own fools at home. In my time, the follies of the town crept slowly among us, but now they travel faster than a stage-coach. Its fopperies come down, not only as inside passengers, but in the very basket.[2]

Mrs. Hard. Ay, *your* times were fine times, indeed; you have been telling us of *them* for many a long year. Here we live in an old rumbling mansion, that looks for all the world like an inn, but that we never see company. Our best visitors are old Mrs. Oddfish, the curate's wife,

[1 Mitford suggested to Mr. Forster that the first title originated in Dryden's—

"But kneels to conquer, and but stoops to rise."

The second title was originally the only one (see p. 289); but was rejected as undignified. Reynolds wanted to christen the play *The Belle's Stratagem*, a name afterwards used by Mrs. Cowley. *The Old House a New Inn* was also debated.]

[2 A large wicker receptacle fixed on the hind axle-tree, sometimes used for luggage, sometimes for passengers, occasionally for both. See Hogarth's *Country Inn Yard*, 1747, and note to p. 279.

and little Cripplegate, the lame dancing-master : And all
our entertainment your old stories of Prince Eugene and
the Duke of Marlborough.   I hate such old-fashioned
trumpery.

Hard. And I love it.   I love everything that's old :
old friends, old times, old manners, old books, old wine ;
and, I believe, Dorothy (*taking her hand*), you'll own I
have been pretty fond of an old wife.

Mrs. Hard. Lord, Mr. Hardcastle, you're for ever at
your Dorothys and your old wifes.   You may be a
Darby, but I'll be no Joan, I promise you.   I'm not
so old as you'd make me, by more than one good year.
Add twenty to twenty, and make money of that.

Hard. Let me see ; twenty added to twenty, makes
just fifty and seven !

Mrs. Hard. It's false, Mr. Hardcastle : I was but
twenty when I was brought to bed of Tony, that I had
by Mr. Lumpkin, my first husband ; and he's not come
to years of discretion yet.

Hard. Nor ever will, I dare answer for him.   Ay, you
have taught *him* finely !

Mrs. Hard. No matter, Tony Lumpkin has a good
fortune.   My son is not to live by his learning.   I don't
think a boy wants much learning to spend fifteen hundred
a year.

Hard. Learning, quotha !   A mere composition of
tricks and mischief !

Mrs. Hard. Humour, my dear : nothing but humour.
Come, Mr. Hardcastle, you must allow the boy a little
humour.

Hard. I'd sooner allow him a horse-pond !   If burning the footmen's shoes, frightening the maids, and
worrying the kittens, be humour, he has it.   It was but
yesterday he fastened my wig to the back of my chair,
and when I went to make a bow, I popped my bald head
in Mrs. Frizzle's face ! [1]

Mrs. Hard. And am I to blame ?   The poor boy was
always too sickly to do any good.   A school would be

[1 A trick played on Goldsmith himself by Lord Clare's daughter.
(Forster's *Life of Goldsmith*, Bk. iv., ch. 15, n. 4.)]

his death. When he comes to be a little stronger, who know what a year or two's Latin may do for him?

Hard. Latin for him! A cat and fiddle! No, no, the ale-house and the stable are the only schools he'll ever go to!

Mrs. Hard. Well, we must not snub the poor boy now, for I believe we shan't have him long among us. Anybody that looks in his face may see he's consumptive.

Hard. Ay, if growing too fat be one of the symptoms.

Mrs. Hard. He coughs sometimes.

Hard. Yes, when his liquor goes the wrong way.

Mrs. Hard. I'm actually afraid of his lungs.

Hard. And truly, so am I; for he sometimes whoops like a speaking-trumpet—(TONY *hallooing behind the Scenes.*)—O, there he goes.—A very consumptive figure, truly!

Enter TONY, *crossing the stage*

Mrs. Hard. Tony, where are you going, my charmer? Won't you give papa and I a little of your company, lovey?

Tony. I'm in haste, mother, I cannot stay.

Mrs. Hard. You shan't venture out this raw evening, my dear: You look most shockingly.

Tony. I can't stay, I tell you. The Three Pigeons expects me down every moment. There's some fun going forward.

Hard. Ay; the ale-house, the old place: I thought so.

Mrs. Hard. A low, paltry set of fellows.

Tony. Not so low, neither. There's Dick Muggins the exciseman, Jack Slang the horse doctor, Little Aminadab that grinds the music-box, and Tom Twist that spins the pewter platter.

Mrs. Hard. Pray, my dear, disappoint them for one night, at least.

Tony. As for disappointing *them*, I should not much mind; but I can't abide to disappoint *myself!*

Mrs. Hard. (*Detaining him.*) You shan't go.

Tony. I will, I tell you.

Mrs. Hard. I say you shan't.

Tony. We'll see which is strongest, you or I.

[*Exit hauling her out.*

HARDCASTLE *solus*

Hard. Ay, there goes a pair that only spoil each other. But is not the whole age in a combination to drive sense and discretion out of doors? There's my pretty darling Kate; the fashions of the times have almost infected her too. By living a year or two in town, she is as fond of gauze, and French frippery, as the best of them.

Enter Miss HARDCASTLE

Hard. Blessings on my pretty innocence! Dressed out as my usual, my Kate! Goodness! What a quantity of superfluous silk hast thou got about thee, girl! I could never teach the fools of this age, that the indigent world could be clothed out of the trimmings of the vain.

Miss Hard. You know our agreement, sir. You allow me the morning to receive and pay visits, and to dress in my own manner; and in the evening, I put on my housewife's dress, to please you.

Hard. Well, remember, I insist on the terms of our agreement; and, by-the-bye, I believe I shall have occasion to try your obedience this very evening.

Miss Hard. I protest, sir, I don't comprehend your meaning.

Hard. Then to be plain with you, Kate, I expect the young gentleman I have chosen to be your husband from town this very day. I have his father's letter, in which he informs me his son is set out, and that he intends to follow himself shortly after.

Miss Hard. Indeed! I wish I had known something of this before. Bless me, how shall I behave? It's a thousand to one I shan't like him; our meeting will be so formal, and so like a thing of business, that I shall find no room for friendship or esteem.

Hard. Depend upon it, child, I'll never control your choice; but Mr. Marlow, whom I have pitched upon, is the son of my old friend, Sir Charles Marlow, of whom you have heard me talk so often. The young gentleman has been bred a scholar, and is designed for an employment in the service of his country. I am told he's a man of an excellent understanding.

Miss Hard. Is he?

Hard. Very generous.

Miss Hard. I believe I shall like him.

Hard. Young and brave.

Miss Hard. I'm sure I shall like him.

Hard. And very handsome.

Miss Hard. My dear papa, say no more (*kissing his hand*), he's mine, I'll have him!

Hard. And, to crown all, Kate, he's one of the most bashful and reserved young fellows in all the world.

Miss Hard. Eh! you have frozen me to death again. That word reserved has undone all the rest of his accomplishments. A reserved lover, it is said, always makes a suspicious husband.

Hard. On the contrary, modesty seldom resides in a breast that is not enriched with nobler virtues. It was the very feature in his character that first struck me.

Miss Hard. He must have more striking features to catch me, I promise you. However, if he be so young, so handsome, and so everything, as you mention, I believe he'll do still. I think I'll have him.

Hard. Ay, Kate, but there is still an obstacle. It is more than an even wager, he may not have *you.*

Miss Hard. My dear papa, why will you mortify one so?—Well, if he refuses, instead of breaking my heart at his indifference, I'll only break my glass for its flattery. Set my cap to some newer fashion, and look out for some less difficult admirer.

Hard. Bravely resolved! In the meantime I'll go prepare the servants for his reception; as we seldom see company, they want as much training as a company of recruits the first day's muster.   [*Exit.*

Miss Hardcastle *sola*

Miss Hard. Lud, this news of papa's puts me all in a flutter. Young, handsome; these he put last; but I put them foremost. Sensible, good-natur'd; I like all that. But then reserved, and sheepish, that's much against him. Yet can't he be cured of his timidity, by being taught to be proud of his wife. Yes, and can't I— But I vow I'm disposing of the husband before I have secured the lover!

Enter Miss Neville

Miss Hard. I'm glad you're come, Neville, my dear. Tell me, Constance, how do I look this evening? Is there anything whimsical about me? Is it one of my well-looking days, child? Am I in face to-day?

Miss Neville. Perfectly, my dear. Yet, now I look again—bless me!—sure no accident has happened among the canary birds or the goldfishes? Has your brother or the cat been meddling? Or has the last novel been too moving?

Miss Hard. No; nothing of all this. I have been threatened—I can scarce get it out—I have been threatened with a lover!

Miss Neville. And his name——

Miss Hard. Is Marlow.

Miss Neville. Indeed!

Miss Hard. The son of Sir Charles Marlow.

Miss Neville. As I live, the most intimate friend of Mr. Hastings, *my* admirer. They are never asunder. I believe you must have seen him when we lived in town.

Miss Hard. Never.

Miss Neville. He's a very singular character, I assure you. Among women of reputation and virtue, he is the modestest man alive: but his acquaintance give him a very different character among creatures of another stamp: you understand me?

Miss Hard. An odd character, indeed! I shall never be able to manage him. What shall I do? Pshaw, think no more of him, but trust to occurrences for success. But how goes on your own affair, my dear? Has my mother been courting you for my brother Tony, as usual?

Miss Neville. I have just come from one of our agreeable *tête-à-têtes.* She has been saying a hundred tender things, and setting off her pretty monster as the very pink of perfection.

Miss Hard. And her partiality is such, that she actually thinks him so. A fortune like yours is no small temptation. Besides, as she has the sole management of it, I'm not surprised to see her unwilling to let it go out of the family.

Miss Neville. A fortune like mine, which chiefly consists in jewels, is no such mighty temptation. But, at any rate, if my dear Hastings be but constant, I make no doubt to be too hard for her at last. However, I let her suppose that I am in love with her son, and she never once dreams that my affections are fixed upon another.

Miss Hard. My good brother holds out stoutly. I could almost love him for hating you so.

Miss Neville. It is a good-natur'd creature at bottom, and I'm sure would wish to see me married to anybody but himself. But my aunt's bell rings for our afternoon's walk through the improvements. *Allons.* Courage is necessary, as our affairs are critical.

Miss Hard. Would it were bed-time and all were well.[1]   *[Exeunt.*

SCENE—*An Alehouse Room. Several shabby fellows, with punch and tobacco.* TONY *at the head of the table, a little higher than the rest: a mallet in his hand.*

Omnes. Hurrea, hurrea, hurrea, bravo!

First Fellow. Now, gentlemen, silence for a song The 'Squire is going to knock himself down for a song.

Omnes. Ay, a song, a song.

[1 *Henry* IV. Act v. Sc. 1.]

Tony.   Then I'll sing you, gentlemen, a song I made upon this ale-house, the Three Pigeons.

SONG

Let school-masters puzzle their brain,
  With grammar, and nonsense, and learning;
Good liquor, I stoutly maintain,
  Gives genus *a better discerning,*
Let them brag of their Heathenish Gods,
  Their Lethes, their Styxes, and Stygians;
Their Quis, and their Quæs, and their Quods,
  They're all but a parcel of Pigeons.

                    Toroddle, toroddle, toroll !

When Methodist preachers come down,
  A-preaching that drinking is sinful,
I'll wager the rascals a crown,
  They always preach best with a skinful.
But when you come down with your pence,
  For a slice of their scurvy religion,
I'll leave it to all men of sense,
  But you, my good friend, are the pigeon.

                    Toroddle, toroddle, toroll !

Then come, put the jorum about,
  And let us be merry and clever,
Our hearts and our liquors are stout,
  Here's the Three Jolly Pigeons for ever.
Let some cry up woodcock or hare,
  Your bustards, your ducks, and your widgeons:
But of all the birds in the air,
  Here's a health to the Three Jolly Pigeons.

                    Toroddle, toroddle, toroll !

Omnes.   Bravo, bravo !
First Fellow.   The 'Squire has got spunk in him.
Second Fellow.   I loves to hear him sing, bekeays he never gives us nothing that's *low.*[1]

[1 Goldsmith, Fielding, and other contemporary humorists much objected to this particular form of depreciation on the part of the sentimentalists. In the whole of this discussion, the author, no doubt, had in mind the rejection of the Bailiff scene in *The Good-Natur'd Man* (cf. p. 131, " Preface ").

Third Fellow. O damn anything that's *low*, I cannot bear it!

Fourth Fellow. The genteel thing is the genteel thing at any time. If so be that a gentleman bees in a concatenation accordingly.

Third Fellow. I like the maxum of it, Master Muggins. What, though I am obligated to dance a bear, a man may be a gentleman for all that. May this be my poison if my bear ever dances but to the very genteelest of tunes. Water Parted,[1] or the minuet in Ariadne.[2]

Second Fellow. What a pity it is the 'Squire is not come to his own. It would be well for all the publicans within ten miles round of him.

Tony. Ecod, and so it would, Master Slang. I'd then show what it was to keep choice of company.

Second Fellow. O, he takes after his own father for that. To be sure, old 'Squire Lumpkin was the finest gentleman I ever set my eyes on. For winding the straight horn, or beating a thicket for a hare, or a wench, he never had his fellow. It was a saying in the place, that he kept the best horses, dogs, and girls in the whole county.

Tony. Ecod, and when I'm of age I'll be no bastard, I promise you. I have been thinking of Bet Bouncer and the miller's grey mare to begin with. But come, my boys, drink about and be merry, for you pay no reckoning. Well, Stingo, what's the matter?

Enter LANDLORD

Landlord. There be two gentlemen in a post-chaise at the door. They have lost their way upo' the forest; and they are talking something about Mr. Hardcastle.

Tony. As sure as can be, one of them must be the gentleman that's coming down to court my sister. Do they seem to be Londoners?

Landlord. I believe they may. They look woundily like Frenchmen.

[1 The song of Arbaces in Arne's *Artaxerxes*, 1762.]
[2 By Handel. The minuet came at the end of the overture, and is said to have been the best thing in the opera.]

Tony. Then desire them to step this way, and I'll set them right in a twinkling. (*Exit Landlord.*) Gentlemen, as they mayn't be good enough company for you, step down for a moment, and I'll be with you in the squeezing of a lemon.   [*Exeunt Mob.*

TONY *solus*

Tony. Father-in-law has been calling me whelp, and hound, this half year. Now, if I pleased, I could be so revenged upon the old grumbletonian. But then I'm afraid—afraid of what? I shall soon be worth fifteen hundred a year, and let him frighten me out of *that* if he can!

Enter LANDLORD, *conducting* MARLOW *and* HASTINGS

Marlow. What a tedious uncomfortable day have we had of it! We were told it was but forty miles across the country, and we have come above threescore!

Hastings. And all, Marlow, from that unaccountable reserve of yours, that would not let us enquire more frequently on the way.

Marlow. I own, Hastings, I am unwilling to lay myself under an obligation to every one I meet; and often stand the chance of an unmannerly answer.

Hastings. At present, however, we are not likely to receive any answer.

Tony. No offence, gentlemen. But I'm told you have been enquiring for one Mr. Hardcastle, in these parts. Do you know what part of the country you are in?

Hastings. Not in the least, sir, but should thank you for information.

Tony. Nor the way you came?

Hastings. No, sir, but if you can inform us——

Tony. Why, gentlemen, if you know neither the road you are going, nor where you are, nor the road you came, the first thing I have to inform is, that—you have lost your way.

Marlow. We wanted no ghost to tell us that.[1]

[[1] *Hamlet*, Act I., Sc. 5.]

Tony. Pray, gentlemen, may I be so bold as to ask the place from whence you came?

Marlow. That's not necessary towards directing us where we are to go.

Tony. No offence; but question for question is all fair, you know. Pray, gentlemen, is not this same Hardcastle a cross-grained, old-fashioned, whimsical fellow with an ugly face; a daughter, and a pretty son?

Hastings. We have not seen the gentleman, but he has the family you mention.

Tony. The daughter, a tall, trapesing, trolloping, talk-ative maypole—— The son, a pretty, well-bred, agreeable youth, that everybody is fond of!

Marlow. Our information differs in this. The daughter is said to be well-bred and beautiful; the son, an awk-ward booby, reared up and spoiled at his mother's apron-string.

Tony. He-he-hem—then, gentlemen, all I have to tell you is, that you won't reach Mr. Hardcastle's house this night, I believe.

Hastings. Unfortunate!

Tony. It's a damned long, dark, boggy, dirty, danger-ous way. Stingo, tell the gentlemen the way to Mr. Hardcastle's. (*Winking upon the Landlord.*) Mr. Hardcastle's of Quagmire Marsh, you understand me.

Landlord. Master Hardcastle's! Lack-a-daisy, my masters, you're come a deadly deal wrong! When you came to the bottom of the hill, you should have crossed down Squash Lane.

Marlow. Cross down Squash Lane!

Landlord. Then you were to keep straight forward, until you came to four roads.

Marlow. Come to where four roads meet!

Tony. Ay, but you must be sure to take only one of them.

Marlow. O, sir, you're facetious!

Tony. Then, keeping to the right, you are to go side-ways till you come upon Crack-skull common: there you must look sharp for the track of the wheel, and go forward, till you come to farmer Murrain's barn. Coming to the farmer's barn, you are to turn to the right, and then to the left, and then to the right about again, till you find out the old mill——

Marlow. Zounds, man! we could as soon find out the longitude![1]

Hastings. What's to be done, Marlow?

Marlow. This house promises but a poor reception, though, perhaps, the landlord can accommodate us.

Landlord. Alack, master, we have but one spare bed in the whole house.

Tony. And to my knowledge, that's taken up by three lodgers already. (*After a pause, in which the rest seem disconcerted.*) I have hit it. Don't you think, Stingo, our landlady could accommodate the gentlemen by the fire-side, with——three chairs and a bolster?

Hastings. I hate sleeping by the fire-side.

Marlow. And I detest your three chairs and a bolster.

Tony. You do, do you?—then let me see—what—if you go on a mile further, to the Buck's Head; the old Buck's Head on the hill, one of the best inns in the whole country?

Hastings. Oh, oh! so we have escaped an adventure for this night, however.

Landlord (*apart to Tony*). Sure, you ben't sending them to your father's as an inn, be you?[2]

Tony. Mum, you fool, you. Let *them* find that out. (*To them.*) You have only to keep on straight forward, till you come to a large old house by the roadside. You'll see a pair of large horns over the door. That's the sign. Drive up the yard, and call stoutly about you.

Hastings. Sir, we are obliged to you. The servants can't miss the way?

[1 This was a popular inquiry in the last century, owing to the reward of £20,000 offered by Parliament in 1714 for the discovery of a means of accurately ascertaining the longitude at sea. The father of Johnson's friend, Miss Williams, is said by Boswell to have made "many ingenious advances" in this direction; but the reward was finally gained by John Harrison.]

[2 This was the recollection of a trick played upon Goldsmith himself in his youth. Inquiring at Ardagh, with boyish importance, for the "best house" (*i. e.* inn) he was directed by a practical joker to the residence of the local magnate, Squire Featherstone.]

Tony. No, no : But I tell you though, the landlord is rich, and going to leave off business ; so he wants to be thought a gentleman, saving your presence, he ! he ! he ! He'll be for giving you his company, and, ecod, if you mind him, he'll persuade you that his mother was an alderman, and his aunt a justice of the peace !

Landlord. A troublesome old blade, to be sure ; but 'a keeps as good wines and beds as any in the whole country.

Marlow. Well, if he supplies us with these, we shall want no further connection. We are to turn to the right, did you say ?

Tony. No, no ; straight forward. I'll just step myself, and show you a piece of the way. (*To the Landlord.*) Mum.

Landlord. Ah, bless your heart, for a sweet, pleasant ——damned mischievous son of a whore.

[*Exeunt.*

END OF THE FIRST ACT

ACT II

SCENE—*An old-fashioned House*

Enter HARDCASTLE, *followed by three or four awkward Servants*

Hard. Well, I hope you're perfect in the table exercise I have been teaching you these three days. You all know your posts and your places, and can show that you have been used to good company, without ever stirring from home.

Omnes. Ay, ay.

Hard. When company comes, you are not to pop out and stare, and then run in again, like frightened rabbits in a warren.

Omnes. No, no.

Hard. You, Diggory, whom I have taken from the

barn are to make a show at the side-table; and you, Roger, whom I have advanced from the plough, are to place yourself behind *my* chair. But you're not to stand so, with your hands in your pockets. Take your hands from your pockets, Roger; and from your head, you blockhead, you. See how Diggory carries his hands. They're a little too stiff, indeed, but that's no great matter.

Diggory. Ay, mind how I hold them. I learned to hold my hands this way, when I was upon drill for the militia. And so being upon drill——

Hard. You must not be so talkative, Diggory. You must be all attention to the guests. You must hear us talk, and not think of talking; you must see us drink and not think of drinking; you must see us eat and not think of eating.

Diggory. By the laws, your worship, that's parfectly unpossible. Whenever Diggory sees yeating going forward, ecod, he's always wishing for a mouthful himself.

Hard. Blockhead! Is not a bellyful in the kitchen as good as a bellyful in the parlour? Stay your stomach with that reflection.

Diggory. Ecod, I thank your worship, I'll make a shift to stay my stomach with a slice of cold beef in the pantry.

Hard. Diggory, you are too talkative. Then, if I happen to say a good thing, or tell a good story at table, you must not all burst out a-laughing, as if you made part of the company.

Diggory. Then, ecod, your worship must not tell the story of Ould Grouse in the gun-room:[1] I can't help laughing at that—he! he! he!—for the soul of me! We have laughed at that these twenty years—ha! ha! ha!

Hard. Ha! ha! ha! The story is a good one. Well, honest Diggory, you may laugh at that—but still remember to be attentive. Suppose one of the company should call for a glass of wine, how will you behave?

[1 This story has escaped identification, like "Taffy in the Sedan Chair," in Letter xxvii. of *The Citizen of the World.*]

A glass of wine, sir, if you please (*to* DIGGORY)—Eh, why don't you move?

Diggory. Ecod, your worship, I never have courage till I see the eatables and drinkables brought upo' the table, and then I'm as bauld as a lion.

Hard. What, will nobody move?

First Servant. I'm not to leave this pleace.

Second Servant. I'm sure its no pleace of mine.

Third Servant. Nor mine for sartain.

Diggory. Wauns, and I'm sure it canna be mine.

Hard. You numskulls! and so while, like your betters, you are quarrelling for places, the guests must be starved. O, you dunces! I find I must begin all over again.— But don't I hear a coach drive into the yard? To your posts, you blockheads! I'll go in the meantime and give my old friend's son a hearty reception at the gate.

[*Exit* HARDCASTLE.

Diggory. By the elevens, my pleace is gone quite out of my head!

Roger. I know that my pleace is to be everywhere!

First Servant. Where the devil is mine?

Second Servant. My pleace is to be nowhere at all; and so I ze go about my business!

[*Exeunt Servants, running about as if frighted, different ways.*

Enter SERVANTS *with Candles, showing in* MARLOW *and* HASTINGS

Servant. Welcome, gentlemen, very welcome. This way.

Hastings. After the disappointments of the day, welcome once more, Charles, to the comforts of a clean room and a good fire. Upon my word, a very well-looking house; antique but creditable.

Marlow. The usual fate of a large mansion. Having first ruined the master by good housekeeping, it at last comes to levy contributions as an inn.

Hastings. As you say, we passengers are to be taxed to pay all these fineries. I have often seen a good sideboard, or a marble chimney-piece, though not actually put in the bill, inflame a reckoning confoundedly.

Marlow. Travellers, George, must pay in all places. The only difference is, that in good inns, you pay dearly for luxuries ; in bad inns, you are fleeced and starved.

Hastings. You have lived pretty much among them. In truth, I have been often surprised, that you who have seen so much of the world, with your natural good sense, and your many opportunities, could never yet acquire a requisite share of assurance.

Marlow. The Englishman's malady.   But tell me, George, where could I have learned that assurance you talk of ?   My life has been chiefly spent in a college, or an inn, in seclusion from that lovely part of the creation that chiefly teach men confidence.   I don't know that I was ever familiarly acquainted with a single modest woman—except my mother—but among females of another class, you know—

Hastings. Ay, among them you are impudent enough of all conscience !

Marlow. They are of *us*, you know.

Hastings. But in the company of women of reputation I never saw such an idiot, such a trembler ; you look for all the world as if you wanted an opportunity of stealing out of the room.

Marlow. Why, man, that's because I *do* want to steal out of the room.   Faith, I have often formed a resolution to break the ice, and rattle away at any rate.   But I don't know how, a single glance from a pair of fine eyes has totally overset my resolution.   An impudent fellow may counterfeit modesty, but I'll be hanged if a modest man can ever counterfeit impudence.

Hastings. If you could but say half the fine things to them that I have heard you lavish upon the barmaid of an inn, or even a college bedmaker—

Marlow. Why, George, I can't say fine things to them. They freeze, they petrify me.   They may talk of a comet, or a burning mountain, or some such bagatelle. But to me, a modest woman, dressed out in all her finery, is the most tremendous object of the whole creation.

Hastings. Ha! ha! ha!   At this rate, man, how can you ever expect to marry!

Marlow. Never, unless, as among kings and princes, my bride were to be courted by proxy. If, indeed, like an Eastern bridegroom, one were to be introduced to a wife he never saw before, it might be endured. But to go through all the terrors of a formal courtship, together with the episode of aunts, grandmothers and cousins, and at last to blurt out the broad staring question of, *madam, will you marry me?* No, no, that's a strain much above me, I assure you!

Hastings. I pity you. But how do you intend behaving to the lady you are come down to visit at the request of your father?

Marlow. As I behave to all other ladies. Bow very low. Answer yes, or no, to all her demands—But for the rest, I don't think I shall venture to look in her face, till I see my father's again.

Hastings. I'm surprised that one who is so warm a friend can be so cool a lover.

Marlow. To be explicit, my dear Hastings, my chief inducement down was to be instrumental in forwarding your happiness, not my own. Miss Neville loves you, the family don't know you, as my friend you are sure of a reception, and let honour do the rest.

Hastings. My dear Marlow! But I'll suppress the emotion. Were I a wretch, meanly seeking to carry off a fortune, you should be the last man in the world I would apply to for assistance. But Miss Neville's person is all I ask, and that is mine, both from her deceased father's consent and her own inclination.

Marlow. Happy man! You have talents and art to captivate any woman. I'm doomed to adore the sex, and yet to converse with the only part of it I despise. This stammer in my address, and this awkward prepossessing visage of mine, can never permit me to soar above the reach of a milliner's apprentice, or one of the duchesses of Drury Lane. Pshaw! this fellow here to interrupt us.

Enter HARDCASTLE

Hard. Gentlemen, once more you are heartily welcome. Which is Mr. Marlow? Sir, you're heartily welcome. It's not my way, you see, to receive my friends with my back to the fire. I like to give them a hearty reception in the old style at my gate. I like to see their horses and trunks taken care of.

Marlow (*aside*). He has got our names from the servants already. (*To him.*) We approve your caution and hospitality, sir. (*To* HASTINGS.) I have been thinking, George, of changing our travelling dresses in the morning. I am grown confoundedly ashamed of mine.

Hard. I beg, Mr. Marlow, you'll use no ceremony in this house.

Hastings. I fancy, George, you're right : the first blow is half the battle. I intend opening the campaign with the white and gold.

Hard. Mr. Marlow—Mr. Hastings—gentlemen—pray be under no constraint in this house. This is Liberty Hall, gentlemen. You may do just as you please here.

Marlow. Yet, George if we open the campaign too fiercely at first, we may want ammunition before it is over. I think to reserve the embroidery to secure a retreat.

Hard. Your talking of a retreat, Mr. Marlow, puts me in mind of the Duke of Marlborough, when we went to besiege Denain. He first summoned the garrison——

Marlow. Don't you think the *ventre d'or* waistcoat will do with the plain brown.

Hard. He first summoned the garrison, which might consist of about five thousand men——

Hastings. I think not : brown and yellow mix but very poorly.

Hard. I say, gentlemen, as I was telling you, he summoned the garrison, which might consist of about five thousand men——

Marlow. The girls like finery.

Hard. Which might consist of about five thousand men,

well appointed with stores, ammunition, and other implements of war. "Now," says the Duke of Marlborough to George Brooks, that stood next to him—you must have heard of George Brooks; "I'll pawn my Dukedom," says he, "but I take that garrison without spilling a drop of blood!" So——

Marlow. What, my good friend, if you gave us a glass of punch in the meantime, it would help us to carry on the siege with vigour.

Hard. Punch, sir!——(*Aside.*) This is the most unaccountable kind of modesty I ever met with!

Marlow. Yes, sir, punch! A glass of warm punch, after our journey, will be comfortable. This is Liberty Hall, you know.

Hard. Here's cup, sir.

Marlow (*aside*). So this fellow, in his Liberty Hall, will only let us have just what he pleases.

Hard (*taking the cup*). I hope you'll find it to your mind. I have prepared it with my own hands, and I believe you'll own the ingredients are tolerable. Will you be so good as to pledge me, sir? Here, Mr. Marlow, here is our better acquaintance! [*Drinks.*

Marlow (*aside*). A very impudent fellow this! but he's a character, and I'll humour him a little. Sir, my service to you. [*Drinks.*

Hastings (*aside*). I see this fellow wants to give us his company, and forgets that he's an innkeeper, before he has learned to be a gentleman.

Marlow. From the excellence of your cup, my old friend, I suppose you have a good deal of business in this part of the country. Warm work, now and then, at elections, I suppose?

Hard. No, sir, I have long given that work over. Since our betters have hit upon the expedient of electing each other, there's no business *for us that sell ale.*

Hastings. So, then you have no turn for politics, I find.

Hard. Not in the least. There was a time, indeed, I fretted myself about the mistakes of government, like other people; but finding myself every day grow more

angry, and the government growing no better, I left it to
mend itself. Since that, I no more trouble my head
about *Heyder Ally*,[1] *Ally Cawn*,[2] than about *Ally Croker*.[3]
Sir, my service to you.

Hastings. So that, with eating above stairs, and drinking below, with receiving your friends within, and amusing them without, you lead a good pleasant bustling life
of it.

Hard. I do stir about a great deal, that's certain.
Half the differences of the parish are adjusted in this
very parlour.

Marlow (*After drinking*). And you have an argument
in your cup, old gentleman, better than any in Westminster Hall.

Hard. Ay, young gentleman, that, and a little philosophy.

Marlow (*aside*). Well, this is the first time I ever heard
of an innkeeper's philosophy.

Hastings. So then, like an experienced general, you
attack them on every quarter. If you find their reason
manageable, you attack it with your philosophy; if you
find they have no reason, you attack them with this.
Here's your health, my philosopher.   [*Drinks.*

Hard. Good, very good, thank you; ha! ha! Your
generalship puts me in mind of Prince Eugene, when he
fought the Turks at the battle of Belgrade. You shall
hear.

Marlow. Instead of the battle of Belgrade, I believe
it's almost time to talk about supper. What has your
philosophy got in the house for supper?

Hard. For supper, sir!——(*Aside.*) Was ever such a
request to a man in his own house!

Marlow. Yes, sir, supper, sir; I begin to feel an

[1 The famous Sultan of Mysore, 1717–82.]
[2 Cossim Ali Cawn, Subah of Bengal.]
[3 This is the Irish ditty beginning—

"There lived a man in Ballinacrasy
Who wanted a wife to make him *unasy*."

It was described as "a *new* Song" in the *Universal Magazine*
for October, 1753.

appetite. I shall make devilish work to-night in the larder, I promise you.

Hard. (*aside*). Such a brazen dog sure never my eyes beheld. (*To him.*) Why, really, sir, as for supper I can't well tell. My Dorothy, and the cook maid, settle these things between them. I leave these kind of things entirely to them.

Marlow. You do, do you?

Hard. Entirely. By-the-bye, I believe they are in actual consultation upon what's for supper this moment in the kitchen.

Marlow. Then I beg they'll admit *me* as one of their privy council. It's a way I have got. When I travel, I always choose to regulate my own supper. Let the cook be called. No offence, I hope, sir.

Hard. O, no, sir, none in the least; yet, I don't know how: our Bridget, the cook maid, is not very communicative upon these occasions. Should we send for her, she might scold us all out of the house.

Hastings. Let's see your list of the larder, then. I ask it as a favour. I always match my appetite to my bill of fare.

Marlow (*To* HARDCASTLE, *who looks at them with surprise*). Sir, he's very right, and it's my way, too.

Hard. Sir, you have a right to command here. Here, Roger, bring us the bill of fare for to-night's supper. I believe it's drawn out. Your manner, Mr. Hastings, puts me in mind of my uncle, Colonel Wallop. It was a saying of his, that no man was sure of his supper till he had eaten it.

Hastings (*aside*). All upon the high ropes! His uncle a colonel! We shall soon hear of his mother being a justice of peace. But let's hear the bill of fare.

Marlow (*Perusing*). What's here? For the first course; for the second course; for the desert. The devil, sir, do you think we have brought down the whole Joiners' Company, or the Corporation of Bedford, to eat up such a supper? Two or three little things, clean and comfortable, will do.

Hastings. But let's hear it.

Marlow (Reading). For the first course at the top, a pig, and prune sauce.

Hastings. Damn your pig, I say!

Marlow. And damn your prune sauce, say I!

Hard. And yet, gentlemen, to men that are hungry, pig, with prune sauce, is very good eating.

Marlow. At the bottom, a calf's tongue and brains.

Hastings. Let your brains be knocked out, my good sir; I don't like them.

Marlow. Or you may clap them on a plate by themselves, I do.

Hard. (aside). Their impudence confounds me. (*To them.*) Gentlemen, you are my guests, make what alterations you please. Is there anything else you wish to retrench or alter, gentlemen?

Marlow. Item. A pork pie, a boiled rabbit and sausages, a florentine, a shaking pudding, and a dish of tiff—taff—taffety cream!

Hastings. Confound your made dishes, I shall be as much at a loss in this house as at a green and yellow dinner at the French ambassador's table. I'm for plain eating.

Hard. I'm sorry, gentlemen, that I have nothing you like, but if there be anything you have a particular fancy to——

Marlow. Why, really, sir, your bill of fare is so exquisite, that any one part of it is full as good as another. Send us what you please. So much for supper. And now to see that our beds are aired, and properly taken care of.

Hard. I entreat you'll leave all that to me. You shall not stir a step.

Marlow. Leave that to you! I protest, sir, you must excuse me, I always look to these things myself.

Hard. I must insist, sir, you'll make yourself easy on that head.

Marlow. You see I'm resolved on it.—(*Aside.*) A very troublesome fellow this, as ever I met with.

Hard. Well, sir, I'm resolved at least to attend you.—

(*Aside.*) This may be modern modesty, but I never saw anything look so like old-fashioned impudence.

[*Exeunt* MARLOW *and* HARDCASTLE.

HASTINGS *solus*

Hastings. So I find this fellow's civilities begin to grow troublesome. But who can be angry at those assiduities which are meant to please him! Miss Neville, by all that's happy!

Enter Miss NEVILLE

Miss Neville. My dear Hastings! To what unexpected good fortune? to what accident am I to ascribe this happy meeting?

Hastings. Rather let me ask the same question, as I could never have hoped to meet my dearest Constance at an inn.

Miss Neville. An inn! sure you mistake! my aunt, my guardian, lives here. What could induce you to think this house an inn?

Hastings. My friend, Mr. Marlow, with whom I came down, and I, have been sent here as to an inn, I assure you. A young fellow whom we accidentally met at a house hard by directed us hither.

Miss Neville. Certainly it must be one of my hopeful cousin's tricks, of whom you have heard me talk so often, ha! ha! ha! ha!

Hastings. He whom your aunt intends for you? He of whom I have such just apprehensions?

Miss Neville. You have nothing to fear from him, I assure you. You'd adore him if you knew how heartily he despises me. My aunt knows it too, and has undertaken to court me for him, and actually begins to think she has made a conquest.

Hastings. Thou dear dissembler! You must know, my Constance, I have just seized this happy opportunity of my friend's visit here to get admittance into the family. The horses that carried us down are now fatigued with their journey, but they'll soon be refreshed; and then if my dearest girl will trust in her faithful Hastings, we shall soon be landed in France, where even among slaves the laws of marriage are respected.[1]

Miss Neville. I have often told you, that though ready to obey you, I yet should leave my little fortune behind with reluctance.   The greatest part of it was left me by my uncle, the India Director, and chiefly consists in jewels.   I have been for some time persuading my aunt to let me wear them.   I fancy I'm very near succeeding. The instant they are put into my possession you shall find me ready to make them and myself yours.

Hastings. Perish the baubles ! Your person is all I desire.   In the meantime, my friend Marlow must not be let into his mistake.   I know the strange reserve of his temper is such, that if abruptly informed of it, he would instantly quit the house before our plan was ripe for execution.

Miss Neville. But how shall we keep him in the deception ?   Miss Hardcastle is just returned from walking; what if we still continue to deceive him ?— This, this way——   [*They confer.*

Enter MARLOW

Marlow. The assiduities of these good people tease me beyond bearing.   My host seems to think it ill manners to leave me alone, and so he claps not only himself, but his old-fashioned wife on my back.   They talk of coming to sup with us, too ; and then, I suppose, we are to run the gauntlet through all the rest of the family.—What have we got here ?—

Hastings. My dear Charles ! Let me congratulate you !—The most fortunate accident !—Who do you think is just alighted ?

Marlow. Cannot guess.

Hastings. Our mistresses, boy, Miss Hardcastle and Miss Neville.   Give me leave to introduce Miss Constance Neville to your acquaintance.   Happening to dine in the neighbourhood, they called, on their return

[1 This was regarded as an oblique allusion to the marriage of the Duke of Gloucester with Lady Waldegrave, which was one of the causes of the restrictive " Royal Marriage Act" of 1772.]

to take fresh horses, here. Miss Hardcastle has just stept into the next room, and will be back in an instant. Wasn't it lucky? eh!

Marlow (aside). I have just been mortified enough of all conscience, and here comes something to complete my embarrassment.

Hastings. Well! but wasn't it the most fortunate thing in the world?

Marlow. Oh! yes. Very fortunate—a most joyful encounter——But our dresses, George, you know, are in disorder——What if we should postpone the happiness till to-morrow?——To-morrow at her own house——It will be every bit as convenient——And rather more respectful——To-morrow let it be.   [*Offering to go.*

Miss Neville. By no means, sir. Your ceremony will displease her. The disorder of your dress will shew the ardour of your impatience. Besides, she knows you are in the house, and will permit you to see her.

Marlow. O! the devil! how shall I support it? Hem! hem! Hastings, you must not go. You are to assist me, you know. I shall be confoundedly ridiculous. Yet, hang it! I'll take courage. Hem!

Hastings. Pshaw, man! it's but the first plunge, and all's over. She's but a woman, you know.

Marlow. And of all women, she that I dread most to encounter!

Enter Miss HARDCASTLE, as returned from walking, a Bonnet, &c.

Hastings (introducing them). Miss Hardcastle, Mr. Marlow, I'm proud of bringing two persons of such merit together, that only want to know, to esteem each other.

Miss Hard. (aside). Now, for meeting my modest gentleman with a demure face, and quite in his own manner. (*After a pause, in which he appears very uneasy and disconcerted.*) I'm glad of your safe arrival, sir—— I'm told you had some accidents by the way.

Marlow. Only a few, madam. Yes, we had some. Yes, madam, a good many accidents, but should be sorry

—madam—or rather glad of any accidents—that are so agreeably concluded. Hem!

Hastings (*To him*). You never spoke better in your whole life. Keep it up, and I'll insure you the victory.

Miss Hard. I'm afraid you flatter, sir. You that have seen so much of the finest company can find little entertainment in an obscure corner of the country.

Marlow (*Gathering courage*). I have lived, indeed, in the world, madam ; but I have kept very little company. I have been but an observer upon life, madam, while others were enjoying it.

Miss Neville. But that, I am told, is the way to enjoy it at last.

Hastings (*To him*). Cicero never spoke better. Once more, and you are confirmed in assurance for ever.

Marlow (*To him*). Hem! Stand by me, then, and when I'm down, throw in a word or two to set me up again.

Miss Hard. An observer, like you, upon life, were, I fear, disagreeably employed, since you must have had much more to censure than to approve.

Marlow. Pardon me, madam. I was always willing to be amused. The folly of most people is rather an object of mirth than uneasiness.

Hastings (*To him*). Bravo, bravo. Never spoke so well in your whole life. Well, Miss Hardcastle, I see that you and Mr. Marlow are going to be very good company. I believe our being here will but embarrass the interview.

Marlow. Not in the least, Mr. Hastings. We like your company of all things. (*To him.*) Zounds! George, sure you won't go? How can you leave us?

Hastings. Our presence will but spoil conversation, so we'll retire to the next room. (*To him.*) You don't consider, man, that we are to manage a little *tête-à-tête* of our own. [*Exeunt.*

Miss Hard. (*After a pause*). But you have not been wholly an observer, I presume, sir. The ladies, I should hope, have employed some part of your addresses.

Marlow (*Relapsing into timidity*). Pardon me, madam,

I—I—I—as yet have studied—only—to—deserve them.

Miss Hard. And that some say is the very worst way to obtain them.

Marlow. Perhaps so, madam. But I love to converse only with the more grave and sensible part of the sex. ——But I'm afraid I grow tiresome.

Miss Hard. Not at all sir; there is nothing I like so much as grave conversation myself: I could hear it for ever. Indeed, I have often been surprised how a man of *sentiment* could ever admire those light airy pleasures, where nothing reaches the heart.

Marlow. It's—a disease—of the mind, madam. In the variety of tastes there must be some who, wanting a relish for—um-a-um.

Miss Hard. I understand you, sir. There must be some, who, wanting a relish for refined pleasures, pretend to despise what they are incapable of tasting.

Marlow. My meaning, madam, but infinitely better expressed. And I can't help observing—a——

Miss Hard. (*aside*). Who could ever suppose this fellow impudent upon some occasions. (*To him.*) You were going to observe, sir——

Marlow. I was observing, madam——I protest, madam, I forget what I was going to observe.

Miss Hard. (*aside*). I vow and so do I. (*To him.*) You were observing, sir, that in this age of hypocrisy—something about hypocrisy, sir.

Marlow. Yes, madam. In this age of hypocrisy, there are few who upon strict enquiry do not—a—a—a——

Miss Hard. I understand you perfectly, sir.

Marlow (*aside*). Egad! and that's more than I do myself!

Miss Hard. You mean that in this hypocritical age there are few that do not condemn in public what they practise in private, and think they pay every debt to virtue when they praise it.

Marlow. True, madam; those who have most virtue in their mouths, have least of it in their bosoms. But I'm sure I tire you, madam.

Miss Hard. Not in the least, sir; there's something so agreeable and spirited in your manner, such life and force——pray, sir, go on.

Marlow. Yes, madam. I was saying——that there are some occasions——when a total want of courage, madam, destroys all the——and puts us——upon a—— a——a

Miss Hard. I agree with you entirely, a want of courage upon some occasions assumes the appearance of ignorance, and betrays us when we most want to excel. I beg you'll proceed.

Marlow. Yes, Madam. Morally speaking, madam ——but I see Miss Neville expecting us in the next room. I would not intrude for the world.

Miss Hard. I protest, sir, I never was more agreeably entertained in all my life. Pray go on.

Marlow. Yes, Madam. I was——But she beckons us to join her. Madam, shall I do myself the honour to attend you?

Miss Hard. Well then, I'll follow.

Marlow (aside). This pretty smooth dialogue has done for me. [*Exit.*

Miss Hardcastle *sola*

Miss Hard. Ha! ha! ha! Was there ever such a sober sentimental interview? I'm certain he scarce looked in my face the whole time. Yet the fellow, but for his unaccountable bashfulness, is pretty well, too. He has good sense, but then so buried in his fears, that it fatigues one more than ignorance. If I could teach him a little confidence, it would be doing somebody that I know of a piece of service. But who is that somebody?—that, faith, is a question I can scarce answer. [*Exit.*

Enter Tony *and Miss* Neville, *followed by Mrs.* Hardcastle *and* Hastings

Tony. What do you follow me for, cousin Con? I wonder you're not ashamed to be so very engaging.

Miss Neville. I hope, cousin, one may speak to one's own relations, and not be to blame.

Tony. Ay, but I know what sort of a relation you want to make me, though ; but it won't do. I tell you, cousin Con, it won't do, so I beg you'll keep your distance, I want no nearer relationship.

[*She follows coquetting him to the back scene.*

Mrs. Hard. Well! I vow, Mr. Hastings, you are very entertaining. There's nothing in the world I love to talk of so much as London, and the fashions, though I was never there myself.

Hastings. Never there! You amaze me! From your air and manner, I concluded you had been bred all your life either at Ranelagh, St. James's, or Tower Wharf.

Mrs. Hard. O! sir, you're only pleased to say so. We country persons can have no manner at all. I'm in love with the town, and that serves to raise me above some of our neighbouring rustics ; but who can have a manner, that has never seen the Pantheon, the Grotto Gardens, the Borough, and such places where the nobility chiefly resort? All I can do is to enjoy London at second-hand. I take care to know every *tête-à-tête* from the Scandalous Magazine,[1] and have all the fashions as they come out, in a letter from the two Miss Rickets of Crooked Lane. Pray how do you like this head, Mr. Hastings?

Hastings. Extremely elegant and *degagée*, upon my word, madam. Your friseur is a Frenchman, I suppose?

Mrs. Hard. I protest, I dressed it myself from a print in the Ladies' Memorandum-book for the last year.

Hastings. Indeed. Such a head in a side-box, at the Play-house, would draw as many gazers as my Lady Mayoress at a City Ball.

Mrs. Hard. I vow, since inoculation began, there is no such thing to be seen as a plain woman ; so one must dress a little particular or one may escape in the crowd.

[1 In allusion to the bust portraits called "Tête-à-Têtes," published, with satirical biographies in the *Town and Country Magazine.* Lady Waldegrave and the Duke of Gloucester came early in the series.]

Hastings. But that can never be your case, madam, in any dress ! (*Bowing.*)

Mrs. Hard. Yet, what signifies *my* dressing when I have such a piece of antiquity by my side as Mr. Hardcastle : all I can say will never argue down a single button from his clothes. I have often wanted him to throw off his great flaxen wig, and where he was bald, to plaster it over like my Lord Pately, with powder.

Hastings. You are right, madam ; for, as among the ladies there are none ugly, so among the men there are none old.

Mrs. Hard. But what do you think his answer was ? Why, with his usual Gothic vivacity, he said I only wanted him to throw off his wig to convert it into a *tête* for my own wearing !

Hastings. Intolerable ! At your age you may wear what you please, and it must become you.

Mrs. Hard. Pray, Mr. Hastings, what do you take to be the most fashionable age about town ?

Hastings. Some time ago forty was all the mode ; but I'm told the ladies intend to bring up fifty for the ensuing winter.

Mrs. Hard. Seriously. Then I shall be too young for the fashion !

Hastings. No lady begins now to put on jewels till she's past forty. For instance, miss there, in a polite circle, would be considered as a child, as a mere maker of samplers.

Mrs. Hard. And yet Mrs. Niece thinks herself as much a woman, and is a fond of jewels as the oldest of us all.

Hastings. Your niece, is she ? And that young gentleman, a brother of yours, I should presume ?

Mrs. Hard. My son, sir. They are contracted to each other. Observe their little sports. They fall in and out ten times a day, as if they were man and wife already. *To them.*) Well, Tony, child, what soft things are you saying to your cousin Constance, this evening ?

Tony. I have been saying no soft things ; but that it's very hard to be followed about so. Ecod ! I've not a place in the house now that's left to myself but the stable.

Mrs. Hard. Never mind him, Con, my dear. He's in another story behind your back.

Miss Neville. There's something generous in my cousin's manner. He falls out before faces to be forgiven in private.

Tony. That's a damned confounded——crack.

Mrs. Hard. Ah! he's a sly one. Don't you think they're like each other about the mouth, Mr. Hastings? The Blenkinsop mouth to a T. They're of a size, too. Back to back, my pretties, that Mr. Hastings may see you.[1] Come, Tony.

Tony. You had as good not make me, I tell you.

　　　　　　　　　　　　　　　　　　　[Measuring.

Miss Neville. O lud! he has almost cracked my head.

Mrs. Hard. O, the monster! For shame, Tony. You a man, and behave so!

Tony. If I'm a man, let me have my fortin. Ecod! I'll not be made a fool of no longer.

Mrs. Hard. Is this, ungrateful boy, all that I'm to get for the pains I have taken in your education? I that have rocked you in your cradle, and fed that pretty mouth with a spoon! Did not I work that waistcoat to make you genteel? Did not I prescribe for you every day, and weep while the receipt was operating?

Tony. Ecod! you had reason to weep, for you have been dosing me ever since I was born. I have gone through every receipt in the complete housewife ten times over; and you have thoughts of coursing me through *Quincy*[2] next spring. But, ecod! I tell you, I'll not be made a fool of no longer.

Mrs. Hard. Wasn't it all for your good, viper? Wasn't it all for your good?

Tony. I wish you'd let me and my good alone, then.

[1 Cf. *The Vicar of Wakefield*, 1766, i. 158–9.]
[2 John Quincy, M.D. (d. 1723), author of a highly popular *Complete English Dispensatory*, a fourteenth edition of which was published in 1772.]

Snubbing this way when I'm in spirits. If I'm to have any good, let it come of itself; not to keep dinging it, dinging it into one so.

Mrs. Hard. That's false; I never see you when you're in spirits. No, Tony, you then go to the alehouse or kennel. I'm never to be delighted with your agreeable, wild notes, unfeeling monster!

Tony. Ecod! Mamma, your own notes are the wildest of the two.

Mrs. Hard. Was ever the like? But I see he wants to break my heart, I see he does.

Hastings. Dear Madam, permit me to lecture the young gentleman a little. I'm certain I can persuade him to his duty.

Mrs. Hard. Well! I must retire. Come, Constance, my love. You see, Mr. Hastings, the wretchedness of my situation. Was ever poor woman so plagued with a dear, sweet, pretty, provoking, undutiful boy.

[*Exeunt Mrs.* HARDCASTLE *and Miss* NEVILLE. HASTINGS, TONY

Tony (*singing*). *There was a young man riding by, and fain would have his will. Rang do didlo dee.* Don't mind her. Let her cry. It's the comfort of her heart. I have seen her and sister cry over a book for an hour together, and they said, they liked the book the better the more it made them cry.

Hastings. Then you're no friend to the ladies, I find, my pretty young gentleman?

Tony. That's as I find 'um.

Hastings. Not to her of your mother's choosing, I dare answer! And yet she appears to me a pretty, well-tempered girl.

Tony. That's because you don't know her as well as I. Ecod! I know every inch about her; and there's not a more bitter cantankerous toad in all Christendom!

Hastings (*aside*). Pretty encouragement, this, for a lover

Tony. I have seen her since the height of that. She has as many tricks as a hare in a thicket, or a colt the first day's breaking.

Hastings. To me she appears sensible and silent!

Tony. Ay, before company. But when she's with her playmates she's as loud as a hog in a gate.

Hastings. But there is a meek modesty about her that charms me.

Tony. Yes, but curb her never so little, she kicks up, and you're flung in a ditch.

Hastings. Well, but you must allow her a little beauty. —Yes, you must allow her some beauty.

Tony. Bandbox! She's all a made up thing, mun. Ah! could you but see Bet Bouncer of these parts, you might then talk of beauty. Ecod, she has two eyes as black as sloes, and cheeks as broad and red as a pulpit cushion. She'd make two of she.

Hastings. Well, what say you to a friend that would take this bitter bargain off your hands?

Tony. Anon.

Hastings. Would you thank him that would take Miss Neville, and leave you to happiness and your dear Betsy?

Tony. Ay; but where is there such a friend, for who would take *her*?

Hastings. I am he. If you but assist me, I'll engage to whip her off to France, and you shall never hear more of her

Tony. Assist you! Ecod, I will, to the last drop of my blood. I'll clap a pair of horses to your chaise that shall trundle you off in a twinkling, and may be get you a part of her fortin besides, in jewels, that you little dream of.

Hastings. My dear 'Squire, this looks like a lad of spirit.

Tony. Come along then, and you shall see more of my spirit before you have done with me.   [*Singing.*

> *We are the boys*
> *That fears no noise*
> *Where the thundering cannons roar.*
>
> [*Exeunt.*

END OF THE SECOND ACT

ACT III

Enter HARDCASTLE *solus*

Hard. What could my old friend Sir Charles mean by recommending his son as the modestest young man in town? To me he appears the most impudent piece of brass that ever spoke with a tongue. He has taken possession of the easy chair by the fireside already. He took off his boots in the parlour, and desired me to see them taken care of. I'm desirous to know how his impudence affects my daughter.—She will certainly be shocked at it.

Enter Miss HARDCASTLE *plainly dressed*

Hard. Well, my Kate, I see you have changed your dress as I bid you; and yet, I believe, there was no great occasion.

Miss Hard. I find such a pleasure, sir, in obeying your commands, that I take care to observe them without ever debating their propriety.

Hard. And yet, Kate, I sometimes give you some cause, particularly when I recommended my *modest* gentleman to you as a lover to-day.

Miss Hard. You taught me to expect something extraordinary, and I find the original exceeds the description!

Hard. I was never so surprised in my life! He has quite confounded all my faculties!

Miss Hard. I never saw anything like it: And a man of the world, too!

Hard. Ay, he learned it all abroad,—what a fool was I, to think a young man could learn modesty by travelling. He might as soon learn wit at a masquerade.

Miss Hard. It seems all natural to him.

Hard. A good deal assisted by bad company and a French dancing-master.

Miss Hard. Sure, you mistake, papa! a French dancing-

master could never have taught him that timid look,—
that awkward address,—that bashful manner——

Hard. Whose look? whose manner? child!

Miss Hard. Mr. Marlow's: his *mauvaise honte*, his
timidity struck me at the first sight.

Hard. Then your first sight deceived you; for I think
him one of the most brazen first sights that ever astonished
my senses!

Miss Hard. Sure, sir, you rally! I never saw anyone
so modest.

Hard. And can you be serious! I never saw such a
bouncing swaggering puppy since I was born. Bully
Dawson [1] was but a fool to him.

Miss Hard. Surprising! He met me with a respectful
bow, a stammering voice, and a look fixed on the
ground.

Hard. He met me with a loud voice, a lordly air, and
a familiarity that made my blood freeze again.

Miss Hard. He treated me with diffidence and respect;
censured the manners of the age; admired the prudence
of girls that never laughed; tired me with apologies for
being tiresome; then left the room with a bow, and,
madam, I would not for the world detain you.

Hard. He spoke to me as if he knew me all his life
before. Asked twenty questions, and never waited for
an answer. Interrupted my best remarks with some silly
pun, and when I was in my best story of the Duke of
Marlborough and Prince Eugene, he asked if I had not
a good hand at making punch. Yes, Kate, he asked
your father if he was a maker of punch!

Miss Hard. One of us must certainly be mistaken.

Hard. If he be what he has shown himself, I'm
determined he shall never have my consent.

Miss Hard. And if he be the sullen thing I take him,
he shall never have mine.

Hard. In one thing then we are agreed—to reject
him.

[1 A Whitefriars bully and gutter-blood. He is immortalized in
Spectator, No. 2, as having been kicked in a coffee-house by Sir
Roger de Coverley.]

Miss Hard. Yes. But upon conditions. For if you should find him less impudent, and I more presuming; if you find him more respectful, and I more importunate —I don't know—the fellow is well enough for a man— Certainly we don't meet many such at a horse race in the country.

Hard. If we should find him so—— But that's impossible. The first appearance has done my business. I'm seldom deceived in that.

Miss Hard. And yet there may be many good qualities under that first appearance.

Hard. Ay, when a girl finds a fellow's outside to her taste, she then sets about guessing the rest of his furniture. With her, a smooth face stands for good sense, and a genteel figure for every virtue.

Miss Hard. I hope, sir, a conversation begun with a compliment to my good sense won't end with a sneer at my understanding?

Hard. Pardon me, Kate. But it young Mr. Brazen can find the art of reconciling contradictions, he may please us both, perhaps.

Miss Hard. And as one of us must be mistaken, what if we go to make further discoveries?

Hard. Agreed. But depend on't I'm in the right.

Miss Hard. And depend on't I'm not much in the wrong.   [*Exeunt.*

Enter TONY *running in with a casket*

Tony. Ecod! I have got them. Here they are. My Cousin Con's necklaces, bobs and all. My mother shan't cheat the poor souls out of their fortin neither. O! my genus, is that you?

Enter HASTINGS

Hastings. My dear friend, how have you managed with your mother? I hope you have amused her with pretending love for your cousin, and that you are willing to be reconciled at last? Our horses will be refreshed in a short time, and we shall soon be ready to set off.

Tony. And here's something to bear your charges by

the way. (*Giving the casket.*) Your sweetheart's jewels. Keep them, and hang those, I say, that would rob you of one of them!

Hastings. But how have you procured them from your mother?

Tony. Ask me no questions, and I'll tell you no fibs. I procured them by the rule of thumb. If I had not a key to every drawer in mother's bureau, how could I go to the alehouse so often as I do? An honest man may rob himself of his own at any time.

Hastings. Thousands do it every day. But to be plain with you; Miss Neville is endeavouring to procure them from her aunt this very instant. If she succeeds, it will be the most delicate way at least of obtaining them.

Tony. Well, keep them, till you know how it will be. But I know how it will be well enough, she'd as soon part with the only sound tooth in her head!

Hastings. But I dread the effects of her resentment, when she finds she has lost them.

Tony. Never you mind her resentment, leave *me* to manage that. I don't value her resentment the bounce of a cracker. Zounds! here they are! Morrice, Prance!
                                      [*Exit* HASTINGS.

Tony, *Mrs.* Hardcastle, *Miss* Neville

Mrs. Hard. Indeed, Constance, you amaze me. Such a girl as you want jewels? It will be time enough for jewels, my dear, twenty years hence, when your beauty begins to want repairs.

Miss Neville. But what will repair beauty at forty, will certainly improve it at twenty, madam.

Mrs. Hard. Yours, my dear, can admit of none. That natural blush is beyond a thousand ornaments. Besides, child, jewels are quite out at present. Don't you see half the ladies of our acquaintance, my lady Kill-daylight, and Mrs. Crump, and the rest of them, carry their jewels to town, and bring nothing but paste and marcasites [1] back?

Miss Neville. But who knows, madam, but somebody

[1 A mineral often mistaken for gold and silver ore.]

that shall be nameless would like me best with all my little finery about me?

Mrs. Hard. Consult your glass, my dear, and then see, if with such a pair of eyes, you want any better sparklers. What do you think, Tony, my dear, does your cousin Con. want any jewels, in your eyes, to set off her beauty?

Tony. That's as thereafter may be.

Miss Neville. My dear aunt, if you knew how it would oblige me.

Mrs. Hard. A parcel of old-fashioned rose and table-cut[1] things. They would make you look like the court of king Solomon at a puppet-show. Besides, I believe I can't readily come at them. They may be missing, for aught I know to the contrary.

Tony (*apart to Mrs.* HARD.). Then why don't you tell her so at once, as she's so longing for them. Tell her they're lost. It's the only way to quiet her. Say they're lost, and call me to bear witness.

Mrs. Hard. (*apart to Tony*). You know, my dear, I'm only keeping them for you. So if I say they're gone, you'll bear me witness, will you? He! he! he!

Tony. Never fear me. Ecod! I'll say I saw them taken out with my own eyes.

Miss Neville. I desire them but for a day, madam. Just to be permitted to show them as relics, and then they may be locked up again.

Mrs. Hard. To be plain with you, my dear Constance, if I could find them, you should have them. They're missing, I assure you. Lost, for aught I know; but we must have patience wherever they are.

Miss Neville. I'll not believe it; this is but a shallow pretence to deny me. I know they're too valuable to be so slightly kept, and as you are to answer for the loss.

Mrs. Hard. Don't be alarmed, Constance. If they be lost, I must restore an equivalent. But my son knows they are missing, and not to be found.

Tony. That I can bear witness to. They are missing, and not to be found, I'll take my oath on't!

[1 Table-cut stones have flat upper surfaces. They are only cut in angles at the sides.]

Mrs. Hard. You must learn resignation, my dear; for though we lose our fortune, yet we should not lose our patience. See me, how calm I am!

Miss Neville. Ay, people are generally calm at the misfortunes of others.

Mrs. Hard. Now, I wonder a girl of your good sense should waste a thought upon such trumpery. We shall soon find them; and, in the meantime, you shall make use of my garnets till your jewels be found.

Miss Neville. I detest garnets!

Mrs. Hard. The most becoming things in the world to set off a clear complexion. You have often seen how well they look upon me. You *shall* have them. [*Exit.*

Miss Neville. I dislike them of all things. You shan't stir.—Was ever anything so provoking to mislay my own jewels, and force me to wear her trumpery.

Tony. Don't be a fool. If she gives you the garnets, take what you can get. The jewels are your own already. I have stolen them out of her bureau, and she does not know it. Fly to your spark, he'll tell you more of the matter. Leave me to manage *her.*

Miss Neville. My dear cousin!

Tony. Vanish. She's here, and has missed them already. Zounds! how she fidgets and spits about like a Catharine wheel.

Enter Mrs. HARDCASTLE

Mrs. Hard. Confusion! thieves! robbers! We are cheated, plundered, broke open, undone!

Tony. What's the matter, what's the matter, mamma? I hope nothing has happened to any of the good family!

Mrs. Hard. We are robbed. My bureau has been broke open, the jewels taken out, and I'm undone!

Tony. Oh! is that all? Ha! ha! ha! By the laws, I never saw it better acted in my life. Ecod, I thought you was ruined in earnest, ha, ha, ha!

Mrs. Hard. Why, boy, I *am* ruined in earnest. My bureau has been broke open, and all taken away.

Tony. Stick to that; ha, ha, ha! stick to that. I'll bear witness, you know, call me to bear witness.

Mrs. Hard. I tell you, Tony, by all that's precious, the jewels are gone, and I shall be ruined for ever.

Tony. Sure I know they're gone, and I am to say so.

Mrs. Hard. My dearest Tony, but hear me. They're gone, I say.

Tony. By the laws, mamma, you make me for to laugh, ha ! ha ! I know who took them well enough, ha ! ha ! ha !

Mrs. Hard. Was there ever such a blockhead, that can't tell the difference between jest and earnest. I tell you I'm not in jest, booby !

Tony. That's right, that's right : You must be in a bitter passion, and then nobody will suspect either of us. I'll bear witness that they are gone.

Mrs. Hard. Was there ever such a cross-grained brute, that won't hear me ! Can you bear witness that you're no better than a fool ? Was ever poor woman so beset with fools on one hand, and thieves on the other ?

Tony. I can bear witness to that.

Mrs. Hard. Bear witness again, you blockhead, you, and I'll turn you out of the room directly. My poor niece, what will become of *her* ? Do you laugh, you unfeeling brute, as if you enjoyed my distress ?

Tony. I can bear witness to that.

Mrs. Hard. Do you insult me, monster ? I'll teach you to vex your mother, I will !

Tony. I can bear witness to that.

[*He runs off, she follows him.*

Enter Miss HARDCASTLE *and* Maid

Miss Hard. What an unaccountable creature is that brother of mine, to send them to the house as an inn, ha ! ha ! I don't wonder at his impudence.

Maid. But what is more, madam, the young gentleman as you passed by in your present dress, asked me if you were the barmaid ? He mistook you for the barmaid, madam !

Miss Hard. Did he ? Then as I live I'm resolved to keep up the delusion. Tell me, Pimple, how do you like my present dress? Don't you think I look something like Cherry in the Beaux' Stratagem?[1]

Maid. It's the dress, madam, that every lady wears in the country, but when she visits or receives company.

Miss Hard. And are you sure he does not remember my face or person?

Maid. Certain of it!

Miss Hard. I vow, I thought so; for though we spoke for some time together, yet his fears were such, that he never once looked up during the interview. Indeed, if he had, my bonnet would have kept him from seeing me.

Maid. But what do you hope from keeping him in his mistake?

Miss Hard. In the first place, I shall be *seen*, and that is no small advantage to a girl who brings her face to market. Then I shall perhaps make an acquaintance, and that's no small victory gained over one who never addresses any but the wildest of her sex. But my chief aim is to take my gentleman off his guard, and like an invisible champion of romance examine the giant's force before I offer to combat.

Maid. But you are sure you can act your part, and disguise your voice, so that he may mistake that, as he has already mistaken your person?

Miss Hard. Never fear me. I think I have got the true bar cant.—Did your honour call?——Attend the Lion there.——Pipes and tobacco for the Angel.—The Lamb has been outrageous this half hour!

Maid. It will do, madam. But he's here.

[*Exit* Maid.

Enter MARLOW

Marlow. What a bawling in every part of the house; I have scarce a moment's repose. If I go to the best room, there I find my host and his story. If I fly to the gallery, there we have my hostess with her curtsey down

[1 By George Farquhar. "Cherry" is the daughter of Boniface, the landlord of the inn at Lichfield. The part was played by Steele's friend Mrs. Bicknell.]

to the ground. I have at last got a moment to myself, and now for recollection. [*Walks and muses.*

Miss Hard. Did you call, sir? did your honour call?

Marlow (musing). As for Miss Hardcastle, she's too grave and sentimental for me.

Miss Hard. Did your honour call?

[*She still places herself before him, he turning away.*

Marlow. No, child! (*Musing.*) Besides from the glimpse I had of her, I think she squints.

Miss Hard. I'm sure, sir, I heard the bell ring.

Marlow. No! no! (*Musing.*) I have pleased my father, however, by coming down, and I'll to-morrow please myself by returning.

[*Taking out his tablets, and perusing.*

Miss Hard. Perhaps the other gentleman called, sir?

Marlow. I tell you, no.

Miss Hard. I should be glad to know, sir. We have such a parcel of servants.

Marlow. No, no, I tell you. (*Looks full in her face.*) Yes, child, I think I did call. I wanted——I wanted—— I vow, child, you are vastly handsome!

Miss Hard. O la, sir, you'll make one ashamed.

Marlow. Never saw a more sprightly malicious eye. Yes, yes, my dear, I did call. Have you got any of your —a—what d'ye call it in the house?

Miss Hard. No, sir, we have been out of that these ten days.

Marlow. One may call in this house, I find, to very little purpose. Suppose I should call for a taste, just by way of trial, of the nectar of your lips; perhaps I might be disappointed in that, too!

Miss Hard. Nectar! nectar! that's a liquor there's no call for in these parts. French, I suppose. We keep no French wines here, sir.

Marlow. Of true English growth, I assure you.

Miss Hard. Then it's odd I should not know it. We brew all sorts of wines in this house, and I have lived here these eighteen years.

Marlow. Eighteen years! Why one would think,

child, you kept the bar before you were born. How old are you?

Miss Hard. O! sir, I must not tell my age. They say women and music should never be dated.

Marlow. To guess at this distance, you can't be much above forty. (*Approaching.*) Yet nearer I don't think so much. (*Approaching.*) By coming close to some women they look younger still; but when we come very close indeed. (*Attempting to kiss her.*)

Miss Hard. Pray, sir, keep your distance. One would think you wanted to know one's age as they do horses, by mark of mouth.

Marlow. I protest, child, you use me extremely ill. If you keep me at this distance, how is it possible you and I can be ever acquainted?

Miss Hard. And who wants to be acquainted with you? I want no such acquaintance, not I. I'm sure you did not treat Miss Hardcastle that was here awhile ago in this obstropalous manner. I'll warrant me, before her you looked dashed, and kept bowing to the ground, and talked, for all the world, as if you was before a justice of peace.

Marlow (*aside*). Egad! she has hit it, sure enough. (*To her.*) In awe of her, child? Ha! ha! ha! A mere awkward, squinting thing, no, no! I find you don't know me. I laughed, and rallied her a little; but I was unwilling to be too severe. No, I could not be too severe, curse me!

Miss Hard. O! then, sir, you are a favourite, I find, among the ladies?

Marlow. Yes, my dear, a great favourite. And yet, hang me, I don't see what they find in me to follow. At the Ladies' Club in town [1] I'm called their agreeable Rattle. Rattle, child, is not my real name, but one I'm known by. My name is Solomons. Mr. Solomons, my dear, at your service. (*Offering to salute her.*)

[1 See the *Gentleman's Magazine* for 1770, pp. 414–5, which gives the rules of the so-called *Female Coterie* in Albemarle Street here intended, together with a list of the members. Horace Walpole, his friend Conway, the Waldegraves, Mr. and Mrs. Damer, C. J. Fox, Selwyn and many persons of quality belonged to it.]

Miss Hard. Hold, sir ; you were introducing me to your club, not to yourself.   And you're so great a favourite there you say ?

Marlow. Yes, my dear.   There's Mrs. Mantrap, Lady Betty Blackleg, the Countess of Sligo, Mrs. Longhorns, old Miss Biddy Buckskin,[1] and your humble servant, keep up the spirit of the place.

Miss Hard. Then it's a very merry place, I suppose.

Marlow. Yes, as merry as cards, suppers, wine, and old women can make us.

Miss Hard. And their agreeable Rattle, ha ! ha ! ha !

Marlow (aside). Egad ! I don't quite like this chit. She looks knowing, methinks.   You laugh, child !

Miss Hard. I can't but laugh to think what time they all have for minding their work or their family.

Marlow (aside). All's well, she don't laugh at me. (*To her.*) Do *you* ever work, child ?

Miss Hard. Ay, sure.   There's not a screen or a quilt in the whole house but what can bear witness to that.

Marlow. Odso ! Then you must show me your embroidery.   I embroider and draw patterns myself a little.   If you want a judge of your work you must apply to me.   [*Seizing her hand.*

Miss Hard. Ay, but the colours don't look well by candle light.   You shall see all in the morning.

[*Struggling.*

Marlow. And why not now, my angel ?   Such beauty fires beyond the power of resistance.——Pshaw ! the father here !   My old luck : I never nicked seven that I did not throw ames-ace[2] three times following.

[*Exit* MARLOW.

Enter HARDCASTLE, *who stands in surprise*

Hard. So, madam !   So I find *this* is your *modest* lover.   This is your humble admirer that kept his eyes fixed on the ground, and only adored at humble distance.

[[1] This is said to have been meant for Miss Rachael Lloyd, an elderly member of the *Female Coterie*.]

[[2] Ambs-ace, *i. e.* a cast of double ace.   "And *Ames-Ace* loses what kind *Sixes* won"—says a poem attributed to Prior.]

Kate, Kate, art thou not ashamed to deceive your father so?

Miss Hard. Never trust me, dear papa, but he's still the modest man I first took him for, you'll be convinced of it as well as I.

Hard. By the hand of my body, I believe his impudence is infectious! Didn't I see him seize your hand? Didn't I see him haul you about like a milkmaid? and now you talk of his respect and his modesty, forsooth!

Miss Hard. But if I shortly convince you of his modesty, that he has only the faults that will pass off with time, and the virtues that will improve with age, I hope you'll forgive him.

Hard. The girl would actually make one run mad! I tell you I'll not be convinced. I am convinced. He has scarcely been three hours in the house, and he has already encroached on all my prerogatives. You may like his impudence, and call it modesty. But my son-in-law, madam, must have very different qualifications.

Miss Hard. Sir, I ask but this night to convince you.

Hard. You shall not have half the time, for I have thoughts of turning him out this very hour.

Miss Hard. Give me that hour then, and I hope to satisfy you.

Hard. Well, an hour let it be then. But I'll have no trifling with your father. All fair and open, do you mind me?

Miss Hard. I hope, sir, you have ever found that I considered your commands as my pride; for your kindness is such, that my duty as yet has been inclination.

[*Exeunt.*

END OF THE THIRD ACT

ACT IV

Enter Hastings *and Miss* Neville

Hastings. You surprise me! Sir Charles Marlow expected here this night? Where have you had your information?

Miss Neville. You may depend upon it. I just saw his letter to Mr. Hardcastle, in which he tells him he intends setting out a few hours after his son.

Hastings. Then, my Constance, all must be completed before he arrives. He knows me; and should he find me here, would discover my name, and perhaps my designs, to the rest of the family.

Miss Neville. The jewels, I hope, are safe.

Hastings. Yes, yes. I have sent them to Marlow, who keeps the keys of our baggage. In the meantime, I'll go to prepare matters for our elopement. I have had the Squire's promise of a fresh pair of horses; and, if I should not see him again, will write him further directions. [*Exit.*

Miss Neville. Well! success attend you. In the meantime, I'll go amuse my aunt with the old pretence of a violent passion for my cousin. [*Exit.*

Enter Marlow, *followed by a* Servant

Marlow. I wonder what Hastings could mean by sending me so valuable a thing as a casket to keep for him, when he knows the only place I have is the seat of a post-coach at an Inn-door. Have you deposited the casket with the landlady, as I ordered you? Have you put it into her own hands?

Servant. Yes, your honour.

Marlow. She said she'd keep it safe, did she?

Servant. Yes, she said she'd keep it safe enough; she asked me how I came by it? and she said she had a great mind to make me give an account of myself. [*Exit* Servant.

Marlow. Ha! ha! ha! They're safe, however. What an unaccountable set of beings have we got amongst! This little barmaid though runs in my head most strangely, and drives out the absurdities of all the rest of the family. She's mine, she must be mine, or I'm greatly mistaken!

Enter HASTINGS

Hastings. Bless me! I quite forgot to tell her that I intended to prepare at the bottom of the garden. Marlow here, and in spirits too!

Marlow. Give me joy, George! Crown me, shadow me with laurels! Well, George, after all, we modest fellows don't want for success among the women.

Hastings. Some women, you mean. But what success has your honour's modesty been crowned with now, that it grows so insolent upon us?

Marlow. Didn't you see the tempting, brisk, lovely little thing that runs about the house with a bunch of keys to its girdle?

Hastings. Well! and what then?

Marlow. She's mine, you rogue, you. Such fire, such motion, such eyes, such lips——but egad! she would not let me kiss them though.

Hastings. But are you sure, so very sure of her?

Marlow. Why, man, she talked of showing me her work above-stairs, and I am to improve the pattern.

Hastings. But how can *you*, Charles, go about to rob a woman of her honour?

Marlow. Pshaw! pshaw! we all know the honour of the barmaid of an inn. I don't intend to *rob* her, take my word for it, there's nothing in this house, I shan't honestly *pay* for!

Hastings. I believe the girl has virtue.

Marlow. And if she has, I should be the last man in the world that would attempt to corrupt it.

Hastings. You have taken care, I hope, of the casket I sent you to lock up? It's in safety?

Marlow. Yes, yes. It's safe enough. I have taken care of it. But how could you think the seat of a post-coach

at an Inn-door a place of safety? Ah! numbskull! I
have taken better precautions for you than you did for
yourself.——I have——

Hastings. What!

Marlow. I have sent it to the landlady to keep for you.

Hastings. To the landlady!

Marlow. The landlady.

Hastings. You did!

Marlow. I did. She's to be answerable for its forth-
coming, you know.

Hastings. Yes, she'll bring it forth with a witness.

Marlow. Wasn't I right? I believe you'll allow that
I acted prudently upon this occasion?

Hastings (aside). He must not see my uneasiness.

Marlow. You seem a little disconcerted, though, methinks. Sure nothing has happened?

Hastings. No, nothing. Never was I in better spirits
in all my life. And so you left it with the landlady,
who, no doubt, very readily undertook the charge?

Marlow. Rather too readily. For she not only kept
the casket, but, through her great precaution, was going
to keep the messenger too. Ha! ha! ha!

Hastings. He! he! he! They're safe, however.

Marlow. As a guinea in a miser's purse.

Hastings (aside). So now all hopes of fortune are at
an end, and we must set off without it. (*To him.*)
Well, Charles, I'll leave you to your meditations on the
pretty barmaid, and, he! he! he! may you be as successful for yourself as you have been for me.   [*Exit.*

Marlow. Thank ye, George! I ask no more. Ha!
ha! ha!

Enter HARDCASTLE

Hard. I no longer know my own house. It's turned
all topsy-turvy. His servants have got drunk already.
I'll bear it no longer, and yet, from my respect for his
father, I'll be calm. (*To him.*) Mr. Marlow, your
servant. I'm your very humble servant.   [*Bowing low.*

Marlow. Sir, your humble servant. (*Aside.*) What's
to be the wonder now?

Hard. I believe, sir, you must be sensible, sir, that no man alive ought to be more welcome than your father's son, sir. I hope you think so?

Marlow. I do, from my soul, sir. I don't want much entreaty. I generally make my father's son welcome wherever he goes.

Hard. I believe you do, from my soul, sir. But though I say nothing to your own conduct, that of your servants is insufferable. Their manner of drinking is setting a very bad example in this house, I assure you.

Marlow. I protest, my very good sir, that's no fault of mine. If they don't drink as they ought *they* are to blame. I ordered them not to spare the cellar, I did, I assure you. (*To the side scene.*) Here, let one of my servants come up. (*To him.*) My positive directions were, that as I did not drink myself, they should make up for my deficiencies below.

Hard. Then they had your orders for what they do! I'm satisfied!

Marlow. They had, I assure you. You shall hear from one of themselves.

Enter Servant, *drunk*

Marlow. You, Jeremy! Come forward, sirrah! What were my orders? Were you not told to drink freely, and call for what you thought fit, for the good of the house?

Hard (*aside*). I begin to lose my patience.

Jeremy. Please your honour, liberty and Fleet Street for ever! Though I'm but a servant, I'm as good as another man. I'll drink for no man before supper, sir, dammy! Good liquor will sit upon a good supper, but a good supper will not sit upon——hiccup——upon my conscience, sir.

Marlow. You see, my old friend, the fellow is as drunk as he can possibly be. I don't know what you'd have more, unless you'd have the poor devil soused in a beer-barrel.

Hard. Zounds! He'll drive me distracted if I contain myself any longer. Mr. Marlow. Sir; I have submitted to your insolence for more than four hours, and I see no likelihood of its coming to an end. I'm now resolved to be master here, sir, and I desire that you and your drunken pack may leave my house directly.

Marlow. Leave your house!—Sure, you jest, my good friend! What, when I'm doing what I can to please you!

Hard. I tell you, sir, you don't please me; so I desire you'll leave my house.

Marlow. Sure, you cannot be serious! At this time of night, and such a night! You only mean to banter me!

Hard. I tell you, sir, I'm serious; and, now that my passions are roused, I say this house is mine, sir; this house is mine, and I command you to leave it directly.

Marlow. Ha! ha! ha! A puddle in a storm. I shan't stir a step, I assure you. (*In a serious tone.*) This your house, fellow! It's my house. This is my house. Mine, while I choose to stay. What right have you to bid me leave this house, sir? I never met with such impudence, curse me, never in my whole life before!

Hard. Nor I, confound me if ever I did! To come to my house, to call for what he likes, to turn me out of my own chair, to insult the family, to order his servants to get drunk, and then to tell me *This house is mine, sir.* By all that's impudent, it makes me laugh. Ha! ha! ha! Pray, sir, (*Bantering.*) as you take the house, what think you of taking the rest of the furniture? There's a pair of silver candlesticks, and there's a fire-screen, and here's a pair of brazen-nosed bellows, perhaps you may take a fancy to them?

Marlow. Bring me your bill, sir, bring me your bill, and let's make no more words about it.

Hard. There are a set of prints, too. What think you of the Rake's Progress [1] for your own apartment?

Marlow. Bring me your bill, I say; and I'll leave you and your infernal house directly.

[¹ The set of engravings by Hogarth.]

Hard. Then there's a mahogany table, that you may see your own face in.

Marlow. My bill, I say.

Hard. I had forgot the great chair, for your own particular slumbers, after a hearty meal.

Marlow. Zounds! bring me my bill, I say, and let's hear no more on't.

Hard. Young man, young man, from your father's letter to me, I was taught to expect a well-bred modest man, as a visitor here, but now I find him no better than a coxcomb and a bully; but he will be down here presently, and shall hear more of it.   [*Exit.*

Marlow. How's this! Sure, I have not mistaken the house? Everything looks like an inn. The servants cry "coming." The attendance is awkward; the barmaid, too, to attend us. But she's here, and will further inform me. Whither so fast, child? A word with you.

Enter Miss HARDCASTLE

Miss Hard. Let it be short, then. I'm in a hurry.— (*Aside.*) I believe he begins to find out his mistake, but it's too soon quite to undeceive him.

Marlow. Pray, child, answer me one question. What are you, and what may your business in this house be?

Miss Hard. A relation of the family, sir.

Marlow. What? A poor relation?

Miss Hard. Yes, sir. A poor relation appointed to keep the keys, and to see that the guests want nothing in my power to give them.

Marlow. That is, you act as the barmaid of this inn.

Miss Hard. Inn! O law!—What brought that in your head? One of the best families in the county keep an inn! Ha, ha, ha, old Mr. Hardcastle's house an inn!

Marlow. Mr. Hardcastle's house! Is this house Mr. Hardcastle's house, child?

Miss Hard. Ay, sure. Whose else should it be.

Marlow. So then all's out, and I have been damnably imposed on. O, confound my stupid head, I shall be laughed at over the whole town. I shall be stuck up in caricature in all the print-shops. The Dullissimo Macaroni.[1] To mistake this house of all others for an inn, and my father's old friend for an innkeeper! What a swaggering puppy must he take me for. What a silly puppy do I find myself. There again, may I be hanged, my dear, but I mistook you for the barmaid!

Miss Hard. Dear me! dear me! I'm sure there's nothing in my *behaviour* to put me upon a level with one of that stamp.

Marlow. Nothing, my dear, nothing. But I was in for a list of blunders, and could not help making you a subscriber. My stupidity saw everything the wrong way. I mistook your assiduity for assurance, and your simplicity for allurement. But it's over—this house I no more show *my* face in!

Miss Hard. I hope, sir, I have done nothing to disoblige you. I'm sure I should be sorry to affront any gentleman who has been so polite, and said so many civil things to me. I'm sure I should be sorry (*Pretending to cry.*) if he left the family upon my account. I'm sure I should be sorry people said anything amiss, since I have no fortune but my character.

Marlow (aside). By heaven, she weeps. This is the first mark of tenderness I ever had from a modest woman, and it touches me. (*To her.*) Excuse me, my lovely girl, you are the only part of the family I leave with reluctance. But to be plain with you, the difference of our birth, fortune and education, make an honourable connexion impossible; and I can never harbour a thought of seducing simplicity that trusted in my honour, or bringing ruin upon one whose only fault was being too lovely.

Miss Hard. (*aside*). Generous man! I now begin to admire him. (*To him.*) But I'm sure my family is as good as Miss Hardcastle's, and though I'm poor, that's

[1 At this date the print-shops, and especially Matthew Darly's in the Strand, were filled with engravings, generally satirizing well-known individuals and having titles of this kind, *e.g.*, *The Lilly Macaroni* (Lord Ancrum), *The Southwark Macaroni* (Mr. Thrale), *The Martial Macaroni* (Goldsmith's friend, Ensign Horneck), and so forth. See note, p. 90, on the Macaronies.]

no great misfortune to a contented mind, and, until this moment, I never thought that it was bad to want fortune.

Marlow. And why now, my pretty simplicity?

Miss Hard. Because it puts me at a distance from one, that if I had a thousand pound I would give it all to.

Marlow (aside). This simplicity bewitches me, so that if I stay I'm undone. I must make one bold effort, and leave her. (*To her.*) Your partiality in my favour, my dear, touches me most sensibly, and were I to live for myself alone, I could easily fix my choice. But I owe too much to the opinion of the world, too much to the authority of a father, so that—I can scarcely speak it—it affects me! Farewell!   [*Exit.*

Miss Hard. I never knew half his merit till now. He shall not go, if I have power or art to detain him. I'll still preserve the character in which I stooped to conquer, but will undeceive my papa, who, perhaps, may laugh him out of his resolution.   [*Exit.*

Enter TONY, *Miss* NEVILLE

Tony. Ay, you may steal for yourselves the next time. I have done my duty. She has got the jewels again, that's a sure thing; but she believes it was all a mistake of the servants.

Miss Neville. But, my dear cousin, sure, you won't forsake us in this distress. If she in the least suspects that I am going off, I shall certainly be locked up, or sent to my aunt Pedigree's, which is ten times worse.

Tony. To be sure, aunts of all kinds are damned bad things. But what can I do? I have got you a pair of horses that will fly like Whistlejacket,[1] and I'm sure you can't say but I have courted you nicely before her face. Here she comes, we must court a bit or two more, for fear she should suspect us.

[*They retire, and seem to fondle.*

Enter Mrs. HARDCASTLE

Mrs. Hard. Well, I was greatly fluttered, to be sure. But my son tells me it was all a mistake of the servants.

[1] A famous racer, painted by Stubbs.

I shan't be easy, however, till they are fairly married, and then let her keep her own fortune. But what do I see! Fondling together, as I'm alive! I never saw Tony so sprightly before. Ah! have I caught you, my pretty doves! What, billing, exchanging stolen glances, and broken murmurs! Ah!

Tony. As for murmurs, mother, we grumble a little now and then, to be sure. But there's no love lost between us.

Mrs. Hard. A mere sprinkling, Tony, upon the flame, only to make it burn brighter.

Miss Neville. Cousin Tony promises to give us more of his company at home. Indeed, he shan't leave us any more. It won't leave us, cousin Tony, will it?

Tony. O! it's a pretty creature. No, I'd sooner leave my horse in a pound, than leave you when you smile upon one so. Your laugh makes you so becoming.

Miss Neville. Agreeable cousin! Who can help admiring that natural humour, that pleasant, broad, red, thoughtless, (*Patting his cheek.*) ah! it's a bold face.

Mrs. Hard. Pretty innocence!

Tony. I'm sure I always loved cousin Con's hazel eyes, and her pretty long fingers, that she twists this way and that, over the haspicholls,[1] like a parcel of bobbins.

Mrs. Hard. Ah, he would charm the bird from the tree. I was never so happy before. My boy takes after his father, poor Mr. Lumpkin, exactly. The jewels, my dear Con, shall be your's incontinently. You shall have them. Isn't he a sweet boy, my dear? You shall be married to-morrow, and we'll put off the rest of his education, like Dr. Drowsy's sermons, to a fitter opportunity.

Enter DIGGORY

Diggory. Where's the 'Squire? I have got a letter for your worship.

[1 Goldsmith does not seem to have invented this delightful perversion, for Gray uses it in a letter to his friend Chute. He has "not seen the face of a *Haspical*, since he came home." Foote also used the expression in Act i. of *Taste*, 1752. Probably it was a popular vulgarism.]

Tony. Give it to my mamma. She reads all my letters first.

Diggory. I had orders to deliver it into your own hands.

Tony. Who does it come from?

Diggory. Your worship mun ask that of the letter itself.

Tony. I could wish to know, though. (*Turning the letter, and gazing on it.*)

Miss Neville (aside). Undone, undone! A letter to him from Hastings. I know the hand. If my aunt sees it we are ruined for ever. I'll keep her employed a little if I can. (*To Mrs.* HARDCASTLE.) But I have not told you, madam, of my cousin's smart answer just now to Mr. Marlow. We so laughed—you must know, madam —this way a little, for he must not hear us. (*They confer.*)

Tony (Still gazing). A damned cramp piece of penmanship, as ever I saw in my life. I can read your print-hand very well. But here there are such handles, and shanks, and dashes, that one can scarce tell the head from the tail. *To Anthony Lumpkin, Esquire.* It's very odd, I can read the outside of my letters, where my own name is, well enough. But when I come to open it, it's all— buzz. That's hard, very hard; for the inside of the letter is always the cream of the correspondence.

Mrs. Hard. Ha! ha! ha! Very well, very well. And so my son was too hard for the philosopher!

Miss Neville. Yes, madam; but you must hear the rest, madam. A little more this way, or he may hear us. You'll hear how he puzzled him again.

Mrs. Hard. He seems strangely puzzled now himself, methinks.

Tony (Still gazing). A damned up and down hand, as if it was disguised in liquor. (*Reading.*) *Dear Sir.* Ay, that's that. Then there's an *M*, and *a T*, and an *S*, but whether the next be an *izzard* or an *R*, confound me, I cannot tell!

Mrs. Hard. What's that, my dear? Can I give you any assistance?

Miss Neville. Pray, aunt, let me read it. Nobody reads a cramp hand better than I. (*Twitching the letter from her.*) Do you know who it is from?

Tony. Can't tell, except from Dick Ginger the feeder.[1]

Miss Neville. Ay, so it is. (*Pretending to read.*) Dear 'Squire, Hoping that you're in health, as I am at this present. The gentlemen of the Shakebag club has cut the gentlemen of Goose-green quite out of feather. The odds—um—odd battle—um—long fighting—um, here, here, it's all about cocks, and fighting; it's of no consequence, here, put it up, put it up.

[*Thrusting the crumpled letter upon him.*

Tony. But I tell you, miss, it's of all the consequence in the world! I would not lose the rest of it for a guinea! Here, mother, do you make it out? Of no consequence!

[*Giving Mrs.* HARDCASTLE *the letter.*

Mrs. Hard. How's this! (*Reads.*) Dear 'Squire, I'm now waiting for Miss Neville, with a post-chaise and pair, at the bottom of the garden, but I find my horses yet unable to perform the journey. I expect you'll assist us with a pair of fresh horses, as you promised. Dispatch is necessary, as the *hag* (ay, the hag) your mother, will otherwise suspect us. Yours, Hastings. Grant me patience. I shall run distracted! My rage chokes me.

Miss Neville. I hope, madam, you'll suspend your resentment for a few moments, and not impute to me any impertinence, or sinister design that belongs to another.

Mrs. Hard. (*Curtseying very low.*) Fine spoken, madam, you are most miraculously polite and engaging, and quite the very pink of courtesy and circumspection, madam. (*Changing her tone.*) And you, you great ill-fashioned oaf, with scarce sense enough to keep your mouth shut. Were you too joined against me? But I'll defeat all your plots in a moment. As for you, madam, since you have got a pair of fresh horses ready, it would be cruel to disappoint them. So, if you please, instead of running away with your spark, prepare, this very

[1 That is—the cock-feeder. Compare the *Vicar of Wakefield,* 1766, i. 57.]

moment, to run off with *me*. Your old aunt Pedigree will keep you secure, I'll warrant me. You too, sir, may mount your horse, and guard us upon the way. Here, Thomas, Roger, Diggory, I'll show you that I wish you better than you do yourselves. [*Exit.*

Miss Neville. So now I'm completely ruined.

Tony. Ay, that's a sure thing.

Miss Neville. What better could be expected from being connected with such a stupid fool, and after all the nods and signs I made him.

Tony. By the laws, miss, it was your own cleverness, and not my stupidity, that did your business. You were so nice and so busy with your Shakebags and Goose-greens, that I thought you could never be making believe.

Enter HASTINGS

Hastings. So, sir, I find by my servant, that you have shown my letter, and betrayed us. Was this well done, young gentleman?

Tony. Here's another. Ask miss there who betrayed you. Ecod, it was her doing, not mine.

Enter MARLOW

Marlow. So I have been finely used here among you. Rendered contemptible, driven into ill manners, despised, insulted, laughed at.

Tony. Here's another. We shall have old Bedlam broke loose presently.

Miss Neville. And there, sir, is the gentleman to whom we all owe every obligation.

Marlow. What can I say to him, a mere boy, an idiot, whose ignorance and age are a protection.

Hastings. A poor contemptible booby, that would but disgrace correction.

Miss Neville. Yet with cunning and malice enough to make himself merry with all our embarrassments.

Hastings. An insensible cub.

Marlow. Replete with tricks and mischief.

Tony. Baw! damme, but I'll fight you both one after the other,—— with baskets.

Marlow. As for him, he's below resentment. But your conduct, Mr. Hastings, requires an explanation. You knew of my mistakes, yet would not undeceive me.

Hastings. Tortured as I am with my own disappointments, is this a time for explanations? It is not friendly, Mr. Marlow.

Marlow. But, sir—

Miss Neville. Mr. Marlow, we never kept on your mistake, till it was too late to undeceive you. Be pacified.

Enter Servant

Servant. My mistress desires you'll get ready immediately, madam. The horses are putting to. Your hat and things are in the next room. We are to go thirty miles before morning.   [*Exit* Servant.

Miss Neville. Well, well; I'll come presently.

Marlow (*To* HASTINGS). Was it well done, sir, to assist in rendering me ridiculous? To hang me out for the scorn of all my acquaintance? Depend upon it, sir, I shall expect an explanation.

Hastings. Was it well done, sir, if you're upon that subject, to deliver what I entrusted to yourself, to the care of another, sir?

Miss Neville. Mr. Hastings. Mr. Marlow. Why will you increase my distress by this groundless dispute? I implore, I entreat you——

Enter Servant

Servant. Your cloak, madam. My mistress is impatient.

Miss Neville. I come. Pray be pacified. If I leave you thus, I shall die with apprehension!

Enter Servant

Servant. Your fan, muff, and gloves, madam. The horses are waiting.

Miss Neville. O, Mr. Marlow! if you knew what a scene of constraint and ill-nature lies before me, I'm sure it would convert your resentment into pity.

Marlow. I'm so distracted with a variety of passions, that I don't know what I do. Forgive me, madam. George, forgive me. You know my hasty temper, and should not exasperate it.

Hastings. The torture of my situation is my only excuse.

Miss Neville. Well, my dear Hastings, if you have that esteem for me that I think, that I am sure you have, your constancy for three years will but increase the happiness of our future connection. If—

Mrs. Hard. (*Within*). Miss Neville. Constance, why, Constance, I say.

Miss Neville. I'm coming. Well, constancy. Remember, constancy is the word. [*Exit.*

Hastings. My heart! How can I support this! To be so near happiness, and such happiness!

Marlow (*To* Tony). You see now, young gentleman, the effects of your folly. What might be amusement to you, is here disappointment, and even distress.

Tony (*From a reverie*). Ecod, I have hit it. It's here. Your hands. Yours and yours, my poor Sulky. My boots there, ho! Meet me two hours hence at the bottom of the garden; and if you don't find Tony Lumpkin a more good-natur'd fellow than you thought for, I'll give you leave to take my best horse, and Bet Bouncer into the bargain! Come along. My boots, ho!
[*Exeunt.*

END OF THE FOURTH ACT

ACT V

SCENE—*Continues*

Enter Hastings *and* Servant

Hastings. You saw the old lady and Miss Neville drive off, you say?

Servant. Yes, your honour. They went off in a post-

coach, and the young 'Squire went on horseback.
They're thirty miles off by this time.

Hastings. Then all my hopes are over.

Servant. Yes, sir. Old Sir Charles is arrived. He
and the old gentleman of the house have been laughing
at Mr. Marlow's mistake this half hour. They are
coming this way.

Hastings. Then I must not be seen. So now to my
fruitless appointment at the bottom of the garden. This
is about the time.   [*Exit.*

Enter Sir CHARLES *and* HARDCASTLE

Hard. Ha! ha! ha! The peremptory tone in which
he sent forth his sublime commands.

Sir Charles. And the reserve with which I suppose
he treated all your advances.

Hard. And yet he might have seen something in me
above a common innkeeper, too.

Sir Charles. Yes, Dick, but he mistook you for an
uncommon innkeeper, ha! ha! ha!

Hard. Well, I'm in too good spirits to think of anything but joy. Yes, my dear friend, this union of our
families will make our personal friendships hereditary:
and though my daughter's fortune is but small——

Sir Charles. Why, Dick, will you talk of fortune to
me? My son is possessed of more than a competence
already, and can want nothing but a good and virtuous
girl to share his happiness and increase it. If they like
each other, as you say they do——

Hard. If, man! I tell you they *do* like each other.
My daughter as good as told me so.

Sir Charles. But girls are apt to flatter themselves,
you know.

Hard. I saw him grasp her hand in the warmest
manner myself; and here he comes to put you out of
your *ifs*, I warrant him.

Enter MARLOW

Marlow. I come, sir, once more, to ask pardon for
my strange conduct. I can scarce reflect on my
insolence without confusion.

Hard. Tut, boy, a trifle. You take it too gravely. An hour or two's laughing with my daughter will set all to rights again. She'll never like you the worse for it.

Marlow. Sir, I shall be always proud of her approbation.

Hard. Approbation is but a cold word, Mr. Marlow; if I am not deceived, you have something more than approbation thereabouts. You take me.

Marlow. Really, sir, I have not that happiness.

Hard. Come, boy, I'm an old fellow, and know what's what, as well as you that are younger. I know what has past between you; but mum.

Marlow. Sure, sir, nothing has past between us but the most profound respect on my side, and the most distant reserve on her's. You don't think, sir, that my impudence has been past upon all the rest of the family.

Hard. Impudence! No, I don't say that—Not quite impudence—Though girls like to be played with, and rumpled a little too, sometimes. But she has told no tales, I assure you.

Marlow. I never gave her the slightest cause.

Hard. Well, well, I like modesty in its place well enough. But this is over-acting, young gentleman. You *may* be open. Your father and I will like you the better for it.

Marlow. May I die, sir, if I ever——

Hard. I tell you, she don't dislike you; and as I'm sure you like her——

Marlow. Dear sir—I protest, sir——

Hard. I see no reason why you should not be joined as fast as the parson can tie you.

Marlow. But hear me, sir——

Hard. Your father approves the match, I admire it, every moment's delay will be doing mischief, so——

Marlow. But why won't you hear me? By all that's just and true, I never gave Miss Hardcastle the slightest mark of my attachment, or even the most distant hint to suspect me of affection. We had but one interview, and that was formal, modest and uninteresting.

Hard. (*aside*). This fellow's formal modest impudence is beyond bearing.

Sir Charles. And you never grasped her hand, or made any protestations!

Marlow. As heaven is my witness, I came down in obedience to your commands. I saw the lady without emotion, and parted without reluctance. I hope you'll exact no further proofs of my duty, nor prevent me from leaving a house in which I suffer so many mortifications.

[*Exit.*

Sir Charles. I'm astonished at the air of sincerity with which he parted.

Hard. And I'm astonished at the deliberate intrepidity of his assurance.

Sir Charles. I dare pledge my life and honour upon his truth.

Hard. Here comes my daughter, and I would stake my happiness upon her veracity.

Enter Miss Hardcastle

Hard. Kate, come hither, child. Answer us sincerely, and without reserve; has Mr. Marlow made you any professions of love and affection?

Miss Hard. The question is very abrupt, sir! But since you require unreserved sincerity, I think he has.

Hard. (*To Sir* Charles.) You see.

Sir Charles. And pray, madam, have you and my son had more than one interview?

Miss Hard. Yes, sir, several.

Hard. (*To Sir* Charles.) You see.

Sir Charles. But did he profess any attachment?

Miss Hard. A lasting one.

Sir Charles. Did he talk of love?

Miss Hard. Much, sir.

Sir Charles. Amazing! And all this formally?

Miss Hard. Formally.

Hard. Now, my friend, I hope you are satisfied.

Sir Charles. And how did he behave, madam?

Miss Hard. As most professed admirers do. Said some civil things of my face, talked much of his want of merit, and the greatness of mine; mentioned his heart, gave a short tragedy speech, and ended with pretended rapture.

Sir Charles. Now I'm perfectly convinced, indeed I know his conversation among women to be modest and submissive. This forward, canting, ranting manner by no means describes him, and I am confident he never sat for the picture.

Miss Hard. Then what, sir, if I should convince you to your face of my sincerity? If you and my papa, in about half-an-hour, will place yourselves behind that screen, you shall hear him declare his passion to me in person.

Sir Charles. Agreed. And if I find him what you describe, all my happiness in him must have an end.

[*Exit.*

Miss Hard. And if you don't find him what I describe—I fear my happiness must never have a beginning.   [*Exeunt.*

Scene—*Changes to the back of the Garden*

Enter Hastings

Hastings. What an idiot am I, to wait here for a fellow, who probably takes a delight in mortifying me. He never intended to be punctual, and I'll wait no longer. What do I see? It is he, and perhaps with news of my Constance.

Enter Tony, *booted and spattered*

Hastings. My honest 'Squire! I now find you a man of your word. This looks like friendship.

Tony. Ay, I'm your friend, and the best friend you have in the world, if you knew but all. This riding by night, by-the-bye, is cursedly tiresome. It has shook me worse than the basket of a stage-coach.[1]

Hastings. But how? Where did you leave your fellow-travellers? Are they in safety? Are they housed?

[1 Cf. C. P. Moritz, *Travels in England in* 1782. See also note to p. 217.]

Tony. Five and twenty miles in two hours and a half is no such bad driving. The poor beasts have smoked for it : Rabbit me, but I'd rather ride forty miles after a fox, than ten with such *varmint.*

Hastings. Well, but where have you left the ladies ? I die with impatience.

Tony. Left them ? Why, where should I leave them, but where I found them ?

Hastings. This is a riddle.

Tony. Riddle me this, then. What's that goes round the house, and round the house, and never touches the house ?

Hastings. I'm still astray.

Tony. Why, that's it, mon. I have led them astray. By jingo, there's not a pond or slough within five miles of the place but they can tell the taste of.

Hastings. Ha, ha, ha, I understand ; you took them in a round, while they supposed themselves going forward. And so you have at last brought them home again.

Tony. You shall hear. I first took them down Feather-bed-lane, where we stuck fast in the mud. I then rattled them crack over the stones of Up-and-down Hill—I then introduced them to the gibbet on Heavy-tree Heath, and from that, with a circumbendibus, I fairly lodged them in the horsepond at the bottom of the garden.

Hastings. But no accident, I hope.

Tony. No, no. Only mother is confoundedly frightened. She thinks herself forty miles off.[1] She's sick of the journey, and the cattle can scarce crawl. So, if your own horses be ready, you may whip off with cousin, and I'll be bound that no soul here can budge a foot to follow you.

Hastings. My dear friend, how can I be grateful ?

Tony. Ay, now it's dear friend, noble 'Squire. Just now, it was all idiot, cub, and run me through the guts. Damn *your* way of fighting, I say. After we take a

[1 A trick of this kind was afterwards played by Sheridan on Madame de Genlis (*Memoirs*, 1825, iv. 113–8.)]

knock in this part of the country, we kiss and be friends. But if you had run me through the guts, then I should be dead, and you might go kiss the hangman.

Hastings. The rebuke is just. Bur I must hasten to relieve Miss Neville; if you keep the old lady employed, I promise to take care of the young one.

[*Exit* HASTINGS.

Tony. Never fear me. Here she comes. Vanish. She's got from the pond, and draggled up to the waist like a mermaid.

Enter Mrs. HARDCASTLE

Mrs. Hard. Oh, Tony, I'm killed. Shook. Battered to death. I shall never survive it. That last jolt that laid us against the quickset hedge has done my business.

Tony. Alack, mamma, it was all your own fault. You would be for running away by night, without knowing one inch of the way.

Mrs. Hard. I wish we were at home again. I never met so many accidents in so short a journey. Drenched in the mud, overturned in a ditch, stuck fast in a slough, jolted to a jelly, and at last to lose our way! Whereabouts do you think we are, Tony?

Tony. By my guess we should be upon Crackskull Common, about forty miles from home.

Mrs. Hard. O lud! O lud! the most notorious spot in all the country. We only want a robbery to make a complete night on't.

Tony. Don't be afraid, mamma, don't be afraid. Two of the five that kept here are hanged, and the other three may not find us. Don't be afraid. Is that a man that's galloping behind us? No; its only a tree. Don't be afraid.

Mrs. Hard. The fright will certainly kill me.

Tony. Do you see anything like a black hat moving behind the thicket?

Mrs. Hard. O death!

Tony. No, it's only a cow. Don't be afraid, mamma, don't be afraid.

Mrs. Hard. As I'm alive, Tony, I see a man coming

towards us. Ah! I'm sure on't. If he perceives us, we are undone.

Tony (aside). Father-in-law, by all that's unlucky, come to take one of his night walks. (*To her.*) Ah, it's a highwayman, with pistols as long as my arm. A damned ill-looking fellow.

Mrs. Hard. Good heaven defend us! He approaches.

Tony. Do you hide yourself in that thicket, and leave me to manage him. If there be any danger I'll cough and cry hem. When I cough be sure to keep close.

[*Mrs. Hardcastle hides behind a tree in the back scene.*

Enter Hardcastle

Hard. I'm mistaken, or I heard voices of people in want of help. Oh, Tony, is that you? I did not expect you so soon back. Are your mother and her charge in safety?

Tony. Very safe, sir, at my aunt Pedigree's. Hem.

Mrs. Hard. (*From behind*). Ah! I find there's danger.

Hard. Forty miles in three hours; sure, that's too much, my youngster.

Tony. Stout horses and willing minds make short journeys, as they say. Hem.

Mrs. Hard. (*From behind*). Sure he'll do the dear boy no harm.

Hard. But I heard a voice here; I should be glad to know from whence it came.

Tony. It was I, sir, talking to myself, sir. I was saying that forty miles in four hours was very good going. Hem. As to be sure it was. Hem. I have got a sort of cold by being out in the air. We'll go in if you please. Hem.

Hard. But if you talked to yourself, you did not answer yourself. I am certain I heard two voices, and am resolved (*Raising his voice.*) to find the other out.

Mrs. Hard. (*From behind*). Oh! he's coming to find me out. Oh!

Tony. What need you go, sir, if I tell you? Hem. I'll lay down my life for the truth—hem—I'll tell you all, sir.   [*Detaining him.*

Hard. I tell you I will not be detained. I insist on seeing. It's in vain to expect I'll believe you.

Mrs. Hard. (*Running forward from behind*). O lud, he'll murder my poor boy, my darling. Here, good gentleman, whet your rage upon me. Take my money, my life, but spare that young gentleman, spare my child, if you have any mercy.

Hard. My wife! as I'm a Christian. From whence can she come, or what does she mean?

Mrs. Hard. (*Kneeling*). Take compassion on us, good Mr. Highwayman. Take our money, our watches, all we have, but spare our lives. We will never bring you to justice, indeed we won't, good Mr. Highwayman.

Hard. I believe the woman's out of her senses. What, Dorothy, don't you know *me?*

Mrs. Hard. Mr. Hardcastle, as I'm alive! My fears blinded me. But who, my dear, could have expected to meet you here, in this frightful place, so far from home. What has brought you to follow us?

Hard. Sure, Dorothy, you have not lost your wits! So far from home, when you are within forty yards of your own door! (*To him.*) This is one of your old tricks, you graceless rogue, you! (*To her.*) Don't you know the gate, and the mulberry-tree; and don't you remember the horsepond, my dear?

Mrs. Hard. Yes, I shall remember the horsepond as long as I live; I have caught my death in it. (*To* TONY.) And is it to you, you graceless varlet, I owe all this? I'll teach you to abuse your mother, I will.

Tony. Ecod, mother, all the parish says you have spoiled me, and so you may take the fruits on't.

Mrs. Hard. I'll spoil you, I will.

[*Follows him off the stage.   Exit.*

Hard. There's morality, however in his reply.

[*Exit.*

Enter HASTINGS and Miss NEVILLE

Hastings. My dear Constance, why will you deliberate thus? If we delay a moment, all is lost for ever. Pluck up a little resolution, and we shall soon be out of the reach of her malignity.

Miss Neville. I find it impossible. My spirits are so sunk with the agitations I have suffered, that I am unable to face any new danger. Two or three years' patience will at last crown us with happiness.

Hastings. Such a tedious delay is worse than inconstancy. Let us fly, my charmer. Let us date our happiness from this very moment. Perish fortune. Love and content will increase what we possess beyond a monarch's revenue. Let me prevail.

Miss Neville. No, Mr. Hastings, no. Prudence once more comes to my relief, and I will obey its dictates. In the moment of passion, fortune may be despised, but it ever produces a lasting repentance. I'm resolved to apply to Mr. Hardcastle's compassion and justice for redress.

Hastings. But though he had the will, he has not the power to relieve you.

Miss Neville. But he has influence, and upon that I am resolved to rely.

Hastings. I have no hopes. But since you persist, I must reluctantly obey you. [*Exeunt.*

SCENE—*Changes*

Enter Sir CHARLES *and Miss* HARDCASTLE

Sir Charles. What a situation am I in! If what you say appears, I shall then find a guilty son. If what he says be true, I shall then lose one that, of all others, I most wished for a daughter.

Miss Hard. I am proud of your approbation; and, to show I merit it, if you place yourselves as I directed, you shall hear his explicit declaration. But he comes.

Sir Charles. I'll to your father, and keep him to the appointment. [*Exit Sir* CHARLES.

Enter MARLOW

Marlow. Though prepared for setting out, I come once more to take leave, nor did I, till this moment, know the pain I feel in the separation.

Miss Hard. (*In her own natural manner*). I believe these sufferings cannot be very great, sir, which you can so easily remove. A day or two longer, perhaps, might lessen your uneasiness, by showing the little value of what you think proper to regret.

Marlow (*aside*). This girl every moment improves upon me. (*To her.*) It must not be, madam. I have already trifled too long with my heart. My very pride begins to submit to my passion. The disparity of education and fortune, the anger of a parent, and the contempt of my equals, begin to lose their weight; and nothing can restore me to myself but this painful effort of resolution.

Miss Hard. Then go, sir. I'll urge nothing more to detain you. Though my family be as good as hers you came down to visit, and my education, I hope, not inferior, what are these advantages without equal affluence? I must remain contented with the slight approbation of imputed merit; I must have only the mockery of your addresses, while all your serious aims are fixed on fortune.

Enter HARDCASTLE *and Sir* CHARLES *from behind*

Sir Charles. Here, behind this screen.

Hard. Ay, ay, make no noise. I'll engage my Kate covers him with confusion at last.

Marlow. By heavens, madam, fortune was ever my smallest consideration. Your beauty at first caught my eye; for who could see that without emotion? But every moment that I converse with you, steals in some new grace, heightens the picture, and gives it stronger expression. What at first seemed rustic plainness, now appears refined simplicity. What seemed forward assurance, now strikes me as the result of courageous innocence, and conscious virtue.

Sir Charles. What can it mean? He amazes me!

Hard. I told you how it would be. Hush!

Marlow. I am now determined to stay, madam, and I have too good an opinion of my father's discernment, when he sees you, to doubt his approbation.

Miss Hard. No, Mr. Marlow, I will not, cannot detain

you. Do you think I could suffer a connection, in which there is the smallest room for repentance? Do you think I would take the mean advantage of a transient passion, to load you with confusion? Do you think I could ever relish that happiness, which was acquired by lessening yours?

Marlow. By all that's good, I can have no happiness but what's in your power to grant me. Nor shall I ever feel repentance, but in not having seen your merits before. I will stay, even contrary to your wishes; and though you should persist to shun me, I will make my respectful assiduities atone for the levity of my past conduct.

Miss Hard. Sir, I must entreat you'll desist. As our acquaintance began, so let it end, in indifference. I might have given an hour or two to levity; but, seriously, Mr. Marlow, do you think I could ever submit to a connection, where *I* must appear mercenary, and *you* imprudent? Do you think I could ever catch at the confident addresses of a secure admirer?

Marlow (*Kneeling*). Does this look like security? Does this look like confidence? No, madam, every moment that shows me your merit, only serves to increase my diffidence and confusion. Here let me continue——

Sir Charles. I can hold it no longer. Charles, Charles, how hast thou deceived me! Is this your indifference, your uninteresting conversation!

Hard. Your cold contempt! your formal interview! What have you to say now?

Marlow. That I'm all amazement! What can it mean?

Hard. It means that you can say and unsay things at pleasure. That you can address a lady in private, and deny it in public; that you have one story for us, and another for my daughter!

Marlow. Daughter!—this lady your daughter!

Hard. Yes, sir, my only daughter. My Kate, whose else should she be?

Marlow. Oh, the devil.

Miss Hard. Yes, sir, that very identical tall squinting lady you were pleased to take me for. (*Curtseying.*) She that you addressed as the mild, modest, sentimental man of gravity, and the bold, forward, agreeable Rattle of the ladies' club : ha, ha, ha !

Marlow. Zounds, there's no bearing this ; it's worse than death !

Miss Hard. In which of your characters, sir, will you give us leave to address you ? As the faltering gentleman, with looks on the ground, that speaks just to be heard, and hates hypocrisy : or the loud confident creature, that keeps it up with Mrs. Mantrap, and old Miss Biddy Buckskin, till three in the morning ; ha, ha, ha !

Marlow. Oh, curse on my noisy head. I never attempted to be impudent yet, that I was not taken down. I must be gone.

Hard. By the hand of my body, but you shall not. I see it was all a mistake, and I am rejoiced to find it. You shall not, sir, I tell you. I know she'll forgive you. Won't you forgive him, Kate ? We'll all forgive you. Take courage, man.

[*They retire, she tormenting him to the back scene.*

Enter Mrs. HARDCASTLE, TONY

Mrs. Hard. So, so, they're gone off. Let them go, I care not.

Hard. Who gone ?

Mrs. Hard. My dutiful niece and her gentleman, Mr. Hastings, from town. He who came down with our modest visitor, here.

Sir Charles. Who, my honest George Hastings ? As worthy a fellow as lives, and the girl could not have made a more prudent choice.

Hard. Then, by the hand of my body, I'm proud of the connection.

Mrs. Hard. Well, if he has taken away the lady, he has not taken her fortune, that remains in this family to console us for her loss.

Hard. Sure, Dorothy, you would not be so mercenary ?

Mrs. Hard. Ay, that's my affair, not yours.   But you know, if your son when of age, refuses to marry his cousin, her whole fortune is then at her own disposal.

Hard. Ay, but he's not of age, and she has not thought proper to wait for his refusal.

Enter HASTINGS *and Miss* NEVILLE

Mrs. Hard. (*aside*). What! returned so soon?   I begin not to like it.

Hastings (*To* HARDCASTLE). For my late attempt to fly off with your niece, let my present confusion be my punishment.   We are now come back, to appeal from your justice to your humanity.   By her father's consent, I first paid her my addresses, and our passions were first founded in duty.

Miss Neville. Since his death, I have been obliged to stoop to dissimulation to avoid oppression.   In an hour of levity, I was ready even to give up my fortune to secure my choice.   But I'm now recovered from the delusion, and hope from your tenderness what is denied me from a nearer connection.

Mrs. Hard. Pshaw, pshaw! this is all but the whining end of a modern novel.

Hard. Be it what it will, I'm glad they're come back to reclaim their due.   Come hither, Tony, boy.   Do you refuse this lady's hand whom I now offer you?

Tony. What signifies my refusing?   You know I can't refuse her till I'm of age, father.

Hard. While I thought concealing your age, boy, was likely to conduce to your improvement, I concurred with your mother's desire to keep it secret.   But since I find she turns it to a wrong use, I must now declare, you have been of age these three months.

Tony. Of age!   Am I of age, father?

Hard. Above three months.

Tony. Then you'll see the first use I'll make of my liberty. (*Taking Miss* NEVILLE's *hand*.) Witness all men by these presents, that I, Anthony Lumpkin, Esquire, of BLANK place, refuse you, Constantia Neville, spinster, of no place at all, for my true and lawful wife.

So Constance Neville may marry whom she pleases, and Tony Lumpkin is his own man again!

Sir Charles. O brave 'Squire!

Hastings. My worthy friend!

Mrs. Hard. My undutiful offspring!

Marlow. Joy, my dear George, I give you joy sincerely. And could I prevail upon my little tyrant here to be less arbitrary, I should be the happiest man alive, if you would return me the favour.

Hastings (*To Miss* HARDCASTLE). Come, madam, you are now driven to the very last scene of all your contrivances. I know you like him, I'm sure he loves you, and you must and shall have him.

Hard. (*Joining their hands*). And I say so, too. And Mr. Marlow, if she makes as good a wife as she has a daughter, I don't believe you'll ever repent your bargain. So now to supper, to-morrow we shall gather all the poor of the parish about us, and the Mistakes of the Night shall be crowned with a merry morning; so boy, take her; as you have been mistaken in the mistress, my wish is, that you may never be mistaken in the wife.

EPILOGUE

BY DR. GOLDSMITH [1]

WELL, having stooped to conquer with success,
And gained a husband without aid from dress,
Still as a Barmaid, I could wish it too,
As I have conquered him to conquer you:
And let me say, for all your resolution,
That pretty Barmaids have done execution.
Our life is all a play, composed to please,
"We have our exits and our entrances." [2]
The first act shows the simple country maid,
Harmless and young, of everything afraid;
Blushes when hired, and with unmeaning action,
I hopes as how to give you satisfaction.
Her second act displays a livelier scene,—
Th' unblushing Barmaid of a country inn.
Who whisks about the house, at market caters,
Talks loud, coquets [3] the guests, and scolds the waiters.
Next the scene shifts to town, and there she soars,
The chop-house toast of ogling connoisseurs.
On 'Squires and Cits she there displays her arts,
And on the gridiron broils her lovers' hearts—
And as she smiles, her triumphs to complete,
Even Common Councilmen forget to eat.
The fourth act shows her wedded to the 'Squire,
And madam now begins to hold it higher;
Pretends to taste, at Operas cries *caro*,
And quits her *Nancy Dawson*,[4] for *Che Faro*.[5]

[1 This was spoken by Mrs. Bulkley as "Miss Hardcastle." According to Cunningham, vol. iv. of *A Collection of Prologues and Epilogues*, 1779, contains a full-length portrait of Mrs. Bulkley in the dress she wore on this occasion.]

[2 *As you like it*, Act ii., Sc. 7. What follows is of course a variation on the speech of Jaques.]

[3 Coquet, to entertain with compliments (Johnson).]

[4 See note to p. 93.

[5 *Che faro senza Euridice* in Glück's *Orfeo*, 1764.]

Doats upon dancing, and in all her pride,
Swims round the room, the *Heinel* [1] of Cheapside:
Ogles and leers with artificial skill,
Till having lost in age the power to kill,
She sits all night at cards, and ogles at spadille.[2]
Such, through our lives, the eventful history—
The fifth and last act still remains for me.
The Barmaid now for your protection prays,
Turns female Barrister, and pleads for Bayes.[3]

[1 See note to p. 91.]
[2 The ace of spades,—first trump in Ombre.]
[3 A character in Buckingham's *Rehearsal*, 1672, intended for Dryden. Here it is used by extension for "poet" or "dramatist."

EPILOGUE[1]

To be spoken in the character of TONY LUMPKIN

BY J. CRADOCK ESQ.[2]

WELL—now all's ended—and my comrades gone,
Pray what becomes of *mother's nonly son?*
A hopeful blade !—in town I'll fix my station,
And try to make a bluster in the nation.
As for my cousin Neville, I renounce her,
Off—in a crack—I'll carry big Bet Bouncer.

Why should not I in the great world appear?
I soon shall have a thousand pounds a year;
No matter what a man may here inherit,
In London—'gad, they've some regard for spirit.
I see the horses prancing up the streets,
And big Bet Bouncer bobs to all she meets;
Then hoikes to jiggs and pastimes ev'ry night—
Not to the plays—they say it a'n't polite,
To Sadler's-Wells[3] perhaps, or Operas go,
And once by chance, to the roratorio.
Thus here and there, for ever up and down,
We'll set the fashions too, to half the town;
And then at auctions—money ne'er regard,
Buy pictures like the great, ten pounds a yard:
Zounds, we shall make these London gentry say,
We know what's damned genteel, as well as they.

[1 "This came too late to be spoken" (Goldsmith's note.)]
[2 See note to p. 75.]
[3 A popular pleasure garden by the New River Head, the scene of Hogarth's *Evening.*]

SCENE FROM THE GRUMBLER:

A FARCE

[*The Grumbler*, **never** printed, was adapted by Goldsmith from *Le Grondeur* of Brueys and Palaprat, or rather from Sir C. Sedley's version of that play, produced in 1702. It was written for John Quick, (d. 1831) the actor of "Tony Lumpkin," and produced at his benefit, in May, 1773. Prior printed the accompanying scene in the *Miscellaneous Works*, 1837, from the Licenser's copy. It exhibits the final expedient adopted by the heroine, who is in love with Sourby's son, to free herself from the unwelcome proposals of the father.]

DRAMATIS PERSONÆ

Sourby (The Grumbler)   Mr. Quick.
Octavio (his Son)   Mr. Davis.
Wentworth (Brother-in-Law to
    Sourby)   Mr. Owenson
Dancing Master (called Signior
    Capriole in the Bills)   Mr. King.
Scamper (Servant)   Mr. Saunders.
Clarissa (in love with Octavio) Miss Helme.
Jenny (her Maid)   Miss Pearce.

SCENE FROM THE GRUMBLER

Enter SCAMPER (SOURBY'S *servant*) *to* SOURBY, *and his intended wife's maid* JENNY

Scamper. Sir, a gentleman would speak with you.

Jenny. Good. Here comes Scamper;—(*Aside.*) he'll manage you, I'll warrant me.

Sourby. Who is it?

Scamper. He says his name is Monsieur Ri—Ri—stay, sir, I'll go and ask him again.

Sourby (*Pulling him by the ears*). Take that, sirrah, by the way.

Scamper. Ahi! Ahi! [*Exit.*

Jenny. Sir, you have torn off his hair, so that he must now have a wig: you have pulled his ears off; but there are none of them to be had for money!

Sourby. I'll teach him!—'Tis certainly Mr. Rigaut, my notary; I know who it is, let him come in. Could he find no time but this to bring me money? Plague take the blockhead!

Enter DANCING MASTER *and his Fiddler*

Sourby. This is not my man. Who are you, with your compliments?

Dancing Master (*Bowing often*). I am called Rigaudon, sir, at your service.

Sourby (*To* JENNY). Have not I seen that face somewhere before?

Jenny. There are a thousand people like one another.

Sourby. Well, Mr. Rigaudon, what is your business?

Dancing Master. To give you this letter from Madame Clarissa.

Sourby. Give it to me—I would fain know who taught Clarissa to fold a letter thus. What contains it?

Jenny (*Aside ; while he unfolds the letter*).   A lover, I believe, never complained of that before.

Sourby (*Reads*).   " Everybody says I am to marry the most brutal of men.   I would disabuse them ; and for that reason you and I must begin the ball to-night."   She is mad !

Dancing Master.   Go on, pray, sir.

Sourby (*Reads*).   " You told me you cannot dance ; but I have sent you the first man in the world."

[SOURBY *looks at him from head to foot*

Dancing Master.   Oh Lord, sir !

Sourby (*Reads*).   " Who will teach you in less than an hour enough to serve your purpose."   I learn to dance !

Dancing Master.   Finish, if you please.

Sourby (*Reads*).   " And if you love me, you will learn the Allemande."[1]   The Allemande !   I, the Allemande !   Mr. the first man in the world, do you know you are in some danger here ?

Dancing Master.   Come, sir, in a quarter of an hour, you shall dance to a miracle.

Sourby.   Mr. Rigaudon, do you know I will send you out of the window if I call my servants ?

Dancing Master (*Bidding his man play*).   Come, brisk, this little prelude will put you in humour ; you must be held by the hand ; or have you some steps of your own ?

Sourby.   Unless you put up that d——d fiddle, I'll beat it about your ears !

Dancing Master.   Zounds, sir ! if you are thereabouts, you shall dance presently—I say presently.

Sourby.   Shall I dance, villain ?

Dancing Master.   Yes.   By the heavens above shall you dance.   I have orders from Clarissa to make you dance.   She has paid me, and dance you shall ; first let him go out.

[*He draws his sword, and puts it under his arm.*

Sourby.   Ah ! I'm dead.   What a madman has this woman sent me !

Jenny.   I see I must interpose.   Stay you there, sir ;

[[1] A German dance movement in triple time.]

let me speak to him; sir, pray do us the favour to go and tell the lady that it's disagreeable to my master.

Dancing Master. I will have him dance.

Sourby. The rascal! the rascal!

Jenny. Consider, if you please, my master is a grave man.

Dancing Master. I'll have him dance.

Jenny. You may stand in need of him.

Sourby (*Taking her aside*). Yes, tell him that when he will, without costing him a farthing, I'll bleed and purge him his bellyful.

Dancing Master. I have nothing to do with that; I'll have him dance, or have his blood.

Sourby. The rascal! (*muttering*).

Jenny. Sir, I can't work upon him; the madman will not hear reason; some harm will happen—we are alone.

Sourby. 'Tis very true.

Jenny. Look on him; he has an ill look.

Sourby. He has so (*trembling*).

Dancing Master. Make haste, I say, make haste.

Sourby. Help! neighbours! murder!

Jenny. Aye, you may cry for help; do you know that all your neighbours would be glad to see you robbed and your throat cut? Believe me, sir, two Allemande steps may save your life.

Sourby. But if it should come to be known, I should be taken for a fool.

Jenny. Love excuses all follies; and I have heard say that when Hercules was in love, he spun for Queen Omphale.

Sourby. Yes, Hercules spun, but Hercules did not dance the Allemande.

Jenny. Well, you must tell him so; the gentleman will teach you another.

Dancing Master. Will you have a minuet, sir?

Sourby. A minuet; no.

Dancing Master. The loure.[1]

Sourby. The loure; no.

Dancing Master. The passay!

[1 A grave dance *à deux temps*.]

Sourby. The passay ; no.

Dancing Master. What then? The trocanny, the tricotez,[1] the rigadon? Come, choose, choose.

Sourby. No, no, no, I like none of these.

Dancing Master. You would have a grave, serious dance, perhaps?

Sourby. Yes, a serious one, if there be any—but a very serious dance.

Dancing Master. Well, the courante, the hornpipe, the brocane, the saraband?

Sourby. No, no, no!

Dancing Master. What the devil then will you have? But make haste, or—death?

Sourby. Come on, then, since it must be so; I'll learn a few steps of the—the——

Dancing Master. What, of the—the——

Sourby. I know not what.

Dancing Master. You mock me, sir; you shall dance the Allemande, since Clarissa shall have it so, or——

[*He leads him about, the fiddle playing the Allemande.*

Sourby. I shall be laughed at by the whole town if it should be known. I am determined, for this frolic, to deprive Clarissa of that invaluable blessing, the possession of my person.

Dancing Master. Come, come, sir, move, move.

(*Teaching him.*)

Sourby. Cockatrice!

Dancing Master. One, two three! (*Teaching.*)

Sourby. A d——d, infernal——

Enter WENTWORTH

Sourby. Oh! brother, you are in good time to free me from this cursed bondage.

Wentworth. How! for shame, brother, at your age to be thus foolish.

Sourby. As I hope for mercy——

Wentworth. For shame, for shame—practising at sixty what should have been finished at six!

[1 An old lively dance.]

Dancing Master. He's not the only grown gentleman I have had in hand.

Wentworth. Brother, brother, you'll be the mockery of the whole city.

Sourby. Eternal babbler! hear me; this cursed confounded villain will make me dance perforce.

Wentworth. Perforce!

Sourby. Yes; by order, he says, of Clarissa; but since I now find she is unworthy, I give her up—renounce her for ever.

APPENDIX

[Goldsmith was scarcely critical in the modern sense of the word, and he had strong prejudices. His account of poetry under Anne and George the First, and the short notes here reprinted were probably written without much premeditation. But they are interesting as representing his off-hand opinions upon the subject, as distinguished from those which he might have expressed with fuller detail, or even with variations, had he been engaged in sustaining an argument, or stating the results of special study. It is notable that in 1767 it was possible to put forth a representative selection of *Beauties of English Poesy* in which Shakespeare, Spenser, Chaucer and Herrick have no part, while there are specimens of Smollett, Shenstone, Savage, and the fabulist Edward Moore.]

I

ON POETRY UNDER ANNE AND GEORGE THE FIRST

[The following is an extract from Letter XVI, Vol. ii, of *An History of England in a Series of Letters from a Nobleman to his Son*, which was published by John Newbery in two volumes in June, 1764.]

BUT, of all the other arts, poetry in this age was carried to the greatest perfection. The language, for some ages, had been improving, but now it seemed entirely divested of its roughness and barbarity. Among the poets of this period we may place John Philips, author of several poems, but of none more admired than that humourous one entitled, *The splendid Shilling;* he lived in obscurity, and died just above want. William Congreve deserves also particular notice; his comedies, some of which were but coolly received upon their first appearance, seemed to mend upon repetition; and he is, at present, justly allowed the foremost in that species of dramatic poesy. His wit is ever just and brilliant; his sentiments new and lively; and his elegance equal to his regularity. Next him Vanbrugh is placed, whose humour seems more natural, and characters more new; but he owes too many obligations to the French, entirely to pass for an original; and his total disregard to decency, in a great measure, impairs his merit. Farquhar is still more lively, and, perhaps, more entertaining than either; his pieces still continue the favourite performances of the stage, and bear frequent repetition without satiety; but he often mistakes pertness for wit, and seldom strikes his characters with proper force or originality. However, he died very young; and it is remarkable, that he continued to improve as he grew older; his last play, entitled *The Beau[x'] Stratagem*, being the best of his productions. Addison, both as a poet and prose writer, deserves the highest regard and imitation. His *Campaign*, and letter to Lord Halifax from Italy, are master-pieces in the former, and his Essays published in the *Spectator* are inimitable specimens of the latter. Whatever he treated of was handled with elegance and precision; and that virtue which was taught in his writings, was enforced by his example. Steele was Addison's friend and admirer;

his comedies are perfectly polite, chaste, and genteel; nor were his other works contemptible; he wrote on several subjects, and yet it is amazing, in the multiplicity of his pursuits, how he found leisure for the discussion of any. Ever persecuted by creditors, whom his profuseness drew upon him, or pursuing impracticable schemes, suggested by ill-grounded ambition. Dean Swift was the professed antagonist of both Addison and him. He perceived that there was a spirit of romance mixed with all the works of the poets who preceded him; or, in other words, that they had drawn nature on the most pleasing side. There still therefore was a place left for him, who, careless of censure, should describe it just as it was, with all its deformities; he therefore owes much of his fame, not so much to the greatness of his genius, as to the boldness of it. He was dry, sarcastic, and severe; and suited his style exactly to the turn of his thought, being concise and nervous. In this period also flourished many of subordinate fame. Prior was the first who adopted the French elegant easy manner of telling a story; but if what he has borrowed from that nation be taken from him, scarce anything will be left upon which he can lay claim to applause in poetry. Rowe was only outdone by Shakespeare and Otway as a tragic writer; he has fewer absurdities than either; and is, perhaps, as pathetic as they; but his flights are not so bold, nor his characters so strongly marked. Perhaps his coming later than the rest may have contributed to lessen the esteem he deserves. Garth had success as a poet; and, for a time, his fame was even greater than his desert. In his principal work, the *Dispensary*, his versification is negligent; and his plot is now become tedious; but whatever he may lose as a poet, it would be improper to rob him of the merit he deserves for having written the prose dedication and preface to the poem already mentioned; in which he has shown the truest wit, with the most refined elegance. Parnell, though he has written but one poem, namely, the *Hermit*, yet has found a place among the English first-rate poets. Gay, likewise, by his *Fables* and *Pastorals*, has acquired an equal reputation. But of all who have added to the stock of English poetry, Pope, perhaps, deserves the first place. On him foreigners look as one of the most successful writers of his time; his versi- fication is the most harmonious, and his correctness the most remarkable of all our poets. A noted contemporary of his own, calls the English the finest writers on moral topics, and Pope the noblest moral writer of all the English. Mr. Pope has somewhere named himself the last English Muse; and, indeed, since his time, we have seen scarce any production that can justly lay claim to immortality; he carried the language to its highest perfection; and those who have attempted still farther to improve it, instead of ornament, have only caught finery.

II

ON CERTAIN ENGLISH POEMS

[The following are the introductory notes prefixed to the poems contained in *The Beauties of English Poesy*. *Selected by Oliver Goldsmith*, and published by Griffin in two volumes in April, 1767.]

THE RAPE OF THE LOCK.—This seems to be Mr. Pope's most finished production, and is, perhaps, the most perfect in our language. It exhibits stronger powers of imagination, more harmony of numbers, and a greater knowledge of the world, than any other of this poet's works: and it is probable, if our country were called upon to show a specimen of their genius to foreigners, this would be the work here fixed upon.

THE HERMIT.—This poem is held in just esteem, the versification being chaste, and tolerably harmonious, and the story told with perspicuity and conciseness. It seems to have cost great labour, both to Mr. Pope, and Parnell himself, to bring it to this perfection. It may not be amiss to observe, that the fable is taken from one of Dr. Henry More's Dialogues.

IL PENSEROSO AND L'ALLEGRO.—I have heard a very judicious critic say, that he had an higher idea of Milton's style of poetry from the two following poems, than from his "Paradise Lost." It is certain the imagination shown in them is correct and strong. The introduction to both in irregular measure is borrowed from the Italians, and hurts an English ear.

AN ELEGY WRITTEN IN A COUNTRY CHURCHYARD.— This is a very fine poem, but overloaded with epithet.[1] The

[1 Cf. Cradock's *Memoirs*, 1826, i, 230, where Goldsmith, rallying his friend upon his devotion to Hurd, Gray, Mason, and "that formal school," proposes to mend the *Elegy* "by leaving out an idle word in every line."]

heroic measure with alternate rhyme is very properly adapted to the solemnity of the subject, as it is the slowest movement that our language admits of. The latter part of the poem is pathetic and interesting.

LONDON. IN IMITATION OF THE THIRD SATIRE OF JUVENAL.—This poem of Mr. Johnson's is the best imitation of the original that has appeared in our language, being possessed of all the force and satirical resentment of Juvenal. Imitation gives us a much truer idea of the ancients than even translation could do.

THE SCHOOL-MISTRESS. IN IMITATION OF SPENSER.— This poem is one of those happinesses in which a poet excels himself, as there is nothing in all Shenstone which anyway approaches it in merit; and, though I dislike the imitations of our old English poets in general, yet, on this minute subject, the antiquity of the style produces a very ludicrous solemnity.

COOPER'S HILL.—This poem, by Denham, though it may have been exceeded by later attempts in description, yet deserves the highest applause, as it far surpasses all that went before it : the concluding part, though a little too much crowded, is very masterly.

ELOISA TO ABELARD.—The harmony of numbers in this poem [by Mr. Pope] is very fine. It is rather drawn out to too tedious a length, altho' the passions vary with great judgment. It may be considered as superior to anything in the epistolary way; and the many translations which have been made of it into the modern languages, are, in some measure, a proof of this.

AN EPISTLE FROM MR. PHILIPS TO THE EARL OF DORSET.—The opening of this poem is incomparably fine. The latter part is tedious and trifling.

A LETTER FROM ITALY, TO THE RIGHT HONOURABLE CHARLES LORD HALIFAX. IN THE YEAR MDCCI.—Few poems have done more honour to English genius than this [by Mr. Addison]. There is in it a strain of political thinking that was, at that time, new in our poetry. Had the harmony of this been equal to that of Pope's versification, it would be incontestably the finest poem in our language; but there is a dryness in the numbers which greatly lessens the pleasure excited both by the poet's judgment and imagination.

Appendix

ALEXANDER'S FEAST; OR, THE POWER OF MUSIC. AN ODE, IN HONOUR OF ST. CECILIA'S DAY.—This ode [Dryden's] has been more applauded, perhaps, than it has been felt; however, it is a very fine one, and gives its beauties rather at a third, or fourth, than at a first, perusal.

ODE FOR MUSIC ON ST. CECILIA'S DAY.—This ode [Pope's] has by many been thought equal to the former. As it is a repetition of Dryden's manner, it is so far inferior to him. The whole hint of Orpheus, with many of the lines, have been taken from an obscure Ode upon Music, published in "Tate's Miscellanies."

THE SHEPHERD'S WEEK. IN SIX PASTORALS.—These are Mr. Gay's principal performance. They were originally intended, I suppose, as a burlesque on those of Philips; but, perhaps without designing it, he has hit the true spirit of pastoral poetry. In fact, he more resembles Theocritus than any other English pastoral writer whatsoever. There runs through the whole a strain of rustic pleasantry which should ever distinguish this species of composition; but how far the antiquated expressions used here may contribute to the humour, I will not determine; for my own part, I could wish the simplicity were preserved, without recurring to such obsolete antiquity for the manner of expressing it.

MAC FLECKNOE.—The severity of this satire, and the excellence of its versification, give it a distinguished rank in this species of composition. At present, an ordinary reader would scarce suppose that Shadwell, who is here meant by Mac Flecknoe, was worth being chastised, and that Dryden's descending to such game was like an eagle's stooping to catch flies.[1] The truth, however, is, Shadwell, at one time, held divided reputation with this great poet. Every age produces its fashionable dunces, who, by following the transient topic, or humour, of the day, supply talkative ignorance with materials for conversation.

ON POETRY. A RHAPSODY.—Here follows one of the best versified poems in our language, and the most masterly production of its author. The severity with which Walpole is here treated, was in consequence of that minister's having refused to provide for Swift in England, when applied to for that purpose in the year 1725 (if I remember right). The

[1 Aquila non capit muscas.]

severity of a poet, however, gave Walpole very little uneasiness. A man whose schemes, like this minister's, seldom extended beyond the exigency of the year, but little regarded the contempt of posterity.

OF THE USE OF RICHES.—This poem, as Mr. Pope tells us himself, cost much attention and labour; and, from the easiness that appears in it, one would be apt to think as much.

FROM THE "DISPENSARY." CANTO VI.—This sixth canto of the Dispensary, by Dr. Garth, has more merit than the whole preceding part of the poem, and, as I am told, in the first edition of this work it is more correct than as here exhibited; but that edition I have not been able to find. The praises bestowed on this poem are more than have been given to any other; but our approbation, at present, is cooler, for it owed part of its fame to party.

PERSIAN ECLOGUES.—The following eclogues, written by Mr. Collins, are very pretty: the images, it must be owned, are not very local; for the pastoral subject could not well admit of it. The description of Asiatic magnificence and manners, is a subject as yet unattempted amongst us, and, I believe, capable of furnishing a great variety of poetical imagery.

THE SPLENDID SHILLING. BY MR. J. PHILIPS.—This is reckoned the best parody of Milton in our language: it has been an hundred times imitated without success. The truth is, the first thing in this way must preclude all future attempts; for nothing is so easy as to burlesque any man's manner, when we are once shown the way.

A PIPE OF TOBACCO: IN IMITATION OF SIX SEVERAL AUTHORS.—Mr. Hawkins Browne, the author of these, as I am told, had no good original manner of his own, yet we see how well he succeeds when he turns an imitator; for the following are rather imitations, than ridiculous parodies.

A NIGHT-PIECE, ON DEATH.—The great fault of this piece, written by Dr. Parnell, is, that it is in eight syllable lines, very improper for the solemnity of the subject; otherwise the poem is natural, and the reflections just.

A FAIRY TALE. BY DR. PARNELL.—Never was the old manner of speaking more happily applied, or a tale better told, than this.

Appendix

PALEMON AND LAVINIA.—Mr. Thomson, though, in general, a verbose and affected poet, has told this story with unusual simplicity: it is rather given here for being much esteemed by the public, than by the editor.

THE BASTARD.—Almost all things written from the heart, as this certainly was, have some merit. The poet here describes sorrows and misfortunes which were by no means imaginary; and, thus, there runs a truth of thinking through this poem, without which it would be of little value, as Savage is, in other respects, but an indifferent poet.

THE POET AND HIS PATRON.—Mr. Mo[o]re was a poet that never had justice done him while living; there are few of the moderns have a more correct taste, or a more pleasing manner of expressing their thoughts. It was upon these fables he chiefly founded his reputation; yet they are, by no means, his best production.

AN EPISTLE TO A LADY.—This little poem, by Mr. Nugent,[1] is very pleasing. The easiness of the poetry, and the justice of the thoughts, constitute its principal beauty.

HANS CARVEL.—This bagatelle, for which, by the bye, Mr. Prior has got his greatest reputation, was a tale told in all the Old Italian collections of jests, and borrowed from thence by Fontaine. It had been translated once or twice before into English, yet was never regarded till it fell into the hands of Mr. Prior. A strong instance how much everything is improved in the hands of a man of genius.

BAUCIS AND PHILEMON. FROM SWIFT.—This poem is very fine; and, though in the same strain with the preceding, is yet superior.

TO THE EARL OF WARWICK, ON THE DEATH OF MR. ADDISON.—This elegy (by Mr. Tickell) is one of the finest in our language: there is so little new that can be said upon the death of a friend, after the complaints of Ovid, and the Latin Italians, in this way, that one is surprised to see so much novelty in this to strike us, and so much interest to affect.

COLIN AND LUCY. A BALLAD.—Through all Tickell's works there is a strain of ballad-thinking, if I may so express it; and, in this professed ballad, he seems to have

[[1 See p. 47, note to *The Haunch of Venison*.]

surpassed himself. It is, perhaps, the best in our language in this way.

THE TEARS OF SCOTLAND. WRITTEN IN THE YEAR MDCCXLVI.—This ode, by Dr. Smollett, does rather more honour to the author's feelings than his taste. The mechanical part, with regard to numbers and language, is not so perfect as so short a work as this requires; but the pathetic it contains, particularly in the last stanza but one, is exquisitely fine.

ON THE DEATH OF THE LORD PROTECTOR.—Our poetry was not quite harmonized in Waller's time; so that this, which would be now looked upon as a slovenly sort of versification, was, with respect to the times in which it was written, almost a prodigy of harmony. A modern reader will chiefly be struck with the strength of thinking, and the turn of the compliments bestowed upon the usurper. Everybody has heard the answer our poet made Charles II.; who asked him how his poem upon Cromwell came to be finer than his panegyric upon himself. "Your Majesty," replies Waller, "knows, that poets always succeed best in fiction."

THE STORY OF PHŒBUS AND DAPHNE, APPLIED.[1]—The French claim this as belonging to them. To whomsoever it belongs the thought is finely turned.

NIGHT THOUGHTS. BY DR. YOUNG.—These seem to be the best of the collection; from whence only the two first are taken. They are spoken of differently, either with exaggerated applause or contempt, as the reader's disposition is either turned to mirth or melancholy.

SATIRE I.—Young's Satires were in higher reputation when published, than they stand in at present. He seems fonder of dazzling than pleasing; of raising our admiration for his wit, than our dislike of the follies he ridicules.

A PASTORAL BALLAD. IN FOUR PARTS.—These ballads of Mr. Shenstone are chiefly commended for the natural simplicity of the thoughts, and the harmony of the versification. However, they are not excellent in either.

PHŒBE. A PASTORAL.—This by Dr. Byrom is a better effort than the preceding.

[1 By Waller.]

A SONG.—This ["Despairing beside a clear stream"], by Mr. Rowe, is better than anything of the kind in our language.

AN ESSAY ON POETRY.—This work, by the Duke of Buckingham, is enrolled among our great English productions. The precepts are sensible, the poetry not indifferent, but it has been praised more than it deserves.

CADENUS AND VANESSA.—This is thought one of Dr. Swift's correctest pieces; its chief merit, indeed, is the elegant ease with which a story, but ill-conceived in itself, is told.

ALMA; OR THE PROGRESS OF THE MIND.—What Prior meant by this poem I can't understand: by the Greek motto to it one would think it was either to laugh at the subject or his reader.[1] There are some parts of it very fine; and let them save the badness of the rest.

III

ON LAUGHING AND SENTIMENTAL COMEDY

[The honour of inaugurating the French *comédie larmoyante* is claimed for Nivelle de La Chaussée, 1691 ?-1754, whose life and work have recently been made the subject of an exhaustive study by M. G. Lanson (Hachette, 1887). His semi-serious method, coloured considerably during its progress by the influence of Rousseau and Richardson, was developed by Voltaire, Diderot (*Le Fils Naturel* and *Le Père de Famille*), Sedaine (*Le Philosophe sans le savoir*), and in the earlier plays of Beaumarchais. Passing to England, it took the form of "Sentimental Comedy", —its most successful exponents being Kelly and Cumberland; its bitterest foes, Foote, Goldsmith and Sheridan, with whose side the victory finally remained. In 1780, when George Colman the elder wrote his "Prologue" to Miss Lee's *Chapter of Accidents*, he says that "the word *sentiment*" was at that date as much dreaded as "*low*" had been in the past, and he makes penitent acknowledgment of Goldsmith's part in the reformation :—

> "When Fielding, Humour's fav'rite child, appear'd,
> *Low* was the word—a word each author fear'd !
> 'Till chac'd at length, by pleasantry's bright ray
> Nature and mirth resum'd their legal sway ;
> And Goldsmith's genius bask'd in open day."

[1 Πάντα γέλωσ, καὶ πάντα κόνισ, καὶ πάντα τὸ μηδέν·
Πάντα γὰρ ἐξ ἀλόγων ἐστὶ τὰ γιγνόμενα."
Incert. ap. Stobæum.]

In the Essay here reprinted Goldsmith is obviously endeavouring to pave the way for *She Stoops to Conquer*, which was produced a few weeks after it first appeared.]

AN ESSAY ON THE THEATRE

OR,

A COMPARISON BETWEEN LAUGHING AND SENTIMENTAL COMEDY

[This essay first appeared in the *Westminster Magazine* for January, 1773, from which it is here reproduced. It was accepted as Goldsmith's by Reed and Percy.]

THE Theatre, like all other amusements, has its Fashions and its Prejudices; and when satiated with its excellence, Mankind begin to mistake Change for Improvement. For some years, Tragedy was the reigning entertainment, but of late it has entirely given way to Comedy, and our best efforts are now exerted in these lighter kinds of composition. The pompous Train, the swelling Phrase, and the unnatural Rant, are displaced for that natural portrait of Human Folly and Frailty, of which all are judges, because all have sat for the picture.

But as in describing Nature it is presented with a double face, either of mirth or sadness, our modern Writers find themselves at a loss which chiefly to copy from; and, it is now debated, Whether the Exhibition of Human Distress is likely to afford the mind more Entertainment than that of Human Absurdity?

Comedy is defined by Aristotle to be a picture of the Frailties of the lower part of Mankind, to distinguish it from Tragedy, which is an exhibition of the Misfortunes of the Great. When Comedy therefore ascends to produce the Characters of Princes or Generals upon the Stage, it is out of its walk, since Low Life and Middle Life are entirely its object. The principal question therefore is, Whether in describing Low or Middle Life, an exhibition of its Follies be not preferable to a detail of its Calamities? Or, in other words, Which deserves the preference? The Weeping Sentimental Comedy, so much in fashion at present, or the Laughing and even Low Comedy, which seems to have been last exhibited by Vanbrugh and Cibber?

If we apply to authorities, all the Great Masters in the Dramatic Art have but one opinion. Their rule is, that as Tragedy displays the Calamities of the Great ; so Comedy should excite our laughter by ridiculously exhibiting the Follies of the Lower Part of Mankind. Boileau, one of the best modern Critics, asserts, that Comedy will not admit of Tragic Distress.

Le Comique, ennemi des soupirs et des pleurs,
N'admet point en ses vers de tragiques douleurs.[1]

Nor is this rule without the strongest foundation in Nature, as the distresses of the Mean by no means affect us so strongly as the Calamities of the Great. When Tragedy exhibits to us some Great Man fallen from his height, and struggling with want and adversity, we feel his situation in the same manner as we suppose he himself must feel, and our pity is increased in proportion to the height from whence he fell. On the contrary, we do not so strongly sympathise with one born in humbler circumstances, and encountering accidental distress ; so that while we melt for Belisarius, we scarce give halfpence to the Beggar who accosts us in the street. The one has our pity ; the other our contempt. Distress, therefore, is the proper object of Tragedy, since the Great excite our pity by their fall ; but not equally so of Comedy, since the Actors employed in it are originally so mean, that they sink but little by their fall.

Since the first origin of the Stage, Tragedy and Comedy have run in distinct channels, and never till of late encroached upon the provinces of each other. Terence, who seems to have made the nearest approaches, yet always judiciously stops short before he comes to the downright pathetic ; and yet he is even reproached by Cæsar for wanting the *vis comica*. All the other Comic Writers of antiquity aim only at rendering Folly or Vice ridiculous, but never exalt their characters into buskined pomp, or make what Voltaire humorously calls a *Tradesman's Tragedy*.

Yet, notwithstanding this weight of authority, and the universal practice of former ages, a new species of Dramatic Composition has been introduced under the name of *Sentimental* Comedy, in which the virtues of Private Life are exhibited, rather than the Vices exposed ; and the Distresses, rather than the Faults of Mankind, make our interest in the

[1] Boileau (*Art Poétique, Chant* iii.), who borrows his precept from Horace.]

piece. These Comedies have had of late great success, perhaps from their novelty, and also from their flattering every man in his favourite foible. In these Plays almost all the Characters are good, and exceedingly generous; they are lavish enough of their *Tin* Money on the Stage, and though they want Humour, have abundance of Sentiment and Feeling. If they happen to have Faults or Foibles, the Spectator is taught not only to pardon, but to applaud them, in consideration of the goodness of their hearts; so that Folly, instead of being ridiculed, is commended, and the Comedy aims at touching our Passions without the power of being truly pathetic: in this manner we are likely to lose one great source of Entertainment on the Stage; for while the Comic Poet is invading the province of the Tragic Muse, he leaves her lovely Sister quite neglected. Of this, however, he is no way solicitous, as he measures his fame by his profits.

But it will be said, that the Theatre is formed to amuse Mankind, and that it matters little, if this end be answered, by what means it is obtained. If Mankind find delight in weeping at Comedy, it would be cruel to abridge them in that or any other innocent pleasure. If those Pieces are denied the name of Comedies; yet call them by any other name, and if they are delightful, they are good. Their success, it will be said, is a mark of their merit, and it is only abridging our happiness to deny us an inlet to Amusement.

These objections, however, are rather specious than solid. It is true, that Amusement is a great object of the Theatre; and it will be allowed, that these Sentimental Pieces do often amuse us: but the question is, Whether the True Comedy would not amuse us more? The question is, Whether a Character supported throughout a Piece with its Ridicule still attending, would not give us more delight than this species of Bastard Tragedy, which only is applauded because it is new?

A friend of mine who was sitting unmoved at one of these Sentimental Pieces, was asked, how he could be so indifferent. "Why truly," says he, "as the Hero is but a Tradesman, it is indifferent to me whether he be turned out of his Counting-House on Fish-street Hill, since he will still have enough left to open shop in St. Giles's."

The other objection is as ill-grounded; for though we should give these Pieces another name, it will not mend their efficacy. It will continue a kind of *mulish* production, with all the defects of its opposite parents, and marked with sterility. If we are permitted to make Comedy weep, we have an equal right to make Tragedy laugh, and to set down in Blank Verse the Jests and Repartees of all the Attendants in a funeral Procession.

But there is one Argument in Favour of Sentimental Comedy which will keep it on the Stage in spite of all that can be said against it. It is, of all others, the most easily written. Those abilities that can hammer out a Novel, are fully sufficient for the production of a sentimental Comedy. It is only sufficient to raise the Characters a little, to deck out the Hero with a Ribbon, or give the Heroine a Title ; then to put an Insipid Dialogue, without Character or Humour, into their mouths, give them mighty good hearts, very fine clothes, furnish a new set of Scenes, make a Pathetic Scene or two, with a sprinkling of tender Melancholy Conversation through the whole, and there is no doubt but all the Ladies will cry, and all the Gentlemen applaud.

Humour at present seems to be departing from the Stage, and it will soon happen, that our Comic Players will have nothing left for it but a fine Coat and a Song. It depends upon the Audience whether they will actually drive those poor Merry Creatures from the Stage or sit at a Play as gloomy as at the Tabernacle. It is not easy to recover an art when once lost ; and it would be but a just punishment that when, by our being too fastidious, we have banished Humour from the Stage, we should ourselves be deprived of the art of Laughing.

EVERYMAN'S LIBRARY

A LIST OF THE 983 VOLUMES
ARRANGED UNDER AUTHORS

Anonymous works are given under titles.

Anthologies, Dictionaries, etc., are arranged at the end of the list.

LONDON: J. M. DENT & SONS LTD.

NEW YORK: E. P. DUTTON & CO. INC.

*The Publishers regret that, owing to wartime
difficulties and shortages, some of the volumes
may be found to be temporarily out of print.*